Thailand

THE MODERNIZATION OF A BUREAUCRATIC POLITY

FRED W. RIGGS

EAST-WEST CENTER PRESS   HONOLULU

To

Amara Raksasataya

and to Kangwan

Salai

Tatsani

Titaya

Vithun

Warin

Wilawan

ACKNOWLEDGMENTS

The trail from initial conception to completion has been, in the case of the book which follows, a long one. I wish to acknowledge herewith the generous support and patient forbearance of those without whose aid the trail could not have been pursued.

To the Public Administration Clearing House, which allowed me, in 1955/56, to launch my investigations of public administration in Southeast Asia; and especially to Charles S. Ascher, then director of the New York office of PACH, untiring critic and meticulous mentor, who watched over these first halting steps.

To the Social Science Research Council, which provided a research grant, enabling me to spend the academic year of 1957/58 in Thailand. Without this grant and the support of Gabriel Almond, Bryce Wood, Lucian Pye, and others in the Committee on Comparative Politics, I would not have been able to carry out the field work which gave me, a nonspecialist on Southeast Asia, the temerity to undertake so brash a task.

To the Social Science Association of Thailand and Dean Kasem Udyanin, whose generous provision of supplementary funds greatly facilitated my field work and permitted me to employ the services of Kangwan Thephastin, Miss Wilawan, and Miss Tatsani of Kasetsart University, and Mr. Salai Niratisayakun of Chulalongkorn University.

To the Cornell Research Center and its director, David A. Wilson, who provided a base of operations and legitimized my work in Thailand. I want particularly to thank Nai Vithun, Nai Titaya, and Nai Warin for their friendly and effective help at various stages of my work. Several American scholars associated with the Center at different times gave me new insights into the Thai scene, notably David Wilson himself, but also Lauriston Sharp, Herbert Phillips, Robert Textor, and Lucian Hanks.

To the Division of Agricultural Economics and its chief, Sawaeng Kulthongkan, who provided desk space for my work in the Ministry of Agriculture and greatly facilitated my research. His colleague, Kamol Janleka, was particularly instructive. To Prince Chakrabandhu Pensiri Chakrabandhu, director-general of the Department of Rice, and his associates, notably Dr. Sala Desananda, Dr. Krui Punyasingh, and M. R. Debriddhi Devakun, who were especially kind in responding to my many and often, I fear, impertinent questions. They facilitated field visits in various parts of Thailand, where I interviewed and observed the work of experiment stations, extension agents, and rice farmers.

Members of the staff of the United States Operations Mission in Bangkok were always co-operative, including Brice M. Mace, chief of the Agricultural Divison, and John More, chief of the Public Administration Division. My greatest debt of thanks goes to Jameson Bell, technical adviser extraordinary, who permitted me to accompany him on many field trips and whose penetrating questions and friendly counsel added much to whatever I learned about Thailand, its people, and its institutions.

International agencies operating in Thailand were also helpful, and I wish to record my special obligation to Professor M. R. Balakrishnan of India and the World Health Organization. His great warmth enveloped all who came near him. He welcomed me as a son and virtually adopted my family. Our most memorable days in Thailand include visits to his experimental station at Samchook and the sugar factory at Suphanburi. He gave me many new insights into problems of agronomy, as well as of Thai culture and administration.

The Institute of Public Administration at Thammasat University, under the direction of Dean Malai Huvanandana, became one of my regular haunts, and members of the Institute staff rendered many services which facilitated my research. I wish to record my special gratitude to colleagues from Indiana University who were working there under contract, notably Edgar Shor and Fred Horrigan, with whom I spent many hours in friendly debate and who shared useful materials with me. Marnop Debhavalya deserves a grateful note of thanks for his companionship, help, and insights.

My efforts to understand the problems of the Chinese rice millers and merchants and their relations with government agencies were greatly facilitated by the friendly co-operation of S. Y. Lee, an informed and objective participant-observer of these matters.

Among the American scholars resident in Thailand with whom I exchanged views frequently and from whom I derived most helpful information—in addition to those associated with the Cornell Research Center —were Fred Ayre, Ed Schuler, and David Davies. Larry Judd, a remarkably perceptive and able Christian fraternal worker, took me on an extended field trip into remote areas of Nan province. John Loftus, economic adviser, shared his experience and official reports, as did members of the International Bank mission, staff experts at the United States Embassy, faculty members of Oregon State University working at Kasetsart University, and others too numerous to mention.

The following year, 1958/59, at the Institute of Public Administration, University of the Philippines, I was unable to continue working on my Thai materials, but Jose Soberano, whose desk adjoined mine, spent many hours discussing with me problems of fact and interpretation which helped to shape the theoretical framework that informs this volume.

Returning to Indiana University in 1959, I found myself engrossed in teaching and other urgent duties which made further work on Thailand impossible at that time. Moreover, I devoted much of my spare time to reflection and writing on more general theoretical problems about the characteristics of politics and administration in transitional societies, leading to the publication in 1964 of *Administration in Developing Countries: The Theory of Prismatic Society.*

During 1960/61, however, a grant for third-time study from Indiana University, made possible by support received from the Ford Foundation and an Indiana University committee under the chairmanship of Edward Buehrig, provided an opportunity for me to resume work on the Thai book. The following year, as a senior scholar at the East-West Center, University of Hawaii, I was able to continue my writing. During this period I benefited greatly from the criticism and help of Dr. Amara Raksasataya, member of the faculty of the Institute of Public Administration, Thammasat University, who was also a senior scholar at the Center. I wish to acknowledge my profound gratitude to him for his advice and counsel.

After returning to Indiana University, the pressure of other duties, especially the direction of the International Development Research Center, again impeded progress on the manuscript, and it was not until the summer and fall of 1964 that I was able to complete my writing. During this period I received assistance from an able staff, including

Mrs. Doris Tennyson, Miss Flora Dalacanog, Mr. Sam Lam, and Miss Surak Vunnag, who typed, proofread, and mimeographed the lengthening text. Indiana University, through a faculty research grant, financed this clerical phase of production.

Such were the circumstances accompanying the prolonged gestation and birth of a study which had to be sandwiched in among the many rival claims of a busy life.

My family had to bear the brunt of living with a preoccupied husband and father and sacrificed the many hours I should have spent with them. To Clara-Louise, Wendy, and Ron I wish, therefore, to express my affectionate thanks for their patience and forbearance.

With all these helping hands, I feel that it is not I but they who are the true authors—mine but the instrument. Yet I cannot avoid accepting full responsibility for whatever errors of fact and interpretation may be found in this work. These are mine alone.

A word of warning should be added. I do not claim to be a specialist on Thailand. To the specialist, weaknesses in detail will be readily apparent—notably, in the system of transliteration of Thai words and names, which avoids the diacritical marks essential for a literal transcription. However, an attempt has been made to keep the spelling of individual names consistent and to reflect the sound more than the Siamese orthography. Appendix A provides the full names of the cabinet politicians, permitting the use in the text of shortened names, with code numbers for identification. In justification of this approach, let me say that the book is primarily designed not for the area specialist but for readers concerned with comparative studies and the theory of political and administrative development. The research upon which this study was based terminated in 1963.

Fred W. Riggs

May, 1965

CONTENTS

LIST OF TEXT ILLUSTRATIONS

LIST OF TABLES

THAILAND

THE MODERNIZATION OF A BUREAUCRATIC POLITY

Introduction

"Neither policy makers nor scholars have produced a doctrine of political development. . . ." [1] This bald assertion by an eminent political scientist and government planner may strike the reader as little short of calamitous in an age when the "cold war" and growing technological interdependence make the future, not only of America, but of the world as well, dependent on the capacity of states to solve a swelling torrent of urgent and fateful problems. The result, according to Wriggins, is that "until a workable doctrine is elaborated and confirmed, each government operator must use his own judgment on an *ad hoc* basis, guessing rather than judging the consequences of events or of actions."

The present work is an attempt, albeit admittedly a highly speculative and personal one, to confront some of the problems involved in political development, with special reference to the role of bureaucracy and bureaucratization in the modernization of Thailand. The personal and even impressionistic character of the work stems from the way in which it was constructed.

The primary observations on which the study rests were collected during a field trip to Thailand in 1957 to 1958. [2] In the usual course of academic research, one is supposed to launch field investigations with a well-defined set of hypotheses in mind. Armed with a battery of questionnaires, one corners a proper sample of willing or unwilling informants, as the case may be, subjecting them to interviews or asking them to fill out forms that can, in due course, be tabulated and computed. Eventually one emerges with the proof—or disproof—of his initial hypotheses.

The difficulty with this method is that it assumes the prior existence of useful hypotheses. To confess that one lacks such hypotheses is virtually to admit, like the fabulous emperor, that one's new clothes are purely imaginary. There are, of course, those who claim that theories, models, propositions, and hypotheses are all irrelevant for the study of strange and exotic societies which can be understood only by research "in depth," which seems to mean the collection of more and more quantities of data about smaller and smaller places. Implicit propositions, however, can be tortured out from between the lines of such writings as may result from these exercises. They may include the notion that all facts are equal, that everything must have a function, or that the familiar Western patterns are modal, everything else being evaluated as worse—or better—than these norms. By now, however, the need for theory as a basis for discriminating between relevant and irrelevant facts has become increasingly accepted. One should embark on a field study in a country like Thailand only if one has at his disposal the requisite theoretical "tool kit."

If I nevertheless confess the poverty of theory which structured my Thai inquiries, I do so now only because Howard Wriggins has at last provided a face-saving "out." Since, by 1962, according to Wriggins, neither scholars nor policy-makers had devised a doctrine of political development, I might be excused for not having had such a basic intellectual engine in 1957.

In this perspective one may ask whether there are not occasions which justify putting the cart before the horse. Can one, indeed, reasonably collect data before he knows what to do with it? If one lacks hypotheses, not just because he hasn't given the matter some thought but because he lacks enough empirical knowledge to suggest meaningful new relationships, and if the available hypotheses seem for the most part irrelevant or misleading because they were framed to meet the realities of a different social and political order, then perhaps one must risk proceeding awkwardly, with a hobbled horse of theory scrambling behind a sluggish cart full of inert data.

If one's primary purpose is to generate theory rather than to amass data, then may it not be useful to set aside the prevailing doctrinal baggage of one's discipline as far as possible and open oneself to reality in field observations with a minimum of preconceptions? If one can do this (difficult, even dangerous, as it may be), then the collection of data becomes not an end in itself or even a means of validating theory, but rather it might be used, however riskily, to generate new understandings or at least a fresh interpretation of reality. Such, at least, was the mood in which I approached my self-assigned task.

Not, of course, that I lacked a "research design" or even a body of makeshift "theory" before leaving for Bangkok. Who, in this age of planned research, could hope to gain financial support for a costly expedition without first having offered such a framework as a prerequisite? I had, indeed, certain notions about the characteristics of both traditional and modern societies, for our literature is not unsophisticated at these levels. Political scientists and sociologists have examined American and other Western societies closely enough to derive propositions about "developed" polities, and social anthropologists and historians have given us enough insight into traditional or folk societies to enable us to theorize with some confidence about their characteristics. We have, consequently, a series of dichotomies for the analysis of these contrastive types. I had already sought to clarify in my own mind the basic elements of these polar systems, even to the point of creating abstract models of them.[3]

However, I had perceived but dimly the possible characteristics of an intermediate model, of a transitional system between the traditional and the modern extremes. My observations in Thailand, plus the opportunity which the Institute of Public Administration at the University of the Philippines gave me to spend the following year reflecting on these problems and discussing them with Filipino colleagues, enabled me to construct the "prismatic model" which has served at least a heuristic purpose in helping to clarify some relationships between phenomena which often puzzle observers of transitional societies.[4]

Against this background, I decided merely to "expose" myself to the Thai scene as much as I could in the brief space of an academic year. Taking advantage of the presence in Bangkok of colleagues from Indiana University who were involved in a contract program designed to establish an Institute of Public Administration at Thammasat University, I devoted myself primarily to the study of the Thai bureaucracy, to open-ended, largely unstructured interviews with Thai officials, and to field trips with them, designed to give me a feeling for their way of life and problems.

In order to narrow the focus of my inquiries somewhat more, I decided to concentrate on problems related to rice. Many government agencies, ranging from the experiment stations and extension services which seek to improve the cultivation of rice to those concerned with marketing, credit, milling, taxing, and exporting rice, were brought within the purview of my inquiries. I gave some attention also to private organizations interested in rice production and distribution.

Rice, of course, was not my sole preoccupation. I had no desire to become a specialist in agriculture or marketing. My chief concern, rather, was with the administrative and political aspects of the groups, both governmental and private, which were concerned with various programs and problems related to rice.

The choice of rice as a subject of study was dictated in part by considerations of research tactics. I felt it desirable to have a subject of general interest and relative neutrality. Everyone is interested in rice in Thailand, and the subject has amazing ramifications. Its significance for the country is suggested by the following statement by John Loftus, American economic adviser to the Thai government:

> Thailand's economy has for most of the last 100 years been characterized by a disturbingly high degree of dependence upon rice production and export. This dependence means not only that most of the producers (who are most of the population) depend upon the world market (which they cannot control) for a single commodity—rice; but Government depends primarily upon revenues (in the form of export duties and premia) directly attributable to this commodity; much of the Government's other revenue-raising capacity can be traced clearly though indirectly to rice income; much of the activity in the business sector of the community is in one way or another concerned with the handling, the processing, the storage and the shipping of rice; and the banking system would have few if any customers here were it not for the ramifications of the trade in rice.[5]

In a relatively short period of time I was able to amass considerable material, through interviews, observation, and documentation, about the operations of government agencies concerned with rice in its many transformations. I then found myself in the position of Pirandello's roles in search of a play. I was tempted merely to describe some of these rice-oriented activities, to give vignettes of interesting and colorful personalities, to describe the operations of an experiment station director, an extension agent, the inspector of rice exports, or an agricultural economist calculating prices in the rice markets. But what do all these activities add up to?

To a certain extent, of course, they provided the basic data which first suggested and then illustrated propositions about the "prismatic model." The shock of recognition is a familiar experience, but it acquires a special aura when one perceives an idea rather than a face. I recall the circumstances under which the notion of "formalism" first bore down upon me, not simply as one aspect of life in a transitional society, but as a pervasive theme. I had arrived at a district office in the interior about noon one day. Noting a clean new privy behind the building, I approached it only to discover that it was locked. Further investigations disclosed that the only key was on the person of the district officer, who had gone home for lunch. No doubt he would have been waiting attendance on a visiting inspector from the public health program or an official of WHO, to show that his district was in the vanguard of progress. As a lowly private scholar, I did not rate this particular status symbol.

I mention this particular episode not because of its intrinsic or jocular interest or even because a locked privy could be considered typical—for it was not. Rather, it was the symbolism of the situation that suddenly struck my attention and dramatized the significance of formalism. The introduction of a new structure, alien to indigenous practices and life ways, but adapted to serve new functions, different from those served elsewhere: this is the essence of formalism and, as I discovered, a central characteristic of the prismatic model.

Another example, less quaint perhaps but more immediately relevant to administrative and political development, occurred to me one day when I inquired in an agricultural agency about the regulatory legislation which provided a basis for its program. Two basic laws were mentioned, whereupon I naturally asked to see copies. It shortly became apparent, after a rapid search of the files, that no text could be found. I was told that a more thorough search would surely turn up the documents and that if I would stop by in a week or two, I could obtain copies. However, when I returned later, I was informed that the agency lacked any copies of the legislation it was presumably enforcing, but I was told that I could obtain copies by going to the book store of the university law school. There seemed to be little awareness of the anomalous nature of this situation. It was explained to me that, as a matter of fact, these laws were difficult to enforce and only antagonized the farmers. In practice, the agency preferred to do what the people wanted and hence limited itself to service-type activities.

Again, I do not mean to assert that this situation was typical. Far from it, for many Thai agencies make vigorous use of regulatory legislation. But the episode struck me because it was surprising. I had not inquired about the laws in the expectation of finding that they were not enforced. Rather, I had perhaps started with an "input-output" model of decision-making, assuming that formally adopted rules would be implemented by the administrative machinery. It came, therefore, as rather a shock to discover that officials could blithely disregard laws which, officially, they were supposed to be enforcing. It is the kind of shock that one experiences when he tries to open a door that is normally un-locked and discovers that it is locked. In more extreme cases, he dis-covers that a door can never be opened because it is an imitation carved in the wall. The prismatic situation is like a room in which all the con-spicuous doors cannot move, and egress must be sought through moving panels controlled by hidden buttons.

Field work in Thailand, then, operated at two levels: the first in-volved the collection of data based on a chosen strategy—the investiga-tion of rice programs in all their manifestations; the second required an unstructured openness to experience which, I hoped, would suggest new relationships or questions that had not occurred to me before. The significance of this distinction was impressed upon me by a conversation I had after my return to the United States. I was challenged by a col-league who felt that I must somehow have failed to accomplish my mis-sion since I did not bring my research trip to a close with a neatly completed monograph. I learned that this tidy-minded person always begins his field inquiries by writing his final report. He then proceeds to the task of collecting data. In other words, he not only has full posses-sion of the hypotheses he wants to test, but he also has reached his major conclusions. He uses his research opportunities to collect data to sub-stantiate his report and, he explained, to revise his original formulations whenever he discovers that they cannot be sustained by his findings.

I do not report this conversation with any sense of smug superiority. Rather, I confess awe in the presence of a man who possesses such a confident command of his basic premises and is thereby able to predict, within narrow margins, just how much time it will take him to carry to completion any particular scholarly investigation. For my part, I admit my lack of a priori conclusions and hence a shamefully imprecise and unpredictable research methodology. In the light of Wriggins' statement about the lack of basic doctrines in the field of political development, however, I feel that I share a historically determined disability which can at least ease the burden of private guilt.

My research method, in other words, was one designed to open peepholes, if not doors, on the political and administrative processes of a transitional society. I believe I returned home having gained several such glimpses into unfamiliar but fascinating scenes. I had learned some-thing about the logically related characteristics of a transitional society. But the insights were only partial, and I returned also with a set of questions to which I had no answer; yet the questions were so perplexing and tantalizing that I felt I could not make effective use of my data until I had found some answers to these questions.

For example, even if one can see a logical progression between several stages, one need by no means understand the dynamics of change from one stage to another. One can understand differences between species, between birds and fish or between men and apes, without knowing how one species might be transformed into another. Hypotheses about the "survival of the fittest" and "genetic sports" form part of the effort to explain biological evolution. But, as Wriggins has indicated, we lack such a theory for political development. Wriggins himself identifies some functional requisites of a developed political system. He suggests that, as a matter of policy, we ought to help other societies change so as to attain these political requisites. But there is a giant step from the recognition of a developed model to an understanding of how it can be created or even how it ever came into being. If a human reformer were to lecture a class of chimpanzees on their need to acquire a bigger brain, we would regard the spectacle as absurd. Is it not equally ludicrous to think that by defining the requisites of a particular stage of development one can, through conscious effort, bring it into being?

This, of course, was the difficulty I faced in thinking about transitional societies. I could not help feeling that contemporary "underdeveloped" countries such as Thailand were quite different from traditional societies. The more I learned about conditions in Siam a hundred years ago, the more convinced I became that vast transformations had taken place. The dramatic contrasts between contemporary Thailand and conditions in Western lands produce a foreshortened perspective which makes us consider the country "traditional." Yet similarities between the "modernizing" societies and those that think of themselves as fully "modern" can be marked. I have often had the experience, after describing what seemed like a particularly distinctive or unique feature of Thai administration, of hearing a listener say, "Oh, but we have exactly the same thing in southern Indiana." Surely the identification of contemporary Thailand with traditional Siam is based on equally numerous parallels between the two systems.

The point is that we are dealing with political systems as configurations of variables. The differences between systems lie in the contrasting magnitudes of shared variables, the divergent ways in which similar elements can be combined. And, of course, we know quite well from historical evidence that one kind of system evolves into another. We often confuse being "modern" with being "Western," yet we realize, when we think about it, that the Western world of the tenth century was anything but "modern." Do the differences between American and Thai politics arise because one is "Western" and the other "Eastern"? Alternatively, in terms of some indices of change, is one just more "developed" than the other? Surely, I thought, the evidence from Thailand—and, no doubt, similar conclusions might have been reached from a study of Turkey, Tunisia, or Tanganyika—should give us some clues, if only we had the wit to see them, as to how a social order changes from one level to another. How do "traditional" societies become "transitional"? If we could answer this question, then we might also learn something about the dynamics of change from the "transitional" to the "modern."

On the other hand, if the key differences are of the Eastern-Western sort, then no amount of analysis can bridge the Kipling gap. East would forever remain Eastern, and no amount of modernization could result in meaningful "Westernization." Or are these two conceptions of the nature of social change merely polar extremes? Could a country like Thailand in some sense become "modern" while remaining "Eastern"? What, exactly, was central to the developmental process and what merely incidental? Could we untangle from the twisted skeins of social change a variety of elements, some subject to "development" and others not?

Questions of this order have long perplexed me, and I do not pretend to have found an answer. Yet I venture to offer in this work some speculations which may, I hope, contribute to a better understanding of such questions. Surely, at least, they go beyond a merely historicist viewpoint in which the reason that something happened is typically given as the fact of its occurrence. In these terms, of course, the "reason" for the modernization of Thailand may be simply the forceful personality of King Chulalongkorn. We know that he made reforms, that he lived a long time, and that he was a powerful monarch. We know that the revolution against the absolute monarchy took place in 1932, and that a series of "constitutions" were subsequently promulgated by a succession of governments which followed each other with bewildering frequency.

But what do these facts explain? Why did Chulalongkorn carry out reforms? Why did not King Mindon or Thibaw in Burma carry out equivalent reforms? Was it just a matter of personality? Or was it because the British wanted to conquer Burma and didn't want to conquer Siam? But if so, why didn't the British want to make a colony of Siam, whereas they did want to make a colony of Burma? Was it purely a British idiosyncrasy that they coveted Burma but not Siam, or were there differences in Burmese and Siamese society such that the Siamese polity would have resisted conquest more effectively, or made conquest more costly, thereby making the fruits of imperial domination less desirable? The mere description of the raw events which marked the transformation of traditional Siam into transitional Thailand suggests more questions than it answers. Without a theory that identifies causal interdependencies and shows how changes in one variable in a system affect other elements, we cannot explain anything. We can only describe.

In an early draft, I planned to start this book with a formal presentation of a theory of development or of change, for which the Thai data might then serve as illustrative material. By this procedure I hoped to emulate the pattern employed by Lucian Pye and Leonard Binder in recent works; [6] both of these books are deeply concerned with problems of modernization and development, and both offer extensive theoretical essays as a prelude to the country analysis.

Preliminary work on the theoretical material, however, convinced me that it would be advantageous to reserve these speculations for future publication as a separate monograph. Much more reflection and analysis are needed to raise them to a level suitable for public presentation. Meanwhile, it seemed useful to write some background essays on the modernization of the Thai polity which would help to explain some of the paradoxes I encountered in my field work on the administration of agricultural programs. At the same time, I hoped by this means to provide some data that could be used in subsequent work of a more theoretical character.

The present work is, accordingly, divided into three parts: the traditional polity; patterns of modernization; and the modernized "bureaucratic polity." The first part is an effort to characterize the traditional Siamese polity in terms both of its typical and its distinctive features. The second part describes some processes of change in Thai politics and administration which occurred between the mid-nineteenth and the mid-twentieth century. The third part describes the contemporary Thai government as a fully realized example of what may be called a "bureaucratic polity," a system of government that is neither "traditional" nor "modern" in character.

The first part of the book begins with a comparison of the responses of Siam and Burma to the impact of the West. By this exercise I seek to clarify some of the distinctive features which characterized the traditional Siamese polity by contrast with those of its nearest and most similar neighbor. The second chapter offers a view of the traditional Siamese polity which—while differing from the more usual image of such a system—elucidates some of the essential features which the Siamese mode of government shared with its contemporary neighbors. By this means I have tried to make evident not only the "typical" but also the "unique" features of the classical Siamese polity.

The transformation of this polity in response to the threat of Western domination is the subject of the second part of the book. Chapter III shows how the monarchy gradually transformed itself from a sacred into a secular, politically oriented institution, thereby enabling it to serve a modernizing function. The fourth chapter describes the functionalization of the bureaucracy which accompanied this process, as both a consequence and a cause; the fifth deals with the extension of bureaucratic control throughout the realm. The sixth and seventh chapters examine the unsuccessful efforts made by Thai reformers to create a new power base for projecting popular control over the expanding bureaucracy—at both the central and local levels of government—as a substitute for the waning power of the monarchy.

The third part of the book deals with the contemporary "bureaucratic polity," beginning with an analysis, in Chapter VIII, of the cabinet as its most distinctive and powerful organ. The inner power structure and working dynamics of the cabinet are characterized, in so far as the operations of this elusive system can be discerned by an outside observer. The ninth chapter carries the inquiry further by examining some of the economic and social aspects of this distinctive cabinet system. The tenth chapter is devoted to a survey of the Thai bureaucratic system as a whole, taking into account relationships between the cabinet and career structures and stressing their administrative dimensions and implications. The concluding chapter summarizes the main argument of the book in terms of a theoretical framework or model of bureaucratic polity.

These essays are by no means intended to provide a complete picture of the Thai political system or of its bureaucracy and its administrative problems. The recent works of such authors as David Wilson and William Siffin make such an effort redundant.[7] It is hoped, rather, that these essays will shed some supplementary light on the politics of modernization and the administrative implications of bureaucratic proliferation in a fascinating and lovely country. Hopefully, also, they will provide some empirical data that may prove helpful in the subsequent formulation of theories concerning development, especially the development of political and administrative institutions and practices.

PART ONE: THE TRADITIONAL POLITY

CHAPTER I

The Modernization of Siam
and Burma

A convenient point of departure for examining the modernization of
Thailand is provided by comparing modern Burmese and Siamese history.* Fundamental similarities between the two neighboring countries
make the differences in their patterns of modernization particularly instructive. Whereas the Burmese monarchy, despite frantic last-minute
efforts, failed to modernize sufficiently to preserve its independence or
even the continued existence of the monarchy as an institution, the
Siamese monarchy was able not only to maintain the country's independence but also to preserve the dynasty—if not as an absolutism, at
least as a constitutional economic, political, social, and administrative
regime.

An examination into the reasons or means by which this result was
accomplished should help us assess the rising levels of performance
achieved in Thailand. The comparable failures in Burma afford, by contrast, some measures of that regime's inability to raise performance
levels sufficiently to preserve either its independence or its monarchic
institutions.

As we shall see later, changing levels of performance are not equivalent to developmental changes. It will be argued that, under the impact

---

*The terms "Burmese" and "Burman," "Siamese" and "Thai" are used, for the most
part, as synonyms. However, in some contexts it is useful to think of the Burmese
as the Buddhist, Burmese-speaking populations of the central and lower valley
regions, in contrast to the Burmans as citizens, regardless of ethnic background,
of the state of Burma. The opposite usage is sometimes employed, so the reader
must beware. Similarly, Siamese may refer largely to the people of the lower
Chao Phya area, and Thai to a larger linguistic family, including Thai-speaking
people outside the boundaries of the Siamese state. Alternatively, Siam may be
used for the absolute monarchy to distinguish it from post-revolutionary Thailand,
although actual usage is, again, not so clear-cut.

of British rule, Burma experienced greater development than Thailand, but the malintegrative pressures accompanying development served to impede growth, i.e., rising levels of performance.

GENERAL SIMILARITIES BETWEEN THE NEIGHBORING COUNTRIES

To justify comparisons between these adjacent countries, let us review briefly some of their essential similarities.

The fact that they are neighbors geographically is less important than the fact that they are comparable in size and population. Both are relatively small countries, whose populations have grown from around six million at the middle of the nineteenth century to over twenty million at the middle of the twentieth (Table 1). In area Thailand has

TABLE 1

POPULATION ESTIMATES

(*in millions*)

	Burma	*Thailand*
Nineteenth Century	1.9 (British Burma, 1861)	4.5 to 6.0 (1850)
" "	6.1 (All Burma, 1870)	
1911	12.2	8.3
1931	14.7	11.5 (1929)
1941	16.8	14.5 (1937), 17.4 (1947)
1953	19.3	19.6
1957	20.1	24.2
1960	20.7	27.2
1962	22.3	28.0

SOURCES: United Nations, *Monthly Bulletin of Statistics* (July, 1963).
        Statistical Yearbook of Thailand, Vol. 1, No. 22.
        James C. Ingram, *Economic Change in Thailand Since 1850* (Stanford
            University Press, 1955), pp. 7, 46.
        J. S. Furnivall, *Colonial Policy and Practice* (New York University
            Press, 1958), pp. 80, 117, 186.

almost 200,000 square miles, Burma about 260,000. Perhaps more significant, both are tropical lands oriented around the alluvial plains of a river valley system. The chief cities have been river ports, both in the delta regions and farther upstream at important junctions, transshipment points, and in fertile tributary valleys. Rice has been the main crop, raised by traditional peasant farming methods in flooded fields. The majority of the population have been farmers living in relatively compact or strip villages following the water courses. In both countries, economic development has been marked by the expansion of rice cultivation and exports, augmented by production of export materials, notably teak and rubber.

Surrounding the valley areas are hills, plateaus, and mountains, in which live ethnic minorities, tribal peoples under more or less direct control of, or paying tribute to, the valley peoples. In both countries, significant cultural distinctions can also be found between the lower valley peoples and the inhabitants of upper valley and plateau regions: the Burmese in relation to the Shan; the Siamese in relation to the Laos peoples.

The dominant ethnic or linguistic groups of both Burma and Thailand were derived from China, by way of its southwestern frontier lands, and belong to related Sino-Thai and Tibeto-Burman stocks. However, more significant influences on the traditional culture—in terms of politics and administration, if not of village and family life—came from India. They included the strongly Brahmanic strains in the organization of court life and the conception and role of monarchy.[1] They also included the Theravada Buddhist order, which prevails in both countries, especially among the dominant valley peoples. Thus, the cosmologically oriented monarchic and ruling institutions and the Buddhistically based social order provided the warp and woof of the traditional society. The former has been undermined, if not destroyed, by the impact of the West, but the latter appears to remain as vigorous as ever.

Full cultural homogeneity, however, was never attained in either society. Foreigners from the West have had a gradually accelerating impact over a period of more than four hundred years. Portuguese traders arrived in the sixteenth century and became involved as mercenaries in the armies of both countries. Later the Dutch, French, and British became increasingly active in the affairs of these kingdoms; this activity reached a climax in the nineteenth century, when Franco-British imperial rivalries stimulated both countries to intensify their interventions. They began to annex frontier provinces to their growing empires. But a striking contrast emerges at this point, for the process began somewhat earlier in the Burman case and ended only with the complete absorption of the Burmese realm in the British-Indian empire, whereas the Siamese monarchy was able to preserve most of its territory from imperial conquest.

Asian foreigners also became important minorities in both countries, playing major roles in their financial and commercial development. However, it is notable that whereas the Indians played a dominant role and the Chinese a minor role in Burma, the position was reversed in Siam, where the number of Chinese greatly exceeded that of the Indians. Their presence has contributed to modernization, yet also hampered it.

Indigenous ethnic minorities have also adhered to contrasting culture patterns. The mountain peoples, for the most part, have retained their animistic beliefs and linguistic, cultural distinctiveness into modern times, although Christian missionary efforts have achieved their greatest successes among these peoples. Islam has also spread into both countries and aggravated local communalism. The Muslim population is concentrated in the southern Thai provinces adjacent to Malaya and in the western Burman areas of Arakan, adjoining Bengal (East Pakistan). No doubt there were important differences in degree of homogeneity between the two countries, for greater ethnic unity was achieved in Siam than in Burma. This difference was probably a fundamental contributory factor to the contrasting patterns of modernization. However, both countries shared the common experience of attempting to deal with minority groups under the control of Buddhist ruling communities organized around a Brahmanical absolute monarchy.

The dynastic history of the two countries also affords some striking parallels. The Alaungpaya dynasty of Burma reigned from 1752 to 1885. The current Chakri house of Thailand may be dated from 1767 or 1782, but it survives to the present day. The Alaungpaya dynasty was, in a sense, a successor to the rulers of Ava, whose period of domination extended from 1364 to the middle of the sixteenth century. Both dynasties exercised their control from capitals on the upper Irrawaddy: from Ava, Amarapura, and Mandalay. Similarly, the Chakri dynasty succeeded the rulers of nearby Ayuthia (1350–1767), both regimes being based near the mouth of the Menam Chao Phya.

A rather significant difference in dynastic histories may be noted here and related to the phenomenon of ethnic diversity. As in other river valley kingdoms, it is useful to distinguish upper from lower regions and to identify intermediate regions which frequently played important marginal roles by swinging their support to the upper or lower areas, but rarely by bringing both under their own control. In the Burmese case, the upper region may be identified with the Ava/Mandalay area, the lower with Pegu/Rangoon. The Siamese counterparts are Chiengmai and Ayuthia/Bangkok. Intermediate zones may be represented by Toungoo in Burma and Sukhotai in Siam. At different periods, of course, the names and locations of the key cities have changed within some, if not all, of these regions.

The power of the lower Chao Phya—identified with Ayuthia and Bangkok—tended to prevail, in the long run, over the rival powers of the upper valley. This should be related, whether as cause or consequence, to the gradual assimilation by the Siamese of the more ancient Mons of the lower valley areas. By contrast, in Burma the kingdoms of the upper region tended to prevail, so that the lower valley alternated between periods of subjection and autonomy. This, again, may be associated with the persistence of Mon separatism and self-consciousness up to modern times. The difficulties experienced by the upper valley Burmese in pacifying the conquered Mons both heightened their own anxiety and defensiveness and provided pretexts for British intervention.[2]

MODERNIZING MONARCHS

Against this background of cultural, geographic, historical, and international similarities, let us begin by comparing the personal careers of two great innovating monarchs, King Mindon of Burma and King Mongkut of Siam. They were contemporaries, Mindon ruling from 1853 to 1878, and Mongkut from 1851 to 1868. Both men concluded treaties with European powers, notably the British, which substantially opened their realms to foreign trade and cultural influences, thereby accelerating the impact of the West upon their political, social, and economic institutions: Mongkut in 1855 and Mindon in 1862 and 1867.

The importance of these treaties can scarcely be exaggerated, since they paved the way for a flood of transformations which followed. To take the Siamese case first, we find Sir John Bowring, who negotiated the treaty with Mongkut, writing that its provisions "involved a total revolution in all the financial machinery of the Government." [3] The basic provision of the treaty was an agreement to permit free trade by private merchants, subject only to an import duty of 3 per cent ad valorem on imports. Thus, the existing system of royal monopolies and the special privileges of many of the highest officials and nobles were undermined. This, in turn, meant that the government would have to devise a new financial system to provide adequate compensation in the form of salaries for its officials, thereby necessitating a basic change in the system of taxation and financial administration.

Under the traditional system in both Burma and Siam, officials had received royal grants or payments from time to time, but the basic sources of their income were derived from land, the services of their clients, and a variety of tax or tribute payments exacted from those under their immediate jurisdiction. Part of what was collected was transmitted to the court, according to specified rules, but often actual collections greatly exceeded what the officials were formally entitled to receive. The true situation is suggested by a term widely used for territorial officials who exercised their authority in a quasi-feudalistic manner. In Burma, "royal princes and high officials of the bureaucracy were assigned, as *myosas* ("town eaters"), the enjoyment of the government's share of the revenues collectible from designated towns or village districts scattered throughout the kingdom." [4]

A Thai equivalent of the Burmese *myosa* was the *kin-muang* (also, to "eat the realm"), a term applied to the king himself, as well as to his officials. Thus, Vella writes that a Siamese official "was expected to raise his income from those beneath him. He might, depending upon his position, obtain goods and services from the people or retain a share of the taxes he collected or fines he imposed." [5]

Under the terms of the treaty with Great Britain—followed shortly thereafter (1856–62) by similar treaties with France, the United States, Denmark, Portugal, Holland, and Prussia—the basis for official revenues was undermined, and the pressure for new and more reliable royal revenues to finance the bureaucracy became acute. Mongkut successfully launched a process of transformation which was carried to fruition by his son, King Chulalongkorn (Rama V), 1868–1910. The character of this transformation will be examined in more detail below.

Meanwhile, it is worth noting that another provision of these treaties, perhaps almost as far-reaching in its long-run implications, was the acceptance of extraterritoriality for the British (and subsequently for other Western) residents of Siam. Actually, traditional monarchies frequently, if not always, preferred to deal with minority ethnic or religious communities through their own leaders. If such resident communities were permitted, then it was always easier to have them settle their own disputes according to their own customs, provided their leaders would accept certain obligations of loyalty and service to the monarchy. As Hall points out, the system had been applied also to the European trading companies in earlier centuries. [6]

By the early nineteenth century, however, these rights were not enjoyed by Europeans in Siam; it was, therefore, an innovation at the time to recognize the right of foreign consuls to exercise jurisdiction over civil and criminal cases arising among their resident subjects. In the course of time this right of extraterritoriality, in Siam as elsewhere in Asia, protected the commercial activities of foreign businessmen whose expanding activities cut ever more deeply into the spheres of autonomy of the indigenous polity. In Siam, this provoked a serious effort to reform the traditional legal system and eventually to introduce modern-type legal codes and judicial administration. These reforms were successful enough to induce the foreign powers, during the nineteen-twenties and thirties, to surrender their extraterritorial privileges.[7]

Similar events took place in Burma. The treaty of 1862 provided for reciprocal abolition of duties on goods in transit between Mindon's Upper Burma and British Lower Burma, which had been annexed as a result of the second Anglo-Burman war in 1852. (It should perhaps be mentioned here that the Burmese monarchy had never recognized this annexation, and negotiations carried on in the spring of 1853 for a peace treaty proved abortive.) According to the 1862 treaty, traders from British Burma were to be permitted along the whole course of the Irrawaddy on a basis of reciprocity. There was no provision for extraterritoriality, but a British agent was authorized to take up residence in Mandalay.[8]

Five years later, in 1867, a second commercial treaty was signed. King Mindon promised to abandon all his trading monopolies except for those on rubies, earth-oil, and timber, and to reduce customs duties to 5%. Extraterritoriality was also granted, including jurisdiction by the British agent over cases between British subjects, with a mixed court, composed of the agent and a Burmese official, authorized to try cases involving British and Burmese subjects. British steamers were granted the right to navigate the Irrawaddy as far as Bhamo, near the Chinese border. An underlying motive was the strong desire of British trading interests to open a channel for trade with China, through Yunnan. In 1872, commercial treaties were also concluded with France and Italy by a Burmese mission to these countries.

As in Siam, the foreign treaties necessitated far-reaching domestic reforms. As early as 1861, Mindon promulgated a series of reforms, including the abolition of the *myosa* system of revenue collection by a reform of taxation and the introduction of regular salaries and stipends for royal officials. "To finance the salary system, Mindon introduced in 1862 [the year of the first treaty] the *thathameda* household income tax throughout all of Upper Burma, except apparently within Mandalay itself. The tax was assessed annually on a flexible pattern in April or May, following the harvesting of the crops and according to the observed prosperity of particular geographical units." This tax provided about two-thirds of the royal revenues for the next two decades, supplemented by the retained monopolies—teak, oil, rubies—and by customs and transit duties.[9] Thus, with differences in detail, both Mongkut and Mindon signed treaties with European powers which entailed far-reaching financial and judicial transformations.

It is also interesting to compare the personal careers and the domestic policies of Mongkut and Mindon. Each man succeeded a brother who had grasped the throne upon the death of his father. Both were devout Buddhists who spent much of their lives in monasteries before their accession to the throne.[10] Mindon also spent much of his life in a monastery and came out only to seize power from his brother at the height of the second Anglo-Burman war, when disaster faced his country.[11] Thus, both men devoted themselves to religious projects and endeared themselves to their subjects by their support of Buddhistic enterprises. Mindon, in 1871, "convened at Mandalay the Fifth Great Buddhist Synod or Council. Its major accomplishment was the recitation of the corrected Pali texts of the Buddhist Tripitaka scriptures." The corrected texts were then inscribed on seven hundred and twenty-nine marble slabs. In the same year, "the king prepared a bejeweled *hti* (umbrella tip) replacement for the Shwe Dagon pagoda at Rangoon and, with British consent, saw it put in place. Another of King Mindon's noteworthy adornments of Mandalay was the beautiful *Atumashi* pagoda, which was finally destroyed in World War II. The king also made his court the center of Burmese literary activity. Mandalay was known as Shwemyo or Golden City." [12] Mandalay was a new capital built by Mindon after he became king. Comparable feats of Buddhist piety were accomplished by Mongkut. They will be discussed in more detail later.

THE IMPERIALIST CHALLENGE: 1818–55

Both Mongkut and Mindon were acutely aware of the need to modernize their countries if they were to prevent further conquest of their territories by European empires. The impact of imperial conquest, however, was much greater upon Mindon's Burma than on Mongkut's Siam, and the Siamese response was more effective than the Burmese.

The Ava kingdom had lost Arakan and Tenasserim in 1826, at the end of the first Anglo-Burman war, and British-supported rajahs had been installed in the Burmese tributary areas of Assam and Manipur. The Treaty of Yandabo imposed a crushing indemnity of ten million rupees, recognition of the loss of the border territories, and a requirement that Burma receive a British resident in the royal capital, then Amarapura.

The second Anglo-Burman war, in 1852, resulted in the loss of Pegu and all of Lower Burma, thereby linking Tenasserim with Arakan and denying Burma any direct access to the sea. These military defeats by the British power in India constituted a major challenge to the Burmese monarchy, and it would have been surprising if the new king had not responded by an attempt to reshape his greatly reduced realm so that it could withstand further assaults.

The impact of European imperial power on Siam had also been sharp, but not nearly so devastating as its impact on Burma. An imperial challenge of England to Siam arose almost contemporaneously with the British annexation of Arakan and Tenasserim, and for similar reasons. The Arakan problem arose out of the military conquests of the Burmese on this southwestern frontier (1784–1824) and the resultant flight of Arakan leaders to British territory in Bengal (Chittagong). The Burmese were, indeed, poised for an invasion of Bengal in hot pursuit of Arakanese rebels when the British countered by an attack on Rangoon that forced the Burmese to withdraw in order to defend a more strategic front. Disaster led to the humiliating treaty of 1826.

Similarly, the Siamese faced an aggressive British power on a troubled frontier. They had long considered the Malay sultanates as tributary states, but the actual extent of Siamese control over these southern lands fluctuated. The new Bangkok dynasty vigorously sought to recapture the domain formerly ruled by Ayuthia, and in the early nineteenth century it was attempting to re-establish its supremacy in the Malayan sultanates.[13] In 1786, the Sultan of Perak had ceded the island of Penang to Francis Light of the East India Company in the expectation that the British would help him maintain the independence of his sultanate. Apparently the Company, in accepting the island, did not accept the commitment. In 1818, Bangkok ordered the Sultan of Kedah to force his neighbor, the Sultan of Perak, to send tribute to the Siamese king. When Kedah refused, the Siamese army invaded the state, and the Sultan fled to Penang, followed by many other refugees. The British refused to give military aid to the Sultan to recover his throne, but John Crawfurd was sent to Bangkok to negotiate in 1822. He failed to regain the Sultan's throne for him but, according to Hall, did indirectly secure Siamese recognition of the British position in Penang.[14] The Anglo-Siamese treaty of 1826, negotiated later by Henry Burney, contained a Siamese promise not to obstruct English trade in Trengganu and Kelantan, in exchange for a British promise not to "attack or disturb" these states. The Siamese response to the British challenge was, it appears, moderately realistic.

The Burmese, however, in 1826 were unable to recognize and deal effectively with the advancing power of Great Britain. The Burmese image of their perilous condition was remote from reality. Their chronicles recorded that the "white strangers from the west" had been permitted to advance as far as Yandabo, "for the King, from motives of piety and regard for life, made no preparations whatever to oppose them. The strangers had spent vast sums of money in their enterprises, so that by the time they reached Yandabo their resources were exhausted, and they were in great distress. They then petitioned the King, who in his clemency and generosity sent them large sums of money to pay their expenses back, and ordered them out of the country." [15]

The British apparently assumed that the Burmese court, after the shock of military defeat, would adopt a realistic policy of adaptation to Western power and diplomatic procedures. In practice the reaction was quite different. "King Bagyidaw became subject to recurring fits of melancholia, which ultimately led to insanity. The cruel loss of face that it had suffered made the Court not less but more arrogant. There was the same elementary ignorance of the outside world, the same refusal to learn. Above all, Burmese pride continued to revolt against the humiliation of having to carry on diplomatic relations with a mere viceroy." [16]

In 1837, the king's brother, Prince Tharawaddy, seized the throne and promptly repudiated the treaty of 1826. The British resident, Captain Henry Burney (who had previously negotiated the treaty of 1826 with Siam), now withdrew from the capital in disgust. Relations between the British and the Burmese court continued to deteriorate, and tensions mounted until the outbreak of the second Anglo-Burman war in 1852.

The Siamese response in 1826 to the British challenge had been significantly different, although British aspirations were also more modest. Burney went to Bangkok with no great expectations. He was instructed to reassure the Siamese that the conquest of Tenasserim was not intended as a threat and would not be followed by conquest of the Malay Peninsula. Rama I (1782–1809), a generation earlier, had sent military expeditions into Tenasserim to re-establish Siam's historic claims in Mergui and Tavoy, but he had to abandon these provinces to the Burmese in 1792.[17] When the first Anglo-Burman war broke out in 1826, the British considered inviting the Siamese to join them as allies. Siam might have retaken Tenasserim while the British were occupying Arakan; but Bangkok did not actually participate in the fighting. However, the Treaty of Yandabo does provide, in Article X, that "the good and faithful ally of the British Government, His Majesty the King of Siam, having taken a part in the present war, will, to the fullest extent, as far as regards His Majesty and his subjects, be included in the above treaty." [18]

Hall states that the British contemplated the cession of Tenasserim to Siam but, because of the intransigence of Bangkok, did not raise the possibility in the negotiations.[19] He also writes that "Siamese fears of a possible British attack were so great that everything he [Burney] did was regarded with the utmost suspicion." [20]

Under these circumstances, it appears that the Siamese gained less than they might have had they been less fearful. A trade of Tenasserim for their flimsy rights in Kedah, Perak, Trengganu, and Kelantan would, in time, have given Thailand a highly strategic port on the Bay of Bengal. But, as compared with the Burmese, this encounter with Western imperial power left the Siamese in a much more favorable position. They did not, after all, lose any territories, and their great fears of British conquests were shown to be empty. Thus, the Siamese response was one of relief, reassurance, and self-confidence, in contrast to the Burmese sense of utter humiliation.

The second wave of British expansion in Burma and Siam in the fifties and sixties also had contrasting results in the two countries. As Burmese resentment and fury against the British mounted following the humiliation of 1826, the capacity of the monarchy to maintain control over its realm declined, even in terms of traditional political forces. In 1846, Tharawaddy was succeeded by King Pagan. Hall writes of his reign that "his first chief ministers . . . carried out a systematic spoliation of his richer subjects by procuring their deaths on trumped-up charges. During their two years of power more than 6,000 people are said to have been put out of the way, and the public fury at last rose to such a pitch that to save himself the king handed over his favourites to be tortured to death. He rarely attended to business, and local officers could do much as they pleased so long as the due amount of revenue was paid regularly to the capital. Local officers . . . were as independent as mediaeval marcher lords in Europe." [21]

Hall attributes the outbreak of the second Anglo-Burman war to this breakdown of central control. The local officials in Pegu and Rangoon were particularly irresponsible, according to the British, in their treatment of English commercial interests. A sequence of incidents led finally to a British ultimatum, which was rejected, and the immediate occupation of Rangoon and Martaban in April, 1852. It appears that the initial aim of the British had been merely, by military pressure, to compel the Burmese court to negotiate, pay reparations, and establish normal relationships. But Ava refused, and the British, after a long wait, decided to annex the coastal area. At the end of the year they occupied the province of Pegu and on December 20, 1852, announced, unilaterally, the annexation of this province. London, in sanctioning the occupation, had stipulated that the court of Ava must sign a treaty recognizing the cession.

At the very moment that the British proclamation of annexation was being read, a revolution against King Pagan started in Amarapura. Prince Mindon, a half-brother of Pagan, raised the flag of revolt and in February, 1853, was able to gain the throne. Negotiations were immediately opened. Mindon apparently hoped that the British would return Pegu, but he found them adamant in their insistence that they keep what they had conquered, although they offered to trade a strip of timber-rich land north of Pegu, which they had also seized, in exchange for a treaty acknowledging the territorial transfer. This Mindon refused to accept, and negotiations were terminated in March, 1853.[22]

Clearly, the underlying aims of British policy at this time were to secure conditions under which trade could be carried on by their merchants with security of life and property. The inability of the Burmese polity to provide such conditions, owing to internal weaknesses, aggravated by their unwillingness to enter into regular communications with the British, exacerbated misunderstandings and mutual hostility to the point where war broke out, followed by the British annexation of Lower Burma.

Simultaneously, the British were making demands on the Siamese. In 1850, before the outbreak of the Anglo-Burman war, Sir James Brooke (of Sarawak) went to Bangkok to negotiate a new commercial treaty to replace the unsatisfactory agreement of 1826. The ailing King Rama III was unable to deal personally with the British envoy. He died in April, 1851, and was succeeded by Mongkut. The Siamese officials who dealt with Brooke found various reasons to put him off, including the fact that his credentials were two years old and had been signed by Lord Palmerston, not Queen Victoria.[23] Just as Mindon's accession followed a crisis in Anglo-Burmese relations, so now did Mongkut's enthronement follow the collapse of Brooke's mission. But the sequels were quite different.

ROYAL RESPONSES: 1855, 1867

In 1855, a second British mission, under Sir John Bowring, came to Bangkok. This time the English were rewarded with a treaty which laid the basis for the modernization of Siam, as we have noted above. But the circumstances surrounding the negotiation of this treaty were utterly different from those attending the contemporaneous ending of the Anglo-Burman war. The British annexation of Pegu in 1853 must have been well known to Mongkut, and he was therefore well aware that disastrous consequences might follow should he fail to satisfy the minimal demands of the British.

To mitigate anticipated difficulties and to lessen the possible humiliation of capitulating under pressure to British demands, Mongkut determined to launch in advance some of the reforms that he knew, from Brooke's mission, would be on the agenda. He also played for time to establish his own royal authority before having to face the British representatives. Brooke had been instructed to go to Bangkok in 1851, shortly after the accession of the new monarch. Mongkut, however, wrote almost immediately, in May, to the governor of Singapore requesting that no envoy be sent until after the cremation of the late king had taken place. Meanwhile, within a few months, Mongkut proclaimed several major reforms affecting import duties and rice exports. This reduced the pressure for immediate negotiations, and the British withdrew the Brooke mission.[24] It was not, therefore, until 1855, four years later, that the Bowring mission was dispatched.

How carefully Mongkut worked to assure the success of these negotiations is shown by the fact that he himself took the initiative in suggesting a mission and in nominating a candidate of his own choice to head it. In mid-1854, Mongkut wrote Bowring, with whom he had previously carried on a personal correspondence, suggesting that he announce, at least three months in advance, his time of arrival, so that preparations could be made to receive the mission "with all suitable honors and respect," and, moreover, so that steps could be taken "to quell the fears of the people, who are of various races, and prevent exaggerated reports, because it is very seldom foreign vessels of war or steamers visit Siam." [25] In the same letter, Mongkut asked Bowring to indicate, in a private communication, the nature of his mission, "so that I might consult with my Council, and know what clauses in the proposed Treaty they would be willing to agree to, and what they would not. I would therefore inform you of the same for your consideration, and thereby will save a good deal of time and discussions after Your Excellency's arrival here." [26] Six months later he wrote again, informing Bowring that everything was satisfactory and the royal government was prepared to receive him.

This sequence of events affords a striking contrast to those which took place in Burma. Understandably, many of the nobles and high officials of the Siamese court were fearful and suspicious of foreigners, especially as they must have known that the proposed abolition of state monopolies would undermine their sources of income. Any demands for change, backed by demonstrations of force, would have confirmed the worst fears of these elements. Moreover, the unexpected appearance at the royal capital of foreign representatives making unprecedented demands would have given little or no opportunity for those who might have been willing to negotiate to pave the way for agreement. Instead, fearful and threatened elements could immediately have spread reports that would have mobilized the population in support of fierce resistance.

Mongkut, however, was able to take the precautions needed to prepare the population for the outlandish visitors and to mobilize support among his own officials for those changes which he foresaw would be unavoidable. Indeed, by launching his own reforms several years before the arrival of Bowring, he was able to ease the costs of transition. That his policy was well conceived is demonstrated by the fact that the actual negotiations took less than a month. Bowring arrived on March 27, 1855, and the treaty was signed on April 18.

Having broken ground with the British treaty, Mongkut subsequently entertained a succession of representatives from the European great powers, each of whom was granted similar privileges. Siam thus not only opened its doors to international trade, but also established itself as an independent state in the "family of nations." All of this was done without resort to violence on either side. No doubt the Burmese example, coming shortly after the Opium War which had shown that even the great Chinese Empire could not withstand the British navy, dramatized for Mongkut and his leading officials the real dangers that a refusal to accede to the British demands might entail. By accepting at face value the proposition that the chief British interest was in the expansion of trade, not in further additions to the imperial territories, the Siamese were able to succeed where the Burmese had so disastrously failed.

In contrast to Mongkut, who started to pave the way for a treaty with the British upon reaching the throne, Mindon waited almost ten years after his accession to power to reach the point where he could sign an agreement that was less far-reaching than the Anglo-Siamese accord. The man who negotiated the Burmese treaty was Colonel (Sir) Arthur Phayre. He had become commissioner of Pegu upon its annexation in 1852. Three years later he headed a mission to Amarapura and held long conversations with Mindon in an attempt to win a general treaty of friendship. There was to be no mention of the humiliating loss of Burmese territory. Although the treaty was not concluded, a basis of mutual understanding was established between Mindon and Phayre, who had learned to speak Burmese and was well acquainted with the country's history, literature, and religion.[27]

By 1862, Phayre had become chief commissioner of British Burma, which had just been formed by consolidating the conquered districts. Mindon now welcomed Phayre as an old friend when he returned to Mandalay, the new capital, and a commercial treaty was signed which provided for reciprocal trading privileges. But the old system of monopolies was not abolished, and the treaty was much less thoroughgoing than the Siamese treaty signed seven years previously. Even the subsequent Anglo-Burman treaty of 1867, which, on paper at least, abolished most of the monopolies and established extraterritorial rights, did not prove as satisfactory to the British as its Siamese counterpart of 1855.[28]

The basic differences between the Burmese and Siamese responses to the impact of the West had become clear by the eighteen-fifties and sixties. Yet the points of similarity were also striking, especially in the secular reforms launched by the contemporaries, Mindon and Mongkut. The comparable reforms of Mongkut will be discussed in more detail below, but it is worth pointing here to the policies of Mindon. Furnivall, who calls him "probably the best sovereign of his line," notes that he introduced coinage,[29] restructured the taxation system, abolished royal monopolies, and built a fleet of river steamers. "He dispatched missions to Europe, sent lads abroad to study English and French, and had others trained in telegraphy in Rangoon, subsequently introducing a telegraph system based on the Morse Code adapted to the Burmese alphabet. He encouraged industry by erecting factories with European machinery and in some cases under European management, for the manufacture of lac, cutch, sugar, and of cotton and silk piece goods; with a view to making Upper Burma less dependent on British Burma he stimulated the cultivation of rice, apparently with no little success. These experiments were costly, and he was 'induced under the stress of financial difficulties to obtain all the cotton he could to meet the requirements of certain European houses to whom he was in debt, and to pay the cost of machinery and steamers he was persuaded to order from Europe.' This, however, was in line with his general fiscal policy of reducing taxation by deriving revenue from trade. . . .

"During his reign there was a great increase in the value of the trade between British territory and independent Burma." Imports from British Burma rose from 4 million rupees in 1858/59 to 18 million by 1877/78, while exports grew from 3 to 20 million during the same period.[30]

Anticipating the reforms in territorial administration introduced almost a generation later in Siam by King Chulalongkorn, King Mindon tried to consolidate royal control over the Burmese provinces by setting up ten new regions, each under the control of a *kayaingwun,* charged with responsibility for supervising the work of provincial *myowuns* (*monthon* and *muang,* respectively, in Siam). "The *Kayaingwuns* were charged with inspecting each *myowun* court three times a year and with transmitting information, complaints, and petitions to the *Hlutdaw* [royal council] on a bimonthly basis covering matters of administration. The *Kayaingwuns* exercised no original court jurisdiction, but they reviewed criminal decisions by the *Myowun* and referred to the *Hlutdaw* cases involving extreme punishment." [31]

Yet Mindon had not been able to carry his reforms to fruition when he died in 1878. "The reforming faction at court," Cady notes, "was still in the ascendancy, although their attempts to carry on under King Thibaw sadly miscarried." [32] The dramatic contrast between the Siamese and Burmese records is pointed up by the miserable failure of Mindon's successor, Thibaw, and the striking success of Chulalongkorn, who followed Mongkut.

The reign of King Thibaw, indeed, was short-lived and disastrous. It was soon terminated by the third Anglo-Burman war. The *Kinwun Mingyi*, a major holdover official from the Mindon period, did indeed try to carry forward the reform policy. "He proposed to distribute governmental responsibilities between fourteen functional departmental heads, who would operate as a kind of cabinet in the European fashion. [Chulalongkorn was not able to make a basic reform of this character until 1892.] He assigned control of tax revenues and expenditures (key powers) plus the operation of royal monopolies to the four *Atwinwuns*, while three *Wungyis* took over departments covering royal lands, waterways, elephants, the arsenals, and the army. The other departments covering judicial appeals, foreign diplomatic and commercial relations, police, and civil administration were assigned to men of *Wundauk* rank." [33]

These reforms, Cady writes, had no chance of adoption. "On the eve of Thibaw's final quarrel with British Burma, in 1884–1885, the Burma administration was in a sad state of confusion, with lawless bands in actual control of much of the area. Rebels holding Sagaing, almost directly across the river from Mandalay, were defying the government. The renewal of the slaughter of followers of one of the exiled princes in 1884 stimulated demands at Rangoon for intervention or annexation. A formidable Shan rebellion began in June, 1883, and the Kachins invaded Upper Burma in force in 1884–1885. Concurrently, Chinese freebooters, in 1884, helped Burmese authorities repel a Kachin attack upon Bhamo and the Chinese then themselves burned and sacked the city." [34]

Such were the conditions in Upper Burma when the British, on October 22, 1885, issued an ultimatum giving the Burmese only twenty days in which to accede to a list of stringent demands. When the court rejected most of the demands, the British promptly launched an attack, taking Mandalay on November 28. Thibaw was exiled to Madras, and the Burmese monarchy was extinguished. Upper Burma was added to Britain's Indian Empire.

SIAMESE STRATEGIES

The international pressures which destroyed the Burmese monarchy in 1885 had their counterpart in Siam. Mongkut's success in negotiating treaties with the great powers, beginning in 1855, by no means assured him the tranquil possession of his throne. Indeed, in the last decade of his reign he confronted mounting pressures from both the British and the French which made him increasingly uneasy for the future. These episodes are worth describing as evidence of the continuing growth of Siamese capabilities for dealing with Europeans.

It will be recalled that the treaty of 1826 had, in effect, confirmed the royal prerogatives of Siam in Trengganu and Kelantan, while British rights to trade there were also recognized. In fact, however, these sultanates were substantially autonomous and carried on their own rather chaotic diplomacy with both the British and the Siamese. In 1862, the Siamese decided to take advantage of some dynastic disputes to reassert their control over these Malayan states. They supported the claims of a refugee pretender to the throne of Trengganu. Thereupon the British in Singapore sent a warship to compel the Siamese protégé in Trengganu to surrender. When the sultan refused to comply, the British shelled his fort, causing him to flee for refuge into the interior.

This bombardment caused a sensation in Bangkok which "changed to near panic when presently it was learned that the ships which had bombarded Trengganu had arrived at the mouth of the Chao Phya." [35] The way in which Mongkut dealt with this crisis is perhaps best stated in his own words, as described in his letter to a nephew. He begins by telling how the British warships had come to the mouth of the river and there anchored while sending a request for permission to sail up to Bangkok. Mongkut's letter then outlines his own speculations about the various possible aims of the British commodore, Lord John Hay, and the probable consequences of alternative courses of action. These views were communicated to his chief ministers, and agents were dispatched to determine the opinion of the foreign traders and other elements of the population. Mongkut wrote:

> Since it was not certain whether Lord John Hay might not do to Bangkok what he had already done to Trengganu, the merchants were warned by the [British] Consul to take good care of their own goods and personal safety.
> These wild whispers put the more weak-minded part of the population on the verge of panic, but the situation was not so serious, since I remained firm. . . .
> Since Lord John Hay was determined to bring his ship up to Bangkok, and since the fortresses at Paknam and Paklat were unprepared and could not be made ready within a single day nor in a single night, it was thought that if any dispute should arise out of our refusal to allow entry to the British warship, the British might make a forced entry into the river, and

at whatever fortress they arrived at, they might make their way into it to spike and dismantle the guns in the manner similar to what they had done in China and elsewhere.

It was agreed, therefore, to send Lord John Hay a written permission and to accord him treatment suitable to a visitor from a friendly nation.

Subsequently, emissaries were sent to welcome the British commodore and to invite him to proceed to Bangkok, where he was received with all due ceremony and escorted to a public audience with the king. Mongkut continues:

> I offered them my greetings and enquired after the purpose of their visit. Lord John Hay replied that he had no other purpose than to pay his respects to me, whom he had heard to have taken so great an interest in the British people as to have endeavoured to learn their language.[36]

So ended without untoward consequences what at first looked to the Siamese court like a threatening *détente*. Had they acted with less presence of mind, the affair might well have led to an ugly incident. As it was, in the spring of the following year, 1863, Bangkok, after protesting the bombardment of Trengganu, withdrew their protégé and abandoned further efforts to bring the sultanate under control.

In nearby Pahang, the Siamese had also supported a candidate for the throne. In this case, however, the matter settled itself when, after a civil war, the Siamese protégé took power and the British offered no objections.[37]

No doubt the British home government was less than enthusiastic for new imperial adventures, and the Singapore authorities, much as they might have welcomed an incident that would afford pretexts for a more forward policy among the Malay states, decided to move more cautiously.

The dangers from the British side were no doubt magnified in Mongkut's mind because he was simultaneously under pressure from the French. In 1861, the French, who had just decided to turn their conquests in Cochin China into a permanent colony, notified the king of Cambodia that they would be happy to help him maintain his independence of Siam. The Siamese, who had carved their own kingdom out of the ruins of the ancient Khmer empire, had frequently fought and subdued the Cambodian kings and at this time regarded Cambodia as a tributary state. The current Cambodian king, Norodom, had just ascended the throne in 1860. He had obtained his education in Bangkok, however, and replied to the French that the Siamese were his faithful allies and had helped his country maintain its freedom from the Vietnamese.

Moreover, shortly after claiming the throne, Norodom had to flee to Siam to seek help against a rebellion led by his younger brother. Bangkok supplied a steamer to take Norodom back to his own country in March, 1862, but failed to supply a supporting army. Meanwhile, Norodom's supporters, with some help from the French, had put down the rebellion, and the king was able to resume his throne peacefully. The French now began to demand that the tribute which had formerly been paid to the Vietnamese in Hué should be paid to the French. It soon became apparent, however, that the Siamese resident in the Cambodian capital of Oudong was more influential than the king himself. In July, 1863, Admiral Lagrandière, who had already played a leading role in the conquest of Cochin China, came to Oudong and "offered" to protect the Cambodians against Siam. Apparently Norodom felt he had little option, and so he complied with the French demand.

The Siamese, with British support—now that the Malayan situation had been composed—protested that, as a Siamese vassal state, Cambodia could negotiate only through Bangkok. The Siamese resident in Oudong insisted that Norodom sign a document (December, 1863) acknowledging his tributary status and changing his title to Viceroy of Cambodia. Mongkut, in return, was to go to Oudong to preside at the coronation ceremonies. When the French objected strenuously, Mongkut proposed that Norodom should come to Bangkok for the coronation, especially since the Cambodian regalia were there in safekeeping. The French then threatened to take the Cambodian capital by force, and naval reinforcements were mobilized. On April 17, 1864, having turned back from his abortive trip to Bangkok, Norodom signed the treaty of protection with France.[38]

Clearly the French felt that their position in Cambodia would be improved if the Siamese could be induced to accept it. Accordingly, a French naval officer, Gabriel Aubaret, who had been appointed consul in Bangkok, was instructed to open negotiations for a Franco-Siamese treaty on Cambodia. An agreement was signed in 1865 whereby Siam recognized the French protectorate in Cambodia and annulled the agreement of 1863, with Norodom confirming his vassalage to Bangkok. France, in return, acknowledged that Cambodia was an independent kingdom, that it might pay tribute to Siam if it wished, and that it could continue having its princes educated in Bangkok. Moreover, the French confirmed the status of Battambang, Angkor, and some adjacent territory as parts of the Siamese realm.

When this agreement was submitted to Paris for ratification, however, it was rejected as too favorable to Bangkok, and Aubaret was instructed to seek a revision. Mongkut now decided to draw the line and refused to offer further concessions. Aubaret then began to conduct himself in a very rude manner, and thoroughly antagonized the king. Eventually, in January, 1867, after six months of acrimonious disputation, Mongkut decided to send a mission to Paris to negotiate the treaty. He apparently considered the possibility of using Sir John Bowring, his old friend, as his representative, but finally abandoned the project, feeling that he could trust only one of his own countrymen.

That Mongkut felt his kingdom to be in most precarious circumstances is evident from a letter he addressed to his embassy in Paris. "The British and the French," he wrote,

can entertain no other feeling for each other than mutual esteem as fellow human beings, whereas the likes of us who are wild and savage, can only be regarded by them as animals. We have no means of knowing whether or in what way they have contrived beforehand to divide our country among themselves. . . .

With France's increasing animosity against Siam, where could she turn? Siam would be driven by the fear of France to seek protection from Great Britain, thereby to continue to be forever under that protection, in the like manner as many states in Hindustan have done and as Burma is doing at the present moment. . . .

As regards the French, they are distinguished for their vainglorious disposition. Their Emperor, famed for his descent from a line of tigers and cobras, would, after his ascent to the Throne, seek colonies that are rich and vast, so that he might exercise his power over them. These lands between Annam and Burma must appear to him to be ownerless and therefore desirable.[39]

Aware as he was of the Scylla and Charybdis between which his kingdom drifted, Mongkut reflected on the alternatives open to him. He recognized that the slightest false move could lead to disaster. On no account must pretexts be given either great power for moving against him. "The Annamites," he wrote, "have been as deaf, dumb and stubborn as the Siamese in previous reigns. Their stubbornness caused them to turn small incidents into serious ones, with the result that their country became a French Colony in the end." Perhaps, he reflected hopefully, the policies of Aubaret were his own and not those of Paris. If so, the Siamese mission in France should be able to arrive at a reasonable agreement. If not, ". . . if you should be forced to give in to all of Aubaret's demands, you must be ready to make sacrifices, so as to bring the whole unpleasant business to a close." [40]

Mongkut concludes his letter with these paragraphs:

If, however, they refuse to remove Aubaret from Bangkok but insist on keeping him here with full power, then the matter would be beyond my endurance. If you fail to get Aubaret removed, then you may cross over to Britain and ask for whatever assistance that you may think fit from the responsible ministers, from the English lords both in and out of office and from Sir John Bowring. I have my own reasons for this decision.

Since we are now being constantly abused by the French because we will not allow ourselves to be placed under their domination like the Cambodians, it is for us to decide what we are going to do; whether to swim up-river to make friends with the crocodile or to swim out to sea and hang on to the whale. . . .

It is sufficient for us to keep ourselves without our house and home; it may be necessary for us to forego some of our former power and influence.[41]

A revised treaty with France was signed on July 15, 1867. Siam again recognized France's protectorate over Cambodia and renounced its vassalage agreement of 1863. But there was no recognition, on the French side, of Cambodia's independence or of its right to offer tribute to Bangkok. The Cambodian provinces of Battambang and Angkor were renounced in favor of Siam—but without consultation with Norodom. The French were given the right to trade and travel up the Mekong and its tributary rivers. Aubaret was shortly thereafter transferred from Bangkok.

Little more than a year later, on October 1, 1868, King Mongkut died. He had sacrificed portions of his empire to the advancing British and French empires, but he had succeeded in keeping the greater part of it intact. He turned over to his son and successor, King Chulalongkorn, most of the royal heritage.

BETWEEN THE CROCODILE AND THE WHALE

The major crisis of the Siamese state, however, was not to come for another twenty-five years. In 1893, eight years after the liquidation of the Burmese monarchy, the French almost brought an end to the independence of Siam. The absorption of Upper Burma into British Burma in 1886 was keenly resented by the French, who had been negotiating with the court in Mandalay at that time. They promptly accelerated their efforts to extend their Vietnamese holdings westward. In May, 1886, they had made a provisional agreement with Bangkok for the appointment of a French vice-consul in Luang Prabang, thereby implicitly acknowledging Siamese sovereignty over Laos. Yet, in 1889, the French ambassador in London suggested to the British prime minister that Siam ought to be regarded as a buffer state between the French and British empires, but that the boundary between French Indo-China and Siam should, for the most part, follow the Mekong, thus assimilating most of the Laotian territory to the French empire.

Two years later, Paris made a new proposal that the British and French governments agree not to extend their influence beyond the Mekong. Since the Shan states tributary to Burma which Britain had already annexed extended to the east of the Mekong, and since French control did not yet reach as far west as the Mekong, the British rejected this proposal. Meanwhile the Siamese, having accepted a demarcation of their frontier with British Burma, sought the aid of London to counter further extensions of French imperial control.

In March, 1893, the French ambassador declared that France regarded all the territory east of the Mekong as traditionally tributary to Vietnam and hence as not a part of Siam. Bangkok appears to have relied heavily on British support to sustain its position, but at this point the British foreign minister, Lord Rosebery, adopted a posture of "cautious diplomatic reserve." [42]

Meanwhile, the French had been preparing for the annexation of all the trans-Mekong territories of Siam, and their representative in Bangkok, Auguste Pavie, who had long played a leading role in these developments, demanded that Siam evacuate certain disputed areas. In April, 1893, military forces seized the Laotian areas claimed by France. Bangkok, recognizing the futility of armed resistance to the French, offered to arbitrate and appealed to Britain for assistance. London replied that the Siamese should avoid any actions that might provoke France to resort to war.

However, it was scarcely possible for a country faced with military aggression on its frontiers to avoid "incidents." To make a long story short, the resulting clashes were used by the French to justify the dispatch of warships to Bangkok in July. The British also sent several naval vessels as a precautionary measure. Earlier treaties had specified that foreign warships would not proceed beyond Paknam, at the river's mouth, except with permission. The French ships, however, started to sail up the river. The Siamese fort at Paknam then fired on the French vessels, which returned the fire, causing casualties on both sides. At this critical point, according to Hall, "the Siamese committed the serious blunder of firing the first shots in the encounter. By disregarding Rosebery's reiterated advice, they had played into the hands of the French." The two ships proceeded on to Bangkok, where Siamese diplomacy manifested itself at its best. "Prince Devawongse [the foreign minister] rose to the occasion by congratulating their commander on his skill and daring in forcing an entrance. His admirable suavity and restraint probably saved the situation." [43]

On July 20, the French delivered an ultimatum demanding that all the territory east of the Mekong, including Luang Prabang, be ceded to France. In addition, an indemnity of three million francs should be paid for the casualties suffered on the French warships, and the Siamese officers responsible should be punished. Prince Devawongse agreed to the first two demands and offered to compromise on the third. The French replied that their demands must be fully met.

The British, who, up to this point, had been content to caution the Siamese not to offend the French, now became alarmed because they saw that the French policy would necessarily precipitate a Franco-British clash in the upper Mekong, where, as we have seen, Shan territories annexed by Britain extended east of the river. When the British now asked the French for clarification of their aims, Paris replied that after Siam had capitulated it would be possible to establish a buffer state between the two European empires. Accordingly, the British now urged Bangkok to accede to the French demands, and the French established a blockade of the Chao Phya. "Two days later Chulalongkorn, who had been in a state of collapse throughout the crisis and had left matters entirely to Prince Devawongse, accepted the terms of the ultimatum unconditionally." [44]

Not content with these dramatic gains, the French next insisted that the Siamese evacuate Battambang and Angkor, withdraw their troops for a distance of twenty-five kilometers from the west bank of the Mekong, and permit the French to occupy the Siamese province of Chantabun in the southeast as a guarantee. In subsequent treaty negotiations, the French also added new demands which appeared to endanger Siam's independence and territorial integrity. The Siamese tried vigorously to resist these demands by diplomatic means, but after another ultimatum from the French, and after the British again advised Chulalongkorn to submit, a treaty was signed on October 3, 1893, in which the French won all they had asked. Further resistance by the Siamese, according to Hall, might well have cost Siam her independence. He continues: "Had matters reached such a pass it is an interesting speculation what action Britain would have taken. As it was, Siam owed her salvation not a little to the consistency with which British diplomacy concentrated upon obtaining from France a guarantee of the independence of the basin of the Menam." [45]

An abortive attempt to create a buffer state on the upper Mekong now took place in true comic-opera fashion. The British and French agreed to send missions to the area to create the buffer state. The local Burmese official, confused by conflicting reports which had come to him, decided to raise a French flag over his court. However, the British mission arrived first and substituted the Union Jack, while the local governor fled. The French party, arriving shortly thereafter, raised a howl of protest, and any hope of a settlement on the spot evaporated. Public opinion in both countries was inflamed. The threat of war seemed real. Diplomatic negotiations between London and Paris, however, eventually resulted in the agreement of January, 1896, whereby Britain abandoned in favor of France its claims to any trans-Mekong territory, in return for a guarantee of the independence of the Chao Phya valley.

Tensions continued to plague Franco-Siamese relations, however, and it was not until 1904 that Paris withdrew its forces in Chantabun in exchange for further revisions of the Laos frontier, the abandonment of Siamese claims to sovereignty over Luang Prabang, and the establishment of a commission on the Cambodian frontier. In 1907, Battambang and Siemreap were surrendered, in exchange for which France gave up extraterritorial jurisdiction over its Asian subjects in Siam.

Two years later, a new Anglo-Siamese treaty provided for the surrender of all Siamese claims over the Malay states of Kelantan, Trengganu, Kedah, and Perlis, in exchange for the abolition of British extraterritorial rights and the extension of a railway construction loan.

THE CAUSES OF SURVIVAL

To what extent did the survival of Siam as an independent monarchy through this nerve-racking period of European imperial expansionism result from Franco-British rivalry and the need of these two

bitterly opposed powers for a buffer zone? Alternatively, can the preservation of Siamese sovereignty be attributed to the skill and effective
performance of the Siamese monarchy and its ruling institutions?

Certainly Franco-British rivalry was also a key factor in Burmese
history. It was the effort of Mindon and his successor, Thibaw, to establish diplomatic and commercial relations with France which had heightened British suspicions and precipitated the final loss of the country's
independence. At the one time when Britain and France did attempt
to create, artificially, a buffer state, the effort collapsed immediately
and never had a chance of succeeding. When British and French imperial ambitions clashed even more dramatically at Fashoda, in 1898,
the result was not, of course, the creation of a Sudanese buffer state,
but the partitioning of this African realm between areas of French and
British control. When Anglo-Russian rivalries shortly thereafter threatened to explode in war over Iran, the nominal independence of the
country was retained, but it was also partitioned, in a sense, by the
creation of "spheres of influence."

It might be argued that the international rivalries of the great powers prevented the partitioning of China and hence preserved that country's independence. A number of striking similarities and differences
between the Siamese and Chinese cases could be examined, but China
was so much larger and hence more difficult to control, and the international rivalries involved so much more complex, that it would be misleading to draw comparisons without more extended discussion. But it
should be noted that during the eighteen-nineties China was being
divided into spheres of influence and seemed destined for partition.

Afghanistan appears to be the only authentic case of a country whose
independence can be clearly attributed to a bargain between competing
European powers. But the other differences between this country and
Siam are striking. Kabul was not the center of an effective monarchy
governing the whole Afghan realm. Rather, there was a congeries of
petty tribal states, so remote from the main channels of commerce, so
intrinsically unattractive from an economic point of view, and so for-
bidding militarily in terms of natural geographic defenses and the
wild will to autonomy of its people that the rival British and Russian
empires were content to draw a *"cordon sanitaire"* around the territory,
give it an artificial name, and recognize its leading city as the capital
of a factitious "state."

The Siamese case differed in all these respects. There was a central
government, although the extent of its effective control tended to de-

cline the farther one went from the capital. The Chao Phya valley was easily accessible to the outside world, and the possible economic value of the area was far greater for European empire-builders than was the Afghan land.

This is not a complete rejection of the thesis that Siamese independence could be attributed to Anglo-French imperial rivalry. Rather, it is my contention that, given the confrontation of these two growing empires, the Chao Phya valley might well have been seized by one or the other, or partitioned by the two. The third possibility, the preservation of its independence, became a practicable solution only because of the relatively effective political and administrative system which the Siamese built, as well as their capacity for diplomatic equanimity. Certainly the Siamese army could not have withstood a determined attack by either Britain or France, yet it could have made a conquest costly. Perhaps more important, by creating a relatively orderly domestic environment in which European commerce and the exploitation of timber and mineral resources could be conducted without great danger, the pretexts for imperial attack were reduced, if not eliminated.

We must remember that policies of imperial conquest were usually, if not always, controversial at home. The history of British imperialism in Asia is remarkable for the continuing struggle between the home government, whether in London or Calcutta, which typically resisted further expansion, and its field agents, who persistently demanded a more aggressive forward policy. To swing headquarters into support of any new military act of expansionism, it was always necessary to show that outrages had been committed and that maintenance of the *status quo* would lead to worse difficulties.

It was recognition of this fact which led the British to caution the Siamese in 1893 against any act that could be used by the French as a provocation. What country would not attempt to resist the intrusion of a warship by a threatening foreign power into its territorial waters? Yet when the Siamese dared to fire upon a French warship starting up the Chao Phya, the occasion was used by Paris as a pretext for demanding indemnities, punishment of the "guilty" officers, and the cession of large areas. Confronted by such a danger, the Siamese foreign minister, with utter *sang froid,* could "congratulate" the French commander on his skill and daring. Nor was the dangerous situation intensified by mob violence, outbreaks of public passion, and reprisals against the persons and property of Frenchmen in Siam, as might well have taken place under such circumstances.

Let us examine some other dimensions of the traditional Siamese polity's performance in order to test the hypothesis offered here—namely, that the preservation of Siam's independence resulted from its political and administrative efficacy as much as from the balance of power generated by Franco-British rivalry. I shall examine first the problem of dynastic successions, and secondly the development of foreign trade.

ROYAL SUCCESSION

In both Burma and Siam, the same basic formulae governed the institution of monarchy. Among these norms was the rule of succession by sons or brothers of the reigning monarch. Unlike the principle of primogeniture which prevails in England and other Western countries, however, it was possible for younger sons or uncles to succeed. Something can be said for both systems, but each has its distinctive difficulties. The rule of primogeniture can bring disaster when the eldest son turns out to be highly incapable of ruling. Then even the availability of more competent siblings may not suffice to save the fortunes of a reigning house.

The lack of such a rule does permit a choice among those members of the royal family who show greatest promise. On the other hand, if disputes arise among rival contenders for the throne, dynastic wars may ensue, followed by destruction of the losers. The dynasty may lose many capable leaders, and the king may become so anxious that the fear of assassination dominates all his policies. Both the Siamese and Burmese monarchies were vulnerable to these evils. However, it is a notable fact that in the nineteenth century these typical difficulties plagued the Burmese throne markedly, whereas they passed lightly over the Siamese ruling house. I cannot explain this difference here, nor, indeed, may it be possible to go far in offering explanations, but I wish at least to demonstrate the fact. Deeper explanations would no doubt require depths of cultural and psychological analysis which cannot be attempted here.

Let us begin with the circumstances preceding and following the reign of kings Mindon and Mongkut, about whom so much has already been said in this chapter. Strangely enough, both men were preceded by their half brothers and followed by their sons; but the successions were marked by violence in Burma, whereas they were peaceful in Siam.

Mindon's half brother Pagan was king during the disaster of the second Anglo-Burman war. At the height of the crisis, in mid-December, 1852, when the position of the Burmese had become desperate, the

Mindon prince went to the ancestral city of Shwebo, from which the founder of the dynasty had come, and there raised the standard of revolt. Dissidence had been gaining ground in the capital (then Amarapura), especially after King Pagan had decided to make a scapegoat of the popular general who had surrendered to the British, together with his whole family. In February, 1853, a number of key ministers threw their support to Mindon, and he entered the city victoriously, amid popular rejoicing. It was characteristic of Mindon, though not of his line, to be generous to his enemies, and so he graciously spared the life of his half brother.[46] Quite different was the usual story.

Mindon hoped to pave the way for a peaceful succession following his own death. Both Burma and Siam had an interesting institution for the heir apparent, who was given dignities and important responsibilities as a way of preparing for the succession. The office was known as *Einshemin* (Lord of the Eastern House) in Burma and *Uparat* or *Wang Na* (Front Palace) in Siam. In the latter case, indeed, the office became so important that it was often referred to, by Europeans, as the "Second King." Mongkut relied heavily on the assistance of his full younger brother, whom he made *Uparat*. This man was more Westernized and spoke better English than the king himself, and Mongkut depended on him for help and advice.

Mindon also appointed a brother as *Einshemin*. As was usual, he was assigned responsibility as presiding officer over the Burmese royal council, the *Hlutdaw*.[47] In 1866, however, two amibitious sons of Mindon broke into the *Hlutdaw* where the *Einshemin* was presiding and assassinated him. The rebels then killed several of his followers and pursued the king himself. Mindon took refuge in his palace, where he endured a night-long siege. The army remained loyal, however, and the next day the rebels were routed. But Mindon was so unnerved by this experience that he never appointed another *Einshemin*. Thus, at his death there was no one to whom the throne could automatically be passed.[48]

On his deathbed in September, 1878, Mindon indicated his preference for one of his sons, the Nyaungyan prince, as his successor. Now one of the standard rules in both Siam and Burma was that the succession should go to a son by a royal queen, not one of commoner origins, but this was by no means an inflexible rule. It so happened that the mother of the Nyaungyan prince was not of royal blood. The chief queen, as luck would have it, had never borne Mindon a son, but she had two daughters. She arranged to have one of these, Supayalat, married to a young and relatively unknown prince, Thibaw. The leading minister, the *Kinwun Mingyi*, who had been a major source of strength to Mindon in his reform policies, decided to support Thibaw for the throne, in the expectation that he would prove a pliable instrument in the hands of the *Hlutdaw* and that, in effect, something like a system of limited monarchy could be introduced.

Under these circumstances, it transpired that when the dying Mindon called for the Nyaungyan prince to be brought to him for designation as his successor, he discovered that control of the palace had already been seized by his chief queen on behalf of her daughter, Supayalat, and of Thibaw. The Nyaungyan prince, accompanied by a brother who had also been regarded as a promising candidate, discreetly took refuge with the British resident. The two princes were smuggled out of the country to India, where they lived the rest of their lives as exiles.[49]

It soon became apparent that the weak Thibaw was to be controlled not by the *Hlutdaw* and the reform-minded *Kinwun Mingyi* but by his power-hungry queen and her henchman, the chief of the palace guard. As soon as they had consolidated their power sufficiently, they arrested several hundred members of the royal family, and on February 18, 1879, thirty-two prisoners, including eight prince-brothers of Thibaw, were executed. An estimated eighty or more additional victims were subsequently killed, including boyhood friends of Thibaw himself who had warned him against his queen and mother-in-law. The new king, who apparently had shown some promise as a scholar and was personally a kind-hearted fellow, took to drink as an escape from the disgraceful predicament in which he found himself. British authorities in Mandalay denounced the orgy of executions, and proposals of intervention on behalf of the Nyaungyan prince were rife. The *Kinwun Mingyi* managed to hold on to his office, but only by surrendering his influence. The succession struggle, in other words, coming at a time when the very existence of the encircled kingdom was at stake, so weakened the monarchy that it was rendered totally incapable of mastering the problems which further disrupted Anglo-Burmese relations, leading to the final catastrophe of 1885.

The Siamese succession after Mongkut was as triumphantly successful as the succession after Mindon was disastrous—for in the former case, a great king was followed by one even greater, whereas in the latter, the great king was succeeded by an utter failure.

That the succession after Mongkut would be successful could by no means have been predicted during the last days of his reign. Often enough, the Siamese *Wang Na* did not survive the king, and in any event there was no occupant of this office to succeed Mongkut when he died. On September 22, 1868, the condition of the ailing monarch had become severe, and he summoned to his royal bedchamber two of his brothers and a high official in whom he placed much confidence, Chao Phya Sri Suriyawongse, the minister of the South (*Kalahom*). He asked these men to take joint responsibility for the conduct of state affairs. Two days later, he wrote a letter which was read aloud before the full council of princes and ministers. It stated:

> It is the King's wish that the person who shall succeed him to the throne, be he a royal brother, a royal son, or a royal nephew, shall do so only with the full approval of the ennobled princes and ministers of state in council. The princes and ministers shall place their choice upon a prince, endowed with the most ability and wisdom, who is best qualified to preserve and further the peace and welfare of the Kingdom.[50]

Now the fifteen-year-old Prince Chulalongkorn was the oldest son of a royal mother and had become the king's favorite, so that he truly favored him for the royal succession. Moreover, the foreigners in Siam, thinking in terms of primogeniture, naturally regarded him as the heir apparent. But Mongkut was fearful that the youth would not be able to defend himself against an ambitious rival, and so was unwilling to name him as his successor. Indeed, he sent a message to Sri Suriyawongse saying that he did not wish Chulalongkorn to become king. "He is not old enough," he said, "to bear the whole burden, and it may be harmful to him."

Later, Sri Suriyawongse visited the king and told him that the consensus of the high officials was that Chulalongkorn should succeed to the throne and that steps had been taken to assure his safety. The king protested that his son was too young and inexperienced. "There are other princes who have experience and wisdom," he said, "and it is for you to choose one of them. My son is so young it is not fair to place him thus in the way of danger!" [51]

The influence of foreign opinion appears to have been an important factor at this point, for Sri Suriyawongse replied:

> It is our opinion, Sire, that if Prince Chulalongkorn is not elevated to the throne a secure and stable future for this Kingdom cannot be ensured. His

Royal Highness is already recognized as your rightful heir in all foreign countries, as evidenced by the royal letter of felicitation and royal gifts sent to him by the Emperor of France. It is our belief that no other successor to the throne except His Royal Highness will be recognized in Europe. We therefore think that, for the security of the State and for the peace and prosperity of the people, Prince Chulalongkorn should be proclaimed King after your demise.

To this, Mongkut is reported to have said, "Let it be as you wish." [52] Later he said, "Since my son Chulalongkorn is also your son-in-law, I will leave him under your care. I am pleased that you have all agreed to offer him the crown, but you must all take care that there should be no political disturbance or assassination at the change of reign, as there has often been in the past. To allow such things to happen would incur a great loss of national prestige." That evening he took a diamond ring and golden Buddhist rosary that had belonged to the first king of the Chakri dynasty and had them sent to Prince Chulalongkorn.[53]

Following Mongkut's death, Sri Suriyawongse, as regent, administered the country from 1868 to 1873, a five-year period during which Mongkut's policies were continued and the young prince was protected and offered opportunities for foreign travel. Vella is of the opinion that the Regent's greatest contribution was his success in assuring dynastic continuity by assuring the accession of Chulalongkorn. Yet Vella also indicates that he was ambitious to lengthen the period of tutelage by controlling the young monarch. Nevertheless, the twenty-year-old prince, upon mounting the throne, began with shrewd self-discipline to assert himself and build political support for his own effective rule.

He once wrote that at the time of his father's death he was so seriously ill that few thought he would survive. "I was like a human trunk, the head of which had just been cut off, propped up merely to serve as a figure head." [54]

How different modern Burmese history might have been if the *Kinwun Mingyi* had been able to serve as an effective regent for the transfer of power from Mindon to a more able son, the Nyaungyan prince, for example. Whatever the reasons might be, the fact is that at this crucial point the Siamese, fully aware of the dangers of foreign intervention, were able to make the problematic transition successfully. The Burmese, faced by the same or even greater perils, were not able to make the same change effectively.

Lest one think that these two episodes in Siamese and Burmese history were exceptional, it should be pointed out that, in fact, they were typical. Let us demonstrate this proposition by tracing the antecedents of Mindon and Mongkut.

The founder of the Burmese dynasty, Alaungpaya, was Mindon's great-great-grandfather (r. 1752–60), who established his reign by the violent destruction of his immediate predecessors, the last Mon rulers of Pegu and the last Burmese rulers of the Toungoo dynasty. Mindon's great-grandfather, Bodawpaya, violently seized the throne in 1781, after two of his brothers had held it in succession. Mindon's father, Tharawaddy, enthroned himself in 1836 after eliminating dangerous relatives, as did Mindon's brother, Pagan, in 1846.

The accession of Bodawpaya is described in these words by Hall:

It began with a blood-bath, in which he made a clean sweep of all possible rivals in the royal family. But a brother who escaped the ceremonial massacre plotted . . . to overthrow him. This caused a second blood-bath, in which they [the plotters], with every member of their families and all their servants, were done to death. Later in the same year 1782 a pretender . . . scaled the palace walls with 200 desperate men. He and his band were overcome and killed by the palace guard. The district . . . where they had hatched their plot was punished by the destruction of every living thing— human beings, animals, fruit trees and standing crops—save for a few people who were made pagoda slaves.[55]

Bodawpaya's successor was his grandson, Bagyidaw, who came to the throne in 1819 and appears not to have killed off his brothers. One of them, Tharawaddy, in 1837—when the king had become progressively incapacitated by insanity and depression—went to Shwebo and organized an insurrection. He subsequently had five ministers of state killed, and he tortured the wife and daughter of the queen's brother, who had become the dominant figure at court during Bagyidaw's last years. Cady thus describes this episode, typifying the "traditional pattern of revolt":

(1) Tharawaddy established at Shwebo a countercenter of strength capable of repelling the halfhearted attacks of the royal troops sent to disperse his band; (2) the forces of rebellion including all enemies of the court party plus irregular troops and bandit elements flocked to his standard; (3) Tharawaddy's agents exploited popular superstitions through the hired services of Brahman priests and other astrologers; (4) maximum confusion and anarchy were deliberately fomented in order to discredit and undermine governmental authority; (5) eventually the rebel army advanced against the dispirited forces at the capital, while endeavoring to foment disaffection and espionage among the defending troops; (6) then came the final collapse of the government and the surrender of the sacred palace fortress itself to the prince pretender. The old officials and *myosas* were quickly replaced by men

drawn in large measure from partisans of the new king and including a number of outright bandit chieftains.[56]

According to Cady, it was only the moderating influence of the British which prevented "the traditional execution of all royal relatives capable of contesting the new king's pre-eminence."

Tharawaddy, like his brother, developed signs of insanity which manifested themselves "in fits of ungovernable rage, during which he committed abominable cruelties." In 1845, his sons combined to bring him under control and then engaged in a fratricidal struggle for power which was won by Pagan Min, "who killed off those of his brothers whom he considered dangerous, together with every member of their households." "His tyranny and atrocities," according to Hall, "were far worse than those of Thibaw and Supayalat which so shocked a later generation of Britishers." [57]

As we have seen, Mindon himself, although humane in his treatment of relatives, came to power by a violent assault on his brother's regime. Thus, five of the last six kings of the Alaungpaya dynasty came to power by violence, and three of them proceeded to "liquidate" potential rivals in the royal family, a fourth being restrained from doing so only by British intervention. Several earlier kings in the dynasty, however, appear to have inherited their thrones peacefully on the death of their predecessors (see Fig. 1).

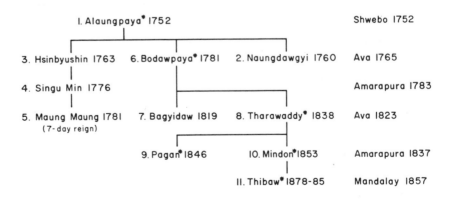

FIGURE 1. The Alaungpaya Dynasty (1752–1885). Rulers who overthrew their predecessors by violence are indicated by an asterisk. The migration of the capital between upper Irrawaddy cities is shown in the column at right.

By contrast, the succession was never taken violently by one king from another during the reign of the Chakri dynasty in Siam. The only exception which might be mentioned was the conquest of power by which Chao Phya Chakri started the dynastic line. Phya Taksin, who had reunited by conquest the fragments of the former Siamese realm (after its utterly savage and devastating occupation by the Burmese under King Hsinbyushin in 1767), had been crowned as King Taksin. Among his commanding officers, Chao Phya Chakri was outstanding. By 1781, however, King Taksin became obsessed by delusions of grandeur and resorted to extremely oppressive measures.[58]

While Chao Phya Chakri was away on a military expedition in Cambodia, an uprising took place in Ayuthia, the capital city. King Taksin was arrested. A rebel leader sought to gain power himself but was overcome by supporters of the popular Chao Phya Chakri who now returned in haste to the capital to be greeted as a savior and crowned king, as Rama Thibodi. Subsequent events are described by Wood in these words:

> The presence of King Taksin was extremely embarrassing; he was incapable of governing, yet he had many adherents in various parts of the country who might be expected to grasp the first opportunity of replacing him on the throne. Cambodia was still disturbed, and a Burmese invasion was thought to be imminent. To ensure the internal tranquillity of the country, all the principal officials urged Chao Phya Chakri to agree to the death of the ex-King; he finally accepted their counsel, and King Taksin was executed.[59]

Upon his death in 1803, King Rama Thibodi was peacefully succeeded by his son, who is now known as Rama II. When Rama II died, there was some question about the succession. It had been assumed that twenty-year-old Prince Mongkut, who was the eldest son by a royal mother, would succeed. He was, at that time, serving as a monk. However, the eldest son, though his mother was a commoner, "was supported by a strong party, as he had for many years taken a prominent part in public affairs, and was thirty-seven years old. He was proclaimed King without any opposition." Mongkut decided to make no protest and remained a monk until his brother's death in 1851, when he himself succeeded to the royal title.[60]

Since the time of Chulalongkorn, there have also been no violent succession disputes, nor has any king of the Chakri dynasty gained power by overthrowing or killing his predecessor. For the genealogy of this Siamese ruling house, see Fig. 2.

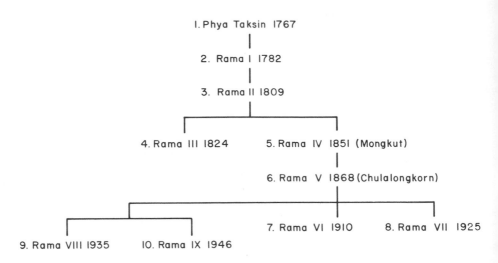

FIGURE 2.   The Bangkok Dynasty (1767 to date)

REIGN PERIODS, ROYAL CAPITALS, AND MILITARY COUPS

It is interesting to compare the average duration of reign in the Burmese and Siamese dynasties. During its rule from 1752 to 1885, a period of 133 years, the Alaungpaya house had 11 kings, or an average reign of 12 years each. The Bangkok dynasty, from 1767 to the present, a period of 196 years, has had 10 kings, averaging 19.6 years each. If we take only the first five Chakri kings, through the reign of Chulalongkorn (from 1782 to 1910, a period of 128 years), we discover that the average reign was 25.5 years. Both houses were fortunate in the relatively long tenure of office of their kings, for when dynastic succession is as problematic as it was for this type of monarchy, longer tenure promoted stability and reduced disruptive civil strife. But during the crucial period of Western imperial expansion, when the fundamental decisions that would determine the fate of the two kingdoms were being made, the average Siamese reign was more than twice as long as that of the Burmese.

Another index of stability was the location of the capital city. King Taksin made his capital in Thonburi, and Rama I moved the capital across the river to Bangkok, where it has remained to the present time.

The Burmese kings continued restlessly to move their capitals from one city to another (see Fig. 1): Shwebo (1752) to Ava (1765), to Amarapura (1783), back to Ava (1823), back to Amarapura (1837), and then to Mandalay (1857).[61] Thus, during the 133-year period, four different capital cities were used, entailing five shifts, at average intervals of only 26.6 years. It may be assumed that shifting a capital city is not only a costly proposition, but also disruptive of normal processes of government and administration. Hence, in this respect also, we can see that the Siamese monarchy during this period attained a higher level of performance than its Burmese counterpart.

Any period of succession from one ruler to another is likely to be accompanied by confusion in governmental operations. Yet the experience of Burma in this regard seems to have been much more disruptive than in Siam. We read, for example, in Cady's history that

even when the succession occurred without serious challenge, all major governmental posts at the capital and in provincial centers and also the *myosa* fief assignments were up for redistribution, so that a considerable measure of political confusion invariably ensued. A crisis would precipitiate a period of general anarchy, during which only the residual authority of the hereditary township headmen was available to hold the villagers under control.[62]

Differences between independent Siam and Burma under British rule and between post-independence Burma and contemporary Thailand involve so many additional variables that comparisons have limited value. Yet it seems significant that, since winning independence of British rule, Burmese history has continued to be plagued by violence. On July 19, 1947, just as negotiations for the transfer of power to independent Burma were being consummated, gunmen in the service of U Saw broke into the room where the embryo cabinet was meeting and massacred the leading and most able politicians of the new state. U Saw, who had himself but recently survived an assassination attempt, was apparently motivated by "a combination of frustrated ambition, anger, and vengeance." He was subsequently convicted of murder and hanged.[63]

No sooner had its independence been established than the Burmese government found itself harassed by rebellions on all sides. A rebellion broke out in Arakan, where the ancient resistance movement against Burmese rule had precipitated the first Anglo-Burman war. The descendants of Arakanese rebels, after more than a century of British administration, were protesting the return of Burmese rule. Similarly, the Karens launched what was to become a long-lasting revolt, accompanied by demands for more rights and privileges. Different communist factions, the Red and White Flags, also raised the standard of revolt.

The ruling AFPFL (anti-Fascist People's Freedom League) soon found itself rent by grievous splits among its component factions. By the spring of 1958, the unity of the League had finally collapsed. "An all-encompassing civil war involving rival elements of the armed forces was narrowly averted. The situation was saved in October, 1958, by the installation of army leadership in the cabinet on an emergency basis." [64]

In February, 1960, U Nu's "clean" AFPFL group won the army-sponsored elections and was permitted to resume power by General Ne Win. However, civilian rule did not last long, for in March, 1962, Ne Win again seized power and created a National Revolutionary Council under military control as the central political force of the country. "A century after Mindon's attempt to modernize Burma's government, the Burmese fell back upon the operative system he thought to discard. The will of the ruler once more was supreme and power within the government again rests with military officers-cum-bureaucrats. The ruling Revolutionary Council has ostensibly turned aside from the legalist, democratic tradition so laboriously nurtured by the British and the AFPFL after independence. A legislative body, the old civil service, popular elections, and a competing opposition are all believed to be obstacles in the path of modernization. Since the formal seizure of power, the Council has ruled by decree and is unabashedly authoritarian. Nevertheless it exercises surprising political power." [65]

Contemporary Siamese history, of course, also has had its share of violence. A revolutionary uprising in 1932 abolished royal absolutism but retained the monarchy as an institution, and the king appears never to have been more genuinely honored and loved by his subjects than he is today. Subsequently, control over the government has been seized on a number of occasions by new ruling groups.[66] For the most part, however, these episodes have been relatively bloodless. Defeated leaders have been allowed to leave the country as exiles, and only a few politicians have been killed.

Although military officers have gained increasingly dominant positions in the Thai government, they have usually been content to rule in a lenient fashion, not seeking to regiment the people or oppress them in extreme fashion.

Throughout the modern period, foreign policy has been conducted with the same shrewd and successful design to preserve the country's independence that marked the policies of Mongkut and Chulalongkorn during the critical period of greatest danger to the country's autonomy. The most severe crisis arose during and immediately after World War II. Recognizing the impossibility of preventing occupation by Japan, the government of Phibun Songkhram, in December, 1941, permitted the Japanese to enter and endured a form of Japanese tutelage throughout the war period. However, substantively, indigenous Siamese administration of domestic affairs persisted. As the likelihood of a defeat of Japan increased, a "Free Thai" movement came into existence and made plans to open a guerrilla movement against the Japanese, but the rather sudden victory of the Allies made it unnecessary to launch any extensive military operations in Thailand.

Anticipating defeat, Phibun resigned as prime minister in July, 1944, paving the way for a "noncollaborator" government that would be able to negotiate more advantageously with the Allied powers, thereby escaping the onus of having, technically, declared war on the side of the Axis. Consequently, Thailand alone of the countries of Southeast Asia escaped serious war devastation and made a relatively smooth transition to the status of an ally of the West and a leading member of the Southeast Asia Treaty Organization.

Whatever judgments foreigners may make of Thai leaders in terms of their own preconceptions and norms, the fact is that the Siamese have successfully accomplished their major objectives, namely, to preserve internal peace and order during a period of international upheavals and to safeguard the independence of the realm against the dangers of imperial conquest. On these counts their performance has continued at a substantially higher level than has been attained by their Burmese neighbors.

ECONOMIC PERFORMANCE

Was an equally high level of economic performance reached? Since this book is primarily concerned with political and administrative rather than with economic and social development, I shall not attempt to deal with this question in any detail. Moreover, James C. Ingram's *Economic Change in Thailand Since 1850* [67] has given such a thorough analysis of the country's economic growth that it is scarcely necessary to do more than call attention to a few indicators and relationships. Comparisons in this field are of limited significance, also, since the imposition of

British rule in Burma, with its emphasis on economic development (or exploitation) makes it possible to judge Burmese performance only up to 1885.

The most important aspect of Siamese economic performance may be indicated by the rise in rice production. At the time of the Bowring treaty in the eighteen-fifties, rice exports were less than a million piculs per year.[68] Annual exports rose gradually to a level of 8 million piculs by the end of the century, and then more rapidly to a peak of more than 25 million by the early thirties. During the war period, exports dropped dramatically, but they made a rapid comeback to the 26 million picul level by 1951. The significance of these figures may be judged from Ingram's statement that "during most of the century under examination, rice cultivation was the chief occupation for 80–90 per cent of the people, and rice exports consistently represented 60–70 per cent of total exports. . . . This 25-fold increase—over the probable maximum volume [of rice exports] at the time of the Bowring Treaty—which took place while the population roughly doubled itself, represents the major economic change in Thailand since 1855. In no other productive activity have the Thai themselves been so deeply involved, nor is there any other productive activity which has concerned such a large part of the population." [69]

We may assume that domestic consumption of rice per capita has remained roughly constant. Thus, the rise in exports was made possible by an increase in rice production relative to population growth. This increase, for the most part, has been achieved by an expansion of the area under cultivation, using traditional techniques of farming. Ingram estimates that the area in rice cultivation in 1850 was about 5.8 million rai (1 rai equals 0.4 acres or 1,600 square meters). By 1905, the area had risen to 9.2 million rai, to 20 million by 1930, 30 million by 1947, and 34.6 million by 1950.[70]

Estimates of rice productivity are not available for the nineteenth century, but figures are available which show, with some margin for error, that the average yield of paddy per rai of planted area dropped from 4.88 piculs in 1906–9 to 4.50 in 1921–24; 3.91 in 1930–34; 3.13 in 1940–44, during the war period. Since the war, productivity has risen to about 3.6 piculs per rai. The postwar improvement in productivity no doubt represents some technical improvement in agricultural practices. The long-run decline in productivity, however, reflects the fact that marginal lands brought under rice cultivation as the total area increased were less fertile, owing largely to inadequacy of the water supply.[71]

Several aspects of this dramatic growth of rice exports need to be noted. Virtually all of the increase in rice cultivation was carried on exclusively by Thai people, but foreigners were engaged in its commercial and industrial aspects. The Chinese were largely responsible for the organization of the domestic rice trade and for establishing the rice mills which processed paddy for export. The exporting was largely carried out by European firms. This picture no longer holds true, since Thais have in recent years, especially through co-operatives and government mills, entered the rice marketing picture, and Chinese firms have become active as exporters. The point, however, is that this phenomenal change in the character of the Siamese economy was made possible by the agricultural activity, primarily by traditional means, of the bulk of the Thai population, whereas the related commercial and industrial enterprises required to transform a self-subsistence into a marketized economy were carried out by foreigners working in Thailand.

Rice has constituted approximately half of Thailand's total exports, although the ratio has fluctuated considerably from year to year. A large part of the rest of the country's exports consisted of tin, teak, and rubber. Ingram notes that these four basic commodities "represented 80–90 per cent of total exports for several decades." [72] It is unnecessary to describe here the fluctuations in the growth of production and exports of the other commodities. The picture is much more confused and fluctuations were greater than in the case of rice. What is perhaps more important for present purposes is to point out the extent to which the entrepreneurship and labor for this development were provided by foreigners, by European firms and Chinese. Rubber, which did not appear as an important export product until the twentieth century, involved a relatively greater contribution by Thai farmers, largely as smallholders.

This picture varies strikingly from that prior to the 1855 treaty. A table of Siamese exports in 1850 prepared by Ingram shows that, out of exports valued at about 5.6 million baht, only 0.15 million consisted of rice, 0.25 of tin and tin products, 0.45 of wood, but not teak. The major items consisted of sugar (0.7 million baht), hides, horns, and skins (0.5 million), and cotton and cotton products (0.65 million).[73]

As the exports of a few basic raw materials expanded, domestic production of manufactured goods, especially homespun cotton and silk, declined in favor of the import of textiles and other manufactures. Again, the complex details need not be presented here.[74]

The relevant point is that the Siamese economy was marketized to a substantial degree, but without any basic institutional transformations in the way of life of the Siamese people. This change was accomplished by specializing in the export of a limited number of raw materials. The most important, rice, was produced by Thai farmers following traditional agricultural practices. The increase in production was made possible simply by a great expansion in the cultivated area. Other exports were produced largely by the enterprise of foreign residents in Thailand, both Chinese and European, and the marketing and processing of rice itself was also largely monopolized by alien residents.

The increase in exports made it possible to import manufactured goods which were cheaper or superior in quality (or both) to equivalent domestic products. The result was a decline in traditional forms of manufacturing and craftsmanship.

On the whole, this pattern of growth permitted a rise in the level of economic performance. Estimates of gross national product or other direct measures of production are not available. It would seem fair to say, however, that the Thai economy expanded and became substantially marketized without fundamental institutional change. Ingram expresses the position in these words:

> In the course of this study we have seen many changes in the economy of Thailand in the last hundred years, but not much "progress" in the sense of an increase in the per capita income, and not much "development" in the sense of the utilization of more capital, relative to labor, and of new techniques. The principal changes have been the spread of the use of money, increased specialization and exchange based chiefly on world markets, and the growth of a racial division of labor.[75]

THE SIAMESE SUCCESS

It is necessary to note some links between these economic changes and governmental policies. In a sense, of course, the fundamental cause of change lay outside Siam. It was the exogenous pressure of European traders and political power which compelled Siam to open its doors to free trade and to abolish the royal monopolies which had played so important a part in the structure of the traditional society.

Yet Siam, like Burma, might well have refused to make even these changes. The result, no doubt, would have been the imposition of colonial rule. But if this had happened, the subsequent changes would have been made by European colonial rulers, not by Siamese governments.

Thus, a full measure of the Siamese performance must take into account their ability to recognize and carry out those minimal changes which would enable the country to withstand pressures from the outside world and to retain control over their own institutions.

The expansion of rice exports resulted from a shrewdly deliberate policy whereby the Thai rulers sought to reconcile internal and external problems. These problems were perceived by King Mongkut, who

. . . saw that the interests of consumers and producers might come into con-flict as rice exports increased. In the edict of 1855 which removed the ban on rice exports, he explained that the ban had been beneficial to those con-sumers who did not grow their own rice, since they had enjoyed low prices of rice. The producers felt otherwise, however, and they suffered so much from the low prices in years of good harvest that they ceased to cultivate all their land, preferring to return part of it to the state. The state thus lost the revenue from land tax. Furthermore, when a poor season came along, the harvest from the reduced acreage was scarcely enough to feed the domestic population, and as a result the price rose greatly. The ban on exports, there-fore, did not prevent distress in years of poor harvest, as it was designed to do. King Mongkut thus recognized the conflicting interests of two large groups within the nation, and he concluded that the general welfare would be best served by allowing the export of rice. In explaining this decision he also noted that the state would receive more revenue.[76]

By encouraging rice exports, then, Mongkut not only met the de-mands of foreign merchants and laid a basis for the augmented revenues which would be necessary for administrative reform, but he also hoped to satisfy domestic producers and consumers of rice.

Ingram has described in some detail the concrete measures adopted by the Siamese government to provide incentives for an expansion of rice cultivation. These included a modification of the land revenue sys-tem to exempt from taxation new lands being brought into cultivation.

In 1857, King Mongkut decreed that "no tax shall be collected from rice land cleared from the jungle for the first year of its cultivation." For the next few years the tax was to be levied at a reduced rate. In justification, Mongkut called attention to the rising price of rice owing to exports, which benefited the merchants and peasants, but not the consuming population. He proposed, therefore, to encourage an increase in the area under cultivation. Later on, King Chulalongkorn continued and strengthened this policy.[77]

If the area of rice cultivation was to be expanded, then the number of cultivators would also have to be increased, assuming that traditional methods of small-scale cultivation would remain unchanged. The old basis of *corvée* service by freemen for the king and their noble patrons had already, by 1850, been substantially undermined by the commutation of service in favor of payments in kind and cash.

King Mongkut decreed that whenever labor could be employed for money, workers should not be compelled to work by conscription. He thus deliberately struck a sharp blow at the declining *corvée* system. As farmers gained exemption from arbitrary demands upon their time, which had often interrupted agricultural work at critical times, the possibility of devoting themselves fully to farming activities grew.

The *corvée* system, although declining, nevertheless persisted. In 1899, however, a head tax was formally substituted for whatever *corvée* obligations remained. This tax was finally eliminated in 1938. "The elimination of the *corvée* system," Ingram notes, "freed a significant amount of labor services, which could then he available for hire or devoted to the land of the cultivator himself." [78] A substantial part of the population had the status of slaves, who were obligated to work for freemen in the cultivation of their fields. These slaves, in large measure, had no obligation to render *corvée* service or to pay taxes. It became apparent to the reforming kings that, by freeing the slaves, the supply of peasant farmers would be increased, and the tax base for the government could simultaneously be enlarged.

King Mongkut had expressed a hope that the increase in trade with the Western powers would reduce the pressure on the poor to sell themselves into slavery. No frontal attack on the institution was made, however, until the time of Chulalongkorn, who decreed in 1874 that anyone born after October 1, 1868, would become free on his twenty-first birthday, if he were then a slave. If such persons were born free, they could be sold into slavery only with their own consent after reaching the age of fifteen. By this rule, existing slaveholders were not suddenly deprived of their property, and the process of freeing slaves was spread over the years as a gradual process, thereby making it possible to cope with whatever opposition or protests may have arisen from slaveowners.

A more comprehensive decree in 1897 made it illegal for anyone to sell himself or to be sold by others, and a final decree in 1905 abolished slavery completely. Undoubtedly, full implementation of the law was not achieved immediately, yet the practice of slavery was gradually eliminated, with no cost to the government and with little social disturbance. In this way, many farmers were released from obligatory service to others and enabled to open new fields on their own account.

Meanwhile, former masters, no longer able to depend on the labor of slaves, had to start cultivating their own land.[79]

It is significant that these measures, which encouraged a substantial increase in the area of rice cultivation, and hence of rice exports, involved little cost for the government, although they depended upon the deliberate adoption of new government policies. More positive—and costly—measures designed to raise the agricultural quality of the land and to help farmers adopt improved cultural practices did not come until much later.

One of the first fields in which such improvements were proposed was irrigation. Yet by the time of Chulalongkorn's death in 1910 little had been done in this sphere. Some canals had been dug, primarily to distribute the floodwaters of the rainy season more evenly over the alluvial plain. In 1903, a Dutch engineer, who was made director of a new Department of Canals, proposed the construction of a major dam and related works which would have made true irrigation possible and thereby permitted a considerable increase in the area that could be effectively cultivated. However, the government was unwilling to undertake the project because of the expense involved, and after some years of frustration, the Dutch engineer resigned his post. The Canal Department was subsequently abolished.[80] However, a Department of Irrigation was established several years later and has now grown into one of the most active and effective departments in the Thai bureaucracy. International assistance has played a large part in this growth. Yet the fact remains that the initial policies which encouraged the expansion of rice production were carried out with governmental support but little expenditure of funds long before the addition of irrigation works made further expansion possible.

Direct assistance to rice farmers by the government in the form of experiment stations and extension services was not started until 1934, when a rice section was established in the Department of Agriculture. In 1938, this section had become a division. Operating at first on a modest scale, it received a strong impetus when, after World War II, American technical assistance was provided in this field. The section was expanded in 1953 to become the Rice Department, and governmental programs designed to support improved rice farming have since been stepped up.

In regard to the other exports which multiplied after the treaties with the Western powers, it is notable that the government did little to encourage or facilitate operations by the Siamese. Rather, it was content to let foreigners take the initiative and carry the main responsibility for operations. Its primary concern was to secure income in the form of royalties from these operations, to prevent disputes and difficulties which might give a pretext for military or diplomatic intervention, to conserve the country's resources, and to prevent speculative activities that might have discredited the government or caused a lowering of prices because of excessive production.

A Department of Mines was established in 1891 to control the further growth of the tin industry. As a result of the government's activities, Ingram notes, "foreign mining companies have received considerate treatment." The government, in turn, "has benefited from the royalties paid by the tin producers." [81]

Similarly, in forestry, the early work of European companies involved much indiscriminate felling of teak trees. Dangerous disputes also arose with local chiefs or princes in the areas, especially in the north, where concessions had been granted. In 1896, King Chulalongkorn invited a British forestry officer to come to Siam from India, where he had been working in the Imperial Forest Service. He established a Siamese Forestry Department which recruited European officers, largely from India, and started to train a Siamese staff, many of whom were sent to the Indian Forest School at Dehra Dun. Royal decrees were promulgated prohibiting forestry operations except under lease, with limitations on the length of the felling cycle, required conservation measures, and stricter control over the payment of royalties. As the original leases expired, more restrictive rules were introduced.[82]

As in the case of mining, it is notable that these regulations permitted the activities of foreign entrepreneurs, without adding materially to the costs of government and without requiring substantial change in the ways of life of the Thai population. Thus, new sources of revenue were created at the same time that the urgent demands of the foreign powers were satisfied. The Siamese monarchy, in short, succeeded in maintaining a neotraditional political system which could, at the same time, meet the primary requirements of the European powers and thereby reduce, if not eliminate, pretexts for imperialist interventions.

THE BURMESE FAILURE

The relative success of the Siamese polity in these respects can be better appreciated if it is compared with the record of the Burmese monarchy in coping with the same problems. In earlier times, the port cities of Burma at the mouths of the Irrawaddy and Salween appear to have been flourishing international trade centers. By the early nineteenth century, however, in the wake of the destruction caused by the military conquest of Lower Burma by the kings of Ava and that wrought by the endemic wars between Burma and Siam, these ports had declined to mere shadows of their former greatness.

"The Burma Government," Cady writes, "forbade the export of rice from Rangoon in order to ensure an ample supply of cheap grain for the capital area." [83] Yet rice prices in Upper Burma remained high, and economic conditions in the south were depressed. According to Cady, "Any change of trading policy permitting the free export by sea of surplus rice from Rangoon, such as the British introduced after 1850, would inevitably transform the trade outlook of the entire country. The consequent development of Lower Burma agriculture would attract large numbers of agriculturalists and laborers from relatively crowded Upper Burma." [84]

After the first Anglo-Burman war, the Ava government was compelled to suppress Mon and Karen rebellions which had flared up in Lower Burma. The resulting civil strife proved so destructive that near-famine conditions resulted, and rice had to be imported from India to this normally productive rice granary. The annexation of Lower Burma by Britain in 1852, of course, brought this delta region under British administration, and steps were then taken by the alien rulers to support the growth of rice production and exports at a rate which soon overtook and surpassed the achievements of the Siamese.

But the monarchy in Upper Burma, having lost its most productive rice lands, attempted to encourage the cultivation of rice in the middle Irrawaddy region.[85] Despite efforts by King Mindon to stimulate increasing production, the price of rice remained high, and it proved impossible to compete with the rapid expansion of rice cultivation in the Lower Burma areas. The loss of its best rice lands also made it impossible for the Burmese monarchy to rival the Siamese by spurring the production and export of rice as a foundation for modernization.

Burma was rich in teak forests, however, and one might have expected that a modernizing Burmese leadership would have taken advantage of every opportunity to stabilize its relations with European forestry concerns, so as to derive income from royalties. Yet it was precisely in this sphere that the breaking point in Anglo-Burmese relations was reached in 1885. In August of that year, the *Hlutdaw* levied a fine of 2.3

million rupees on the Bombay-Burmah Trading Corporation for, allegedly, having illegally taken out more teak logs from its concessions than it had paid royalties for. On September 20, when the Corporation refused to pay the fine, the Burmese stopped log rafts going down the river. The British ultimatum was delivered on October 22.

Although the dispute over logging operations was, admittedly, not the "cause" of the third Anglo-Burman war, it was the precipitating event, and it remains a stark symbol of the inability of the Burmese monarchy to create an effective administration which might, in the first place, have stopped the illegal extraction of teak before the amounts involved had become so large, or, in the face of a *fait accompli,* have recognized more realistically its own perilous condition and the need to avoid further provoking the British if it wished to preserve its independence.

It is, of course, difficult for a weak state, convinced of the righteousness of its cause, to make what it considers unjust concessions to a powerful neighbor. Yet, when its own survival is at stake, it appears wiser to make such concessions than to adhere uncompromisingly to a stand which seems certain to be suicidal. It might be argued that the Siamese took a more realistic view of these dangers because they had already seen their neighbors brought under the heel of European conquerors. Yet the Burmese had themselves already twice experienced catastrophic defeats (in the first and second Anglo-Burman wars), so that they, above all, should have been fully alert to the threat British expansionism posed for their own security.

No doubt had Mindon still been alive, the case of the Bombay-Burmah Trading Corporation would have been handled differently, and it appears that the *Kinwun Mingyi,* Mindon's premier statesman who still held office, though in humbled circumstances, did attempt to mollify the British by urging the *Hlutdaw* to reduce the fine to less than one-tenth of the original amount. His attempt proved abortive. He was working for a Thibaw, not a Chulalongkorn. The measure of Burma's failure lay not in the fact that Thibaw happened to be king, but rather in the fact that the Burmese elite was unable to bring a stronger successor of Mindon to the throne, or to compensate for the weakness of an ineffectual man, once he had been enthroned.

Alternatively, if we accept the Burmese debacle as a typical manifestation of the weakness of traditional regimes when confronted by the far better organized might of an industrial power, then we must be impressed by the truly remarkable performance of the Siamese monarchy, which, confronted by a similar challenge, was nevertheless able, while giving ground on several, and even crucial, fronts, to safeguard its own independence and move into the contemporary world as an autonomous, economically viable, and administratively adequate state.

Our purpose here is not to inquire into the underlying reasons which may help to explain these differences in performance. No doubt there are subtle divergences between the cultural patterns of Siam and Burma which ought to be explored. The characteristic personality structures of Siamese and Burmese elites probably differ from each other in ways that may account for the relatively peaceful successions in Bangkok as contrasted with the characteristic violence of such transitions in Ava and Rangoon.

Other noncultural variables would also have to be examined. The geographic position of Burma adjacent to the Indian empire, as contrasted with the more remote position of Siam, around the great bend of the Malay peninsula and not necessarily a port of call on voyages to the Far East, suggests that Burma may have been subjected to greater external pressure than Siam. Moreover, the preoccupation of both Britain and France with finding new, overland routes to Southwest China led them to focus their attention on the Irrawaddy and Mekong, and hence on the Burmese and Indo-Chinese realms, in contrast to the apparent uselessness of the Siamese Chao Phya as a route to China.

Perhaps more important, the degree of assimilation of conquered earlier inhabitants to the Siamese way of life was certainly greater than in Burma, where both the Mons of the lower valley area and the Shans and other tribal minorities of the highlands, to say nothing of the Arakanese and Assamese, retained their recalcitrant separateness despite the pressure of repeated Burmese conquests. Thus, the challenge confronting Burmese statesmen in seeking to bring their own conquered territories under effective control was far more unnerving than the equivalent task facing the Siamese empire-builders.

When, on top of this, one takes into account the recklessness of Burmese rulers in launching extravagant military campaigns against the Siamese, as compared with the relatively more conservative policies of the Chakri kings, one can suppose that the Burmese polity, in a sense, burned itself out, exhausting its resources of talent and manpower in wild quests for the unattainable.

Are we, however, to regard these extravagant manifestations of the Burmese spirit as "causes" or as "consequences" of their inability to cope with the challenges presented to them by their environment, including the British and French interlopers? It carries us beyond the scope of the present work to do more than mention such questions in passing. Our major inquiry requires that we return now to a more detailed examination of the ways in which the Siamese elites responded to the challenge of the West. Let us begin with an effort to understand the structure of the traditional Thai monarchy, the foundation on which all subsequent changes have been built.

CHAPTER II

The Traditional Polity in Siam

So foreshortened has the perspective of modern Western man become that he can fall, without much resistance, into the habit of lumping together as "non-Western"[1] the widely varied political systems of the world that did not emerge out of European history. Similarly broad dichotomies prevail in the contrast frequently drawn between "traditional" and "modern" political systems, or between the "underdeveloped" and the "developed."[2]

Such frames of reference give us no leverage for distinguishing between the contemporary Thai polity—which is surely non-Western, "underdeveloped," and "pre-industrial or partially industrial"—and the Siamese political system that existed a century or two ago. A recent attempt by Banks and Textor to classify polities in various respects gives us a categorization of the contemporary Thai bureaucracy as "traditional."[3] However, since Banks and Textor are, by definition, concerned only with contemporary polities, it may be supposed that the Thai system is called "traditional" only in contrast to other present-day systems, even though it may be far from traditional if historical Siam is taken as a basis for comparison.

The difficulty that arises out of classifying contemporary Thailand as a "traditional," "underdeveloped," "partially industrial" or "non-Western" polity is that it tends to obscure many important changes that have occurred within the last hundred years. This is scarcely surprising, since comparative government writings are almost innocent of any useful concepts and models for the description of pre-modern traditional politics. Even those who concern themselves with historical Siamese materials tend to reconstruct the past in terms of images drawn from the present. Hence, the historical Siamese polity is glimpsed, as in a curved mirror at a carnival, in grossly distorted forms.

Consider, for example, the way in which A. L. Moffat, in his sympa-
ethic and wholly admirable biography of King Mongkut, quotes a description of the king's death from which he omits an apparently unimportant yet telling final paragraph. The date was October 1, 1868. The
king lay weak and ill, having contracted malaria during a fateful royal
expedition to southern Siam the previous August to observe a total
eclipse of the sun. Following Western methods, he had correctly predicted the time of the eclipse. Indeed, it was reported that his calcula-
tions were more correct, within two seconds, than those of the competing
French astronomers! But the court astrologers were convinced that he
was wrong, and they held, moreover, that the eclipse augured a national
disaster.

Disaster did indeed strike in the form of malaria, which attacked
many of those who had joined the expedition. On that first day of October, the astronomically acute Mongkut spoke more like an astrologer
himself when he said, "The moon will be full to-night. To-day being my
birthday, I feel sure that the end of my life has come." That evening
he did die, but not before dictating a final message in Pali addressed to
the Buddhist Brotherhood, in which he reaffirmed his faith, and declared
that ". . . the six forms of consciousness, the six senses and the six sensa-
tions through the six channels are merely illusory. Hence no man can,
without offense, hold as reality any worldly thing. I believe that all
worldly manifestations are not identifiable to self, being variable according to circumstances. That is to say, such things as we deem ours are
not ours, and such beings as we deem us are not ourselves." With this
message Moffat terminates his account of the king's death.[4]

But the source of his quotations, which was a collection of papers
by and about Mongkut as assembled by the brothers M. R. Seni Pramot
and Kukrit Pramot, ends this poignant description with a final paragraph
in which we read:

8 o'clock and 50 minutes in the evening. The King called for his chamber,
and having passed water he turned his face towards the East and said "I am
about to die this very moment." Then he turned towards the West and again
said "I am dying now." In this position His Majesty remained, slowly but
distinctly calling out the sacred name "Arahang Samma Sam Buddho."

His breath became softer and softer until no sound could be heard, followed by the "unmistakable sound of the death rattle." "At that fateful
moment," the record concludes, "the clock on the Bhuvadol Tower

struck nine, an owl gave a hoot, His Majesty Phra Baht Somdech Phra Paramendr Maha Mongkut Phra Chom Klao Chao Yu Hua was dead."[5]

That Moffat should have considered this final passage not worth including in his book reflects, I think, a characteristic inability of most modern writers to enter into the point of view of a traditional mind. Mongkut, it is true, was to a considerable degree influenced by Western ideas, and his Buddhistic discipline had captured the deepest levels of his conscious thought. But below these layers of rationalized thinking there lay an even deeper stratum that was basically topological and astrological. Why should he, with his dying strength, have turned first to the East and then to the West? Why was he so convinced that the night of the full moon, coming on his birthday, would be his last? Why does the recorder of these events take pains to note that the death rattle came at precisely nine o'clock, and why did an owl choose this precise moment to hoot?

THE COSMOLOGICAL WORLD VIEW

Such questions suggest an escape to the world of fantasy that may have little to do with the subject of this essay. Yet if we dismiss such questions as irrelevant, we shall scarcely comprehend the traditional mind or polity. We can perhaps link the manner of Mongkut's death to the classical order in Siam by referring to Robert Heine-Geldern's insightful essay on politico-religious thought in Southeast Asia. "The primary notion with which we shall have to deal," he writes, "is the belief in the parallelism between Macrocosmos and Microcosmos, between the universe and the world of men. According to this belief humanity is constantly under the influence of forces emanating from the directions of the compass and from stars and planets. These forces may produce welfare and prosperity or work havoc, according to whether or not individuals and social groups, above all the state, succeed in bringing their lives and activities in harmony with the universe. Individuals may attain such harmony by following the indications offered by astrology, the lore of lucky and unlucky days and many other minor rules. Harmony between the empire and the universe is achieved by organizing the former as an image of the latter, as a universe on a smaller scale."[6]

A detailed analysis of the rituals whereby the Siamese kings not only conformed themselves to the cosmological forces of the universe but in so doing assured harmony, life, and prosperity to their people is given by Wales in his book on Siamese royal ceremonies.[7] One of the crucial elements in the royal coronation rites was the ceremony on the octagonal throne. Here, Wales tells us, "The King first sat facing the East, the quarter of the sun, and hence perhaps another indication of the king's early equivalence to the sun." The Brahman priest officiating at this point then said to the king in Pali:

May the Sovereign here give me leave to pronounce his victory. May the Sovereign, turning now towards the East, seated upon his royal throne, extend his protection and exercise his royal authority over all those realms situated to (the east) and all beings that therein dwell. May he remain on earth, further protecting this kingdom, as well as her Buddhist Religion and her people. . . . Whoever creates evil in this eastern quarter, may the Sovereign, through his might, triumph over them all in a righteous manner.

After anointment with water, and further responses, the king turns to the southeast where the same action is repeated, with appropriate changes as to the direction involved, and so on around the compass.[8]

After the formal coronation ceremony is over, the king performs the circumambulation of the Grand Palace. Wales remarks that ". . . this rightwise circumambulation of the King around the city represents the path of the sun, and is important evidence in favor of the solar origin of kings." The idea goes back to Vedic times, for we read in the *Satapatha Brahmana,* that "while the Brahmans perform the *pradaksina,* they think, sunwise this sacred work of ours will be accomplished, and therefore they again walk thrice round sunwise." [9]

It seems unnecessary to review other ceremonies, such as the tonsure and the cremation, for in each, at progressively higher levels, the king is reborn or takes on the attributes of a higher divinity. Of them all, the cremation was traditionally the most elaborate because, as Wales writes, "it signifies the final step in supreme elevation" and because "whatever doubt there might possibly be in the mind of the king himself or of others as to deification during lifetime, the force of inspired tradition, of visions, and of the mystery of the unknown life beyond the grave, could leave no doubt in the minds of the people as to the possibility, indeed the certainty, of deification after death." [10]

By means of these ritual enactments the king and his court were thought to bring life and prosperity to the realm. Thus, at the end of the coronation ceremony "the King scattered gold and silver flowers and coins among the Brahmans, an action which he repeated later, on leaving the hall of audience." He subsequently would pour out a libation of water to the Goddess of Earth.

To the modern mind, such acts seem part of the quaint and colorful pageantry of monarchic institutions, scarcely the essence of political action. Yet if we can recognize the legitimizing or ordering function as basic to the political process, we will see in these ceremonial acts (which had their counterpart, though on a much reduced scale, in the daily life of the Siamese kings) the foundation of the political order.

THE ORGANIZATION OF GOVERNMENT

What concerns us here is not merely the focal role of the divine monarch, but all the implications which flow from it for the nature of the state, its political and social structure. The royal harem and the organization of the government, for example, were conceived as micro-cosmic replicas of the macrocosmic order, in which lesser divinities surrounded greater. And these beings were, of course, cosmologically oriented through palace topographies which duplicated, in miniature, those of Mount Meru, the abode of the gods, and its surrounding lands and seas.

Heine-Geldern describes how the capitals and palaces of Southeast Asia were laid out in cosmological fashion, and how the Burmese queens, for example, were identified with the four cardinal and four secondary directions. Similarly, Wales tells us that, in Siam, "there were normally four queens at the same time, a greater and a lesser of the right, and a greater and a lesser of the left. . . ."[11]

A conception of governmental organization based on cosmological and topographical considerations contrasts strikingly with modern ideas about the place of function, technique, clientele, and territorial jurisdiction as criteria for organizational design. So pervasive have these themes become in contemporary thought that they seem to provide the only framework in which any system of government can be imagined. We find, for example, that Walter Vella—who has provided historical data on nineteenth-century Thailand of great value—characterizes the early Siamese states as "feudalistic" with, accordingly, a "territorial" basis of organization. Following the defeat of the Khmer kingdom and the sacking of Angkor Thom (1431), Vella notes, King Boroma Trailok (1448–88) established a more centralized form of government in which functional specialization replaced, at least in part, the territorial basis of feudal rule.

"By the time of the Bangkok dynasty," Vella writes, the Siamese bureaucracy "had become extremely complex. Its complexities arose primarily from feudal carry-overs into the bureaucratic form of government; the administration was organized partly along territorial, partly along functional lines. Although the hereditary feudal princes with nearly absolute authority in their territories had been replaced by a central government with departments that ideally were to control only one aspect of administration, many of these departments in fact had territorial responsibilities, and the result was an illogical mixture of functional and territorial responsibilities." [12]

James Mosel, writing about the same time as Vella, also reaches the view that Trailok created a "centralized and functionally specialized administrative organization." However, he goes on to say that the basic departments (*krom*) "tended to have both territorial and functional responsibilities, which in time led to considerable confounding and overlap." [13]

While admitting that the traditional Siamese departments had "symbolic significances" which, in the Bangkok period, had "become confused and perhaps not fully understood," Wilson holds that each office "had administrative responsibilities which appear to be quite clear." [14]

Similarly, Siffin, who refers to the extension of the "Khmer system of functionally differentiated administration" in the fifteenth century of the Christian era, observes that "in the absence of powerful and persistent rationalizing forces, the rational system of King Trailok gradually became more and more saturated with traditionalism in content and purpose." [15]

All these interpretations seem to reflect the view of Wales, who continues to be the primary source of information on the traditional Siamese system of government for contemporary Western authors. He attributes to King Trailok the transformation of the political structure, drawing on Khmer practices, by creating "a centralized and functionally differentiated system of administration for the large area now placed under the direct control of the capital." [16]

It is unnecessary to question the proposition that the transformed structure of government under the Ayuthian dynasty involved, in practice, considerable specialization of function in the organization of the bureaucracy. However, it may be important to understand how the structure of government was perceived by the Siamese of that time. If they were conscious of the conceptual distinction between "territorial" and "functional" orientations in organizational practice, as Vella, Mosel, Wilson, Siffin, and Wales suggest, then we could consider the modernizing reforms of Mongkut and Chulalongkorn as merely an extension and elaboration—under Western pressure—of transformations which had already been initiated long before by the great king Trailok, under the guidance of Brahman mentors brought from the conquered city of Angkor Thom.

However, there is another way of thinking about the organization of government which is not rationalistic in its orientation to place, person, technique, and purpose. This is the cosmological viewpoint taken by Heine-Geldern in speaking of a magical correspondence between the microcosmic world of men and the macrocosmic universe of gods. This correspondence applies, as has already been suggested, not only to the role of divine monarch, but also to palace architecture and bureaucratic organization. Indeed, the design of palaces so as to match the universal order provides an architectural framework within which the organization of government takes form. From this standpoint it is not functional or territorial criteria which determine architectural patterns; rather, it is the structure of the palace which shapes the conduct of its inhabitants. Each wing or court of the palace had its corresponding officials, and the salient characteristic of each office, therefore, was its location, or better, its topological identity. Consequently, such categories as east and west, right and left, center, rear, and front are more germane to the traditional perspective than any particular function or domain which may, in the course of time, come to be associated with a given palace or court.

The cosmological basis of royal architecture can be readily seen in the remains of Angkor Thom, the city from which the Brahman advisers came who helped Trailok reorganize his government. "The city was surrounded with a wall and moat forming a square almost two miles on each side, its sides being directed towards the four cardinal points. There are gates in the middle of each side and a fifth one on the East leading to the entrances of the royal palace. The towers above the gates are crowned with the same four-fold faces of Lokesvara as those of the central temple. Thus, that smaller world, the city of Angkor, and through its means the whole Khmer empire were both put under the protection of the 'Lord of the Universe.' " [17]

The structure of government corresponded to this cosmological architecture. "Thus the stage was set," Heine-Geldern writes, "for the enacting of the cosmic roles of king, court, and government." After describing the organization of the harem in cosmological terms, he goes on to the officials, taking Burma as his example:

There were four chief ministers each of whom, in addition to their functions as ministers of state, originally had charge of one quarter of the capital and of the empire. They obviously corresponded to the four Great Kings or Lokapalas, the guardian deities of the four cardinal points in the Buddhist [Hindu?] system. However, the task of representing the four Lokapalas had been delegated to four special officers, each of whom had to guard one side of the palace and of the capital. They had flags in the colors attributed to the corresponding sides of Mount Meru, the one representing Dhattarattha, the Lokapala of the East, a white one, the officer representing Kubera, the Lokapala of the North, a yellow flag, etc. The cosmological principle was carried far down through the hierarchy of officialdom, as revealed by the numbers of office bearers. Thus, there were four undersecretaries of state, eight assistant secretaries, four heralds, four royal messengers, etc.

Very much the same kind of organization existed in Siam, Cambodia, and Java. Again and again we find the orthodox number of four principal queens and of four chief ministers, the four pillars as they were called in Cambodia. In Siam, as in Burma, they originally governed four parts of the kingdom lying toward the four cardinal points. . . .

Throughout the kingdoms of Farther India the system based on the compass was largely supplemented and modified by the division into offices of the right and left hand, right and left in this case referring to the place on the side of the king due to the respective office bearer on ceremonial occasions. As the king, when sitting on the throne, always faced the East, right corresponded to the South and left to the North. In Siam, for instance, there were a major and a lesser queen each of the right and of the left. Civilian officers had their places on the left of the king, officers of the army on his right, i.e. in the South, because the planet Mars, connected with war, was considered to be the planet of the South. Indeed, the population of Siam was divided into the two classes of the right (South) and of the left (North). The former had to render military and the latter civilian services.[18]

PALACE, COURT, AND CHAMBER

No doubt officials, whose essential role was conceived of in cosmological terms, were assigned a range of shifting duties, having both functional and territorial aspects, although not conceived of primarily in these terms. Consequently, it is possible to substitute functional or territorial for cosmological names of agencies, but the result is a distorted and anachronistic image of the system. Thus Vella, in his enumeration of the traditional *krom,* writes:

A list of the principal departments and their functions will illustrate the divided basis of administration: The Mahatthai Department superintended the northern provinces; the Kralahom superintended the southern provinces; the Nakhonban administered the capital; and Na was in charge of lands; the Phrakhlang was in charge of commerce and foreign relations and superintended the seaboard provinces near the capital; and the Wang was in charge of the palace and palace affairs. Other important departments directly responsible to the king were those dealing with church affairs, registry of the people, royal appurtenances, the treasury, literature, the royal elephants, the court Brahmans, and the guarding of the palace. There were also numerous minor departments dependent on the major ones.[19]

Notably absent from this list is an office which Vella discusses later in these terms: "The highest *krom* official was the Heir Apparent (Uparat), who headed the Department of the Heir Apparent (literally, the Department of the Front Palace; that is, the palace in front of the royal palace) and who was frequently called upon to lead an army." [20]

There was also a back palace, whose incumbent frequently played the role of a commanding general. The front and back palaces (*Wang Na* and *Wang Lang*) are not usually thought of in the same context as the other *krom*, because their functions were limited to caring for the high princes who headed them. But this is to superimpose a rationalistic conception upon the organizational structure.

We know how strictly hierarchic was the status system of the Siamese, with its elaborate *sakdi na* numerical grading scale, applying to everyone from the king himself to the meanest slave.[21] What is more natural than that the king, at the center of the palace, should hold the highest cosmological position? Since, when enthroned, he faced the East, it is apparent that the front (eastern) palace would have the next highest rank and should be occupied by a prince second in status only to the monarch himself. The third place would go to the rear (western) palace. The incumbents of these palaces would have so exalted a rank that it would be improper to call upon them to administer the affairs of lower mortals; accordingly, their chief work came to be the care of their royal heads. Other palaces or courts, in descending order, would be assigned successively more humble duties, whose territorial and functional aspects might be quite undifferentiated.

Let us try to reconstruct a hypothetical image of the Siamese governmental organization, starting from cosmological principles. In view of the changes and reorganizations which succeeding reigns imposed, our task may be likened to the reconstruction of an ancient city plan after successive encroachments and reconstructions have all but blotted out the remains of the original design.

Let us first suggest that the Siamese term *krom* be translated not as "department," but rather by a number of words all suggesting architectural locations. To facilitate distinctions as to both rank and historical period, I propose to use the words "palace," "court," and "chamber." [22]

It appears that from the beginning of the Ayuthian period (A.D. 1350) until the reforms of Trailok a century later, there had been a relatively simple four-court organization of government, known as the *Klang, Wang, Muang,* and *Na.* The heads of these courts were called *Senabodi.* It is not definite that the four courts consisted architecturally of buildings oriented to the points of the compass around the king's palace, although this may well have been the case. They may have been thought of as a series of concentric circles, which makes sense if we recall the sequence of annular seas (or moats) surrounding the palace in the ideal image of Mount Meru. The word *klang* apparently means center, and this court was, appropriately enough, charged with responsibility for the royal treasury. The second court, *wang,* became identified with the palace; the *muang* with the royal city; and the *na,* the outlying countryside.

FIGURE 3.
Hypothetical Plan
of the Four Courts

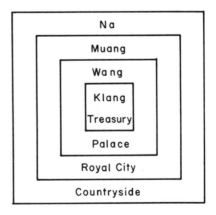

It is worth noting that the four courts, which had Sino-Thai names previously, were given Sanscrit-derived (through Pali) names after Trailok's reforms, as shown below. The transcriptions by Wales are given after transliterations which come closer to current Thai orthography.

English	Sino-Thai (early forms)	Sanscritized (15th century)
Treasury	Klang (Glăṅ)	Kosatibawdi (Kosādhipatī)
Palace	Wang (Văṅ)	Thammatikorn (Dharmādhipatī)
Capital	Muang (Mo'aṅ) or Wiang	Nakornban (Nagarapāla)
Countryside	Na (Nā)	Kasetrabawdi (Ksetrādhipatī)
	(after 1532)	Bolathep (Baladebā)

In the Khmer-influenced reforms of Trailok, the bilateral divison of right and left came to play an important part. However, remembering the front and rear palaces, we may do better to assume that a new set of four palaces was superimposed upon the older set of four courts. It may have seemed easier to make a fresh start, with a new palace complex, than to try to reconstruct or vitalize the old four-court system. But the earlier courts would nevertheless have survived and been brought, gradually, under the domination of the new palaces. Assuming that the front and rear palaces came to play a predominantly ceremonial and ritual function, serving the royal family, the palaces of the right (south) and of the left (north) could well have become the dominant instrumentalities of administration. The southern palace was known as *Kalahom,* the northern as *Mahadthai.* The heads of these palaces were called *Akkhramaha Senabodi.*

Just as the four courts of the earlier period had acquired territorial-functional duties, so the new palaces also acquired novel roles. The population was split into two divisions, the "right" and the "left," whose members were equally distributed throughout the realm. These divisions did not correspond, then, to territorial jurisdictions; members of both divisions lived side by side. We might think of them as "right-ers" and "left-ers." Logically enough, *Kalahom,* as the palace of the right, was assigned authority over the right-ers, and *Mahadthai* took control over the left-ers. The terms here obviously do not imply political tendencies, but, as in the case of the French chamber of deputies, physical location came to have a functional meaning. In the Siamese case, however, this significance moved toward a military-civil distinction. We may formulate the following equations:

Kalahom = right (southern) palace = right-ers (military)
Mahadthai = left (northern) palace = left-ers (civil)

Wales assumes that the *Kalahom* was a kind of "defense department" and the *Mahadthai* a "home" or "interior" ministry.[23] But this may be to impute undue functional differentiation to the palaces. It is clear that the royal officials, from the king himself on down, undertook both to lead military campaigns and to conduct civil-type activities. Ordinary freemen were, for much of the time, farmers; but while on *corvée* duty, they might be called on to serve in nonmilitary capacities or to fight in a campaign. Thus, in time of war—which was frequent—every freeman was liable to military duty, as were all officials, both right-ers and left-ers. In peacetime, however, it may have been the practice to call on right-ers, under *Kalahom,* to take part in relatively permanent guard— hence "military"—duties. In war time, *Mahadthai* may have played a more important part than *Kalahom,* since left-ers were free to join the campaign, whereas right-ers could not be spared from their local security (militia) duties. Alternatively, it is contended that both divisions did guard duty and fought in wars. The distinction may have been used mainly for purposes of enlistment and command.

Over the course of time, the role of the two lateral palaces changed. This change was probably related to the territorial extension of the royal domain. At first, the authority of the *senabodi* was, as Wales observes, confined to the area within the *Ratcha Thani,* or territory ruled directly from the capital, the "royal domain." Outside this area, the lords of the fiefs (or Lands) each held miniature courts in which, on a smaller scale, the cosmological organization of the royal court was duplicated. But gradually, during the Ayuthian period, the royal domain grew, and the populations brought under the jurisdiction of the two palaces increased. As this happened, the royal palaces imposed their direct supervision over their counterpart palaces in the march lands. Wales reports that, at the end of the seventeenth century, it was found desirable, "in order to obtain a unified command of all the men available for service in that part of the country, to place those of both civil and military divisions [left-ers and right-ers] in the southern provinces under the control of the *Kalahom;* while in the same way the *Mahatdaiya* commanded men of both divisions in the northern provinces." This arrangement persisted into the nineteenth century, with the result that Europeans came to refer to the *Mahadthai* as the "Minister of the North," and the *Kalahom* as "Minister of the South." Each controlled all provincial matters concerned with war, justice, and finance in his part of the country.[24]

With the expansion of the royal domain, a further refinement of the right-left division also took place. Each of the great chambers acquired two subsidiary chambers, one charged with responsibility for the conscription of freemen for compulsory service in the outer provinces of its territory, and the other with the same work in the inner area. This development was, however, not peculiar to the great chambers. Thus Wales notes that many other "dependent *krams* [*kroms*] show dual organization, there being *krams* of the left and right, each having a slightly different function but both remaining closely related." [25]

INTERPRETATIONS

In dealing with the bilateral system in Siamese organization, we have passed over the original four-chamber system which, as noted above, seems to have antedated the reforms of Trailok. This older system did not disappear, but was simply combined with the new, thereby illustrating the capacity of the Siamese to innovate by combining new and old structures. While the heads of the two palaces were known as the *Akkhramaha Senabodi,* the *senabodi* who headed the four older courts became known as the *Chatusadom,* or the four supports. Thawatt, on the basis of a review of the available Thai literature as well as of Wales and other Western writers, has concluded that the four *senabodi* were made responsible to the *Mahadthai* in all matters concerning members of the left division, and to the *Kalahom* in all matters concerning the right.[26]

This interpretation seems more reasonable than the following offered by Wales: "The four *senapati* were no doubt at first under the control of . . . the head of the civil division . . . since . . . there were four general officers, each originally in command of one of the four divisions of the army, who were under the command . . . of the military division." [27] It seems more likely to me that the civil-military distinction is an anachronistic reinterpretation, in functional terms, of a subsequent evolution of the offices. Perhaps, over a period of time, *Mahadthai* was able to exercise more control over the four *senabodi* than *Kalahom,* and the latter thereupon created somehow a shadowy counterpart of its own. Whatever the explanation, the fact is that by the Bangkok period there were six *senabodi,* the original four courts, and two of the later palaces. If the Wales interpretation were correct, we would expect to find ten *senabodi,* two "chief ministers," each with four dependent "ministers" or "generals."

According to my interpretation of the situation, there were two prime sets of four, the original four courts being succeeded by a subsequent set of four palaces. However, the second set was differentiated into two pairs: the *Wang Na* (front or east palace) and the *Wang Lang* (rear or west palace) became specialized for the honoring of the highest princes, whereas the *Kalahom* (right or south palace) and the *Mahadthai* (left or north palace) became specialized for higher administrative duties, beginning with the registration and control of the right-ers and left-ers throughout the administered population.

Meanwhile, the four courts continued their older duties, but each came under the domination of the two new palaces in so far as right-ers and left-ers, respectively, were concerned. Later, then, *Mahadthai* began to control the four courts more effectively than *Kalahom*. Moreover, as the domain brought under central control by Bangkok expanded, *Mahadthai* began to exercise more authority in the new northern territories, and *Kalahom* in the south. Thus, the directional designations which had initially been merely cosmological became eventually territorial.

This pattern of change becomes more reasonable when we also take into account the fact that both princes and commoners were assigned to every palace, court, and chamber. Although the initial rank of a prince might affect his assignment to a *krom,* it was also apparent that the rank of a *krom* affected or reinforced the rank of the prince. Only princes of the first and second rank—there was usually just one of each—could be named to *Wang Na* and *Wang Lang*, respectively. The commoners assigned to each *krom* became eventually, if they were not initially, the retainers of its prince and provided support for his establishment. Since the number of clients and the value of the income provided for its incumbent varied with the rank of the *krom,* it can be seen that the appointments carried practical as well as ceremonial advantages.

In matters of royal succession, we can assume that only the highest princes, and therefore the incumbents of *Wang Na* and *Wang Lang,* were actively considered. Hence, these palaces became strongly oriented toward the king and the affairs of the royal family. By contrast, the princes assigned to other *kroms* were not likely to become candidates for succession, and therefore these palaces and courts became more concerned with public administrative matters. Normally, however, it was not the prince himself who took leadership in these questions, but the chief commoner or noble in his entourage. This may explain why two of the new palaces became the leading *krom* for public administration, whereas the other two became identified with the royal household.

So far we have looked only at the palaces and courts. We have yet to mention the chambers. It appears that during the period of the Trailok reforms, a set of six chambers was established, headed by *montri*.

They were assigned such duties as the administration of Buddhist affairs, control of the royal apparel and insignia, the registration of clients, guarding the palace, a royal secretariat, and a supplementary treasury.[28] Wales notes that the six chambers reported directly to the king, not through the four courts or the two palaces. He adds that there were "a large number" of minor *kroms,* but for the most part these seem to have been dependent on one of the major *kroms.* Wales also tells us that "many of these dependent *krams* show dual organization, there being *krams* of the left and right, each having a slightly different function but both remaining closely related." [29]

The pattern of governmental organization, viewed from this perspective, was designed neither for territorial administration nor to carry out a set of functionally differentiated activities. Rather, it corresponded to the cosmologically oriented palace architecture, with a proliferation of minor chambers surrounding, in geometrical fashion, a core complex of palaces and courts. The subsequent assignment of duties possessing both territorial and functional attributes which overlapped each other gave each *krom,* over a period of time, a distinctive range of duties, with their territorial aspect sometimes predominating, their functional aspects prevailing at other times. But the exact duties assigned to each *krom* must have been viewed by the kings and the incumbents themselves as matters of expediency and tradition, rather than as inherent in the constitution of each office.

Quite naturally the tasks carried out by any court or chamber "varied from time to time," as Wales remarks.[30] Such variations no doubt reflected the predispositions and capabilities of the incumbents of each *krom* and their mutual rivalries, as well as conscious efforts by the kings to strengthen the hands of their most loyal supporters and weaken those in whom they had less confidence. In this sense, traditional Thai politics and administration can be seen as a nexus of power and authority flowing from the king to and among a congeries of palaces, courts, and chambers, each somewhat autonomous and a rival of all the others, yet linked together by patterns of mutual dependence and hierarchically structured but mobile linkages of deference and prestige.

LOCAL ADMINISTRATION

In the earliest, half-legendary Sukhotai period (ca. A.D. 1238–1317), the term *Paw-muang* was used for the head of territories within the kingdom. The expression might be translated as "father of the realm." At lower levels, the village head was *Paw-ban,* or "father of the village," and the family head, *Paw-krua,* or "father" in the usual sense.[31]

The imagery suggests a benevolent paternalism, which gives the ancient system a romantic aura in the minds of contemporary Siamese, but it may also be interpreted as a highly decentralized confederation of feudalistic or tribal-type polities, with minimal differentiation of function, the linkages between levels being provided by hierarchically structured relationships between the all-purpose rulers or "fathers" at each level.

Looking to Western history for parallels, we can observe in medieval France the institution of counts, each in control of a county. Originally agents of the monarchy, the counts eventually became hereditary noblemen, whereas the word "county" has come into modern usage as an administrative area. Later the kings appointed bailiffs, whose territorial jurisdiction became known as a bailiwick.[32]

An English near equivalent was the sheriff who both administered the area and presided over judicial hearings in the pre-Norman shires. It is interesting that, whereas the office of count subsequently evolved into a high hereditary title, the terms bailiff and sheriff have come to be used for minor officials with subordinate or specialized functions. In Central Asia today, local landlord-officials are referred to as *khans,* and the area under their jurisdiction may be called a *khanate.* This seems to be a reduction in scale and importance of a title which, under the Mongol empire of Chingiz Khan, was used for the highest office itself. The terms *chagan* and *cham* are other variants of *khan.*

The key term *muang* has, in Siamese usage, acquired a variety of meanings. It may originally have meant something like "city," but came to include the surrounding countryside. We note a similar origin for the English "borough," which once meant a castle or fortification, a manor house, then a fortified town, and eventually a district, usually including or within a city. The German *Burg* retains the meaning of fortress, but in the suffix -bury, as used in the names of some American cities and villages, it has the more expanded meaning.

We find a comparable range of meanings in the word "municipality," which referred originally to office-holding in free cities but has been extended to include the area of jurisdiction. In American usage, this is typically an urban government, but in the Spanish tradition it includes also the surrounding rural area, a territorial unit like the American county, with the *municipio* as its urban core and administrative center.

The Siamese *muang*, however, has acquired an even more expanded meaning, referring not only to districts and regions, but also to the whole realm. Thus, the Siamese today refer to their country as *Muang Thai*, i.e., Thailand. This expansion in meaning, however, should not surprise English-speakers who reflect on the similar changes that have taken place in the meaning of the word "land" itself. Consider the simple meaning of earth or soil, as in the "farmer's land," which becomes a "tract of land," and moves on to become a state (Mary*land*) or a nation (Switzer*land*, New Zea*land*). In German, *Länder* is a state, and a *Landgraf* was a nobleman with territorial jurisdiction. In common usage, a "landlord" is today thought of as an owner who rents land to tenants. Thus the word connotes both private and public domains. Perhaps an appropriate translation for the Siamese term *Chow-muang*, which succeeded *Paw-muang* after the Khmer-inspired reforms of the fifteenth century, would be "Lord of the Land."

In traditional systems we often find appointed territorial officials becoming hereditary nobles (such as the counts and provosts in early French history). The ruler may cope with the resultant weakening of central authority by appointing a new type of territorial administrator. The French sequence from count to provost to bailiff to governor to intendent to prefect, as described by Fesler, has been repeated in other countries under different names.[33]

It is probably too neat a distinction to see the *Paw-muang*, "Father of the Land," as a patriarchal figure, perhaps rooted in clan or tribal structures, and the *Chow-muang* as a royal administrator or provincial governor. No doubt the actual content of each office varied over time, but available records scarcely suffice to give an exact picture of the changes. I suspect that each office started after a period of royal conquest as a royally-appointed generalist official with a territorial jurisdiction, but each tended to become more autonomous and hereditary with the passage of time. Alternatively, the *Paw-muang* might have been local magnates who accepted the suzerainty of the king at first, but later became more and more autonomous. This could account for the apparent "territorialization" of what is today said to have been originally a more "functionally specific" pattern of organization.

Some glimpses of this cyclical movement, involving a gradual erosion of royal power in conquered territories during periods of dynastic decline, followed by renewed extension of control during periods of vigor, can be gained by examining the geographic distribution of Lands around the capital. Let us imagine a series of concentric circles like the ripples caused by a stone dropping into a pool of water. The circles may gradually expand and, in this case, also contract. Secondly, just as the ripples near the center are stronger than the fading circles farther away, so the inner territories are under better control by the monarchy than the outer ones. Moreover, the status of the inner belts is higher than that of the outer rings. To make our image more complex and analogous, suppose that a number of smaller pebbles are thrown into the pool at the same time as a larger stone. We can then see how the rings around the stone dominate the weaker sets of ripples sent out by the pebbles. Yet each pebble creates miniature circles which duplicate those formed by the stone. The farther away a pebble falls, the more clearly marked is its own pattern, since it is overwhelmed less by the ripples spreading from the larger stone.

Following this model, we can imagine the courts of each territorial ruler as replicas, on a smaller scale, of the central court. The sequence from *Paw-khun* to *Paw-muang* to *Paw-ban* to *Paw-krua* epitomizes this succession of miniaturized imitations. A. M. Hocart has shown how many traditional ceremonies and rituals have spread down from a royal court, by emulation, to lower strata and local centers of society.[34]

McKim Marriott, using a somewhat different frame of reference, has spoken of this process as one of "parochialization," whereby the practices and rites of the Great Tradition percolate down to the parochial centers of the Little Traditions.[35]

Each *Paw-muang* or *Chow-muang*, then, may be imagined as the presiding dignitary at a court which duplicates, on a smaller scale, the same cosmologically oriented structure of government as that exhibited in all its grandeur by the royal capital. Each center of government would have, then, its own "southern palace," but the duties actually assigned to the southern palaces might vary considerably, and one cannot imagine a national, functionally specialized "department" or "bureau" linking together all the "southern palaces" of the realm. The linkage, rather, would be provided directly, in a single hierarchic chain, from the king at the center to each Lord of the Land throughout the realm.

Just as the king had to supervise personally each of the subsidiary chambers in the capital, as well as the palaces and courts, so he had to maintain the loyalty of each Lord of the Land to his dynasty if he wanted to hold his realm together. Obviously, the farther away the Land, the more difficult it became to maintain effective control. The consequences can be visualized in the terminology and descriptions that are available to us.

At the center was the *Ratcha Thani* or royal domain. The word *Ratcha* (*Raja*) refers to the king, and *Thani* is a large city. Here the direct administration of the king prevailed, and the apparatus of cosmologically oriented palaces, courts, and chambers could deal directly with the people. The ability of the kings to maintain control over the area tended to fluctuate, however, and so we find the area of the *Ratcha Thani* expanding and contracting.

Expansion of the royal domain would be at the expense of the surrounding Lands, which were known as the *Hua-muang Channok*, or "Outer Lands," each ruled by a *Chow-muang* (Lord of the Land). As areas within this belt became detached and annexed to the *Ratcha Thani*, they formed a new circle, the *Hua-muang Channai*, or "Inner Lands." By a complex subclassification of this domain into first, second, third, and fourth class Lands, following the strategic balance principle elaborated by classical Brahmanic writers, the Siamese kings strove to combat the inherently centrifugal pressures of the traditional polity, to bring the territorial lords under greater central control.

Outside these belts lay a broad domain of tributary states, each under its own hereditary ruler, but all acknowledging some obligations to the Siamese dynasty. These could involve providing soldiers in the event of war and sending tributes to the royal capital. From a different point of view, the provision of troops might be regarded as a sign of alliance rather than of fealty, and the tributes might be looked upon as gifts rather than as homage. A local prince, indeed, might similarly honor several neighboring empires. The Siamese, for their part, paid comparable deference to the great imperial court of China. Nevertheless, especially in the light of more modern ideas about sovereignty, it became possible to view this nexus of traditional obligations as evidence that the Siamese realm had, traditionally, included a broad territory inhabited by tributary dependencies, if not by directly administered provinces.

The monarchy, in practice, resorted to a variety of techniques designed to consolidate its territorial authority. Thus, roving commissioners were sent to observe and report on the performance of the Lords of the Lands. In the same way, the French kings sent out roving bailiffs to inspect and hold court in areas under the permanent control of resident provosts.[36] But if their visits were brief, they could scarcely hope to be effective, and if they stayed too long, they might well be co-opted by local interests. It was difficult to find a way to assure their effectiveness and yet to maintain their loyalties. The Siamese during the Bangkok period used the technique of maintaining an official, the *Yokkabat,* perhaps a "public prosecutor," in each Land. He had somewhat limited functions but was given direct access to Bangkok and the king.[37] He could, therefore, report on any signs of treason, but he could not become a Lord of the Land himself. Thereby his own loyalty to the monarchy was presumably enhanced.

A supplementary control institution was the royal harem whose important cosmological role was stressed in the passage from Heine-Geldern, cited above.[38] But the royal establishment also provided a convenient means for creating bonds of kinship with distant and potentially rebellious princes. Vella has noted this point as follows:

> Some measure of control was exercised over the vassal states and over the distant provinces with hereditary governorships, however, through a system of marriage alliances. It was the policy of Thai kings to acquire the daughters of heads of dependencies to fill the royal harem. These women formed a permanent bond between the Bangkok government and the leaders of vassal states and provinces.[39]

One of the more dramatic methods used by the monarchy to assure the loyalty of the *Chow-muang* was the semi-annual rite of "Drinking the Water of Allegiance." All territorial rulers were required to visit Bangkok, where they took a most solemn and incriminating oath of loyalty, accompanied by the drinking of ritually sanctified water, which was supposed to bring deadly consequences to anyone harboring disloyal or treasonable thoughts. In terms of negative sanctions, the punishments which a king could impose for any signs of disloyalty were extremely severe, involving confiscation of all property, execution of the culprit and his entire family, extending for seven generations, and the use of torture for seven days as a prelude to execution. Mere association between the *Chow-muang* of different Lands could be interpreted as evidence of treason, for which the death penalty was authorized. According to Arsa, the royal code in such matters offers proof "of how conscious the king was of the problems of provincial control, and how aware of the great power of the provincial governors." He concludes that "although historical evidence indicates that the king had always been able to suppress the rebellious acts of the provincial governors, the problem of provincial control remained crucial and serious up to the end of the last century, just prior to the administrative reorganization undertaken during the reign of King Chulalongkorn." [40]

Anyone familiar with contemporary doctrines about the limits of the span of control in administrative organization and the requirements of the scalar principle might well ask how a king could personally supervise and direct the congeries of courts, palaces, and chambers in his own capital city, plus the many appointive and hereditary lords and princes of the surrounding Lands. Surely if the king were required to formulate, authorize, and enforce policies or laws in the modern sense of these words, the task would have been impossible to perform.

The viability of the traditional polity, however, was based on the fact that such rule-making processes were not necessary. In large part, each sub-unit within the realm was an autonomous, self-subsistent, and self-governing social entity. If a king chose to spend all his time with his harem favorites—as some no doubt did—the various component institutions of the social order would have continued to operate with little change. The main effect would have been a dwindling of the royal domain, a weakening of the linkages which assured not so much the welfare of the kingdom as the tributary intake of the royal establishment.

Moreover, the monarchy provided a sense of order, a point of orientation for all the sub-institutions of Siamese society. When that orienting superstructure weakened, then the mutual relationships of the parts of the system began to deteriorate, a sense of disharmony grew, leading to intensified rivalries and civil strife. The main function, in a word, of the traditional monarchy was "system-maintenance." It did not have to provide the positive services and regulatory mechanisms of a modern government. Why and how this could have been true may become clearer if we examine the role and nature of law in traditional Siam.

THE ROLE OF LAW

Could a political system of the type described above carry out the functions we have learned to associate with the model of any political system, as it has been described by Almond? Where in the Siamese polity shall we look for the inputs and outputs in terms of socialization and communication, of interest articulation and aggregation, of rule-making, rule-implementation, and rule-adjudication? [41]

Crucial to this input-output model is the role of law, the "rules."

The Austinian classic conception of law as the "command of the sovereign" provides a framework within which to view the output processes, for what is law in these terms but a set of rules promulgated by the ruler, enforced by his officials, and tested in his courts? John Austin, as an early nineteenth-century conservative, laid no stress upon the input processes whereby the people's interests might be translated into official enactments. Yet it takes only a slight transposition to visualize the "people" as the "sovereign," and hence to see law as the codification of aggregated popular demands.

But if this were the nature of traditional "laws," then the Siamese regime was singularly ill-equipped to formulate and enforce them. Through what mechanism, one might ask, could a king, in the governmental structure described above, formulate, promulgate, and enforce generalized policies? How, had he wished to, could he have received information about popular interests, aggregated them, and translated them into rules?

This is not to say that the traditional Siamese polity lacked a functional equivalent of "law," for there were certainly norms governing the actions of common men as well as those of noblemen and kings. But these were, for the most part, guides to action that had emerged, crescively, over the generations. The anthropological terms "folkways" and "mores" come close to suggesting the character of traditional law. Mores are generally accepted behavior patterns, slow to change, enforced by social pressures. Folkways are similar practices, but the sanctions are lighter than those applying to mores.

When such rules of behavior are codified and buttressed by the authority of king and court, something like traditional (or customary) law results. At least, such was the Siamese situation. Apart from law in this sense, the commands of the sovereign took the form of highly particularistic orders relating to specific individuals in concrete situations, not general rules or policies applicable to many cases. Of course, over a period of time the particular commands of a king might be used as precedents that would later be invoked, not as grounds for changing the law, but as evidence of what the law was.

That the Siamese polity was of this sort is indicated by Lingat in an essay on Burmese and Siamese law in which he shows that the Siamese traditionally lived under the Mon-Hindu *dhammasattham,* or sacred code. Kings, lords, and chiefs, he writes, relied on these rules in governing their people. "They regarded them as the supreme expression of truth and equity, showing to princes the right way for an impartial administration of justice, and they never confused their own authority with that of these sacred precepts. They enjoyed absolute power and could act however they pleased. But their decisions were mere orders, they could not alter the law as revealed by Manu and could not stand as permanent rules. At the best, their authoritativeness could last as long as the ruler who had ordered them was living, but once dead they failed to have any standing, and fell, unless the new ruler was pleased to sanction them." [42] On this basis, Lingat concludes, "There was apparently no place for what we call law."

Similar conclusions were reached years ago by Sir Henry Maine. He spent much time in the Punjab in the latter part of the nineteenth century, and wrote from first-hand observation of its political system under the highly arbitrary but effective rule of Ranjit Singh. This ruler, according to Maine, "was absolutely despotic. Except occasionally on his wild frontier, he kept the most perfect order." Any disobedience to his commands was followed by death or mutilation. "Yet," Sir Henry wrote,

I doubt whether once in all his life he issued a command which Austin would call a law. He took, as his revenue, a prodigious share of the produce of the soil. He harried villages which recalcitrated at his exactions, and he executed great numbers of men. He levied great armies; he had all material of power, and exercised it in various ways. But he never made a law. The rules which regulated the life of his subjects were derived from their immemorial usages, and these rules were administered by domestic tribunals, in families or village-communities.[43]

Maine's wide-ranging studies of legal systems compel attention to his opinions when he says, "The state of political society which I have described as Indian or Oriental is a far more trustworthy clue to the former condition of the greatest part of the world than is the modern social organization of Western Europe as we see it before our eyes." [44] The Siamese polity, then, was not at all atypical, but rather the rule for all such traditional systems.

The traditional system, nevertheless, was not devoid of loopholes for the innovating monarch to make his will felt. Indeed, Lingat himself tells us that it became customary to collect the orders of each Siamese king in a literary form known as *rajasattham,* as distinguished from the sacred and ultimate authority of the *dhammasattham.* Eventually, items of the *rajasattham* came to be incorporated in the *dhammasattham* as derivative materials illustrating how the basic rules had been applied.

"Decisions of kings," Lingat notes, "became henceforward permanent rules, not because they emanated from kings, but because they were illustrations of the Eternal Law and partaking of its authority." [45]

Building on this foundation, the reforming kings of the nineteenth century carried out a radical transformation of the royal role. Thus, Lingat writes that, although Rama I, in codifying the texts which had come down to his period, had in effect made substantial modifications in the sacred law, it was not until the time of Mongkut that we see the old conception of law deliberately and definitely put aside.

The traditional system, then, did provide in a very limited way some basis for the subsequent transformation by which law and administration, in the modern sense of these words, were introduced. Seen in retrospect, these proto-modern elements in the traditional system were magnified to such an extent that it has become difficult for contemporary observers to gain a just perspective on the essential characteristics of the former polity.

Yet it is only by striving for an understanding of the cosmological pattern of governmental organization, the weak linkages between central and territorial regimes, and the sacred, customary quality of the normative or legal system that we can grasp the magnitude of the transformations carried out after the mid-nineteenth century. To think of the contemporary Thai polity as a "traditional," "underdeveloped," or "non-Western" system is to obscure the fundamental and far-reaching changes which have taken place and to mask the striking differences between the governmental structures of contemporary Thailand and classical Siam.

In order to gain a better understanding of these differences, let us turn next to an analysis of some of the steps by which the traditional polity has been modernized and the dynamic forces which have impelled this transformation.

PART TWO: PATTERNS OF MODERNIZATION

CHAPTER III

The Transformation
of the Monarchy

The word "bureaucracy" has become attached to a variety of meanings, ranging from the common-sense notion of red tape and official obstructionism to the idea of rule by an administrative oligarchy, to sociological, Weberian constructs used in empirical analysis. It is in the last sense that I wish to use the term here; yet the other meanings also retain a certain relevance, for all apply, in part at least, to the concrete reality.

To Lasswell and Kaplan, "A bureaucracy is a hierarchy of considerable power and diversification, and low circulation."[1] For them, the term has a descriptive, not a normative, significance. All power groups are not bureaucratic nor, by this definition, are all hierarchies bureaucratic. The exercise of power by members of the hierarchy must be accompanied by diversification of roles and relative continuity of incumbents in these roles, regardless of how recruited—whether by appointment, election, or inheritance.

The notion of hierarchy is emphasized in a sociological definition which states that a bureaucracy is "a graded hierarchy of officials, each of whom is responsible to his superiors." The normative connotations are separated from the empirical by using a different word, "bureaucratism" to refer to such disapproved characteristics as "adherence to routine, more or less inflexible rules, red tape, procrastination, unwillingness to assume responsibility, and refusal to experiment."[2]

A political definition from England states that bureaucracy refers to "(a) the rule of a caste of high officials, (b) this caste itself."[3]

I shall assume that all these definitions apply to the organization of government as found both in the traditional Siamese polity and in the contemporary Thai government. However, I shall take the Lasswell and Kaplan definition as my point of departure. The hierarchic structure of roles will be the focal point of analysis. That the occupants of these roles exercised considerable power and manifested to some degree the characteristics of "bureaucratism" may be taken as probable but not necessary. One may, in other words, assume that a bureaucracy meeting the criteria of hierarchy, diversity, and low circulation might, at the same time, be politically subordinate to a different ruling "caste" or set of institutions, and that it need not display a high degree of "bureaucratism."

The purpose of Part Two will be to examine the respects in which the Siamese bureaucracy was, in fact, changed or transformed during the process of modernization. We shall, in due course, inquire into the effect of these changes upon the power position of the bureaucracy and the extent to which it exhibited bureaucratism.

Meanwhile, three aspects of the bureaucracy will be examined. The first involves the identity of its core institutions and the basis of its legitimacy; the second involves the characteristic patterning of its roles, the types of diversification practiced; and the third involves the domain of the system. I shall argue that the absolute monarchy was displaced by an office-holding elite as the core of the bureaucracy, although the monarchy continued to play an important part in legitimizing the system. The cosmologically oriented structure of roles was displaced by one which, to a considerable degree, is functionally specialized. A decision-making system gradually replaced an ordering and legitimizing regime. The domain of the system expanded in a revolutionary fashion, as a single national hierarchy of officials replaced the concatenation of local officialdoms which had presided over the traditional society.

It may seem strange to link the monarchy to a discussion of the bureaucracy. Yet if we take our key definition seriously—a hierarchy of officials each responsible to his superior—then the superior of all superiors in the traditional system was clearly the king. In a sense, of course, we might include in the concept of bureaucracy only those officials who have a superior to whom to report. We might use "government" as a more inclusive term to include a "principal" and his "agents," in this case, the king and his officials. We have seen how, in the traditional Siamese polity, the whole structure of officialdom gravitated, both politically and topologically, around the throne.

Clearly, any change in the function and role of such a monarchy would have had a fundamental impact upon its dependent bureaucracy. Even if we chose conceptually to detach the bureaucracy from the crown, we could not obtain a coherent picture of the restructuring of the bureaucracy without examining the concurrent changes which took place in the monarchy. It is, therefore, not necessary to solve the terminological riddle posed by the question whether a bureaucracy ought to be thought of as including its key role, the apex of its hierarchic pyramid. We shall just assume that any bureaucracy is fundamentally affected by basic changes in the character of this key role, and that the latter must, therefore, be studied in any examination of changes in the bureaucracy as a whole.

Our interest will focus on the transformation of the monarchic role more than on the specific policies launched by the Siamese kings. These policies, although directed primarily toward transformations in the total polity, indirectly also changed the character and the public image of the monarchy itself. It has been common in writings on Siam, as on other modernizing countries, to depict the chief reformers as though they stood, in some way, outside the system which they ruled and manipulated. Yet the monarchy itself was the central institution of the traditional polity. Any innovative actions on the part of a king would certainly have a retroactive impact upon the role of the monarchy. Despite the saying that a "king can do no wrong," kings cannot violate the normal rules governing their own conduct without upsetting the balance of forces that sustains the kingship as an institution. Thus, kings can wrong only themselves. Viewed from this vantage point, the transformation of the Siamese bureaucracy was due as much to the changes in the character of the monarchy as to the policies of the throne. The chief influence of a modernizing king may not be exercised so much upon the government as an object of policy, as on the royal institution itself.

We have been greatly impressed by the apparent effectiveness of the reforms launched by Mongkut and Chulalongkorn in their efforts to modernize the Siamese polity. We have regarded the decline in the effectiveness of the monarchy during the succeeding reigns of kings Wachirawut (1910–25) and Prachatipok (1925–34) as due to their relative lack of dynamism or competence as compared with their more heroic predecessors. Yet it may be that the changes in the monarchic role made, no doubt unintentionally, by Mongkut and Chulalongkorn, did not become fully apparent until the time of their successors.

The true measure of the success of these innovating kings may be not that they brought into being a modernized bureaucratic polity, but rather that, in doing so, they were able to lay the foundations for maintenance of the monarchy as a legitimizing institution. Siamese society could scarcely have avoided the impact of Western imperialism. On the most superficial level, if Mongkut and Chulalongkorn had not responded adequately to this challenge, they would have forfeited their rule, and Siam would have come under alien domination, the fate which struck Burma, as we have seen in Chapter I.

But on a deeper level, they might have saved the country at the expense of the monarchy. The revolution of 1932 might well have led to the establishment of a republic, as it seemed determined to do in the first flush of victory. But the ability of the Siamese throne to outlast this harrowing crisis and, indeed, to restore in some measure its former aura, if not its power, is a tribute, not so much to Prachatipok and his successors, Ananda and Phumiphon, as to the way in which Mongkut and Chulalongkorn, in the very process of secularizing and expanding the bureaucracy as a decision-making institution, also laid a new foundation for the monarchy as a religious and popular focus of civic loyalties and, hence, of national identifications. As in the case of the Meiji Restoration in Japan, it was the neotraditionalism of the reforming kings which made it possible to carry through a limited program of modernization without the far-reaching and unnerving crises of mind and society which have so deeply devastated neighboring countries such as Burma and Vietnam.[4]

That the monarchy should have been able to pass unscathed through a fundamental transformation of the polity would perhaps not have been thought possible but for the image of the "absolute monarchy" which has come to be widely accepted as literal truth. The kings were generally regarded—by the Siamese themselves no less than by astonished foreign observers—not only as "divine monarchs" in current dogma, but also as virtually god-like in their capacity to rule in Jovian fashion.

Vella, for example, writes that the traditional Siamese monarchy was "probably even more absolutist than its Indian and Cambodian models, for in India and Cambodia the Brahman, or priest, class was strong and acted as a restraining force on the monarchy, whereas in Thailand this class was weak and had relatively little power to influence government policy."[5]

CONTRADICTORY ROYAL ROLES

Two contrasting views have become popular as "explanations" of contemporary Siam. One, accepting the notion of royal absolutism in uncritical fashion, has regarded the relatively painless entry of Thailand into the modern world as a tour de force by its reform-minded and omnipotent rulers. The alternative view is that, despite heroic efforts by its kings, Siamese society and government have remained virtually unchanged. The contemporary polity is equated with the traditional, and Thailand is viewed as a quaint backwater country where time stands still while the rest of the world rushes feverishly by. Both interpretations, in my opinion, fall short of a reality which is both more complex and more interesting.

The absolute monarchy, in practice, was never as powerful as many imagine. Vella himself writes that the effective powers of the "absolute" monarch were sharply limited. "Thailand was not," he records, "in any respect a strong unitary state and the relations between the government and the people were therefore extremely loose. There was a vast difference between the absolute monarchy's ideal of centralization and the fact." [6] This looseness was manifest particularly in the relations of the center to local government. Thus, according to Vella,

> The problem of provincial control was a real one. The ideal was to centralize control as much as possible, but poor transportation and communication facilities made a large degree of decentralization of power inevitable. Thus the principal problem of the central government with regard to provincial administration was to give provincial officials enough power to administer the provinces effectively but not enough to permit the creation of independent provinces. In general, the degree of control maintained by the central government over the provinces tended to decrease as the distance from the capital increased. For many distant provinces the government adopted the practical policy of allowing the position of governor to become hereditary. [7]

Vella also shows how, in local government, the governors, in fact, exercised very little control over the villages, which were, to a considerable extent, self-governing communities. Even at the center itself, Vella points to the fact that royal officials could not depend upon salaries for their support as a major factor contributing to "corruption among the officialdom," which, in turn, indicated the weakness of the king's control over his bureaucracy. [8]

The traditional Siamese monarchy, then, was "absolutist" in name only. In practice it was quite limited, not so much by constitutional or legal restraints as by the law of diminishing returns: the marginal costs of extending control beyond fairly narrow limits tended to exceed whatever marginal benefits to the crown might thereby be gained.

If we look upon the Siamese monarchy in these terms, then we can see that the reforms carried out by the Thai elite during the last decades of the nineteenth century and the first decades of the twentieth brought about a transformation within the structure of the "absolute monarchy" itself. It acquired a capacity for effective power which it had never possessed before. The new technology of administrative organization and procedure, which the Siamese rulers borrowed selectively from the West in order to defend their culture from "Westernization," placed in the hands of the elite new and effective weapons of control over their own people. From this point of view, the seizure of power by a new commoner oligarchy in 1932 was not only a reflection of the absorption of Western constitutional ideals by this group of "returned students," but also a natural symptom of protest against the aggrandizement of power by the king and the royal family.

The "absolute monarchy" of 1932, in other words, was basically different from the "absolute monarchy" of 1832. It had become much more powerful, yet it had undermined its own foundations in the process. But a second paradox needs to be understood: at the same time that one basis of monarchic legitimacy had been withering away, another had been steadily growing. The Hinduistic ideology of the divine kingship had been replaced by the Buddhistic ideal of the Great Man, who rules so that the welfare of all may increase.

The modernization of Siam, then, was not the result of the superhuman exertions of an absolute monarchy. Rather, it took place as a relatively weak governing institution was able to make itself strong, as the nominally "absolute" kings transformed their office into one of effective power-wielding rulers.

But the modernization of Siam was also not a mere façade; it did bring secularization and transformed the bureaucracy into a decision-making organ of government. In so doing, it undermined the basis of legitimacy of the old regime. That the monarchy has survived, though shorn of political power, not only is a tribute to the effectiveness of the kings in creating a new basis of legitimacy, but also reflects the need of the polity for the throne in its new role.

The revolution of 1932 confirmed but did not create a more basic transformation in the structure of the Thai government, which had already taken place. Thus, in 1930, while the absolute monarchy still persisted in name, Wales could write that the "masses" had no real understanding of the rites of tonsure, coronation, and cremation, but they had "an innate love and respect for all forms of royal pageantry, and it is the magnificence of the state procession, the splendour of the Urn enthroned upon the catafalque, or the brilliantly illuminated Brah Meru, that impress them that their King is a great King."[9]

It was this loss of understanding and respect for the rituals which had once led to the deification of the monarch as a living god that made it possible for a group of Siamese rebels to consider overthrowing and displacing the monarchy as a basis for the legitimacy of government. The progressive erosion of the old ideas about the divine kingship dates back to the time of Mongkut himself. To the Western world, he is known as the first modernizing Siamese king, who launched programs of secularization and had his children instructed in Western learning. Thus, Vella writes that "his bias in favor of things Western made converts among the officials and had a lasting influence on his successors, paving the way for more far-reaching Western innovations in later years." But Vella seems to miss an important dimension of Mongkut's role by saying that he was "too closely wedded—in time and in temperament—to the old order of Thai government to contemplate any major changes in it."[10]

MONGKUT AS RELIGIOUS REFORMER

However, I suspect that the eventual verdict of history upon Mongkut will be that it was in the Buddhistic core of his mind that he made the greatest impact upon Thai society, not as a traditionalist, but as an innovator. In so doing, he laid the foundation for the monarchy's survival despite its de-deification.

It is well known that when Rama II died in 1824, Mongkut was only twenty years old, but the oldest prince born of a royal mother. He had just entered a monastery for the usual short period of monkhood. Upon his father's death, his thirty-seven-year-old brother was named king, whether because of a palace intrigue or because the royal council thought a more experienced man should be placed on the throne. In any event, Prince Mongkut decided to stay in the Buddhist Order, where he remained until the death of Rama III and his own coronation in 1851. During this long monastic retreat, Mongkut made use of missionary teachers, both Catholic and Protestant, not only to learn about Christianity, but also to study Latin, English, astronomy, mathematics, geography, physics, and chemistry.

But the major impact of this monastic experience was on the young prince-monk's religious understanding. In a mood of deep self-questioning, he devoted himself to Pali studies and quickly acquired intimate knowledge of the Buddhist scriptures and a sure command of the sacred language. Rama III then named him head of the Board of Pali Examinations, which greatly increased his influence within the Order. In 1837, he was named abbot of a new monastery established by the king, where he and his followers started a movement that was ultimately to take form as the reform Dhammayutta sect, devoted to rigorous promotion of the original Buddhist teachings. "They rejected all practices that had no authority other than custom. They accepted all canonical regulations, not merely following them mechanically, but endeavoring to keep their significance ever present in their consciousness. They were expected to understand the formulas they recited, the reasons for the rules they were subject to, and the meaning of the acts they performed."[11] In effect, he launched a Buddhist reformation.

Griswold tells us that "by his judicious selections and rejections, Prince Mongkut had created a new Buddhism—or, as he more modestly thought, revived the original Doctrine. He was fond of saying that there is nothing in it that conflicts with modern science. He could point to the laws of physics to show that given causes produce given effects. If these laws govern the material universe, is it not reasonable to assume that similar laws govern the moral domain, so that every deed, whether good or evil, is inevitably followed by its appropriate consequence?" Discouraging meaningless acts of "merit," Mongkut encouraged deeds of social value: "while only the rich could afford to build monasteries and hospitals, the poor could bridge a stream with a few bamboo poles or remove sharp thorns from a public path; all could give alms in proportion to their means, in money or in service; all could practice kindness and self-restraint."[12]

The Dhammayutta doctrines, even today, have not been universally accepted among the Siamese, but they have spread widely, exercising a leavening influence. Meanwhile, a solid core of Dhammayutta sectarians seeks to practice the reform doctrines as taught by Mongkut.

In his quest for religious truth, Mongkut sought the advice of foreign experts more than a decade before he engaged in international diplomacy as king. In 1840, five Sinhalese monks came to Siam and stayed at Mongkut's monastery, where they conversed with each other in Pali. Mongkut then sent five of his own followers to Ceylon, where they spent a year in study and returned with forty volumes of the scriptures. Later missions continued the exchange of monks and sacred texts.

"As a result of his discussions with them," Griswold writes, "Prince Mongkut began a copious correspondence with the most learned members of the monkhood in Ceylon on all points of doctrine and discipline. In the course of time the Sinhalese tradition succeeded in tempering his attachment to the Mon practices; both together helped him to revert to the pure Doctrine of the Buddha." [13]

For present purposes, however, the most telling impact of Mongkut's Buddhist "neotraditionalism" was on the monarchy itself, for he began to look self-critically upon the royal role in terms both of Buddhist piety and Western rationalism. Writing to an English correspondent about the expensive preparations being made for the cremation of Rama III, he declared, "Large sums of money are always sacrificed on such occasions from the royal treasury. It costs much labor and time and strength to all classes of the subjects of the kingdom. It appears indeed to be a custom the observance of which is not followed by any advantage. But it is a very old custom of the kingdom, and by all her tributaries well known and revered. And if it should be now disregarded, passing it by with ceremonies only such as are really needed, all the head provinces and tributary kingdoms would find fault and attribute it to base motives." [14]

Similarly, in regard to his own coronation, Mongkut faithfully complied with tradition; but, at least according to Griswold, he viewed it as a secular matter. "As there is no Buddhist substitute for the Brahmin ceremony," he writes, "the most that King Mongkut could do was to revise the ceremony slightly, so as to reinforce the Buddhist elements that had been introduced into it, and add a human touch. All the most conspicuous features necessarily remained Hindu. He had no objection to Brahmanism as long as it did not threaten to contaminate Buddhism itself. To him the Hindu gods were no more than picturesque fancies. They could be admitted as supporters of a Buddhist monarchy, so long as Buddhists did not mistake them for Buddhism." [15]

But from the time of Mongkut on, many of the older customs and ceremonies of the divine kingship were questioned and were either reinterpreted in Buddhist terms, secularized, or neglected and gradually forgotten. Whereas in the Brahmanic tradition the king was a Deva-Raja or human vehicle for the gods, for Vishnu or Siva, in the Buddhist view the king was a man. The Buddhist classical understanding of kingship is well stated by Hocart in the following passage:

. . . the highest rank to which a king could attain in the secular sphere was that of Wheel-monarch [*Charkravartin*] or Emperor; while the summit of a spiritual career was the Buddha or universal Sage. I say secular and spiritual, but in point of fact there is not so very much distinction between the two: the emperor of the Buddhist scriptures is first and foremost a moralist; he conquers his empire peacefully by preaching the law and by upholding it in his dominions, in fact the Buddhist scriptures declare both the Emperor and the Buddha to be the two beings that are born for the welfare of gods and men; they are in fact two varieties of that somewhat obscure conception, the Great Man . . . the difference between them is that the Emperor stays in his palace enjoying the pleasures of the world, while the Buddha goes forth into homelessness; both have come into the world to uphold law, morality, and religion, but one devotes himself exclusively to that purpose, the other combines it with the good things of this world and secular authority. . . .[16]

ROYAL PATRONAGE OF THE KATHIN

It was part of Mongkut's policy not only to reduce the emphasis placed on the royal coronation and cremation ceremonies, as expressions primarily of the old cult of the divine king, but also to give greater attention to the role of the king as leading patron of Buddhist ceremonials and activities. In this spirit Mongkut stressed the importance of the *kathin,* a well-established Buddhist rite which he elevated to an even more conspicuous place. We find Wales writing in 1930:

. . . although it is important to remember that the King of Siam protects *all* Buddhist activities, it is only in the Royal *Kathina* that he takes a predominant part, a part eminently characteristic of the traditional Buddhist monarch. Indeed, the sociological value of the Royal *Kathina* for the maintenance of social integrity and the continued prosperity of the Buddhist religion in Siam is exceeded by no other ceremony, for the following three reasons: (1) the King, by the lavishness of his gifts and his personal profession of faith at the altar, impresses upon the people in a truly regal way his belief in the national religion, and thus the love and respect which the people have for their monarch; (2) the example of the King inspires the people with a desire to emulate his generosity, and by the *Kathinas* of noble and private persons which take place on a smaller scale all over the country, every monastery is provided for and the growth of the Buddhist religion is stimulated; (3) the Royal *Kathina* procession by land and by water are almost the only occasions, other than the Coronation, on which the people can see their monarch pass by in the pomp and circumstance of Old Siam. While the State Processions on these occasions are not so magnificent as those which take place at the Coronation, yet I think they are of greater sociological value, for they take place, not once in a life-time, but every year, and the volume of the crowds that line the route can leave no doubt as to the great hold which royal pageantry still exercises over the minds of the people. Indeed, it is above all the frequency and regularity of these occasions which give them such great value.[17]

In effect, then, the reforms of Mongkut, from the perspective of the people rather than of the European observer, may have had their greatest significance in gradually changing the public image of the monarch from that of a divine king, apotheosized by the magical and supernatural rites of the Brahman priests, to that of the leading human defender and patron of the Buddhist Church. This is an image that persists strongly until the present day, and contemporary Thai kings allow no opportunity to pass to present themselves to the public as exemplary Buddhists, even to the point of taking the vows and becoming, for a while, Buddhist monks, amid great public interest and acclamation.

By leading the way in the *kathin,* the king does not separate himself from the people, but projects his role into the midst of those activities which are most sacred to them, for the *kathin* is truly a national festival of exalted significance. The greatest means of "making merit" for a devout Buddhist is to take the vows of the Order and enter a monastery for a longer or shorter time. Those who remain outside, for their part, make merit by serving those within, and the daily perambulation of the monks to receive alms from the people is one of the most striking sights witnessed by the foreign visitor to Thailand. The genius of this rite is that the act of presenting alms is not regarded as "charity," as something for which the recipient need feel gratitude. Rather, the monk performs a favor for the donor by permitting him or her to "make merit," and thereby to assure a more favorable future in the continuing cycle of rebirths.

But the rhythm of almsgiving reaches its natural climax in the annual *kathin* ceremony at which the whole community goes to the monastery to present to the monks there assembled a supply of robes, alms bowls, soap, and towels, and other simple but necessary items for the monastic life. I once participated in one of these observances, which may be worth reporting because it demonstrated in a striking way some of the important functions served by the ceremony.

The climax of the event was reached in the central shrine of the monastery where some thirty monks were sitting cross-legged in the posture of meditation, lined up, immobile, on a platform along the side of the chamber, with the Buddha figure and altar in front. Here the assembled population seated themselves modestly on the floor, after having with great fanfare conducted the ritual circumambulation of the temple, going three times around, sunwise (clockwise), beginning at the entrance. The leader of the lay community then spoke, giving a public accounting of the source of the contributions, after which, in succession, following status order, members of the congregation each took a gift, decently laid upon a round tray, and kneeling low before one of the monks, beginning with the abbot, presented it.

In this manner did each member of the community add to his personal store of merit. But the presentation ceremony was only the climax of a major community festival. Preceding the ceremony itself there had been a long meeting, with reading from the scriptures and accompanying rituals in the open *sala* or pavilion outside the temple. And this day's events brought to a culmination a merry celebration which had gone on for some time, culminating in a gigantic carnival the evening before. Booths were set up in which plays (the *like*), rhyming verse contests, dancing, minstrel shows, movies, and other entertainment were presented for a large crowd gathered on an open field. Refreshment stands did a thriving business, and in the place of honor was a pavilion where the gifts for the *kathin* were exhibited. The festival began as boats filled with gaily dressed participants and bands playing hilariously converged from all directions upon the scene.

One must visualize such festivities taking place throughout the country, during the October–November period, when the rains have stopped and the most pleasant weather of the year has begun. The Buddhist Retreat is at an end. Thus, the *kathin* is not only a time for making spiritual merit but also a joyous occasion for the whole community, functionally equivalent, perhaps, to Thanksgiving and Christmas in American life, but focused more on public activity and less on the home and the individual, with gift-giving serving a more social and less private function.

How, one might ask, does such an activity help to legitimize the monarchy and the political order? The answer may be suggested by an event in the *kathin* ceremony described above. It was announced, during the course of the observances, that the major contributor to the *kathin*, not only for the gifts to the monks but also for the cost of the entertainment the night before, was the manager of the new sugar factory. This factory, which had but recently been built at great expense, was an innovation of troublesome potentialities, since it involved the employment and housing of labor, imported to a considerable extent from outside the community, and a transformation of the working habits of many farmers who were being urged to grow sugar cane in place of— or in rotation with—their rice crops.

It happened that while I was there, a foreman responsible for the supervision of sugar planting in the fields acquired by the factory had been shot. It was thought that some laborers whom he had discharged may have been responsible. Since he had in his care at the time a large sum of payroll money, there was also speculation that robbery may have been the motive. As luck would have it, the assailant hit him only in the shoulder and was frightened away before further damage was done. But such events were disturbing to the local community. A rumor had been going around that the factory was the work of "Communists," and all kinds of ominous changes and conflicts were in the offing.

By sharing in the local observance of the *kathin* and by footing the bill for a celebration which may well have been more elaborate than usual, the manager of the sugar factory had not only "made merit" in a spiritual sense, but he also had won the gratitude and support of the local population, and especially its leaders. After all, anyone who would contribute so much to a *kathin* could scarcely be an "atheistic Communist!"

To complete our picture, we must appreciate the extent to which Buddhist monks, and especially the local abbot, are community leaders. Despite the formal governmental organization of village and communal headmen, and the district officers and other agents of the central government, the lodestar of community feeling and initiative in Thai villages is often located in the monastery and oriented to the abbot. This is emphasized in the studies of a village near Bangkok carried out by research workers from the Cornell University Southeast Asia program. For example, in their preliminary report we find the following statements:

> The center of most organized social activity in Bang Chan is the wat, built as the monastery and place for the religious exercises of the Buddhist community. The villager has a close identification with this focus of his religious, social and recreational energies. In effect, the wat might be regarded as the functional element which binds the scattered hamlets of Bang Chan into an interacting whole. The wat, therefore, is a symbol whose importance is difficult to overestimate in assessing the patterns of Bang Chan society. . . .
>
> In their functional participation in the community, the priests of Wat Bang Chan do not confine themselves exclusively to supernatural problems,

and they are far from being above the more mundane considerations of life. The great concern of the head-priest with all community affairs is recognized throughout the village. His leadership in the various wat committees for organizing fêtes and raising funds is invaluable, and he is, in fact, a mainspring of social activity. His advice is sought by the laity in both sacred and secular matters. . . .

From even this cursory glance, it will be seen that life in Bang Chan is rich in organized social activity and that the foci of religion, recreation and social cohesion are the wat and its revered occupants. Popular concepts of morality are frequently identified with priestly conduct, aspirations toward acquiring merit are inextricably associated with the wat, and real confidence in social control, unity and continuity is to a large extent dependent upon the wat, its personnel and their services. . . .[18]

A report on a village in northeast Thailand shows the monks in an even more active leadership role. We read, for example:

In various villages of the area, I have seen priests helping to build village wells, sawing wood to be used for the building of the new village school, working with rake and shovel in the building of a village road. In Nong Khon the priests have done work in making village paths more presentable and done a major portion of the direction and physical labor in having the village resthouse built. . . . On such communal tasks as those above, the priests are able to give time which often the villagers do not have, offer superior knowledge and, at the same time, by their presence and their acts encourage more extended efforts on the part of the villager. . . .

The above remarks should of course not lead one to forget the religious role that the priests play. In this sphere, as well, they are far from parasites. For whether it is a birth, marriage, death, housewarming, sickness, etc. the priests play an important role in the given ceremony and, in the minds of the villagers, assure a proper and successful result. They are a vital necessity to the villagers' well being.[19]

In view of the key role which the wat and the monks play in the life of the Thai community, then, it is apparent that the Thai kings, by becoming the chief patrons of the Buddhist Church—as symbolized, above all, by taking the lead in person in annual *kathin* ceremonies— identified themselves as patrons of the most sacred and popular of Siamese institutions. The result has been not only to assure popularity for the king, but also to provide a ready means by which state officials, from the highest to the lowest, can integrate themselves into the social structure. The significant role which King Mongkut personally played in projecting this revised image of the monarchy is suggested by Wales, who notes that, although the great Buddhist festivals, like the *kathin*, became established in Siam from the thirteenth century, the

. . . royal ceremonial remained predominantly Hindu, since the Thai rulers sought to imitate the splendour of their former Khmer suzerains. Even as late as the second half of the seventeenth century there was a Siamese King of Ayudhya (Narayana, 1656–84), who is known to have favoured Brahmanism. On the whole, however, the trend of development was in favour of Buddhism, which culminated in the reign of King Rama IV (1851–68), with the addition of Buddhist modifications to nearly every State Ceremony.[20]

WESTERN CEREMONIES WITH BUDDHIST COLORATION

Emulating Western models, Mongkut also started such secular ceremonies as the King's Birthday and the Coronation Anniversary celebrations. Just as in the coronation rites, Mongkut had strengthened the Buddhist elements in ceremonies which were primarily Brahmanic, so in the new royal anniversaries he adapted Western ceremonial ideas to Buddhist sentiments. Wales tells us that "the King was wise enough to found nearly all the component parts of the new ceremony on rites drawn from the stock of Siamese religion and culture—the material that lay ready to hand and was most easily understood by the people."[21] Mongkut chose these occasions, for example, to confer public degrees of learning on distinguished monks and to present food to priests participating in the ceremony, which was made a gala four-day celebration. The Brahman pundits, however, were not neglected, and secular officials were granted promotions. New orders of merit or honors were presented at these events.

In borrowing the notion of birthday celebrations from the West, Mongkut also instituted a festival to commemorate the Birth, Enlightenment, and Death of the Buddha. It was reported that in ancient India there had been such celebrations, so that the idea could be presented as a traditional revival rather than as an innovation. The king, following his birthday celebrations—in which again promotions were made and the priests accorded a large role—took a ceremonial bath of purification, in which the Brahmans took part, providing the music accompanied by a twenty-one-gun salute furnished by the Army and Navy. In Bangkok, the city was brightly lit, and government offices, private homes, and commercial firms competed to provide brilliant displays.

Building on these foundations, the Thai kings have, in recent years, taken advantage of more Western techniques to project their image. The picture of the king and queen is displayed everywhere, from the greatest public buildings to the humblest home. Every performance in a moving picture theater ends with a picture of the king, while the

audience rises to listen to the national anthem. The tours of the king
and queen are widely heralded and photographed in every press me-
dium, and the occasion of a royal visit is made the excuse for a vast
expenditure of energy to decorate, renovate, and bring every item of
furniture, machinery, and landscaping to an unprecedented degree of
good order. Commemorative programs and brochures with many photo-
graphs are issued and given wide distribution.

The monarchy has now become, in a real sense, the focal point of
loyalty and solidarity for the Thai people, helping the Siamese to become a nation in the modern sense, linking their religious and social
with their political values. For the perpetuation of this sense of nation-
hood the survival of the monarchy would appear to be necessary. We
may conclude that, although the Siamese kings have lost the power to
control decision-making in Thai politics, they have retained the capacity
to legitimize the socio-political order.

Decision-making, however, must be organically related to the legitimizing functions. A society does not accept as binding decisions made
by someone who lacks authority. Hence, one of the important continuing roles of the Thai limited monarchy is to grant the accolade of legitimacy to each succeeding cabinet and each successive constitution. Yet
we cannot assume that the Siamese throne would automatically have
survived the transition from a traditional, sacred regime to a modern,
secular one. We know too many examples—China, Egypt, Iraq, Vietnam, France, Austria, Turkey—where republicanism replaced monarchy.

THE LEGITIMIZING THRONE

Even in Siam, the throne tottered and almost fell during the course
of the 1932 coup d'état. On June 24, the promoters of the revolution
issued a manifesto violently denouncing the monarchy:

The King was above the law as before. He appointed his relatives and
incompetent favorites to important positions without listening to the voice
of the people. He allowed dishonest government officials to abuse their power,
such as by receiving bribes in government building projects and buying supplies, seeking profits in the exchange of government money, and spending
public money extravagantly. He elevated the royal class and gave them many
privileges so as to allow them to oppress the common people. . . .

That the government of the present King could not correct the above
wrongs is due to the fact that it does not rule for the interest of the people
as do the governments of other countries. It regards the people as slaves,
even as animals, not as human beings—the people are called "servants" or

"slaves." Consequently, instead of ruling for the public interest, the government is farming on the backs of the people. . . .

Let us understand that this country belongs to the people, not to the King as we have been deceived into believing. Whereas the ancestors of the common people fought the enemy to maintain national independence, the royalty just reaps the fruits which it does not deserve to have.[22]

Yet, two days later, King Prachatipok returned from his vacation resort at Hua Hin to hold an audience with leaders of the People's Party, who apologized for their actions and especially for the denunciation of the king in the manifesto. The king, in turn, "forgave them and affixed his signature in the law, prepared by Pridi, to pardon all illegal actions made by the People's Party in seizing power." He then signed and promulgated a temporary constitution which brought into existence the system of limited monarchy.[23]

Just as, in the past, Siamese kings had preserved their realms by bowing graciously to the superior military might of British and French imperialism, so on this occasion the king saved his throne by accepting with good grace the *fait accompli* of the revolutionists.

From this nadir, which might well have closed the book on the monarchy, the Siamese kings have gradually risen to a position of unchallenged popularity. The first important step in this revival was taken before the crucial year 1932 had drawn to an end, for, on December 7, the new rulers presented a permanent constitution to the king for his signature. They praised him for helping to carry out a peaceful transformation of the political system, and they admitted that the Chakri dynasty's absolute rule had, "in fact, contributed much progress and modernization to the country." The king replied:

What really gave me great pleasure is the recognition, in your speech of apology, that the Chakri kings and the members of the royal family have made a great contribution to present-day progress in Siam, and this is quite true . . . this should erase all feelings of sorrow and bitterness that other members of the royal family, as well as I myself, have felt before. . . . The confession of your error, I believe, will help you to gain much public confidence. . . .[24]

In all the subsequent crises, coups, and power shifts among the Thai elite, no matter by what means power has been seized, the new rulers have never failed to seek and obtain the king's sanction, and hence to legitimize their rule in the eyes of the masses, for whom the only true order is that which stems from the royal house.

To summarize, we have seen how the Chakri rulers, by transforming the popular image of the monarchy from that of a divine king ruling by supernatural right over a subject population according to Brahmanic rites and doctrines into the image of a great man, serving his people by promoting true religion and morality, were able to create a viable basis for legitimizing the Siamese polity in a time of secularism, populism, and imperialism.

This transformation accompanied and made more palatable the other fundamental change which has received more general recognition, namely, the shift from a traditional, largely ceremonial regime to one in which decision-making and the effective exercise of governmental powers dramatically grew in importance. This change has been well described by Vella:

> Chulalongkon set up a precedent for the monarchy to exercise a legislative power it had never before wielded. The king's traditional duty of adhering to the *Thammasat*, or basic law, was subverted by Chulalongkon in his reformation of the structure and functions of the Thai government. The Thai king was no longer just an executor of traditional law; he became a legislator with unlimited powers to change Thai government and Thai life.[25]

The difference between the two transformations has not been sufficiently recognized. The first, from Brahmanic god-king to Buddhistic human king, gave the Siamese a viable basis for legitimizing the polity and stabilizing the nation—in short, for the maintenance of an integrated social order. The second, from a ritual to a decision-making ruler, was ephemeral for the monarchy but permanent for the polity. Mongkut and Chulalongkorn, in other words, did not reform the government primarily as absolute monarchs. Rather, they transformed, and thereby subverted, the traditional role of the monarchy itself. In so doing, by creating, in effect, the new role of a head of government (as contrasted with head of state), they brought into being a new political function for the polity. But this was a function which could not, over the long run, be monopolized by a hereditary ruling family. Thus, unwittingly, they also undermined the power of the monarchy even as they were creating it. It was their good fortune that, at the same time, they had also built a scaffolding for themselves in another role as legitimizing ceremonial heads of state upon which they could rest after they had moved too far out on the limb of power and modernizing rulership.

To emphasize the difference between the interpretation offered here and those which have been more widely accepted, let me state the following. It was not possible for the Siamese kings, as "absolute monarchs," to act directly upon the polity so as to bring about its transformation. Absolutism traditionally rested on sacred, ritually defined premises, and a modernizing role contradicted these premises. Thus, the kings had to transform the monarchy at the same time that they were trying to modernize the country, a process which necessarily sapped the roots of the traditional conception of the kingship. That the institution survived was due to the fact that, drawing on Buddhistic rather than Brahmanic sources, a new image of the throne was also created, capable of withstanding the erosive forces of modernism and secularism. Therefore, the ability of the Siamese kings to launch modernization was not, in essence, a function of their divinity or absolutism.

The contrasting view, that little if anything has "really" changed in Siam, rests on the fact that, in many respects, social changes in the life of the common people have been minimal. Perhaps more important, the Siamese elite were able to set a pace and a style of modernization that reduced the sense of traumatic discontinuities over time. Thus, to many Siamese the consciousness of sharp breaks with the past has been blurred. Yet if one takes a historical view, contrasting the contemporary Thai government with the traditional regime of a century ago, the contrasts become more evident when one looks at the bureaucracy than if he restricts his view to the rural society.

The primary fruit of the secularizing transformation of the monarchic role was the creation of a new or restructured bureaucracy. Yet this same bureaucracy was to sow the dragon's teeth that would, eventually, topple the monarchy in its new-found decision-making role and substitute commoners, drawn for the most part from the bureaucracy itself. Let us now, therefore, examine in more detail the changes which have taken place within the structure of the bureaucracy.

CHAPTER IV

The Functionalization
of the Bureaucracy

Step-by-step accounts of the events marking the transformation of the Thai bureaucracy have already been provided by Vella and Siffin.[1] We have only to summarize these events briefly in order to present them in perspective, to illumine the basic character of the changes which took place.

Siffin speaks of the old administrative system as an "archaic and untouched pattern of traditional bureaucracy," and notes that the reforms made, especially during the time of King Chulalongkorn, involved a "radical reformation," "a basic reconstruction."[2]

Siffin's views also add support to the idea that the Siamese bureaucracy played a fundamental role both in Thai society and in the processes of modernization. He writes:

> With the possible exceptions of Buddhism and the kingship, no Thai institutions outrank the bureaucracy as a force which has sustained the culture and maintained the vitality of the nation during most of the past century. . . .
>
> The modern bureaucracy helped project ancient Siam into modern statehood. It produced solvency, order, stability, and diplomacy sufficient to avoid excuses for Western seizure. Its needs gave rise to a system of secular education; and bureaucratic careers have fulfilled the expectations of graduates of that system. The stable, neutral bureaucracy has carried on the work of government without breakdown in the face of depression, war, inflation, and a dizzying succession of political changes.[3]

FIVE PERIODS OF TRANSFORMATION

In analyzing the process of modernization in the Thai bureaucracy it is convenient to use a scheme of historical periodization to show the stages by which the transformation was accomplished.

The *first period,* from 1851 to 1873, was a time during which the groundwork was laid, creating a favorable environment for basic structural change. This was the period of Mongkut's reign, during which doors were opened for the intrusion of Western influences, but the basic organization of government remained intact. The period continued through the first years of Chulalongkorn's reign, when he was under the control of a regency which, in effect, perpetuated Mongkut's policies.

The *second period* began in 1873, when Chulalongkorn took over effective control of government, and continued through 1891. In this period several new, functionally specialized "departments" were created, with the help of Western advisers, to carry out essential new activities of limited scope. Basically, they remained outside the established framework of government, which continued without fundamental change.

The *third period* began in 1892 with a sweeping reorganization of core governmental structures, in which many of the old courts and chambers were eliminated, their duties and some of their personnel being absorbed into new "ministries." New departments were also consolidated under ministerial control, although a few of the courts were reoriented as ministries, and some palaces were permitted to continue to exist without substantial modification. In a sense, 1892 was a year of "silent revolution." In more contemporary jargon, it was a time of "take-off." The changes were made possible by the fact that some of the new ministries were established on foundations that had already been laid, and that the more sacred structures of the old regime were permitted to continue without substantial modification, under the guidance of a brilliant leader who had greatly enhanced the effective powers of the monarchy. Moreover, Chulalongkorn was able to wait for the strategic moment to carry out his reforms, thereby permitting the transformation to occur without violence or much apparent break in political continuity. This stage has no clear-cut terminal point, but it may be convenient to think of it as continuing through the eighteen-nineties, by which time the basic pattern of the new regime had been established.

The *fourth period*, which ran from approximately 1900 to 1932, was a stage of consolidation, readjustment, and expansion.

The *fifth stage* began in 1932 with the "revolution." As far as the structure of bureaucracy is concerned, this was a period of the acceleration and consolidation of changes which had already been launched, the deepening of the pattern of functional specialization. But the most important change of 1932 was a basic recasting of the political control structure. Attention has, quite naturally, been focused on the formal changes, the creation of parliamentary and electoral machinery, the abolition of the absolute monarchy, and the launching of a series of written constitutions.

However, the revolution of 1932 was paradoxical in that these new political institutions largely failed to become effective. The developments of that period were dramatic and conspicuous, but they concealed a change of greater real significance. There are several ways to interpret this pattern. The most obvious one is to consider that 1932 marks the dividing line between the old regime and the new, between the absolute monarchy of traditional society and the limited monarchy of a modern polity, between a system of autocratic and arbitrary rule and the dawn of constitutionalism and democracy. But there are other possible interpretations.

If, as has been suggested above, the basic change in the process of Siamese modernization was the transformation of the ceremonial head of state into an effective, decision-making head of government, then the replacement of the "absolute monarchy" by a civilian cabinet in 1932 was a change of personnel more than a basic institutional revolution. By that time, the more fundamental transformation had already taken place.

That this seems to flout common sense and accepted doctrine is owing, no doubt, to our rather ethnocentric view that modernization means progress toward democracy. Such a view requires that we consider a communist, single-party regime, such as that of the Soviet Union, not modern. If, on the contrary, we say that modernization involves a structural transformation of government and society in the direction of more differentiated roles, including subjection of the state bureaucracy by primarily political institutions, then the changes of 1892 constitute a more significant dividing line between traditional and modern governmental institutions in Siam than the events of 1932.

From this point of view, we can argue that the revolution of 1932 involved merely the substitution of one oligarchic elite for another. The transformations of that period may be viewed as more factitious than real. Certainly, in terms of legitimation, the establishment of a largely ineffectual national assembly and the humbling of the king did mark a recognition that the basis of legitimacy had been changed. But this can be interpreted as nothing more than the consolidation and manifestation of a revolution which had already, with all deliberateness, been brought about by Chulalongkorn.

It is possible to adopt an even more radically different point of view. We can argue that, by setting up a functionally specific pattern of ministerial and departmental organization, and imposing a firm though absolutist system of control over the restructured bureaucracy, the king not only had abdicated his ancient role of ceremonial and cosmological ruler, but also had brought into being a new kind of secularized polity. The new system was one in which the state officials had been remade into an instrument of public administration and the monarchy into a central organ of political domination.

Indeed, by establishing the control of the monarchy over the bureaucracy, the Siamese kingdom had made a fundamental break-through in the direction of a more differentiated and modern type of political system. The destruction of monarchic control did not automatically entail the creation of popular controls over the bureaucracy. We can, instead, interpret the events of 1932 as a victory for the bureaucrats in their continuous struggle to escape political domination. From this point of view, the coup d'état was a kind of counter-revolution—while creating a façade of modern parliamentary government, it re-established high officials, notably military officers, as a ruling elite.

THE FIRST TWO STAGES: PREPARATIONS

In order to lay a basis for better understanding of these complex and problematical transformations, let us now explore somewhat more deeply the character of the changes which took place at each stage.

We need scarcely linger over the first stage in which the policies of Mongkut paved the way for "modernization." These involved policies which began to mobilize pressures for change, without themselves achieving any fundamental transformations. Thus, the treaty of 1855 with Great Britain, negotiated by Sir John Bowring, in opening the door for expanded trade, introducing extraterritoriality, and abolishing Siamese control over customs duties, undermined the traditional financial base of the royal government. By 1868, Mongkut had signed eight such treaties with other European powers, extending similar privileges to all of them.

Sir John himself remarked the far-reaching impact of these developments upon the Siamese polity, as noted above, when he wrote that his "success involved a total revolution in all the financial machinery of the Government."[4]

In domestic policy, however, Mongkut contented himself for the most part with issuing experimental policy decisions that served to loosen up traditional norms. As has been pointed out already, he was a thoroughgoing innovator in Buddhist practices, and he did introduce Western knowledge by setting up a printing press and importing European teachers and specialists. According to Vella, "Some eighty-four Europeans entered government service in Thailand during Mongkut's reign; among these were military officers, a tutor in the palace, a harbormaster, a customhouse director, and a head of the police force."[5] Unlike the advisers who served Chulalongkorn in the next period, these men were not used to help reshape the structure of government; their role, more modestly, was to introduce in particular nooks and crannies some of the more specialized and curious techniques of the Westerners.

The second period, beginning with Chulalongkorn's assumption of real power in 1873, was to witness more dramatic innovations (see Fig. 4). Shortly after taking power, in 1874, the king named a royal commissioner to reside in Chiengmai. Thus began a process of the extension of royal control over distant provinces which led, eventually, to the creation of the Ministry of Interior and the imposition of an effective system of local territorial administration. But, at first, this step involved little departure from tradition. Earlier monarchs had frequently extended the area of the royal domain under direct administration, at the expense of feudal rulers in the surrounding border zone.

The Lord of Chiengmai had long been the ruler of one of the richest and most important of these feudal states. It could scarcely be said that he was truly "subject" to the rule of Bangkok. Rather, he may have accepted the nominal suzerainty of the Chakri dynasty in order to gain an ally in his continuing struggles against the expansive Burmese. It should not be forgotten that, in those days, the distance to places like Chiengmai—in terms of travel time—was much greater than it now is from, let us say, New York to any part of the world. When McGilvary, the pioneer missionary, went to Chiengmai in 1867 it took him three months to make the trip. As late as 1905, it took from three to six weeks for the trip by boat, depending on river conditions. When Reginald Le May went there in 1913, he made the journey in eleven days, but he was able to go as far as Den Chai by rail, walking the remaining one hundred and twenty miles.[6]

It was, indeed, in good part a consequence of McGilvary's work that the royal commissioner was sent. When the missionaries first set up their work in the north, they were protected by the local lord, but before long, difficulties arose. In 1869, the rains failed, and antimissionary elements spread the rumor that spirits, angered by the work of the

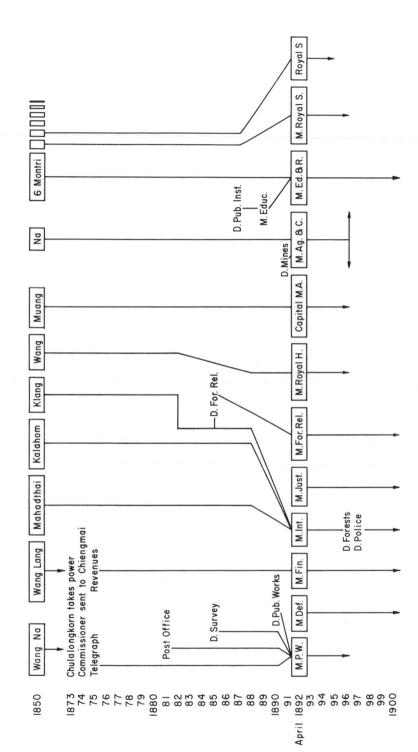

FIGURE 4. Over-all Scheme of Functionalization

Christians, had caused the disaster. The prince then turned against the missionaries, who appealed to Bangkok and to the United States consul for protection. When, shortly thereafter, the prince died, Rama V took advantage of the opportunity to send a high commissioner.

There were also disputes between the Lord of Chiengmai and European lumbermen intent on developing the teak business. Thus, the possible danger of European intervention—whether on behalf of missionary or lumber interests—provided the motive for an extension of royal control which was to help pave the way for a modern system of territorial administration.

Equally, if not more, important were Chulalongkorn's innovations in the field of public finance. In 1875, he established a Revenues Development Office. This was not, of course, a thoroughgoing reform. The existing chambers and courts retained, for the most part, their traditional revenue sources. But the new office was able to consolidate some taxes and carried out an analysis of potential revenue sources, studying the current distribution of taxes and modes of collection. According to a report that had been compiled in 1872, some ten different *krom* shared in the collection of the main taxes, most of which were farmed out to Chinese agents.[7] Inadequate as the new office must have been, it helped pave the way for the establishment of the Ministry of Finance in 1892.

The difficulties of communication with remote provinces have already been mentioned. The new technology available in the West made it possible to start construction of telegraph and telephone services, following the creation of a Royal Telegraph Department in 1875. The creation of a post office in 1881 extended to Siam another new form of service that was also not competitive with the existing chambers. In 1885, a Department of Survey was set up, utilizing the services of James McCarthy who had earlier (1881) helped survey a line between Bangkok and Moulmein for the telegraph service. Siamese surveyors were trained, and this department laid the basis not only for telegraph lines but also for railways, the demarcation of national and provincial boundaries, and the creation of a basis for land registration.[8]

Also in 1885, a Department of Foreign Relations was set up, taking over, perhaps for the first time, an important function which had been performed earlier by one of the chambers, the *Krom Klang*. But this was a matter of intense personal concern to the king, and perhaps the range of Siamese vested interests affected was relatively narrow.

Another agency established during this preparatory period was a new Department of Public Instruction, set up in 1887 under the direction of Prince Damrong, who was later to play a crucial role in the formation of the Ministry of the Interior. Perhaps the experience this gave Damrong was as important, in the long view, as the launching of public education, which scarcely began in earnest until some years later.

THE THIRD STAGE: BREAK-THROUGH

The stage was now set for the great transformation of 1892, to which we can turn next (see Fig. 4). In that year, on April 1, Chulalongkorn promulgated an edict which effectively restructured the entire bureaucracy and laid the foundation upon which the present system of government continues to rest. Core of the reorganization was the new Ministry of the Interior, under the direction of Prince Damrong, who continued to provide effective guidance and control in this major agency until 1915. In it were combined the territorial administrative functions hitherto performed—although quite ineffectively—by the two great chambers of the left and right, the *Mahadthai* and *Kalahom,* and one of the "four chambers," the *Krom Klang.* They had, formally speaking, responsibilities for the provinces of the north, the south, and the gulf areas of the east.

A Ministry of Finance, building on the earlier work of the Revenues Development Office, was given authority to consolidate all the revenue functions hitherto distributed among every chamber. The military functions which had also been widely distributed in several chambers were similarly consolidated in a new Ministry of Defense. In the same way, the scattered judicial functions were to be combined in a new Ministry of Justice.

Other ministries were created by expanding departments of the new type which had already been created during the second period. A Ministry of Education had been established in 1889, organized around the Department of Public Instruction, which, as we have seen, was set up two years earlier. To it were added new hospital and museum departments and one of the older *kroms* belonging to the six *montri,* the *Dharmakara (Thammakan),* or chamber of ecclesiastical affairs. The Ministry of Public Works was formed around the Department of Post and Telegraph, based on foundations built in 1875 and 1881.

Three ministries, reshaped in form, were continuations of three of the old chambers: *Wang, Muang,* and *Na. Wang* continued as the Ministry of the Royal Household, minus its responsibility for the supervision of justice. *Muang* continued as the Ministry of the Capital, responsible for the administration of Bangkok. *Na* was more dramatically reorganized as a Ministry of Agriculture—a matter to which I shall return.

One of the six *montri*, the *Krom Alaksana* (royal scribes) appears to have formed the nucleus for the new Ministry of Royal Services.

It will be seen from this that the most crucial functions—territorial control, defense, foreign affairs, finance, communications, training (education), and justice—were consolidated in new ministries. Other functions, concerned particularly with the immediate affairs of the king's household and the capital, presumably including matters of interest to many members of the royal family and the nobility, continued to be handled by established courts, modified largely in matters of form.

The new Ministry of Agriculture belonged to an intermediate category. New specialized functions were built on older foundations. This foundation, however, later proved so weak that the various agricultural functions were transferred to other ministries, and in 1896 the whole Ministry was abolished, only to be reconstituted in 1899, but on a new basis. The history of this ministry illustrates some of the difficulties encountered in creating a new, functionally specialized structure of government, and I shall, therefore, subject it to closer examination below.

Meanwhile, little more need be said of the third period, which is described in some detail in Siffin's work. A Forest Department was created in 1896 and played an important part in strengthening the territorial control of the central government, as did the Mines Department, both of which were brought within the Ministry of Interior. The Irrigation Department was set up in 1899. A national police service was created in 1897 and also placed in the Ministry of Interior. Schools for the training of technically qualified personnel to staff these new agencies were established. Their graduates supplemented the supply of men who were beginning to return in growing number from their studies overseas. A cabinet or ministerial council was created and replaced the archaic *senabodi*, although the old term continued to be used until 1932. To describe in detail the many other changes which took place at this time would be unnecessary for present purposes.

It is enough to point out the crucial role which the Ministry of Interior played as the focal center and womb of the new governmental structure. In April, 1892, immediately after his return from a tour of Russia, India, and Egypt on behalf of his new Ministry of Education, Prince Damrong was suddenly named head of the new Ministry of Interior. In answer to his protests, Chulalongkorn told him that he would have to take on this assignment because of the danger from "foreign countries who were trying to invade Siam." "If we were not careful, and did not arrange the country's affairs very well," he continued,

it might be very harmful to the country. We might even lose our independence. If this happened how could the Ministry of Education go on working? The administration in the country was much more important at this time and the Ministry of Interior had to be responsible for this much more than any other ministries because all the provinces were in the control of the Ministry of Interior.[9]

As we have already suggested, the Ministry of Interior served as the incubator of a series of new departments, each of which, after having gained strength within Interior, was transferred to another ministry of more specialized function.

In addition to this role, the Ministry of Interior, through its control over territorial administration, provided the matrix within which virtually all the other services were embedded. Siffin writes that the Ministry "was the supporting trunk of domestic government." He points out that the regional, provincial, and district officers were responsible for "*everything*" within their area of jurisdictions. "Functional specialists in agriculture, health, education, and other fields," he continues, "were attached to and administratively subordinate to these generalist officials." Although they were selected and paid by their ministries, these specialists had to go through the territorial administrators to communicate with their own headquarters. Thus, the new "territorial basis of organization, coupled with an impressive growth in the scope of specialized governmental functions, produced a complex pattern of domestic governmental organization" which had become fully formed by 1915, when Prince Damrong retired.[10] If Chulalongkorn had been the architect, it was Damrong who was the master builder. The structure which was built between 1892 and 1915 has been a lasting one, for the system of government which one finds in Thailand today is, in its basic features, the same.

THE MINISTRY OF AGRICULTURE: A CASE STUDY

Although the basic structure remains unchanged, there have been numerous changes in detail, involving the proliferation of specialized units held within the framework of the major ministries. It would certainly be a tiresome and unrewarding task to seek to trace all of these many changes, yet it may be helpful to analyze them in a selected ministry. Partly because of its checkered history, and partly too because of its developmental functions, I have chosen to concentrate on the Ministry of Agriculture.

Let us start again at the beginning and examine the scope of the work of the *Krom Na,* out of which the Ministry was initially formed.

The *History of the Ministry of Agriculture,* an official publication of the Ministry, presents a view of the past strangely colored by contemporary values. It starts out by describing the policies of the Sukhotai period, as revealed by the stone inscription of Ram-kam-hang (ca. 1275–1315). It appears that he encouraged his people to cultivate the land, granting them rights of possession and inheritance over farms which they cleared. There is evidence that he encouraged the construction of irrigation works, but beyond this the agricultural policy of the Sukhotai period remains obscure.

In the Ayuthian period, as we have already indicated, the four chambers were established, including the *Krom Na,* or Chamber of Lands. According to the *History,* the duty of the *Krom Na* during the time of Rama Thibodi I (1350–69), founder of the Ayuthian dynasty, was "to settle the disputes of the people concerning rice, agricultural products, farming and animal husbandry." Subsequently, its duties appear to have expanded to include the supervision of royal paddy lands and the collection of farm taxes paid in paddy.

By the time of King Prasad-Thong (1628–56), the duties of the *Krom Na* were listed as follows: land development, irrigation, promotion of animal husbandry, collection of farm taxes in paddy and their storage, administration of land grants to religious bodies and individuals, settling disputes over land, and the control over agents charged with these responsibilities.

However, the *History* goes on to discuss the activities of the *Krom Na* "in practice," as contrasted with the official prescription. It speaks of the continuous military activities of the Ayuthian dynasty, and states that "the main governmental policy regarding the *Krom Na,* therefore, was to expect it to furnish food, particularly rice, for the government services. Consequently, the actual operations of the *Krom Na* were primarily concerned with the collection of food for the army and other governmental services. In order to carry out this work, the *Krom Na* was authorized to provide land to the people for cultivation and rice production, to issue certificates of land possession, to settle farmers and prevent their disputes, and to collect the farm tax."[11]

From the point of view of a Western scholar, the activities of the *Krom Na* appear somewhat different, but they were still oriented primarily toward land, rice, and taxes. Wales writes:

It was the first duty of this minister to urge a somewhat indolent people to begin the cultivation of the fields at the proper season, himself setting the example at the ceremonial First Ploughing. He also saw that the people did not waste their time when they should be attending to their crops; and he had a court in which he was empowered to try cases connected with lands and cattle, and to settle boundary disputes. The work of draining fields and cutting irrigation canals was under his jurisdiction, and his officers supervised the clearing of jungle. It was through his department that the king allotted lands to distinguished officials in recognition of their services, as royal gifts at cremations and so on. He appointed officers to collect the revenue due from the people on their rice crops and to assemble cattle or buffaloes if they were required by the government.

The important *Kram Chan* was also under the control of this department. Its special duty was the buying of rice and cattle fodder (also, apparently, ivory and leather) for the royal storehouses, and distributing them in accordance with the requirements of the various departments of the central administration, especially in connection with military expeditions.

But the *Senapati Kram Na* only liked the work of buying the royal rice because this was the only work that was profitable to himself; consequently he neglected his other duties. The work of the subordinate officers of this department was particularly fruitful in opportunities for extortion and corruption; and these evils had, by the middle of the Bangkok period, completely undermined the efficiency of the department.[12]

Before the basic structure of the *Krom Na* was modified, a new department of Mines and Geology had been created, by royal proclamation, on January 1, 1891.[13]

CREATION OF THE MINISTRY

As we have seen, the new Ministry of Agriculture and Commerce was created by the royal proclamation of April 1, 1892 (which also established twelve functionally oriented ministries to rationalize and displace the earlier structures of government). This ministry took over the earlier activities of the *Krom Na,* plus the newly created Department of Mines.

But in 1896 the Minister, Chao Phya Surasakdimonti, resigned and recommended the abolition of the Ministry. Accordingly, the Department of Mines was transferred to the Ministry of Interior, where it proved useful in helping to extend the centralized control of the government to remote provinces of the south where European mining

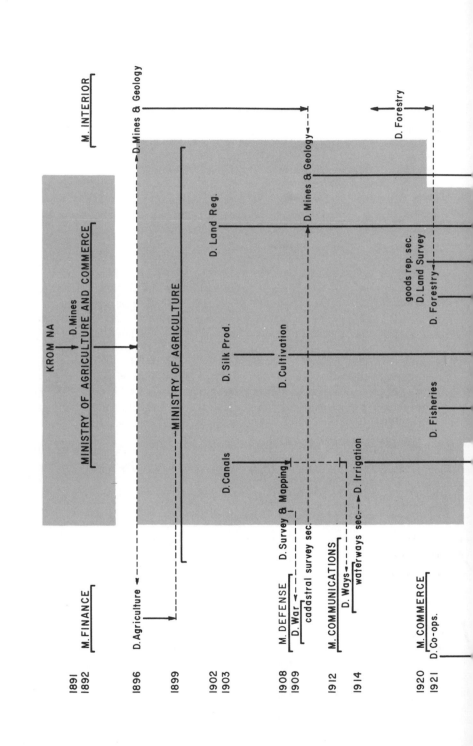

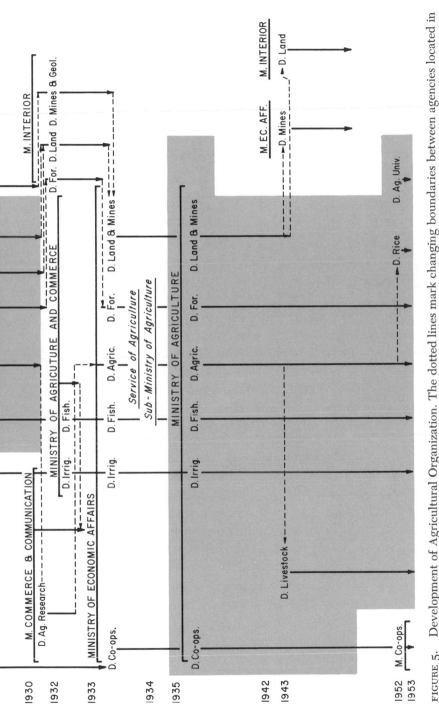

FIGURE 5. Development of Agricultural Organization. The dotted lines mark changing boundaries between agencies located in the Ministry of Agriculture and those transferred to or from other ministries. The tinted areas indicate when the Ministry of Agriculture was first established and twice restored

operations threatened to create difficulties for the embattled kingdom. The old *Krom Na* activities—primarily fiscal in character, as we have seen—were transferred to the Ministry of Finance, where they were reorganized as a Department of Agriculture.[14]

Within three years, however, the new Department of Agriculture had shown sufficient expansive energy to make it no longer convenient to keep it within the Ministry of Finance, and it was accordingly reestablished as a Ministry of Agriculture (see Fig. 5).[15]

It was not long after this that several new departments were created for the revived Ministry of Agriculture. First to come was a Department of Land Registry, created by ministerial notification on February 17, 1902. It was authorized to maintain land records and issue title deeds to owners of farm lands.

Shortly thereafter, in 1903, J. H. van der Heide, a Dutch specialist who had been working in Java, was invited to Siam, in agreement with the Dutch government, to help develop an irrigation program. He was named director-general of a new Canal Department, which was placed in the Ministry of Agriculture. Van der Heide's subsequent studies led to the formation of an elaborate plan for the irrigation of the Chao Phya valley, but lack of funds—or the conservatism of the British financial adviser—made it impossible to implement the plans. (Substantially the same scheme was put into effect after World War II.) Van der Heide resigned in disgust in 1909, and his department was abolished. It was later revived, however, to become one of the most effective departments in the Ministry.[16]

In the same year, 1903, a Japanese silk production expert was brought to the country and made an adviser for the development of the Siamese silk industry. An organizational base was provided for his activities by setting up a Silk Production Department in the Ministry of Agriculture, under the direction of a prince who had recently returned from foreign study of agriculture. The new department gradually expanded the scope of its work to other crops, however, so that in 1908 it was renamed the Department of Cultivation.[17]

One of the interesting features in Siamese legislative history has been the promulgation, from time to time, of general laws organizing or reorganizing the structure of particular ministries and departments. We have already seen how such a proclamation in 1892 set forth a comprehensive framework for the twelve newly established ministries. In 1908, such a regulation was adopted for the Ministry of Agriculture. It provided for an organization containing four substantive departments, plus a headquarters structure containing departments for the director-general, correspondence, and accounts, and six offices for agricultural inspection located in various regions of the country. The four substantive departments included, besides Land Registry, Cultivation, and Canals, a Department of Survey and Mapping.[18] However, the following year this new department was transferred to the Department of War in the Ministry of Defense. But, as if in compensation, a Cadastral Survey Section in the War Department was shifted to the Ministry of Agriculture's Land Registry Department.

Meanwhile, in 1909, the Ministry of Agriculture grew again by the addition of the Department of Mines and Geology which, having now become a well-established agency, was transferred from the Ministry of Interior.[19]

As we have seen, the resignation of van der Heide had been followed by a collapse in the Department of Canals, which, in 1912, was incorporated in the Ministry of Communications (a revamped version of the Ministry of Public Works) as a Department of Ways. The stress was laid on transportation facilities, by land as well as by water. However, irrigation needs were also to be satisfied by the work of a section on waterways within this department. Another foreign influence again brought about reorganization, however, for a British irrigation adviser —perhaps with more influence than his Dutch predecessor—now recommended strengthening the program of water works for agriculture. Accordingly, the section on waterways was taken out of the Department of Ways in the Ministry of Communications and returned in 1914 to the Ministry of Agriculture as a new Department of Irrigation.[20]

In 1920, a proclamation on the service in the Ministry of Agriculture was issued, recognizing five substantive departments: Land Registry, Cultivation, Mines and Geology, Irrigation, and a newly formed Land Survey Department.

A process of continual readjustment and redistribution of functions went on during this period. Some minor changes at this time illustrate this process. In 1920, a new Ministry of Commerce was formed out of a pre-existing Department of Commerce and Statistics which had been in the Ministry of Finance.

It will be recalled that in its first phase the Ministry of Agriculture had been called a Ministry of Agriculture and Commerce, being charged with responsibility for assistance in marketing, as well as production.

Although the commercial aspects of its work were largely removed from the Ministry, some of them continued. Thus, the Land Registry Department contained a Goods Reporting Section, which collected statistics on prices, production of crops and animals, rainfall, water levels, and even foreign commodity prices affecting export markets. With the establishment of a Ministry of Commerce, this section was now transferred to the new ministry, as was a Division of Company Registration which had also been formed in the Ministry of Agriculture.[21]

We have already seen how the Department of Mines and Geology, after a period of gestation in the Department of Interior, was transferred to Agriculture in 1909. A similar change took place in 1921, when the Department of Forestry, which had matured under the control of Interior, was also transferred to Agriculture. As the *History* reports it, "After the service in the Ministry of Agriculture had been well arranged, it was deemed proper to transfer the Department of Forestry" to it. In the same year, a new Department of Fisheries was established and also made a part of the Ministry of Agriculture.[22]

In 1930, another proclamation on the service in the Ministry of Agriculture was issued, confirming the addition of Fisheries and Forestry to the five departments named earlier, which still continued in the Ministry. As of 1958, the basic structure of the Ministry remained substantially the same. It still had seven major departments, but it had lost three and gained three. The departments of Mines, Land Survey, and Land Registry had been transferred elsewhere. The Department of Cultivation had, after several changes, been split into two departments, Agriculture and Rice. A new Department of Animal Husbandry was added in 1943, and the Agricultural University was created in 1952. The twenty years of "revolutionary" change which followed had scarcely made as much difference to the Ministry as the twenty years preceding 1930.

PERIOD OF STRESS AND STRAIN

Yet the few years which were to follow 1930 threatened the very existence of the Ministry. This unsettling process, however, was not so much the consequence of the revolution of 1932 as one of its contributing causes. The world economic depression had brought a decline in foreign trade and retrenchment at home. Significant cuts were made in the number of officials—a decline of 17 per cent in the period between 1925 and 1932, or a loss of 3,000 jobs by the 45,000 men in the career service.[23]

The emergency brought reorganization, as well. The crisis was viewed as one chiefly concerning international markets, rather than agricultural production for domestic consumption. Hence, in 1931 the Department of Cultivation was moved from the Ministry of Agriculture to the Ministry of Commerce, which had meanwhile been combined with Communications into a single ministry. There the Department was renamed the Department of Agricultural Research and charged with responsibility to study foreign markets and find ways to produce more crops suitable for export.

On June 29, 1932, at the height of the coup itself, the movement toward consolidation reached a dramatic climax. The Ministry of Agriculture was united with the Ministry of Commerce and Communication to form a new Ministry of Agriculture and Commerce, which, the following year, was renamed the Ministry of Economic Affairs. Four of the departments previously in Agriculture—Mines and Geology, Forestry, Land Registry, and Land Survey—were handed back to the Ministry of Interior, only to be restored the following year to the new Ministry of Economic Affairs. However, in the process several departmental amalgamations took place. Land Survey and Land Registry had been united into a Department of Land on the first move to Interior. On the next move to Economic Affairs, Land itself was combined with Mines and Geology to become a Department of Land and Mines.[24]

After the dust had cleared, we find in Economic Affairs some ten departments, but five of them are attributable to the commerce and communications part of the merger. The five agricultural departments were Agriculture, Forestry, Irrigation, Fisheries, and Land and Mines. To formalize the distinction, a Service of Agriculture and a Service of Communication were set up in the Ministry of Economic Affairs having jurisdiction, respectively, over these two sets of departments. The next year, in 1934, the services were elevated to the status of "sub-ministries," and later that year the sub-ministry was raised to full status as a Ministry of Agriculture.[25]

All the revolutionary furor, in other words, had amounted to little more than a reshuffling of departments in which, with a few consolidations but without the addition of anything new, the same structure emerged at the end as had entered at the beginning.

One of the curious fruits of this shuffling process, however, was that the Ministry of Agriculture picked up a new department in the process: Co-operatives. This function had begun in a lowly way as a mere section in the Department of Commerce and Statistics of the Ministry of

Finance in 1915. In 1920, it became a department when its parent agency was promoted to become the Ministry of Commerce. In 1932, when the ministries of Commerce, Communications, and Agriculture were combined into a single ministry, Co-operatives was naturally included, and it remained in this setup when the Ministry of Economic Affairs was created. However, when the departments in this ministry were sorted into the two sub-ministries of Agriculture and Commerce and Communication, the Department of Co-operatives was shifted over to the agricultural side, rather than remaining in the commercial side, from which it had first come. When the Ministry of Agriculture was reconstituted in 1935, it found itself consequently with a new protégé, the Department of Co-operatives. However, it was not to be a permanent addition to the agricultural family, for in 1952 the Department was moved again, this time to become a ministry in its own right.

BIRTH OF SECTIONS AND DEPARTMENTS

The expansion of the Department of Co-operatives into a ministry illustrates a process which also took place at lower levels. Sections grew in size until they were reconstituted as divisions, and divisions expanded until they commanded enough support to become departments. This process took place several times in the Ministry of Agriculture during the years from 1934 to 1958. It should be noted, however, that such growth can no more be called a basic structural change than can the reshuffling of departments which took place between 1932 and 1934.

The process began with the launching of higher level training institutions to provide personnel qualified for the increasingly specialized work of the departments. At first, as we have seen, top-level specialists received their training abroad, but as the departments grew in size it seemed more economical to set up special training facilities in Thailand. In 1935, the Forestry Department established a school in the north, at Prae, to train future forestry officers. The Department of Irrigation followed this lead in 1938 by setting up its own school of irrigation. The same year, the Department of Agriculture took over several agricultural training schools from the Ministry of Education, reconstituting them into an agricultural college as a new division.

By 1943, it began to seem irrational to permit the further proliferation of highly specialized agricultural training schools, and so a consolidated University of Agriculture was established as a department in the Ministry of Agriculture. The University consisted of several faculties, each corresponding to a program department in the Ministry. Other faculties were later created to serve the needs of the departments of Fisheries, Animal Husbandry, and Rice. The result was a composite structure in which, although students and teaching facilities were all brought together on a single campus (Bang Kaen, just north of Bangkok), administratively each faculty behaved to a considerable degree as though it were an administrative division of one of the program departments.[26]

Another example of institutional growth from within was the formation of the Livestock Department in 1942. This function had been established in the Department of Agriculture as early as 1933—and probably earlier—as an Animal Promotion Division, having two sections. A year later, the division had expanded to include eight sections. In 1938, it became too large to remain a unit and was accordingly split into two divisions—Animal Husbandry and Animal Care. These two divisions, in 1942, were transferred out of the Department of Agriculture to form a new Department of Livestock and Beasts of Burden. Strangely enough, this was not the end of reshuffling for this department. In 1951, its Animal Husbandry Division was returned to the Department of Agriculture, only to be brought back to the Department of Livestock the next year.[27]

A similar growth, also within the Department of Agriculture, led to the formation of the Department of Rice in 1953. This department was conceived in 1934 as a small section in the Agriculture Development Division of the Agriculture Department. By 1938, it had expanded into a division, containing three sections; by 1942 it have five sections. The energetic division had grown to eight sections by 1951 and was clearly becoming too powerful to remain within the confines of the Department of Agriculture. It is not surprising, therefore, to find that in 1953 it had broken loose and become a new department, partly in response to the impact of an American technical assistance program in the field of rice-breeding.[28]

This brings us up to 1958 in the evolution of the Ministry of Agriculture, but certainly not to the end of the story, which is still in process of unfolding. In 1958, for example, there was a movement under way—with strong prodding from the American technical advisers—to create an instrumentality, whether or not in the form of a new department, which would carry out extension services. Virtually every one of the product-oriented departments had its own extension division dedicated to the dissemination of new techniques and methods. Would it not be more logical—more functional—to transfer all these divisions to a single new extension service which would offer a unified approach to the farmer, channeling to him all the diverse services and resources of the separate departments? But the answer which history will give to this question remains to be disclosed.

At the point where this historical sketch breaks off, the Ministry of Agriculture had settled down to a relatively stable pattern, unchanged since 1953. It included seven basic program departments—Irrigation, Fisheries, Livestock, Agriculture, Forestry, Rice, and the Agricultural University (which was transferred to the prime minister's office in 1959) —plus two overhead offices, one for the ministerial secretary, and the other for the undersecretary. One could scarcely ask for a neater package, better organized in terms of major functions. Certainly it was a far cry from the vague and heterogeneous structure of the *Krom Na,* from which it may trace some historic continuity but little or no basic similarity in structure and function. The modernizing reformers—whether absolute monarchs or constitutionalists—had truly worked a basic transformation. But the historian must note that the restructuring of the bureaucracy on functional lines was carried out before, not after, the revolution of 1932. Since that date, the proliferation and expansion of governmental programs had deepened but not fundamentally changed the course of development which preceded.

In closing this chapter, it may be worth summarizing the changes in the over-all structure of the bureaucracy which took place during this period. We noted earlier that the great transformation made its crucial break-through in 1892 with the establishment of twelve ministries. Significantly, only two ministries were added to the roster as set forth in the act of 1953, which laid down the pattern that still prevailed in 1959, although in 1933 the original twelve had been temporarily reduced to nine. The major functionally oriented departments created by Chulalongkorn—Interior, Defense, Finance, Foreign Affairs, Justice, Education—persisted, but the primarily economic departments of Agriculture, Commerce, and Communications (Public Works) were then consolidated into a Ministry of Economic Affairs. Of the ministries based primarily on the old chambers, only the Royal Household survived, and it was not to last into the 1953 period.

By 1953, the same basic structure of the chief functional ministries —continuous from 1892 to 1933—still remained. The consolidated Ministry of Economic Affairs was split apart again to form three ministries:

Agriculture, Communications, and Economic Affairs (Commerce). The Royal Household Ministry was demoted to an autonomous "bureau," but four new ministries were added: Public Health, Industry, Co-operatives, and Culture, bringing the total up to fourteen, by including the prime minister. Clearly the foundations laid by Chulalongkorn had been lasting. Not only had they created a basic governmental structure which could stand the strain of revolutionary pressures generated by the abolition of the absolute monarchy itself, but they provided, in addition, a floor on which further growth and development would be possible.

In creating a modern-style bureaucratic machine, the absolute monarchs had built more strongly than they could have imagined, for they built something too powerful for them to control, a system which would shoulder them out of the way and go on under its own impetus. Not anticipating their own fate, they had not created (nor could they, indeed, had they tried) an institutional base for controlling a bureaucracy which was destined to become stronger than the monarchy which created it. The great obstacle to further modernization of the Siamese polity lay not in the construction of its bureaucracy, which could surely, if adequately directed, give effective and efficient service. That flaw, rather, lay in the lack of a guiding force outside the bureaucracy capable of setting its goals and keeping its agents under effective control.

The consequences of this unbalanced pattern of development will become clearer in later chapters. Meanwhile, let us examine the way in which the new bureaucracy created by Chulalongkorn spread from Bangkok to bring the whole country under its tutelage.

CHAPTER V

The Consolidation
of Bureaucratic Rule

It has been shown, in Chapter II, how the traditional system of law rested on cosmological and religious foundations. To tamper with the sacred law or *dhammasattham* would have been considered as sacrilegious as for a Christian true believer to propose an amendment to one of the Ten Commandments. Manu was to the Siamese what Moses was to Jews and Christians. Against this standard, the truly innovating posture of King Mongkut may be understood. Lingat writes that he was the first of the Siamese kings to seek to put aside the old conception of the law.

King Mongkut was a progressive minded monarch. He ridiculed the Manu the rishi story [supernatural inspiration of Manu, the lawgiver], and did not feel bound at all by old provisions of law whenever they appeared to him no longer suitable for modern times. With him, and still more with his son and successor King Chulalongkorn, the Law of Manu was over. Many provisions of the old code were repealed and replaced by new enactments relying upon the royal will only.[1]

Mongkut himself was content to issue occasional proclamations beginning with a flourish: "By Royal Command, reverberating like the Roar of a Lion"; his son, on the contrary, launched a thoroughgoing revision of the whole legal system, based on European models. As we have seen, he instituted a Ministry of Justice in 1892, concurrently with his creation of a whole new system of functionally specialized ministries. Belgian, British, Japanese, and French lawyers were invited to advise the new law courts and to help frame new laws. Underlying this drastic scheme of reform was the desire to eliminate extraterritoriality, whereby, since the Bowring treaty of 1855, Europeans on Thai territory had been subject to their own, rather than Siamese, courts.

In 1897, a committee under the chairmanship of the Minister of Justice, the Prince of Rajburi, was named to prepare a penal code.

M. G. Padoux of France was named adviser, and the first Western-type law code, although carefully harmonized with Siamese traditions, was promulgated in 1908. Subsequently, civil and commercial codes were drafted by a predominantly French legal commission, preparing first drafts in English, for subsequent translation into Thai and submission to a Siamese Revising Committee. Later a single Siamese-French commission, under a Siamese chairman, completed the work, leading to promulgation of the codes and elimination of extraterritoriality in the nineteen-twenties and thirties.

René Guyon, who was chief of the drafting committee, has written of this process that, with the greatest care, they

> . . . avoided indulging in the too easy plan of copying any foreign Code, perfect as it might be, and of transferring their provisions with slight alterations, into the Siamese legislation. They have for each Draft, pursued the same methods: first, they have made a general study of the matter as it stands in the existing Siamese texts . . . and in the principal foreign Codes . . . important precisions have been made and a good knowledge of the local needs has in turn enabled the Commissioners to submit drafts which do not consist only in theoretical schemes but are framed according to the actual and real requirements of the country.[2]

Our primary concern here is not with the reform of the legal system but with the implication of these changes for our understanding of the governmental system. As long as the laws of the land were little more than the mores and folkways passed down by tradition, the challenge to government for positive action and enforcement was minimal. The society was virtually self-controlled and self-patrolled. The rulers could safely concentrate their attention on performing the sacred rituals, interfering with society only when the direct interests of the royal court were at stake.

If a traditional monarch were to launch substantive innovations—beyond the imposition of heavier tributes or the conduct of a military campaign—he would quickly discover that, despite his sacred omnipotence, his secular powers were limited. To transform a cosmological head of state into a commonplace head of government required a fundamental recasting of the administrative infrastructure. This was a "fact of life" which King Mongkut himself soon discovered. On one occasion, his scholarly proclivities got the better of his common sense, and he issued an edict ordering everyone to use more proper terms for the fish sauces *kapi* and *nampla,* which are as popular in the Thai cuisine as ketchup and mustard in America. Shortly thereafter he repealed the order, regretfully admitting that the majority of people in the capital still used the old words. "Worse still," he wrote, "advantage is being taken by some rogues who, by impersonating the Nai Amphur, have, on many and increasing occasions, extorted money from the people. Be it, therefore, declared that from now on the people may continue to use the words *kapi* and *nampla* as they have been used to do so from the time immemorial." However, he added, the correct words should be used in the court![3]

Two lessons were pointed up by this episode. First, it demonstrated that even an "absolute monarch" could not compel his subjects to obey all his commands. An effective apparatus for the enforcement of new policies would be necessary. The second lesson was that, in the absence of such an apparatus, new rules could be exploited by opportunists in such a manner as to prevent the accomplishment of the desired goal —or, even worse, to compound the old difficulties with new ones. By the time of Chulalongkorn, it had become abundantly clear that the efforts of a reforming monarch to modernize his country, to enact new laws, would be frustrated unless a new machinery to enforce the laws could be brought into existence.

As late as 1892, when Chulalongkorn launched his major administrative reorganization of government at the top, the machinery for implementing new programs and policies was still largely missing. It was one thing to create a governmental superstructure in Bangkok, but quite a different matter to extend its operations throughout the country, to translate the royal will into effective programs and projects.

Recognizing this fact, Chulalongkorn decided that a Ministry of Interior, with a kingdomwide apparatus of territorial officials, would be a necessary foundation for the creation of an administrative machine capable of enforcing the new laws of the land. Accordingly, he asked his most able and energetic brother, Prince Damrong, to take primary responsibility for creating and organizing this new and basic ministry.

DAMRONG AND THE MINISTRY OF INTERIOR

Damrong had just returned from a foreign tour on behalf of his Ministry of Education when Chulalongkorn gave him his new assignment and sent him out on a tour of the country. He soon discovered that the hinterland was almost as far from the capital, psychologically and politically, as the foreign countries he had visited. The officials whom he met on this trip asked him, with surprise and alarm, why he had come, since a great *senabodi* had never before, they said, come out to supervise their work. Indeed, if anyone ever came from Bangkok, it had always been in response to some crisis, such as a rebellion. During subsequent years he made many such trips in order to supervise personally the dramatic changes which he launched.

The traditional system of local government has been described in Chapter II, above. It should be clear from that account that the first preoccupation of the Siamese kings had been to maintain the loyalty of the local rulers, the *Chow-muang* (Lords of the Land), in the outlying territories. The maintenance of the royal domain required not only that goods and services for the court be supplied, but also that these Lands should be allies, not enemies, in times of war. What Chulalongkorn and Damrong now intended to do was to transform this archaic system by superimposing on it an apparatus of centrally appointed and rotated officials, responsive to the capital and capable of enforcing new rules in the territories to which they would be appointed.

Some measure of the magnitude of this task can be gained from Damrong's own report on his first trip. He discovered that, due to a rise in the cost of living, or an increase in the scale of the *Chow-muang's* establishments, these officials had resorted to increasingly oppressive and extortionate methods. He wrote:

> The money and the things that the governor and his assistants got were not enough for them to live on comfortably. They had to try to think of ways to increase their income such as by farming or doing some business. The governor and his people could control the people, and when they started business on their own, they could use their position for the benefit of their work. For example, if they did farming, they could ask the people to come and help them, or if they did business, they could help the persons who were their partners for the benefit of their own business. Even the tax collectors from Bangkok, if they let the governor and his people have some share of the tax, they could collect it more easily. This was the cause of influential people using their own rank for personal profit.[4]

Damrong goes on to explain that most of the provincial officials belonged to influential local families. "Very few officials who lived in Bangkok would dare to go out to work in the provinces," he said, "because they were afraid of the difficulty of trying to earn their own living. They had to have their own money before daring to venture out of Bangkok or they had to be the in-laws of the influential people in the provinces. Especially the council members had to be chosen from the persons living in those provinces."

In order to increase their effective power, the governors often appointed local persons with many followers, hoping that this would frighten away thieves. However, Damrong concluded that this practice often had perverse results. Indeed, he decided that the council members themselves were often bandits who, in exchange for a free hand, would protect those favored by the governor. Other council members, according to Damrong, were able to make a "profit by collecting rice money from the farmers or by asking the people to help them with the farming in return for their services." Still others, he found, had become corrupt and "sent their own people to steal cows or buffaloes or money from the people."[5]

Apart from the quality of persons holding these local appointments, Damrong discovered that the physical arrangements for housing the work of local administration were quite unsatisfactory. Each governor had to use his own home for official business. He would typically construct a pavilion or *sala,* but discovered that it did no good since they became the personal property of the official's family upon his death, and the next governor would not only live and work in a different house, but often in a different district.

Taking a long look at the purposes of local administration, Damrong reflected that, according to customary views, if there were no bandits in the countryside, it was considered to be well governed. In effect, the administration provided no services to the people. It had no policies to enforce. In case of bandits, rebellion, or invasion, *senabodi* from the capital would intervene. The collection of taxes was left largely in the hands of Chinese tax-farmers, operating on a concession basis. But since the time of Rama IV, and even more so since Rama V came to the throne, Damrong noted that the new idea of government was that it "should bring happiness to the country during peace time."[6]

The conditions which Damrong found in the provinces actually existed in the capital also. *Senabodi,* for example, still conducted most of their business from their own homes, and although they received a bonus from the royal treasury for their work, they had to rely primarily on income from clients for their support. As a result, royal control over high officials was weak, and it was difficult to assure continuity in the conduct of an office from one incumbent to another. In effect, the staff in each court or chamber consisted of the personal clients of the noble who held the high office. Recruitment was aristocratic in the sense that the nobles started out as pages in the royal court, later receiving royal appointments as high officials. The clerks under them would start to work at an early age, doing the substantive work of the courts, with which they became quite familiar. The system was not one designed to assure effective implementation of any complicated policies or to translate innovations into action. However, since the rule-making output of a traditional polity was minimal, little damage was done.

NEW ADMINISTRATIVE PRACTICES

But for a modernizing government, such a bureaucratic machine was clearly inadequate. Damrong notes that the financial office which, as we have seen, was created in 1875 was the first agency to be set up according to European ideas. Officials working there were paid salaries and had to report to duty in the office every day, according to a regular schedule, with the exception of the director-general, a prince, who still insisted on working in his own palace.

When the new Department of Foreign Affairs was created in 1885, the king persuaded Prince Thevavong Paropakarn, the new foreign-educated minister, to start working in the office. According to Damrong, "He was the first *Senabodi* who came to work in the office every day just like the other officials. He was also the first *Senabodi* to receive a salary like the others."

When the great reorganization of 1892 was carried out, the new ministries of Interior and Defense were patterned after the earlier experiments in Finance and Foreign Affairs.

Despite these formal—and highly significant—changes, Damrong moved deliberately to change the methods of work in his new ministry. For the most part, he retained the old staff, although he pensioned off a few. He states that he brought only two new men into his ministry right away. He did this, he writes, to "check the fear of having new and modern people replacing the old ones in the Ministry." Similarly, in reorganizing the work of the Ministry on a functional basis, he retained the old familiar organizational names.

After laying a basis for tighter control over his staff within the headquarters offices of the Ministry of Interior, Damrong turned to the task of creating an effective machine for governing the provinces. One of the first steps was, in a way, an indirect one. Foreign lumber merchants, as we have already seen, had been operating in the north by agreement

with the Lord of Chiengmai. However, they had run into various difficulties, with resulting disputes, causing them to appeal to the British
consul in Bangkok for aid.

Chulalongkorn at this point asked Damrong to organize a Forestry
Department within the Ministry of Interior. It was soon set up with
the assistance of H. Slade, a British forestry expert from India, who was
recruited in 1896. Slade brought other European officers from India and
Burma, who trained a Siamese staff. Thai trainees were sent to the
Indian Forest School at Dehra Dun. Royal decrees were then issued
protecting the forests and specifying conditions under which lumbering operations could be carried out, including the terms of leaseholds
to foreign firms.

It is significant that in this early venture the creation of an administrative apparatus preceded the issuance of a new set of rules. Had
regulations governing the use of forests and lumbering operations by
foreign concessionaires been issued prior to the creation of an organization capable of enforcing the rules, they might well have led to controversies similar to those which brought an end to the Burmese monarchy.

Enforcement, of course, involved not only policing the work of the
lumbering companies but, perhaps even more important, intervening
between foreign interests and the locally entrenched authorities. This
clash was described by Reginald Le May, who viewed them first hand
from Chiengmai.

> In his work in organising the Department Slade naturally met with a
> good deal of opposition from the local northern Chiefs, on whose preserves
> he had naturally to encroach to a large extent; but in the end, after a hard
> fight, he won his battle, and this victory weakened the position of the Chiefs,
> who never regained their former prestige. Slade may be said, therefore, to
> have played an important part in consolidating the Siamese Kingdom, and
> to have been of great assistance to the government in this regard.[7]

Thus Slade served as an effective instrument for Chulalongkorn and
his extraordinary Minister of Interior in extending the control of Bangkok to a northern area which only vaguely recognized the feudalistic
suzerainty of the Chakri dynasty. When Slade left Siam in 1901, he had
helped Damrong win an important battle in his struggle to create a
modern apparatus for policy execution. Damrong himself points out
that by handling complaints from foreign firms in an efficient manner,
his Forest Department was able to induce them to stop going through

the consulates, and thus also helped to reduce the occasions for tension between the Siamese government and foreign powers.[8]

A similar story could be told about the founding of the Department of Mines, which, it will be recalled, was created in 1891 and was subsequently incorporated in the new Ministry of Agriculture. Some European miners had obtained concessions in Siam, but, in the absence of official policies and effective administration, many disputes had arisen. Chulalongkorn again brought in some European advisers to help set up the new Department of Mines, but it was not able to work effectively in the Ministry of Agriculture. Quarrels with local governors and their councilmen led to dangerous tensions. Consequently, Chulalongkorn ordered this department transferred to Interior, where it came under Damrong's personal control, and he again used it as an effective instrument to extend central control over certain provincial governors. The Department of Mines was returned to the Ministry of Agriculture after this function had become less important.

TERRITORIAL ADMINISTRATION

Perhaps the most important reform of Damrong, however, was the creation of a network of officials charged with responsibility for territorial administration. This system, which was called *tesaphiban,* or local government administration, involved the creation of a regional organization in which half a dozen provinces were combined in a *monthon* under the control of a commissioner. Damrong wrote about this plan that, because of the distance and long time consumed in travel, a *senabodi* could not personally visit and supervise all the provinces. He could only send out orders and rules to the governors, but he had no way to make certain that these instructions would be carried out. "I saw that the system of sending out orders to each province was quite a handicap," he wrote, "and tried to solve this problem. The only way was to follow His Majesty's plan of combining the provinces in *Monthons.* . . . The size would not be too big for the high commissioner to supervise the work himself. An official with a rank between *Senabodi* and governor would be sent to supervise the work in every *Monthon.* That person would carry out the orders of the *Senabodi* and would also give advice. This meant that the *Senabodi* had only the duty of laying down the plan and the high commissioners would carry it out."[9]

Thus, without displacing the provincial governors, Damrong was able to bring them gradually under control by superimposing regional

commissioners. These were trusted and carefully chosen men, all salaried, and usually princes, who were sent out as control agents of the
Ministry of Interior, operating from official centers built by the government. This policy was adopted step by step, creating one *monthon*
at a time, and making sure that central control had been consolidated
in one region before moving on to the next. By the end of his administration in 1915, there were seventeen *monthons* covering the whole country.

At a later stage, the control of the governors was also undermined
from within by dividing each province into districts (*amphur*), each
under the control of a district officer who was sent out by the new Department of Interior. By this means, the old network of relatively
autonomous provincial governors was brought within a control system
superimposed from above at the *monthon* level and undermined from
below at the *amphur* level.

FIELD OFFICES OF SPECIALIZED SERVICES

It is against this background that the transformation effected by
King Chulalongkorn, Prince Damrong, and the other reformers, aided
by their Western advisers, should be evaluated. Fundamentally, this
transformation involved creating new, national, functionally specialized
networks of administration, each having its headquarters in Bangkok,
linked with corresponding field officials at the regional, provincial, and
district levels of government.

In time, the need for the regional (*monthon*) level of organization
declined as the provinces were brought under control by career administrators. The cost of maintaining the *monthons* began to seem too high,
and the system was, therefore, curtailed and finally abolished. By this
time the nationwide apparatus of salaried, functionally specialized officials, appointed by and financed from the central government departments, had made it impossible for a governor or district officer to act
as anything but a territorial administrator, rather than as a "Lord of
the Land."

In mentioning the departments of Forestry and Mines, above, I have
merely suggested, rather than fully described, the role which functionally specialized units played from the start in making this transformation possible. The rise of functionally specialized national agencies
took place simultaneously with the change in the character of the territorial administrators. Previously, as Lords of the Land, maintaining
themselves on a *kin-muang* (eat-the-city) basis, their control over all

the functions of government in their own domains meant that they were virtually petty "kings" who could have maintained themselves as independent rulers whenever the direct political, military, or sacred powers of the king in Bangkok declined. Under the new system, some of the former powers of these provincial lords were eroded away and transferred to the new specialized agencies.

In addition, novel functions of government not hitherto performed were established by the royal government, and field offices were set up in the provinces. They also undermined the comprehensive control of the territorial governors by creating needs which they could no longer meet. Perhaps the most fundamental of all these transfers of function was that by which the collection of local revenues was made a duty of new specialists by the creation of a Ministry of Finance, and salary payments were substituted for the archaic *kin-muang* system. All these changes paved the way for creation of a career service of territorial administrators, men who were transferred regularly from post to post, who worked in a public office rather than in the *sala* of their own homes, and who were paid on a regular salary basis.[10] The career pattern came to resemble prototypes in other bureaucratic polities, ranging across the spectrum from Imperial China to Republican France, and including the Indian Civil Service. Normally the new appointee began his career as an assistant district officer and worked his way up through district and provincial posts as prefect or governor, rotating between field and headquarters assignments in the Department of Interior, where control over this network became centralized. Thus, all the *Chow-muang* (Lords of the Land) came to be replaced by regular governors, career administrators under central control, known in Siamese as *Poo Waraja-karn Changwad* (governors) or *Kha-luang* (king's servants).

Let us first examine certain of the old territorial functions which were transferred to new specialized agencies, notably the judicial, the financial, the police, and the military.

OLDER FUNCTIONS REALLOCATED

With the creation of a Ministry of Justice and the promulgation of new law codes, judges were sent out from Bangkok to preside over provincial and district courts.

Similarly, a network of finance officers, appointed by the Revenue Department in the Ministry of Finance, took over control of the fiscal activities of the *Chow-muang*. The system was launched as early as

1896 when an English adviser, F. H. Giles, helped Prince Damrong establish an Outside (Provincial) Revenue Department within the Ministry of Interior.

Control over expenditures perhaps ought to be regarded as a new function, rather than as one of the old functions taken from the *Chow-muang,* since under the traditional system there was generally only a one-way flow of resources from the Lands to the capital. But the creation of a salaried national bureaucracy and the construction of public buildings in the provinces made it necessary to disburse central funds in a systematic way. Accordingly, a Finance (Paymaster) Department was established in the Ministry of Interior, with its local finance officials at the *monthon* and *changwad* levels.[11]

A provincial finance officer or treasurer, the *Klang Changwad,* reporting to the Ministry of Finance, took over primary responsibility for the disbursement of funds allocated to the provincial and district administrations. Centralized accounting and auditing services were provided by a Controller General's Department in the Ministry of Finance and by a State Audit Council in the Council of Ministers. It is unnecessary to spell out here the details of this system or the stages by which it evolved, but clearly the new financial institutions and control procedures made it much more difficult for a governor or other territorial administrator to handle public funds arbitrarily with the aim of building a personal "empire" or "fief."

A third sphere in which the powers of the *Chow-muang* were curtailed was the police function. I have already mentioned the creation of a Police Department in 1897. A national police network staffed by a separate career service of uniformed, armed, and disciplined officers posed a heavy counterweight to the authority of territorial administrators. Although the Police Department is within the Ministry of Interior, it has equal status with the Department of Interior, which controls the provincial and district officers. Although they have nominal authority over the police units stationed within the provinces, governors have been reluctant to exercise this authority. Clearly the police system constitutes a significant basis of functionally specialized countervailing power. The same situation prevails also at the district level, where many problems have arisen in defining the scope of responsibility of the district officer in relation to that of the district police chief, with his local force, often composed of fifteen to twenty-five officers and men.

Arsa, commenting on these relationships, notes:

. . . the governors themselves have been vague and uncertain about the real extent of their authority. Thus, despite their legal power to punish and reward all civil officials under their jurisdictions, most of the governors have not been of a mind to exercise full control over the police except in routine functional relations. Normally, annual increases in salaries of police officials in the provinces are sanctioned by the governors who, on the other hand, would themselves be disinclined to punish the police rather than report them to the Police Department in Bangkok for disciplinary action.[12]

An analogy could be drawn between the position of the provincial and district officers with that of the American ambassador overseas. He has nominal authority over the foreign aid mission and the military establishment, but in practice these are often quite autonomous entities, much more responsive to their own headquarters in Washington than to the titular chief appointed by the State Department. No doubt, as we shall see below, the relative power of the territorial official and the various specialized field offices has fluctuated. Nevertheless, the establishment of these offices brought to a definite end the monopoly of local power formerly exercised by the *Chow-muang.*

Of the four traditional functions of the *Chow-muang* which were separated out institutionally during the period of basic reforms, it may be thought that the military was exceptional in that a civil-military distinction had always been recognized in the traditional Siamese polity. We have already noted the distinction in roles between the *Mahadthai* and *Kalahom.* However, in so far as these did represent a civil-military division, they operated primarily at the central level, not in the localities. Each *Chow-muang* might have, in his own smaller court, counterparts to the *Mahadthai* and *Kalahom,* but in his person he exercised control over both military and civil functions.

Moreover, in the conduct of military operations, nominally "civilian" officials might play as important a role as those formally designated "military." Arsa notes that as late as 1875, when a war was fought with the Haw people, the commanders-in-chief of the Thai armies were both civilian officials. "It was not until after the Military Conscription Act (1903) was promulgated that the real separation between civil and military administration in Thailand was accomplished."[13]

The establishment of a new Ministry of Defense and the creation, with foreign advice, of a modern Army and Navy and, more recently, an Air Force were accompanied by the effective curtailment of the military authority of the governors. Initially the *Chow-muang* had, indeed, regarded the defense of their borders against hostile invasions, as well as the suppression of internal uprisings, as one of their cardinal duties. Now this responsibility passed specifically to the Defense Ministry and also, to some degree, to the Police Department.

NEWER FUNCTIONS ESTABLISHED

The creation of new types of functionally specialized services also added to the number of national bureaucratic networks which extended their field offices into the realm of local administration. These included agencies concerned with agriculture, education, and communications.

Some, such as the railroad, post and telegraph, and irrigation, carved out their own special districts which frequently cut across the boundaries of the established regional, provincial, and district units. Others merely appointed field officials to work within the existing territorial domains of the governors and district officers. But in either case, they provided a growing volume of channels for communication between Bangkok and the field, thereby reducing the scope for arbitrary action by local territorial administrators.

A list of officials attached to the typical *monthon* or regional office shortly after Damrong's retirement in 1915 gives five men reporting in various ways to the Ministry of Interior and seven attached to other ministries. The former group included the deputy commissioner, prosecutor, police commander, penitentiary officer, and public health officer. The latter included a military assistant commissioner, treasury, revenue, customs, agricultural, and educational officers, and an inspector of the post and telegraph service.[14]

The tendency has been for the number and range of functionally specialized activities to increase. Naturally, the number of specialists attached to each provincial governor's office has increased the most; but even the district officer of today has to supervise a considerable array of specialized officials, each responsible more or less directly to a national department. These include men responsible for the functions of police work, education, revenue, excise work, land registration and use, agriculture, veterinary services, public health, forestry, and fisheries.[15]

DISTRIBUTION OF CAREER OFFICIALS

An index of the extent to which the central agencies have increased their functionally specialized field services is provided by the statistics in Table 2, which gives the number of personnel employed in the head-

TABLE 2
MINISTRY OF AGRICULTURE
HEADQUARTERS AND FIELD OFFICERS, 1957
(*by department and rank**)

Departments			Ranks			
	Special	1st gr.	2nd gr.	3rd gr.	4th gr.	Total
Agriculture						
Headquarters	4	9	75	91	180	359
Field services	0	9	43	105	219	376
						735
Rice						
Headquarters	1	6	48	55	84	194
Field services	0	0	4	137	102	243
						437
Irrigation						
Headquarters	6	23	73	108	176	386
Field services	2	44	179	207	250	682
						1068
Forestry						
Headquarters	3	20	61	292	455	831
Field services	0	13	42	51	948	1054
						1885
Fisheries						
Headquarters	2	4	16	24	49	95
Field services	0	1	27	15	72	115
						210
Livestock						
Headquarters	4	12	72	108	286	482
Field services	0	5	76	144	163	388
						870
Total						
Headquarters	20	74	345	678	1230	2347
Field services	2	72	371	659	1754	2858
	22	146	716	1337	2984	5205

*Temporary employees are omitted from this table.
SOURCE: statistics furnished the author by the Ministry of Agriculture.

quarters and field services of the several departments in the Ministry of Agriculture, whose growth we have already examined. By 1957, this ministry had a national apparatus of over 5,000 career employees, of whom 45 per cent (2,347) worked in Bangkok, the rest being scattered about the country in the field services. If we consider that at that time Thailand had 71 provinces (*changwad*) and 488 districts (*amphur*), it may be seen that the average province had about 40 field officials of the Ministry of Agriculture, and the average district about 6.

Within each province there is naturally a larger concentration of officials in the provincial office than in each district, so that the actual number of specialized agricultural officials in the average district office was considerably less than six. Two other considerations affect the distribution of field officials in provincial and district offices: special districts and experiment stations.

Two of the six departments had special districts: Irrigation and Forestry. They also had the largest number of officials: 1,736 field men in Irrigation and Forestry as compared with 1,122 for Agriculture, Rice, Fisheries, and Livestock. With some exceptions, their field staff were assigned to special district offices outside the regular provincial and district headquarters. Moreover, a substantial number of the field staff of the four other departments (Agriculture, Rice, Fisheries, and Livestock) were assigned to experiment stations rather than to regular offices of territorial administration. Although I lack exact figures, it seems safe to estimate that less than 900 men were actually stationed in the *changwad* and *amphur* offices, whereas more than 1,800 were located in experiment station and special district offices. This means that less than two men were available for the average territorial office, and many *amphur* had only one man, or no man at all, for agricultural work. In practice, the specialists assigned to provincial headquarters had either to provide services for these unmanned districts or depend on someone else in the district office to give part-time assistance on a "voluntary" basis.

Although these figures show the extent to which a national apparatus of specialized field offices had penetrated the country, thereby limiting substantially the over-all scope of the power of territorial officials, they also demonstrate that a considerable expansion of these services was still required in 1957 in order to provide complete local coverage for the new technical programs of the government.

CONCLUSION

I do not have similar data for the other ministries, but there is no doubt that comparable distribution patterns would be found. At least, as regards the relationship between the capital and the surrounding countryside, the great reforms carried out under the absolute monarchy had effectively transformed the polity from one which was relatively undifferentiated structurally, with a high degree of localization of power as a consequence, to one in which the scope of power attributable to each agency of government had been considerably narrowed. The result was that the domain of the monarchs was vastly enlarged: the country as a whole was brought effectively under the control of a centralized power structure. The principle of bureaucratic rule had been substantially consolidated.

This meant also, of course, that decisions made in Bangkok on specific matters of national policy and law could now—at least, potentially—be implemented on a national scale, something which had lain beyond the range of possibility for the traditional system of government. In other words, a basic reason that the king could not formerly have been a legislator in the modern sense of rule-making was simply that he lacked the machinery to implement his wishes on a national scale. He had to limit himself to minor modifications of the traditional sacred codes, because he could scarcely conceive of any other mode of operation, and, further, he could not have implemented such policies had he imagined that such a course of action would be desirable.

It should now be clear how, in the modernization of the Thai polity, a fundamental "silent revolution" in the character of the bureaucracy was carried out, not only in the overhead structure of functionally specialized ministries and departments, but also in the expansion of these new agencies to include field staffs potentially capable of implementing enacted laws, regulations, and programs on a country-wide basis.

CHAPTER VI

The Effort to Impose Accountability: Central Government

The revolution of 1932 sought to replace the absolute monarchy, as master of the restructured bureaucracy, by the conventional Western institutions of constitutional government: a parliament, political parties, courts, a responsible cabinet headed by a prime minister, private interest groups, a free press, and an electoral system. If these new institutions had proven effective, then the modernization of the Siamese polity started by Mongkut and Chulalongkorn through royal absolutism might have been completed by popular democracy. Constitutional extrabureaucratic centers of power might have imposed accountability upon the apparatus of public administration in a manner far surpassing the capacity of the kings to compel responsibility and efficiency.

In practice, however, the new institutions of political control remained largely formalistic. They presented an imposing façade of official constitutionalism, but behind this front, real power passed largely to members of the bureaucracy, both military and civilian. Measured in terms of the distribution of power, the revolution of 1932 brought a greater dispersal, as the grip of the monarchy was broken and more people entered the political arena to participate in decision-making processes.

But the new entrants were for the most part in the military and civil bureaucracies, not outside. Thus, the bureaucratic apparatus, instead of serving largely an administrative function, became also the primary arena of political rivalry. It remained in substantial measure, however, a concealed arena. Political struggles began to take place on two levels: an open but largely epiphenomenal façade of parliamentary and constitutional processes; a hidden but substantive core of intrabureaucratic rivalry.

There was an important difference also in the kinds of issues which were decided at these two levels. On the open, parliamentary level the issues ostensibly concerned matters of public policy and the general interest, but at hidden, bureaucratic levels the covert stakes were the perquisites allocated to rival members of the bureaucracy, notably those in the higher echelons, military officers and civilians.[1]

The formal institutions of political accountability were created by fiat of the promoters of the 1932 revolution, under the impetus of doctrines imported by them from France and other Western countries where they had studied. The revolution did not emerge, as constitutional movements did in most Western countries, from a revolt of the middle classes, of industrial workers, of mass-based political parties, or of other widely supported organizations outside the government. Rather, the leaders of the revolution were themselves members—actual, would-be, or recently laid off—of the military and civil bureaucracy. (Who they were and how they acted is described in more detail in Chapter VIII.) Here I shall examine primarily the fate of the constitutional organs created by the revolutionists, notably the parliamentary and electoral machinery which has received the most public attention.

WEAKNESS OF THE NEW ASSOCIATIONS

In focusing attention on these formal structures of ostensible political control I do not mean to slight the importance of underlying substructures such as interest groups, the courts, the press, and prevailing cultural values. In an earlier essay, I have analyzed the role of associations in Thai politics and administration.[2] In that essay, I noted that the number of clubs and associations had risen from two, listed in the *Bangkok Register* for 1888, to eighty mentioned in the 1951 edition. Governmental registration figures brought the total to 591 as of 1958. No doubt the number of formally organized groups has continued to increase. Moreover, the number of Siamese groups relative to non-Siamese continually rose. Associations with a predominantly foreign membership rose in number to a peak of 35 in 1940, thereafter declining rapidly. Groups with a predominantly Thai membership began to be organized in 1910 and had risen to 74 by 1951.

Despite this growth in numbers, interest groups in Thailand remained weak politically. Indeed, they served more often as agents to carry out the will of influential officials than as spokesmen for the public interest in its dealings with the government. Among the reasons for this persistent weakness of private associations were the lack of funds, small memberships, cultural values uncongenial to organizational discipline and co-operative action, beliefs and values which linked ascriptive criteria of membership to functional goals of organizations, the limited extent of the socially mobilized sectors of the population in a small country, and certain legal restrictions on freedom of organization which hampered the growth of associations.

On the basis of such considerations, plus observation of actual interactions between selected groups and government officials, I reached the following conclusions:

In finances, the absolute poverty of private Thai participants as compared with the relative affluence of the government and the considerable degree to which private funds are in the hands of foreign nationals contribute to the relative weakness of Thai associations and their dependence on government support. This in turn makes them, while not fully creatures of government, at least more decisively subject to bureaucratic than to membership control.

Similarly, the predominance of bureaucrats in the membership of associations weakens their capacity to assert independent pressure on the government.

Thai social structure and beliefs, while posing no basic obstacle to the organization of associations, do inhibit their effectiveness. They make it difficult for the members to reach decisions, especially on policy or program goals. Hence the associational interests remain largely potential, only rarely becoming effective or reaching any high degree of intensity. Particularism and eclecticism result in the formation of diffuse programs of a very general character. Lacking specificity and focus, they lose penetrating power and tend to make little impact on government. Hence in finance, membership, internal cohesiveness, direction, and drive, the Thai association tends to be weak in power and more subject to manipulation by government agency than by members.[3]

More often than not, associations which were nominally private were in fact little more than the mouthpieces or weapons of influential officials and competing public agencies. Sometimes rival groups, such as trade unions, were deliberately organized and run by top bureaucratic politicians to augment their own power position.

Comparable phenomena could be found in the business world—as examined below in Chapter IX—and in the sphere of the mass media and the communications networks. In Western countries, it is taken for granted that the formation of public opinions capable of imposing checks upon the arbitrary action of officials is normally shaped and stimulated by the mass media, which feed information and ideas to the public, helping them relate their personal interests to the public scene. The existence of relatively free organs of press and radio is taken for granted as a prerequisite for public opinion to arise and find channels of expression. In the Thai system, one forms a misleading conception of the mass media because of the controversial and antagonistic positions taken by different organs against each other. One might think that here a free press plays a role similar to that performed in Western countries. However, closer investigation reveals that particular bureaucratic agencies and influential officials tend to dominate each of the main outlets. The control patterns of the newspapers are somewhat obscure and indirect, but the various radio stations openly serve as organs for competing units in the bureaucracy. In 1957, for example, the Siamese could listen to broadcasts from the following stations and networks:

1. The National Radio, operated by the Public Relations Department in the office of the prime minister;

2. Thai TV, a nominally "private" radio and television station, but effectively dominated by General Phao and providing extra positions for many officials in his group;

3. An "Experimental Station" run by the Public Relations Department, on a larger scale than the National Radio;

4. An "Experimental Station" run by the Post and Telegraph Department;

5. "Experimental Stations" operated by various branches of the Army, including an extensive radio and TV system run by the Signal Corps; a Regional Radio Division network of eleven stations; a Territorial Army Station; an Armored Car Division Station; and an Anti-Aircraft Regiment Station;

6. "Experimental Stations" operated by three divisions of the Air Force;

7. An "Experimental Station" of the Royal Navy;

8. "Experimental Stations" operated by several divisions of the Police Department;

9. The "Experimental Station" of the Ministry of Education; and

10. The King's Station.

In principle, only the first two stations in this list were licensed to operate on a regular basis. The "experimental stations" were authorized initially on a temporary basis for limited functions, but, in fact, all had become permanent operations, largely self-supporting through the sale of advertising. Apparently only the stations listed above under numbers 1, 9, and 10 did not take commercial advertising.[4]

Perhaps nothing could more clearly illustrate the proposition that interest groups and the mass media in Thailand did not stand outside the government as agents of an organized public capable of imposing constraints on the behavior of its public servants. Nor, however, could this system be likened to that of authoritarian systems in which a single monolithic mass party imposes its control over both the public and the state bureaucracy. In communist systems, for example, the party-controlled press and radio are used to exert pressure on and help direct the state bureaucracy. But the Thai system was marked by a high degree of competition and the free flow of rival, even contradictory, opinions and information. The political struggle, however, was not primarily between political parties, interest groups, and the mass media, all seeking support from a sovereign people. Rather, the public was a plastic and somewhat pliable audience before whom the real power struggle was enacted by competing groups within the bureaucracy itself.

A conspicuous manifestation of this system was the formalism of constitutions, parliamentary bodies, elections, and evanescent political parties, to which we now direct our attention.

FORMALISM OF THE REVOLVING CONSTITUTIONS

To political scientists who regard written constitutions as serious statements of the rules of the game, the parade of revolving charters under which the Thai government has operated since 1932 must appear astonishing indeed. The provisional constitution imposed by the revolutionists of June, 1932, was soon followed by a "permanent" constitution promulgated in December. A new constitution was enacted in 1946, only to be overthrown in 1947 by a second provisional charter, and replaced by another "permanent" constitution in 1949. In 1951, the 1932 constitution was reinstated, and revised in 1952. In 1957, the constitution was temporarily suspended, then reinstated. In 1959, a third provisional (or interim) constitution was announced, while a constituent assembly went to work on another "permanent" charter.[5]

Clearly these constitutional documents cannot be taken seriously as binding statements of the rules of the political game, as expressions of fundamental law. It is apparent that, whenever important shifts in the personnel of the ruling circle took place, the previous charter was suspended to permit the promulgation of new rules more compatible with the interests and inclinations of the winning group. The rules, no doubt, were followed, but only as they proved convenient for the power holders. Constitutionalism was not designed so much to constrain the rulers as to facilitate their rule. The charters, in other words, did not prescribe the effective norms of political behavior, but were used to cast a cloak of legitimacy over the operations of succeeding rulers and to set the stage for a play to be enacted by the extrabureaucratic performers—parliaments, political parties, electors. These performers played their parts, most of the time in cheerful conformity with the prescribed scenarios, although between 1945 and 1947 they almost succeeded in inverting roles with their bureaucratic protagonists. Had they really succeeded, the subsequent political history of Thailand might have been quite different.

As it was, Siamese political parties and parliaments were largely used to legitimize decisions previously taken in the bureaucracy by a ruling circle of military and civil service politicians. To some degree, these constitutional devices also provided a safety vent for criticisms of the group in power, although this outlet could always be closed whenever the cries of protest became too vehement, or when those in power began to feel uneasy about the safety of their offices.

The constitutional history of Thailand is so revealing that it deserves close analysis. The account which follows does little more than skim some of the high spots. In order to facilitate the reading of what must at times appear to be a most complicated story, Table 3 is presented as a chronological guide to the successive constitutions and elections and to the regular and special sessions of parliamentary bodies. A detailed analysis of the underlying political struggles reflected in this formal "constitutional" history is given in Chapter VIII. The full names of Thai cabinet politicians mentioned below are given in Appendix A.

THE PROVISIONAL CONSTITUTION AND THE TUTELAGE IDEA

The Provisional Constitution of June 27, 1932, had obviously been prepared in advance by promoters of the coup d'état, notably by Pridi.[6] The document was an eclectic mixture of Western parliamentary ideas and Soviet doctrines, with an infusion of Sun Yat Sen's theories. Formally, political authority was to rest with a national assembly, and a People's Committee was to be elected by the Assembly as its executive body. This committee was to supervise the government, which would continue to be run, as in the past, by career officials as ministers or *senabodi*.

TABLE 3

CONSTITUTIONS, ELECTIONS, AND LEGISLATIVE SESSIONS

1932,	6/27	PROVISIONAL CONSTITUTION	
	12/10	PERMANENT CONSTITUTION	
	6/28	National Assembly (appointed)	
		6/28/32–4/1/33*	6/22–12/6/33*
1933,	11/15	*First Elections,* 78 first-category members, 1933–37	
		12/10/33–3/31/34	8/1–9/30/34
		12/15/34–3/31/35	
		8/1–10/29/35	2/1–3/31/36
		8/1–10/29/36	12/26–12/28/36
			2/1–3/31/37
			6/24–7/15/37
1937,	11/7	*Second Elections,* 91 first-category members, 1937/38	
		12/10/37–3/19/38	
		6/24–9/11/38 (dissolved)	
1938,	11/12	*Third Elections,* 91 first-category members, 1938–1945	
		12/10/38–3/31/39	
		6/24–10/12/39	
		6/24–9/21/40	11/1–12/6/40
			6/9–6/23/41
		6/24–9/30/41	11/1–12/7/41
			12/9/41–4/16/42
		6/24–12/31/42	1/1–2/25/43
		6/24–9/21/43	11/1–12/31/43
		6/24–9/30/44	11/1–12/30/44
		6/24–10/15/45	
1946,	1/6	*Fourth Elections,* 96 first-category members, 1946	
		1/24–5/9/46	
	5/10	CONSTITUTION OF 1946 (Pridi)—established bicameral Parliament: Senate and House	
		6/1–6/22/46	
	8/5	*Fifth Elections,* 82 additional members of Parliament	
			8/21–12/31/46
		5/10–8/30/47	
1947,	11/9	PROVISIONAL CONSTITUTION "Under-the-Red-Jar"	
		Newly appointed Senate	
		11/24–12/31/47	1/8–1/28/48
1948,	1/29	*Sixth Election,* 99 members of Parliament, lower house	
		2/19–10/1/48	11/1–12/31/48
			1/6–3/3/49
			(*Continued*)

TABLE 3 (*Continued*)
CONSTITUTIONS, ELECTIONS, AND LEGISLATIVE SESSIONS

1949,	3/23	CONSTITUTION OF 1949 (Phibun)—minor changes
	6/5	*Seventh Election,* by-election of 21 for expanded House

6/15–9/12/49	10/20–12/31/49
	1/1–2/24/50
	6/1–8/14/50
10/1–12/29/50	1/1–?/51
10/1–11/29/51	

1951,	11/29	RESTORATION OF 1932 CONSTITUTION, "Silent Coup"
		Appointed Assembly, Senate abolished

	12/1–12/31/51
	1/1–2/29/52

1952,	2/26	*Eighth Election,* 123 first-category members, 1952–1956
	3/8	CONSTITUTION OF 1932, REVISED 1952

3/18–4/10/52	
6/24–9/21/52	11/1–12/31/52
	1/1–1/23/53
	6/24–9/21/53
	11/1–12/31/53
	1/1–2/13/54
6/24–9/25/54	11/1–12/31/54
	1/1–1/17/55
6/24–9/21/55	11/1–12/31/55
	1/1–2/6/56
6/1–9/21/56	11/1–12/31/56

1957,	2/26	*Ninth Election,* 160 first-category members, 1957

3/14–4/11/57
6/24–9/16/57

	9/16	SUSPENSION AND RE-ESTABLISHMENT OF 1932 CONSTITUTION (Sarit)—Appointed Assembly

9/20–11/29/57

	12/15	*Tenth Election,* 160 first-category members

12/26–12/31/57	1/1–1/17/58

1958,	3/30	*Eleventh Election,* by-election for 25 additional members

6/24–9/21/58	4/8–6/23/58

1959,	1/29	INTERIM CONSTITUTION (Sarit)—Constituent Assembly

*Dates in first column are for regular legislative sessions, in the second column for special session.

Data from *Pictorial Book on Members of Parliament, 1932–1959* (in Thai), trans. by Amara Raksasataya and Veeravat Karnjanadul (Bangkok, 1960).

In this respect, the organization of government was supposed to re-semble the Soviet constitution of 1924, in which the Central Executive Committee of the Congress of Soviets had responsibility for appointing and supervising the People's Commissars, who carried administrative responsibility for the conduct of government.

The king, as in the British system, was to remain a constitutional monarch, but he no longer was to be regarded as "Lord of Life" and source of political legitimacy. Political sovereignty was declared to re-side in the "entire people" (Article 1). The Assembly representing the people could try the king, and its endorsement was necessary for a new king to be enthroned. The king was to review and endorse legislation, but his disapproval could be overruled by a simple majority of the Assembly.

The courts were also recognized as having an independent status, and they were to make judicial decisions in accordance with established laws; but the American principle of judicial review of the constitution-ality of laws was not included in the provisional constitution.

A sequential pattern of constitutional development was provided for, based on a three-stage model that had been propounded by Sun Yat Sen, the Chinese revolutionist, as early as 1905. The doctrine re-ceived its fullest expression in Sun's *Three Principles of the People* in the nineteen-twenties and was clearly well known by Pridi. Although parallel to some Marxist and Leninist ideas, the model contained dis-tinctive ideas attributable to Sun himself. The three stages were to be a period of military conquest of power, then a stage of political tutelage (or party dictatorship), and finally full constitutional government.

The first stage was supposed to continue for six months after the coup, or until "the affairs of the country are properly in order" (Article 10). During this stage, the military officers in control of the revolution would name the seventy members of the Assembly and would them-selves exercise power on the people's behalf. Thus, the Assembly was to be controlled by the military promoters of the coup, so that the pro-moters themselves actually determined, indirectly, the membership of the People's Committee.

During the second stage, party tutelage, the Assembly would con-tain the original members plus others elected by provinces in districts having a population of 100,000 or more. The number of members in the elected category was to equal the number appointed. The elections were to be carried out by a system of indirect voting similar to that recommended by Sun Yat Sen. Candidates were to pass examinations pre-scribed by the Assembly—another feature of Sun's scheme—and they would also have to be recommended by the original members of the Assembly.

Complete political democracy would be established in the third stage: when more than half of the population had completed primary school, but not more than ten years after promulgation of the Constitution.

Although the formal terms of the Provisional Constitution reflected in this eclectic fashion some prevailing doctrines of the democratic West, of communist Russia, and of modernizing China, the effective practice of Siamese politics turned out to be distinctively different from all these models. Clearly an assembly appointed by a ruling clique could not, in any significant way, "represent" the people, nor could it be expected to exercise any real power in case it should have the temerity to espouse a point of view contrary to that of the ruling circle.

On April 1, 1933, the Assembly was prorogued and proved helpless to check the government of the day. However, even in this first test of strength, the members of the Assembly had not adopted a view contrary to that of the ruling circle. Rather, the circle itself had split, and the assemblymen found themselves aligned with the weaker faction, namely, that led by Pridi himself, the chief author of the Provisional Constitution. The dismissal of the Assembly took place on the same day that Pridi himself was ousted from the government and forced into exile.

But if these events demonstrated that the National Assembly was to have no more real influence than the Supreme Soviet in Russia or the Legislative Yuan in China, they also made it clear that the People's Party was not equivalent in power to the Bolsheviks or even to the Kuomintang of Nationalist China. Although the Kuomintang was rent with cliques, it actually was a membership organization with local cells; and, under the tutelage of Borodin and his team of Russian advisers, Sun Yat Sen had built, despite its flimsiness, a "grass roots" political movement. What is more, with the help of Galens and the Whampoa Military Academy, Chiang Kai Shek, Chou En Lai, and their fellow officers had mobilized an effective military cadre.

No doubt the splitting of the right and left wings of the Kuomintang, the ouster of the Communists, and the military coup by means of which Chiang seized control of the Nationalist Party have their parallel in the split by which the military man, Phya Song, with the support of

Phya Mano, ousted Pridi in April, 1933. But the differences are greater than the similarities. Chiang Kai Shek, in splitting the Kuomintang leaders, was nevertheless able to take over a membership organization that had become a going concern.

In Siam, the People's Party was scarcely more than a political club. With the ouster of Pridi, the chief protagonist of political organization outside the government had been removed from the scene—at least for a time. The remaining military members of the coup had no interest in promoting a mass membership organization. Moreover, the older bureaucratic members of the government—represented by Phya Mano, the prime minister—were actively opposed to any form of political organization. After the coup of June 20, 1933, which brought the junior members of the People's Party back into power (and also recalled the Assembly) and made Pridi's return to the cabinet possible, an attempt might have been made to organize the party on a larger scale. But the attempt was not even made, and the remaining promoters merely continued their association for a time as a social or political club. Wilson goes so far as to deny that the term "political party" could even be applied to the People's Party:

> From 1932 through World War II, there were no political parties in Thai politics. The People's Party or People's Association which emerged as the public organization of the Promoters of the Coup d'Etat of 1932 cannot properly be so described. The initial intention of the Promoters apparently was to form a large but exclusive party organization to support their position, but they soon abandoned the idea. Shortly after the establishment of the constitutional government, it became public policy not to permit the organization of parties and the People's Party became the People's Association, which appears to have combined social activities with some genteel political education. The usage is somewhat confused, however, since the ruling group continued to refer to themselves as the People's Party. In this sense the term refers to the ruling group associated with the 1932 coup.[7]

The lack of an organizational base for control over the government meant, of course, that the conceptions of Lenin and Sun regarding political tutelage could not be realized in Thailand any more than the ideas of parliamentary control could be fulfilled. The primary base for the exercise of power that remained, after the crushing of the absolute monarchy, was in the bureaucracy itself. The events of 1932 and the succeeding years, therefore, can be best understood in terms of rivalries between political leaders whose primary sources of power were their control over elements and agencies within the government, military and civilian. They are analyzed below in Chapter VIII. Meanwhile, let us examine the later constitutions to discover if they ever provided a set of political rules capable of constraining the ruling circle in its exercise of power.

The Permanent Constitution was drafted by a committee appointed by the Assembly in co-operation with King Prachatipok. Pridi was the only promoter among the nine members of this committee, the others being senior officials during the absolute monarchy, all of whom had been given high positions in the new government. The committee reported its draft to the National Assembly which, doubling as a constituent body, adopted and promulgated the text, with the king's endorsement, on December 10, 1932.

The new charter was much more conciliatory toward the king than the Provisional Constitution had been. It assigned him many prerogatives and powers and made his actions no longer subject to trial by the Assembly. But restrictions carefully written into the text were designed to prevent the king from ever exercising these powers. A member of the drafting committee explained to the Assembly that the listing of royal prerogatives had been put into the charter "for the sake of rhetoric as well as an honor to the King." [8]

The restrictions took primarily the form of stipulations that all ordinary actions of the king must be countersigned by a member of the State Council, and the appointment of a new state council had to be endorsed by the president of the Assembly (Article 57). Thus, the Assembly, through its president, and the members of the State Council could effectively inhibit the exercise of all royal prerogatives.

Mention has been made of the State Council. What was this body, and how did it come into being? We have seen that the Provisional Constitution provided for a People's Committee, elected by the National Assembly, to serve as a central control body, imposing its domination over a body of ministers who would run the government. The model is that of the Central Executive Committee of the Supreme Soviet in relation to the Council of People's Commissars. In the U.S.S.R., the pattern has continued, with modifications in the 1936 constitution, where the Presidium of the Supreme Soviet—still dominated by the party leadership—directs the Council of Ministers.

But in the Thai Permanent Constitution of December, 1932, the People's Committee and the council of ministers were combined into a single body, the State Council, or "cabinet," as it is frequently called. Thus, the original idea of a political body outside the bureaucracy capable of imposing control over the supreme organ of the officials somehow became obscured in the drafting of a new charter. Since it was a group of high officials who prepared the draft, it may not seem surprising that they decided to abolish the People's Committee.

By restoring the dignity—but not the power—of the king, the writers of the Permanent Constitution attracted support from conservative and pro-monarchist elements. In destroying the People's Committee, they capitalized on anticommunist and pro-Western sentiments. The king himself is reported to have proposed abandoning the name "People's Committee" because it might give the impression of having been taken from the Soviet Union's Council of People's Commissars. The State Council was praised for resembling the cabinet in Western parliamentary systems. As in England, the king was to name a prime minister who would appoint his fellow ministers. The Council would be responsible to the Assembly, which would endorse the initial appointments and have the right to approve or disapprove their actions. In principle, the Assembly could overthrow any State Council by a vote of no confidence.

On the surface, the Permanent Constitution seemed to be a logical sequel to the Provisional Constitution. The dignity of the king had been restored but not his power, and the structure of government had been streamlined by consolidating the People's Committee with the body of ministers in a new state council. Under the surface, however, the structure of power had been significantly reshaped. The People's Party, which, in the mind of Pridi at least, had offered a possible base for the direction of the revolution, had been seriously undermined.

In June, 1932, following the coup, Phya Phahon, as leader of the promoters and military controller, had named the members of the new assembly. He included, besides those who took part in the revolution, some twenty-five nonpromoters who had been senior officials with high rank and extensive administrative experience. Chao Phya Thammasak-Montri, who had been minister of education, was chosen Assembly president. The fourteen-member People's Committee had contained eleven promoters of the revolution and three senior officials of the old regime, one of whom, Phya Manoprakorn Nitithada, was named chairman. A council of ministers was then named by the People's Committee. All were senior officials and nonmembers of the People's Party. There was, thus, a clear differentiation between a political control center and the central executive or administrative body.[9]

Following the promulgation of the Permanent Constitution, however, the two bodies, the eight ministers, and the fourteen members of the People's Committee were simply merged to form the State Council. With two overlapping memberships, the total now came to twenty persons. The Council consisted of nine senior officials from the old regime, who held all the cabinet positions, and eleven promoters of the revolution, who were all Council members without portfolio. Mano continued to serve as chairman, or prime minister.

It has been suggested that the promoters hoped to maintain their control over the government by means of their majority in the Council. But the Council scarcely made its key decisions by a vote. Certainly if the Council were to have divided eleven to nine, promoters vs. old officials, the People's Party members could scarcely have counted on getting their way. In practice, factionalism among the promoters quickly manifested itself, and Phya Mano was not slow to capitalize on this dissension in order to maximize his own influence and that of his fellow senior officials.

Thus, the crucial idea of a political group outside the administration capable of imposing its control over the government had been lost in the very structure of the Permanent Constitution, despite its formalistic adherence to the principle of parliamentary responsibility. With an appointed Assembly, it became clear that the State Council would never have to depend for its continued existence on parliamentary approval. The charter actually gave the Assembly no more real power than it gave the king.

It is true that some members of the People's Party did try to consolidate their power position by other means. A number of "unreliable" army and navy officers were transferred to unimportant posts or dismissed, and leading promoters of the coup assumed military command positions. Phahon became commander-in-chief of the Army; Song was named deputy commander-in-chief and director of military operations. Ritthi became commander of artillery, and Phibun was named his deputy. Other key military positions were also filled by members of the People's Party.[10]

The significance of this strategy requires careful analysis. If the People's Party had hoped to gain political control over the government from outside the bureaucracy, they would have had to build an organization similar in structure to the Communist Party, the Kuomintang, or, let us say, the Congress Party or Muslim League in India. In fact, the People's Party, as Wilson has pointed out, was not a real political party, despite its name. It had no popular support on which to base its effort to control the government. Moreover, its members were bureaucrats, in mentality if not in current positions. Many were military officers. To them, the logical means to power, and the gratification of their personal ambitions, took the form of appointments to official positions. As individuals they continued to play key roles, but their influence depended on the solidarity of their cliques within the bureaucracy, not on external support.

By taking official positions and consenting to the formation of the State Council, the promoters of the revolution effectively surrendered their power over the bureaucracy. Thenceforth, political struggles took place within the bureaucracy, between its rival cliques. Both the monarchy and the parliamentary and party apparatus became decorations, utilized and maintained primarily as means of legitimizing decisions made behind the closed doors of the governmental machinery.

THE ABORTIVE RISE OF PARLIAMENTARISM

The Constitution of 1932 remained the formal façade of government until after World War II. At this time, the National Assembly began to play an increasingly important role. Political parties were formed and nominated candidates for election to the Assembly. It appeared possible that real vitality would be infused at last into the long dormant body, and that an organizational framework for instituting political controls over the bureaucracy might come into being.

Several changes in the structure of power may be mentioned as contributory forces. The older system of bureaucratic rule under Phibun had become identified with the Japanese occupation. Pridi, on the other hand, had taken the lead in forming a Free Thai underground movement to collaborate with the Western powers in ousting the Japanese. Although the sudden collapse of the Japanese in August, 1945, meant that the Free Thai never had a real opportunity to display their prowess, Pridi did emerge at the end of the war as the leading pro-Ally figure in Siamese politics. As such, he received substantial external support, while his old rival, Phibun, remained in jail.

But internally Pridi had also gained prestige and potential power by his appointment as regent in December, 1941, when he was dropped from the cabinet in response to Japanese pressure. The young King Ananda Mahidol (Rama VIII) was a student in Switzerland, and the prestige and power of the constitutional monarchy came to be exercised, paradoxically enough, by the allegedy republican Pridi. By helping to form new cabinets and taking the resignation of old ones, he utilized the regency to greater effect than any king had been able to do since the revolution in 1932.

Unlike other top Siamese politicians, Pridi had never entrenched himself in the bureaucracy, although he naturally maintained connections there. His support depended in part on his old associates of the People's Party, notably the members of the civilian faction in the younger clique, of which he was leader, but even more on a new group of leaders in the Free Thai movement which had been created during the war. Members of this Pridi following now organized themselves into political parties, which became important actors for the first time on the Bangkok scene. Pridi's friends and supporters began to form political groups which called themselves "political parties," although they might better be thought of as cliques and factions in a larger movement. The new politicians who had been active in the Free Thai movement set up the *Sahachip*, or Co-operation Party. Pridi's older associates, who had belonged with him to the People's Party, constituted a definite clique and took the lead in forming a larger coalition known as the Constitution Front, designed to include the *Sahachip* and a number of independents and small groups (including a Communist Party member).[11]

During the fall of 1945, a group of intellectuals and loyalist officials who had not joined the revolution in 1932—and some of whom had spent years in jail as a result—formed the Progressive Party under the leadership of Kukrit Pramot, editor of the *Siam Rath*, an influential and often pro-royalist paper.

Upon the successful termination of prolonged diplomatic negotiations between Bangkok and the Allied powers, at the end of 1945, the Seni cabinet resigned, and elections were held on January 6, 1946, for "first-category" members of the National Assembly, in accordance with the 1932 constitution. Candidates nominated by the new political parties ran for election, and Pridi's Constitution Front, with the *Sahachip* taking the lead, won a decisive majority. Under these circumstances, Pridi's political future seemed assured. He commanded the respect and support of the Allies. Internally, he controlled the monarchy through his position as regent. The young King Ananda, returning from Switzerland in December, 1945, enhanced the popularity of his regime. Moreover, victory at the polls gave Pridi a base of authentic popular support never previously enjoyed by other Thai politicians. The time seemed ripe to institutionalize democratic controls over the government, to break the grip of the officials and to establish truly responsible government.

Whether in moving to change the constitution Pridi was animated by an altruistic desire to consolidate a democratic regime, or merely by a wish to safeguard his own position as chief power-holder, can perhaps never be determined. No doubt in serving his own aspirations he could also fulfill some of the political goals for which he had become a symbol. At any rate, on February 14 a committee of fifteen was appointed to draft a new constitution. Pridi himself, after presiding indirectly over the government through associates who acted as prime ministers, decided to take the premiership himself on March 24, following a break with Khuang Aphaiwong, who had resigned the position in protest against Pridi's behind-the-scenes manipulations.

Pridi then turned his attention to the new constitution, which was promulgated on May 10. It provided for abolition of the appointed, second-category members in the National Assembly and for their replacement by additional elected members. To compensate for the presumed stability previously given the Assembly by the appointed members, a second chamber, to be known as the Senate, was to be established, consisting of eighty indirectly elected members, holding office for six-year terms.

The first Senate was named by the existing Assembly. Since Pridi had secure control over that body, he was able to obtain the designation of his supporters for all the positions in the new Senate. The new Senate and the House with its previously elected members then held a regular session in June. Subsequently, on August 5, elections were held for the replacement positions in the House of Representatives, as it now became. Eighty-two new members were elected, bringing the total number of representatives to one hundred and seventy-eight.

Although Pridi dominated the new bicameral parliament, he by no means held a monopoly. His disaffected associate, Khuang, joined forces with Kukrit and his Progressive Party, following the end of the Khuang cabinet on March 24, 1946, to form a new party known as the *Prachatipat* (Democrat Party). During the year and a half which followed, partisan debate in Parliament became more and more acrimonious, while corruption in the government increased, often involving Pridi's Free Thai followers. Pressures, including violence, against Khuang's Democrats rose. In this atmosphere of political tension, Phibun—who had been released from prison in March, 1946—began to gather around him a new coup d'état group (the *Khana Ratapraharn*), which seized power on November 8, 1947.

THE DEMISE OF THE QUIXOTIC ASSEMBLY

The day after this coup, a provisional constitution was promulgated, popularly known as the "Under-the-Red-Jar Constitution." It provided for the abolition of Pridi's Senate and its replacement by the new upper house, to be appointed by the Supreme Council on behalf of the king. The House of Representatives was to be re-elected on the basis of larger constituencies. Members of the new upper house were promptly appointed. They consisted of one hundred elderly gentlemen, predominantly officials who had served the government before 1932. They convened November 24 and acted on behalf of the whole parliament pending the re-election of representatives, which took place on January 29, 1948.

The new parliament met on February 19, but it soon became evident that it no longer provided any basis for political control over the government. On April 6, the military leaders demanded the resignation of Khuang, who had been retained in the premiership as a front man. Khuang never even turned to Parliament for support. After canvassing the military officers in his government and discovering their unwillingness to support him, he resigned. The bureaucracy was again in full control of a government headed by military officers, but many civilian officials also held high posts in the cabinet.

Provision for a constituent assembly of forty members had been made on January 23, 1948, just prior to the elections, but the appointments were not made until July 7, after Phibun had established his supremacy. This body now deliberated and produced a new draft constitution on December 25, 1948, which was subsequently approved by Parliament and regent, and promulgated on March 23, 1949, the fifth charter since 1932.

According to this document, the bicameral legislature was retained. The existing members of both the Senate and House of Representatives were continued in office, but the size of electoral constituencies was reduced from 200,000 to 150,000, causing new elections to be held on

June 5, 1949, to add 21 new members to the House. The Phibun regime thus legitimized itself and created a docile parliament willing to support the new administration.

Meanwhile, ambitious officers who had taken an active part in the 1947 coup remained restlessly in the background, for Phibun chose not to give them cabinet posts. Gradually they gathered their forces for a showdown, while political unrest grew as manifested in the abortive "Manhattan rebellion" of June 26 (see Chapter VIII). On November 29, 1951, they staged the "silent coup." This took the simple form of a radio announcement by rising Police General Phao that the 1949 constitution had been suspended and the 1932 "Permanent Constitution" was being reinstated. The bicameral legislature was, accordingly, abolished, and a split, half-appointive and half-elective assembly was revived. One hundred twenty-three second-category members were promptly appointed, on November 30, 1951, consisting of 64 army officers, 14 navy officers, 13 air force officers, 11 police officers, and 21 civilian officials. Without waiting for the election of first-category members, this "parliament" composed predominantly of military officers met on December 1 and continued to act as a legislature until the elections for first-category members were held on February 26, 1952. Precedents, of course, had been set in June, 1932, and November, 1947.

Meanwhile, steps were taken to adopt certain minor amendments to the 1932 constitution, which was then officially proclaimed on March 8, 1952, ten days after the elections had been held. The new assembly met on March 18, but it was clear to all that the government of military officers had nothing to fear from its reformed and chastened legislature.

The 1932 constitution (as revised) remained in force until September 16, 1957, when a most unusual incident occurred. Two rival cliques had formed within the Phibun government, one headed by Phao, the other by Sarit. Elections for new members of the Assembly had been held on February 26, 1957, at which time Phao's group won decisive support at the polls. The Sarit group loudly accused Phao and his followers of foul play, asserting that local officials had "rigged" the election returns. On September 16, the Sarit clique staged the Military Group coup d'état. Simultaneously, Sarit announced the temporary suspension and reinstatement of the 1952 (1932) constitution. By this ingenious device, he was able to abolish the existing parliament and thus start out with a fresh slate. He proceeded immediately to appoint a new set of officials loyal to his clique to the second-category posts in the Assembly, and announced that new elections for the first-category spots would be held within ninety days, i.e., on December 15, 1957. Meanwhile, the second-category appointed members solemnly met on September 20—following the earlier precedents—to carry on routine legislative business.

PERPLEXITIES OF THE PARTY MEN

The right of a ruling circle under the 1932 constitution to appoint half the members of the Assembly assured control over the legislature. Nevertheless, a vocal opposition among the elected members could seriously embarrass a dominant clique. In the period from the 1947 coup and the "red jar" constitution up to the restoration of the 1932 constitution in November, 1951, political parties continued to flourish as they had during the previous period. However, the pro-Pridi Constitution Front and *Sahachip* were replaced—after a brief florescence of the Democrat Party—by a group of pro-Phibun groups in a loose coalition known as the United Parties. Their main function was to jockey for favors and cabinet positions in exchange for support in the House of Representatives, which remained on an all-elected basis.[12]

After the restoration of the unicameral assembly in 1951, parties were once more forbidden. However, the ruling group needed a mechanism to co-ordinate assembly procedures, and so it set up, under the guidance of Phao as secretary-general, a legislative study committee. This body consisted of the appointed members of the Assembly plus the elected members who expressed willingness to support the government. It met regularly as a caucus to plan legislative strategy. In 1955, political parties were again legalized, and the Legislative Study Committee was transformed into the *Seri Manangkhasila* Party, still under Phao's leadership.[13]

By 1957, several parties had become active on the Thai political scene. As rivalry between the Phao and Sarit cliques in the government grew, Sarit gave his support to a new party, the Unionists, which challenged the Phao-led *Seri Manangkhasila*. The fact that a variety of available perquisites could be dispensed only with the support or consent of the top leaders in the ruling circle meant that the pressures were strong on elected members of the Assembly to identify with one or another of these officially sanctioned political parties.

However, there were also elected members of the Assembly who for one reason or another could not or would not make their peace with the dominant officials in the ruling circle. Around them circulated a rather fluid group of opposition parties. Most stable of these was the Democrat Party, under the continuing leadership of Khuang, to which reference has already been made. During the first half of 1948, when Khuang was prime minister in alliance with Phibun, under the "red jar" constitution, the Democrat Party had experienced a brief heyday as an official party, but when Khuang subsequently went into opposition, the party's fortunes suffered a sharp reverse.

Another important opposition group was the Socialist Front, which brought together a number of assemblymen from the northeast. They claimed that their region was neglected and underdeveloped by contrast with the rest of the country and demanded more assistance. They also pressed for a neutralist foreign policy.

In societies where political parties become centers of influence capable of recruiting members of the elite by nominating candidates for public office and securing their election at the polls, we are accustomed to thinking of legislators as men whose selection reflects relatively stable party identifications and political platforms. Although such identifications could be said to characterize some M.P.'s in the Thai Assembly, especially those of the dissident minorities, the majority members can be better understood as partyless "independents."

An independent is a candidate for the Assembly who simply runs on his own. Relying on his own resources, and with the help of his friends and relatives, he seeks the votes of the electorate. A very substantial number of candidates at the elections in 1957 professed no party affiliation, and for others who did, the connection was purely nominal. As Wilson observed, "No party is sufficiently strong or well organized to either guarantee or deny election to any candidate." Although the Democrat Party was one of the most stable, Wilson noted that ". . . members who had been elected on the Democrat ticket seemed to have little hesitation about shifting their allegiance." [14]

We should come closer to understanding the nature of the Thai political process, therefore, if we thought of the elected assemblymen less as party members than as independents. Party membership becomes something that acquires its main significance *after,* not *before,* an election. As far as the local constituency is concerned, they view themselves as choosing among candidates on the basis of who can bring them the most help from the public purse. The "pork barrel," not policies and ideological issues, then, becomes the governing electoral consideration. Seen from this point of view, it is natural for an elected assemblyman to seek whatever party affiliations will best serve his interests after his election.

Although certain kinds of largess can be distributed with an even hand to all assemblymen, the choicest plums—important posts, major contracts, the allocation of licenses and permits, and free funds for local improvements—are costly and scarce and can be provided only for the favored few. The party system then becomes a means of bargaining assembly votes against favors. M.P.'s who feel that they have been unfairly treated, or that they can enhance their position in this way, move into one of the opposition circles. Those who are most favored become the leaders of pro-government parties. Others, well placed on the gravy train, become the stalwarts of these official parties. Having run substantially as an independent—with or without a party—the M.P. feels no sense of the people's mandate nor of policy orientations. The parties lack any basis for claiming loyalty and discipline in terms of support or meaningful party guidance given during elections. The Assembly, therefore, is a club whose members are free to join any one of several competing cliques and to change cliques whenever it serves their interests to do so.

TYPES OF PARTY POSITION

On this basis we can distinguish three kinds of party situation, reflecting the current structure of power. The first situation is that of the majority of M.P.'s who rally round the ruling circle in the cabinet, forming an *official party*. The second situation is that of the several hard-core deviants who, for one reason or another, cannot make their peace with the ruling circle and form the *opposition parties*. A third situation occurs when a split within the ruling circle becomes apparent. At such times a different kind of opposition arises, based on a close alliance with key power-holders. The connection may be based on the current ability of leaders in the deviant faction to reward their followers, augmented by a shrewd guess that the faction will in due course overthrow the dominant clique, at which time the early supporters of the revolt will obtain their rewards. Let us call such a group a *factional party*.

Clearly, any particular party can shift in its party situation from one type to another. For example, the Progressive Party started in 1945 as an opposition party. When Khuang resigned in 1946 and co-opted the Progressive Party into his new *Prachatipat* (Democrat Party), the organization became a factional party, since Khuang still remained very influential, even though out of the government. After the November coup, when Khuang formed a new government, the Democrat Party became an official party, and expanded rapidly. But after the *coup de main* which overthrew Khuang on April 6, 1948, the Democrat Party virtually disappeared. When parties were revived in 1955, the old faithfuls of the Democrat Party began to play the role of an opposition party.

Tracing the history of the official parties, we recall that the People's Party played this role, though briefly, in 1932 and 1934. Party activities were subsequently suppressed until after the war, when the Constitution Front emerged as the official party. Following the November coup in 1947, the Democrat Party served briefly, under the watchful eyes of a restless military junta, as the official party. Following the coup of April, 1948, the Phibun-supporting United Parties became the official party. Phibun himself is reported to have started a small opposition party, the *Tharmathipat*, in March, 1947, which formed the nucleus later for the United Parties.

When parties were suppressed after the "silent coup" in November, 1951, the Phibun leadership was displaced by the Phao group. In forming the Legislative Study Committee, Phao established a *de facto* official party which tolerated no opposition groups. However, in 1955 this monopolistic position became untenable, and, as parties became legal once more, the Committee was renamed the *Seri Manangkhasila* as an avowed official party.

During this period, the Unionist Party arose as a factional party, following Sarit, chief rival to Phao. When Sarit overthrew Phao in September, 1957, the *Seri Manangkhasila* immediately collapsed, and after the elections of December, 1957, the National Socialist Party came into existence as the official party.[15] This election well illustrates the dynamics of the Thai political process and accordingly is described below as a case study.

DECEMBER, 1957: CASE STUDY OF AN ELECTION

We have already seen that, following the flight of Phao and Phibun, the *Seri Manangkhasila* collapsed. There was, clearly, no grass roots organization to maintain the adherence of politicians whose membership was directly based on the attractions of good standing in an official party. Such attractions, obviously, could no longer be provided by an ousted leadership.

One might have expected, under these circumstances, that the defectors from the *Seri Manangkhasila* would have flocked to Sarit's Unionist Party, the presumed basis of a new official party. However, as indicated above, the Thai parties were unable to help candidates win elections, nor did they provide significant ideological or policy platforms by which to discriminate between supporters and opponents. Perhaps more important, from the viewpoint of Sarit or any ruling group, if most elected assemblymen are at heart independents, regardless of party label, then the real interest of the leader is not in candidates for election but only in those who succeed in getting elected. If the leader's power is already assured, his position does not depend on securing the election of his supporters or of members of his organization.

In accordance with this view, Sarit neither supported the Unionists nor formed a new party during the ninety-day period of electoral campaigns. The election results are revealing. A total of 160 seats were contested. The returns were as follows:

Independents and small personal "parties"	69
Unionists	40
Democrats	39
Socialist Front	12
Total	160

In terms of normal conceptions about political parties and parliamentary systems, one might imagine that an opposition coalition of Democrats and Socialist Front candidates would secure enough allies among the independents to overthrow the government and set up a new one. Nothing, of course, was farther from the realm of possibility. Many of the independents—an estimated thirty-seven, in fact—were former members of the *Seri Manangkhasila.* Some, indeed, had even used this party label in advertising themselves to their constituents even though the party had folded up! They were clearly available to Sarit.

Two days *after* the election, press reports appeared that a new political party would be formed by combining the Unionist group with the former *Seri Manangkhasila* Party members who had campaigned as independents. On December 18, three days after the election, Sarit held a long meeting with the newly elected members of the Unionist Party. The factional party was about to be converted into an official party. On the 20th, the new party, to be headed by Field Marshal Sarit, was formally announced. A spokesman for the group, which was to be called the National Socialist Party, proclaimed that it would stand for "nation, religion, King, democracy and society." [16] Virtually all the second-category assemblymen could be counted on to vote for the new party. There was some confusion about other groups. The *Bangkok Post* carried a report on the same day that the Socialist Front "may be able and willing to co-operate with the new National Socialist Party." However, Khuang declared on the 23rd that he would lead his Democrat Party members as the "chief opposition" to the National Socialists, who, he expected, would control two hundred seats.

Since at that time there were 121 appointed M.P.'s and 160 elected, or a total of 281, Khuang must have been calculating that Sarit would capture the votes of the Unionist and former *Seri Manangkhasila* assemblymen, in addition to the appointed members.

Meanwhile, the leaders of the new party began to formulate a program for the Assembly. On January 7, 1958, it was published as a sixteen-point platform, which began with a declaration of intention to "do everything to promote full happiness of the people, so that this Government will be a genuine government of the people by the people for the people." The second point asserted the government's intention to "uphold democracy under the Constitution of Thailand, uphold the monarchy as an object sacred forever, uphold Buddhism as the national religion, and give patronage to other religions which are worshipped by the people." Remaining points dealt somewhat more specifically with policies to be applied in several fields of government policy, ending with the affirmation, in point sixteen, that the party "believes that capability, efficiency and integrity of officials are necessary for good administration, and will try to achieve this." [17]

On January 9, the Assembly, after a heated debate, endorsed the new National Socialist government of Prime Minister Thanom Kitikhachorn by a vote of 162 to 40. Only the Democrats and a few independents voted against the government. The Socialist Front members abstained. A total of 79 did not vote.[18]

An analysis of the strength of the National Socialists published later in January showed that it was not formed simply by the amalgamation of earlier parties, for there were some members of the parties which joined who refused to go along, and there were other individuals in parties which chose to remain in opposition who decided to break with their former colleagues. According to this account, some members of the opposition parties, especially the "Free Democrats," had decided to defect in favor of the National Socialists. However, we are told, "they do not welcome too much publicity on their defection from the parties under which they sought and won election, and will only gradually admit to the public their membership in the National Socialist Party."

By contrast, the same item reports that several members (from four to seven) of the Unionist Party had decided to leave the National Socialists, ostensibly because they did not want to be associated with former *Seri Manangkhasila* Party men.

Calculating these additional, and somewhat problematic, changes in party allegiance, the report concluded that the National Socialists would command a total of 212 seats in the 283-member Assembly, including 90 elected members and 122 appointed members. The only nonconformist among the second-category members was old Field Marshal Phin Chunnahawan, former minister of agriculture, father-in-law of General Phao, and central figure of the clique which had been overthrown by the Military Group the previous September![19]

PARTY "LEADERSHIP"

In the normal political system, one might assume that the leadership of a major parliamentary party would be considered not only an honor but also an opportunity to enhance one's power and influence. On the assumptions made here, namely, that the real source of power was control over bureaucratic machinery, especially in the armed forces, the leadership of the official party could become a thankless chore. If one assumes that the government could be certain of a majority, then the real task of a party leader would be to help allocate patronage, to cope with unruly members threatening to join opposition groups, and possibly to supply arguments to be used against annoying opponents who refused to join the ranks of the docile majority.

Under Phibun, Phao had managed to make something useful for himself out of the job of party secretary-general. Following this example, Praphas—who replaced Phao as minister of interior in the Thanom government formed on January 1, 1958—was named secretary-general of the new National Socialist Party. Praphas was also vice-premier and had been second in command of the First Army, which was stationed in Bangkok. Clearly, he was an ambitious man and one near the top of the new power structure. On January 6, however, he announced his resignation as secretary-general of the party, offering as his reason the impropriety of his serving concurrently as party leader and minister of interior, "since the job of a Minister of Interior is to ensure clean and just elections and the duty of a party secretary-general is to ensure election of party members. Thanom, the prime minister and deputy party leader, then announced to newsmen that either Lieutenant-General Chitti Nawisathien or Major-General Vichai Pong-anand would probably be named for the leading party post. But four days later it became known that Sarit himself had designated Air Marshal Chalermkiart Watthanangkun, commander-in-chief of the Air Forces, to be secretary-general. When asked by reporters, Chalermkiart said that he would "have to accept the post" if the Supreme Commander insisted.[20] Chalermkiart had held a cabinet post as deputy minister of communications in the last Phibun cabinet, but he was not even a member of Thanom's cabinet, although he had been a promoter of both the 1947 and 1957 coups.

CONCLUSION

In February, on the eve of by-elections for some additional assembly seats, Praphas, who was then identified as "third deputy leader of the Government National Socialist Party," announced that, as minister of interior, he intended to "keep the coming by-elections clean, regardless of political parties." He promised there would be no prejudice in favor of the NSP. On our assumptions, he could not really have cared much who won in each district.

It is difficult to discover how the "average" voter in Thailand felt about all these developments, which were fully described in the local press. But it may be worth referring to a statement by the Undersecretary of Interior on December 17, two days after the December election, to the effect that about 30 per cent of the eligible voters had turned up at the polls. He stated that in no election in Thailand had the turnout exceeded 40 per cent of the eligible electorate, and in most elections the figure had been considerably lower than 30 per cent. However, he declined to compare the turnout with that in the February, 1957, election in which irregularities were alleged. These included the use of "fire-cards" (illegal voting cards) and "paratroopers" (persons not on the eligible lists casting votes).[21]

The effectiveness of an electoral system can scarcely be judged by the percentage of eligible voters who cast their ballots. After all, the highest percentages are normally achieved in totalitarian systems where the voters have little or no choice among candidates. In the typical Thai constituency they had many names to choose among. Siamese elections began to resemble a fiesta or gala social event. No doubt some local political ends were achieved also, and the M.P.'s who exerted themselves and used their private resources to win an election must have found the honor and perquisites of office rewarding. Given the extent to which the outcome of individual elections made little difference in the Bangkok power struggle, it is scarcely surprising that the electoral procedures—with some exceptions, as in the February, 1957, case—were models of decorum and fair play.

But virtuosity at the polling places means little if it is not combined with a party and parliamentary system in which real power is mobilized outside the state bureaucracy. In the Siamese case, such power failed to develop, except to a limited degree during the immediate postwar years.

The Military Group coup in 1957 was atypical in that its guiding spirit was a sick man who had to go abroad for medical treatment shortly after his conquest of power, leaving the government in the hands of one of his lieutenants, Thanom. When he returned in the fall of 1958, he was dissatisfied with the state of affairs and on October 20, 1958, carried out a second coup. The 1952 (1932) constitution was again suspended, this time for good. Parliament was abolished and so was the cabinet. The Military Group, under Sarit's direction, began to rule directly. On January 29, 1959, however, another provisional constitution was proclaimed providing for a new constituent assembly of 240 appointed members to be selected by the ruling group. This assembly convened on February 5, and was authorized to act as a parliament pending its successful drafting of another "permanent" constitution. Meanwhile a new cabinet, under the premiership of Sarit himself, was set up on February 10, with nine civilian and five military career officials as members.

Thailand's experiments with constitutional government have been treated by many observers as a kind of comic-opera performance. They deserve much more serious analysis. The tendency has been to view the sucession of constitutional charters, parliaments, political parties, and elections as a meaningless charade in which the military politicians and the civilians have simply alternated with each other in control of a rubber-stamp government.

The underlying issues were far more important. In 1932, a group of bureaucratic and quasi-bureaucratic reformers combined to oust an absolute monarchy in the name of constitutionalism, of limited monarchy, and of democracy. Having little understanding of the prerequisites for effective political control over a well-organized state bureaucracy, they tried by fiat to institute parliamentary and party government. Both the People's Party and the parliamentary system proved unable to control the dynamism of intrabureaucratic conflict which broke out as the monarchic control system was dislodged.

The disruptions of World War II and the consequent disgrace and demotion of leading officials who had previously come to the fore provided a new opportunity for Pridi, Khuang, and other civilian politicians to lay a new political foundation for popular and constitutional government. They made a promising start in grasping this opportunity, but internal dissensions, increasing corruption and mismanagement, and the rising dissatisfaction of ambitious military officers, brought an end to their experiment. Step by step the bureaucracy reinstated its full control. In the process, one bureaucratic clique struggled against another, setting in motion a pattern of intrabureaucratic politics which had become the dominant style of Siamese politics by the time the decade of the sixties had begun.

CHAPTER VII

The Effort to Impose Accountability: Local Government

The revolution of 1932, as we have seen in the previous chapter, was marked by an effort—largely abortive—to replace the absolute monarchy as the control center of a proliferating bureaucracy by new, constitutional organs of democratic government. In practice, high officials, both military and civil, became the real rulers of the country. It would be a mistake, however, to think that the effort to impose accountability on the state bureaucracy was limited to the central government. Concurrently, a variety of efforts were made to create new organs of local self-government which would guide and correct the officials appointed to serve in provinces and districts throughout the country.

With some exceptions, the efforts to impose accountability through elected councils, boards, and rural officials proved disappointing. For the most part, indeed, the bureaucrats were able to control elected representatives and officers more effectively than the people's spokesmen could control career officials. The main struggle, as in the central government, turned into a contest between various levels and types of bureaucrats in the field offices of central government departments. But this intrabureaucratic arena did provide some levers for imposing accountability in local government. We will, therefore, in this chapter, take a look at both electoral and intrabureaucratic mechanisms and experiments designed to bring local officials under control.

It can be shown that in most "advanced" countries there are institutions of local self-government which help to shape public policy, which often have their own administrative staffs or sub-bureaucracies, and which are able to impose some controls on field officers of the national bureaucracy. These institutions of representative government, however, form part of a larger matrix of organized political action, typically including local chapters of political parties which offer candidates in national as well as local elections and help to shape public policies. This larger matrix also includes a complex fabric of private companies, trade unions, farmers' associations, professional societies, independent newspapers, universities, and schools, all of which help to articulate and aggregate public interests, to set goals, and to impose sanctions on the civil services.

For the most part, such institutions of public participation in the political process have not become strong in Thailand, although they have been formally created—largely by fiat of central bureaucratic authorities—in an attempt to produce by intervention from above what failed to grow spontaneously from below. It should be recognized that the expedient interest of central officials is not necessarily in conflict with local organs of self-government, at least not to the extent that it is with central organs. Sometimes national officials suppose that local representative bodies will absorb the restless energies of dissatisfied elements and divert their attention from efforts to bring the central government under popular control. Office-holders who accept, in principle, the ultimate goal of democratic responsibility may also consider that a population as yet unready to exercise power ought to gain experience in political action at the relatively safe level of village, municipal, and district councils.

A more convincing argument for local self-government under bureaucratic or autocratic central government can be based on the costs of development and the exigencies of intrabureaucratic struggle. If the leadership of the national government has accepted some goals of development—such as the establishment of schools and the construction of rural roads—then it may see local self-government as a convenient way of passing to someone else the responsibility for financing and administering these programs.

Perhaps equally important, but less publicized, is the difficulty faced by any central bureaucracy in maintaining control over its field officials in distant localities. The situation which confronted Prince Damrong as he started to build the central apparatus of the Ministry of Interior has already been discussed. It may well be that central officials, seeking to bring their own subordinates under effective control, think of representative bodies at local levels as their allies. Moreover, such bodies might impose discipline and maintain standards of conduct and efficiency which the headquarters offices could not themselves secure. Headquarters may also hope that local officials, who might be tempted to assert their independence of central authority, would turn to the capital for support when pressed by representative bodies, and so would become more amenable to discipline from above.

Whatever the considerations might be that influenced their actions, the fact is that central officials who strongly oppose the creation of effective instrumentalities of popular control over their actions frequently give support to efforts to strengthen institutions of local self-government. This phenomenon has occurred in many colonial regimes. It arose also under the absolute monarchy in Siam, at the time when the last thing the rulers wanted was to bring their own authority under effective constitutional and parliamentary restraints.[1]

The first efforts to establish local self-government in Thailand were actually made under the absolute monarchy, long before the revolution of 1932. As early as 1905, an experiment in local self-government was launched with the creation of a *sukahpibahn,* or "sanitation district," in a commune of *Samud Sakorn* province, a short distance southwest of Bangkok. Provision was made for the creation of a board all of whose members were appointed ex officio, namely, the village headmen with the commune headman as chairman. (A number of villages or *mu ban* constitute a commune or *tambon,* whose head is chosen from among the headmen of the constituent villages.) This board was authorized to collect certain taxes, largely on houses and building construction, to be used for the maintenance of local public works, such as roads, bridges, and lights, and to enforce local sanitation rules in a congested coastal fishing area.[2]

In 1908 and again in 1915, new acts were promulgated expanding the powers of the *sukahpibahn,* providing that similar boards could be established elsewhere on the recommendation of the provincial governor and the *monthon* (region) head. By the time of the revolution, it is estimated that there were some forty-five *sukahpibahn.*[3]

According to an act promulgated in 1914, qualified voters in each village were authorized to elect their own headman, but the district officer presided over the election. The headmen of all the villages in a commune in turn chose one of their number to be the *tambon* head. Although, in this manner, the rural population was introduced to some of the forms of local self-government, it may be doubted that they experienced much of its reality. Choop points out that the *sukahpibahn,* commune, and village institutions at that time were "always controlled by the central government officials."[4]

LOCAL SELF-GOVERNMENT UNDER THE CONSTITUTIONAL MONARCHY

After the revolution of 1932, more serious and sustained efforts were made to launch a system of effective local self-government. As soon as the promoters of the revolution had seized power in 1932, they publicly announced their devotion to the principles of democratic constitutional government, which was interpreted to mean local self-government as well as representative institutions in national government. At the same time that they were setting up a national assembly, therefore, and planning to democratize the legislative process on the basis of national elections, they were also considering ways to institute local representative processes.

The thinking of the promoters, however, was colored by a deep ambivalence. Although the population at large was formally regarded as the legitimate and ultimate source of sovereignty—an idea which was necessary to justify the attack upon the absolutism of a sacred throne—in practice, it was considered impossible to turn real power over to the people or their elected representatives. Consequently, as we have seen, the National Assembly was set up on an appointive basis to start with, and the principle of military conquest, to be followed by party tutelage, was incorporated in the Provisional Constitution.

The ultimate stage of full popular sovereignty was to be reached by a gradual process of political education in which the choice of representatives by indirect elections was to be used—an idea which Sun Yat Sen had espoused a decade before. According to this idea, which was written into the Provisional Constitution, the village folk would choose representatives, who would then meet in electoral colleges at the district level to choose provincial assemblies; these, in turn, would name members of the National Assembly. These local elections would be limited in function to the selection of national assemblymen, but, potentially at least, they would lay the foundation for a system of local self-government.

The support of the founders, therefore, for the principle of local self-government was inhibited by reservations regarding its practicability, as manifested in sharp limitations on the mode of elections and the scope of power exercised by elected representatives.

Doctrinaire arguments for local self-government were no doubt supplemented, in the minds of central officials (who may still, at heart, have espoused old principles of royal authoritarianism) by the view that the bureaucratic authority of the central government ought to be extended more deeply into rural districts and urban wards, and that some forms of carefully controlled local self-government would serve this purpose. By mobilizing the population for political participation and securing their involvement in programs intended to improve their own welfare, centrally designed programs and goals could be accomplished with lower cost and without seriously compromising the power of the national officials themselves. Accordingly, we find the theme of administrative effectiveness often mixed with the ideal of popular sovereignty in arguments for enhanced local self-government.

A further paradox might be pointed out in this connection. The original tutelage idea, as it was shaped in the Russian and Chinese contexts, envisioned a political organization—the party—as chief guide in the process of mobilization. The party was not only to run the central government; it was also to help the people take the first steps of their political education by nominating candidates for public office and supervising the work of local soviets or councils. However, in the Siamese case, as we have seen, the People's Party turned out to be little more than a short-lived association of promoters of the revolution, without organizational roots in the countryside.

This actually meant that if someone were to play the tutorial role, to help the people gain political experience and to supervise elected bodies, it would have to be officials of the central bureaucracy. Let us make a schematic comparison between three types of systems, as follows:

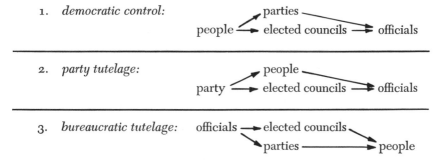

1. *democratic control:* parties / people → elected councils → officials

2. *party tutelage:* people / party → elected councils → officials

3. *bureaucratic tutelage:* officials → elected councils / parties → people

Under the *democratic concept,* the people, choosing among candidates presented by autonomous political parties, elect councils which choose goals, impose taxes, and control officials who carry out these directives. Under the *party tutelage* theory, where the people are not capable of self-activation in this fashion, the party chooses candidates which the people legitimize by casting ballots to elect the single party's nominees; then the party guides the elected councils as they go through the motions of adopting rules which the party, again, enforces by its ability to control the officials. In both these models, the officials are brought under control, either by the people acting through the representatives of their choice, or by the party acting in the name of the people.

What happens under the third model, where the tutelage role is assumed by officials who are themselves supposed, ideally, to be controlled by the elected representatives? One would have to attribute to bureaucrats superhuman qualities of altruism and self-abnegation to assume that, when asked to set up the means of curtailing their own power, they would actually carry out this act of political suicide. It seems more likely that they would try to abolish the electoral procedures as a threat to their self-interests, or bring them under their own control. If they were under compulsion from higher officials to go through with the ritual, then they might comply with the required procedures but, in practice, prevent the elected representatives from gaining effective power. A third possibility must also be considered. Having mastered the technique of controlling the polls and manipulating councilmen, officials might discover that formally elected representatives of the people could actually serve a useful purpose as agents of the administration. In other words, in actual practice, bureaucrats might learn to use official parties and elected councils to control the people. Such a system could be called *bureaucratic tutelage.*

The political history of Thailand, as has already been indicated in our examination of its kaleidoscopic constitutional development, is so complicated that simple generalizations are usually wrong. The development of local government is also difficult to characterize in a few words. Certainly, all the possibilities outlined above have manifested themselves at various times. A historical approach, distinguishing between periods and levels, will provide a framework for preliminary analysis and possibly for the drawing of some general conclusions.

Let us first examine some tendencies of the prewar years, distinguishing what happened at the level of municipal or urban government from developments in the field of territorial or provincial government.

THE PREWAR PERIOD: THE PROMISE OF AUTONOMY

Municipal Government. It has perhaps been normal in Western countries for self-government to find its most vital expression in the autonomy of municipalities. The long history of free cities provides abundant evidence of the ability of urban populations, crowded together and increasingly interdependent, to create mechanisms for their own self-government. It is characteristic of the Siamese pattern of political development, however, that the initiative for municipal self-government did not come from within the cities but from central officials of the absolute monarchy.

The establishment of the sanitation districts (*sukahpibahn*) as early as 1905 has already been mentioned. In 1930, the Ministry of Interior set up a committee headed by a prince, Sakonwanakorn Warawan, which was charged with responsibility for drafting a law on municipal government. This committee had already made considerable progress by 1932. Shortly after coming to power, the revolutionary government decided to continue this work and asked Prince Sakonwanakorn to serve as adviser to implement many of the proposals which he had made earlier.[5]

However, Pridi's concepts as reflected in the Provisional Constitution also helped shape the law on municipal government. In both central and municipal government, "the procedures of holding meetings, questioning, debate, and even the vote of confidence were identical." The governor was to name the mayor, who would choose his executive committee (cabinet), subject to endorsement by the elected council (assembly), just as the king appointed the prime minister and Supreme Council subject to Assembly approval.[6] In practice, however, a major difference appeared at this very point: whereas the appointive powers of the king became purely ceremonial, the appointive power of the governor became increasingly effective.

A law authorizing the creation of municipal governments was promulgated by the National Assembly in 1933. Under this law, cities (*nakorn*) with populations of more than 30,000 persons were to enjoy full municipal government; towns (*muang*) having populations between 5,000 and 30,000, and the seats of provincial governments, were to enjoy a more limited form of town government; and communes (*tambon*) were to have even more limited powers, if so authorized by the Ministry of Interior. By the time the war broke out, three city governments (Bangkok, Thonburi, and Chiengmai) were reported to have city governments, and there were 82 towns and 33 communes with municipal self-government.[7]

The system of municipal self-government did not work well, although it clearly represented a genuine effort to delegate real power to representative bodies. The difficulties experienced at this time have been attributed to the unwillingness or inability of the government to provide the needed support and positive assistance. Vella remarks that "the government was . . . disinclined to give adequate financial support to the councils or to implement fully the democratic provisions of the act. The remarks of two different ministers in 1937 illustrate the government's token implementation of the act. The Minister of the Interior announced that at least one self-governing unit had been created in every province. The Minister of Finance admitted, however, that the budget for these units would be limited because they were not yet ready to take over all their prescribed functions and the government was not yet prepared to hand them over." [8]

Virginia Thompson writes of the elected municipal councils:

Their dependence on loans to supplement their meager revenues kept these assemblies in a state of subservience to the central and provincial governments, and little or nothing was done to help them with long-term planning or train them in efficient methods of municipal administration. [9]

Nevertheless, despite its limitations, this early period of municipal self-government was a period of experimentation and even of vigor. The law did give the elected municipal councils some real authority, which they were eager to use. For example, by rejecting the annual budget or a major ordinance, a council could compel the mayor and his executive committee (or cabinet) to resign. It is apparent that just as members of the National Assembly at first confidently expected that they would be able to exercise real influence over the government, so the elected municipal councilors thought that they would be able to control the city administration.

But popular control over government requires the slow growth of requisites which were scarcely present in the Siamese setting. Local economic resources were inadequate, and the tax base authorized for municipal governments quite limited. The Ministry of Interior had the right to supervise municipal finances and was unable or unwilling to provide needed subventions. Without a base of experience with political parties and organized private groups, without an assimilated commercial and professional middle class, it was probably inevitable that the municipal assemblies should be poorly equipped for the exercise of their new responsibilities. After all, even in the most developed countries municipal self-government is often characterized by gross inefficiency, corruption, and conflict.

The result, in the Thai case, is described by Blanchard as follows:

The governments of the larger municipalities, especially Bangkok and Thon Buri, were travesties of honest and competent urban administration. Assemblymen bickered over small matters or plotted against the mayor; assembly meetings were often boycotted or broken up by incessant wranglings. Mayors came and went with great frequency; some were ousted by their assemblies, others had to leave on charges of incompetence or corruption. Councilors were often incompetent, and the administrative services were over-staffed and poorly run. Corruption pervaded the entire system. The central government sometimes intervened with a heavy hand; thus the Minister of the Interior ousted Bangkok's last elected mayor without even observing the formality of preferring charges against him.[10]

Lacking real power to control the municipal administration, municipal assemblymen clearly became demoralized, and the public increasingly indifferent. Only a small percentage of the eligible voters took the trouble to participate in municipal elections. The central government, disillusioned with the failure of local self-government, or perhaps reinforced in their conviction that it could not work, began to intervene more and more to bring order out of confusion.

In 1938, the municipal law was amended to require that members of municipal executive committees be chosen from among members of the elected council. The right of the council to adopt votes of no confidence was also withdrawn. Thus, the authority of the councils as legislative bodies to impose their will upon the executive officials was curtailed, while the mayors, although restricted in their choice of key administrators, were encouraged to co-opt members of the councils who would help them keep the elected representatives under control. The Ministry of Interior sought to justify these changes by stating that they would assure "full cooperative effort between the municipal council and the executive committee," resulting in "efficient administration."[11]

More meaningfully, perhaps, the changes enhanced the ability of the central bureaucracy to strengthen its controls over the elected municipal councils. Put inversely, the ability of the electorate to impose accountability upon the executive officials was reduced.

Nevertheless, throughout the prewar period, the elected municipal councils did have some independence, and they often struggled valiantly, if chaotically, for a real voice in the conduct of public affairs. But it was a losing battle. The state bureaucracy and the municipal officials, combining legal and institutional resources with personal manipulation, were able gradually to subdue and render powerless the municipal councils. Choop compares the municipal with the national political situation in these terms:

> The executive committee had the same kind of stability as that of the cabinet of the national government. It was dependent upon the ability and personality of the executive committee members to maintain control of the majority of members in the council; otherwise, the council members could request the Minister of the Interior to investigate the executive committee.[12]

The over-all significance of the changes of 1938 and later is summarized by Choop as reflecting a shift in emphasis from "political education" to "efficient administration." In other words, from being an experiment in local self-government designed to impose popular controls over public administrators and to stimulate the growth of democratic political institutions, municipal government came to be seen as an inexpensive way of extending the range of bureaucratic control within the municipalities.

Provincial Government.   The Municipal Government Act of 1933 also provided for the establishment of provincial councils or assemblies (the two words are used here as synonyms). However, they were not intended to serve as organs of self-government, as were the municipal assemblies. Rather, the expectation seems to have been that they would provide a body of leading citizens to advise the governor in the performance of his duties. The law specified various criteria, such as geographic and professional representativeness and minimum standards of age, education, and orientation. Candidates were to be nominated by the governor and appointed officially by the Minister of Interior. The governor himself would preside over meetings of the council and, presumably, set its agenda.

It was expected that eventually at least half of the members of this advisory council would be elected. However, in 1938, a new provincial council act, entirely separate from the municipality legislation, provided for the councils to be fully elected. Thus, whereas the municipal councils were being curtailed in power, the provincial councils were being enhanced. Their main functions were to include consultation with the governor, endorsement of the provincial budget submitted by the governor, and advising the central government upon request. However, virtually no provision was made for provincial revenues, so that the provincial government was fully dependent on central government appropriations. "As a result," Choop writes, "the council never per-formed any real function of local self-government nor exercised admin-istrative or legislative power." [13]

Horrigan reached the same conclusion about the provincial coun-cils. Their lack of formal authority and separate tax resources meant that "they were dominated by the provincial governor." Few members of the public even bothered to vote for the council members. Electoral frauds were widely reported. After the Japanese came, interest in the provincial councils further declined, and no provincial elections were held after 1943.[14]

THE POSTWAR PERIOD: THE FACSIMILE OF DECENTRALIZATION

Throughout the war and the first years thereafter, conditions in municipal self-government continued to deteriorate. Finally, in January, 1953, a municipal reform act was adopted which brought urban gov-ernments directly under the administrative control of the central bu-reaucracy through their governors and district officers. The elected city councils were to be continued, but their powers were reduced to the vanishing point. Mayors and their executive committees were to be appointed by governors, and the equivalent functionaries of commune authorities were to be designated by the district officers. The municipal councils could be dissolved at any time by the provincial governors. Moreover, half of their members were to be appointed and only half elected, following the example set by the constitution of 1932 in or-ganizing the National Assembly. As poor compensation for these losses, the municipalities were promised new revenue sources and greater financial autonomy—a promise that was not kept.[15]

By 1953, in other words, the effort which seemed to have begun with such bold promise in 1932 to create at the local government level effective centers of popular autonomy capable of imposing responsi-bility on administrative officials had petered out, and the long arms of the central bureaucracy, working through the Ministry of the Interior, had gained effective control. It should also be noted that the municipal officials were themselves supposedly independent of the central gov-ernment's career bureaucracy, being chosen by and directly responsible to the elected councils. Moreover, since they were local men, not sub-ject to rotation between territorial assignments, as were the provincial and district officials, the central government always faced the possi-bility that these administrators would become locally entrenched city bosses. From this point of view, the frequent displacement of mayors by elected councils may have been viewed as a safeguard. With the extension of effective territorial controls through the career officials of the Ministry of Interior, however, it became possible to bring the city administrators directly under the domination of the governors and district officers. At this point, the intervention of city councils came to be regarded as more of a nuisance than an asset, and the Municipal Reform Act of 1953 gave formal sanction to the triumph of bureaucratic power.

Against the background of this victory for the officials, it may seem strange that a new movement for local self-government and "decentralization" should have been launched in 1955, at a time when military and civil officers were in firm control of the government. The paradox becomes even more astonishing when we realize that the movement for local government originated within the very stronghold of bureaucratic rule, namely, in the Ministry of Interior.

On April 11, 1955, General Phao offered a memorandum to Prime Minister Phibun. He began by noting that the "Revolutionary Party" in 1932 had intended to set up "a free democratic form of government on the pattern of several other civilized nations." He claimed that "the Central Government manages affairs through the Ministries, Bureaus, and Departments with the Ministers concerned as the Chief Administrators, under the policy direction of the Council of Ministers and with the Prime Minister taking responsibility as the Head." As a result, he wrote:

Central Government administration has fully conformed with the pattern set by foreign countries, while government in the provinces is still backward. Preliminary steps have been taken to set up municipal governments, but they are few in number, and not much attention has been given to the Changwad, which is an important tool of provincial government.

Regarding the *changwad* councils, Phao pointed out that they were composed of elected members, but they had the power "to act merely as advisors in administrative affairs." "Government in the provinces," he concluded, "has therefore not really developed to the extent desired by the Revolutionary Party." [16]

To rectify this situation, Phao proposed a three-point program. First, the *changwad* governors should have two recognized roles. As before, they were to be the field agents of the Ministry of Interior for local administration. But the *changwad* should also be recognized as a legally autonomous unit of government, under the policy direction of the *Changwad* Council, with the governor serving as its executive officer. This system, in Phao's view, would be like that of the county in American government!

The second step in Phao's program called for the authorization of three patterns of municipal government, based on American practice—the mayor-council, commissioner, and city manager forms—which might be chosen by Thai municipalities when they reached appropriate stages of development. Meanwhile, elected committees with limited powers could be established to help pave the way to more self-government.

The third step proposed by Phao seemed a truly radical conception for the Thai polity. When the local units of self-government were ready, he suggested that field officials of central agencies would then be transferred to local government, which would pay their salaries, subject to standard rules laid down by the central government. To finance such a transformation, appropriate revisions in the tax structure would be necessary, granting local government units their own revenue sources.

Phao suggested that the development of such a system would entail the creation of local political parties. He went on to say:

I am of the opinion that we should take an opportunity to link them [local parties] with the state political parties, as today it can be more or less taken that the Government is supported by a political party. The political parties which will be formed in the various localities should be organized as parts of the political party which supports the present government in power through the fact that we shall take initial steps to set them up. If the Government does not take steps to establish links with political parties, the administration of affairs according to the policy of the Government may not be in conjunction with that of the localities.

Phao visualized completion of the first step within the following two years, and the second and third steps by the end of seven years, i.e., by 1962. He noted that his proposals called for "a big and sweeping change in the system of provincial government in Thailand," but he added that he thought this was necessary "to relieve the Government of some of the burden of responsibility by training the people to realize their responsibility and allowing them to take a share in the administration, which is the objective of a perfectly free democracy."[17]

Significance. When interpreting this document, we shall do well not to assume that Phao had suddenly undergone a conversion process, that he had been transformed from an arch-bureaucrat intent on building his political machine to a progressive reformer demanding that power be turned over to the sovereign people and their representatives. We must remember that he was at that time director-general of the Police Department and deputy minister of interior. He had joined Phibun in the coup of 1947, which brought the military officers back into power, and had himself led the "silent coup" of November, 1951, which made him a leading protagonist in the political arena. Moreover, he was the secretary-general of the *Seri Manangkhasila,* the official party of the day. To make sense out of Phao's memorandum, we must reconcile it with his own interests in the various positions he held at that time.

We must also take into account an intrabureaucratic struggle which had been going on for some time, a struggle which will be described in more detail below. Here it is enough to mention that in 1952 there had been enacted an administration of the kingdom act which greatly enhanced the power of the *changwad* governors in their continuing struggle with the provincial officials of the specialized program departments. Although this act reinforced the power of the Ministry of Interior in relation to the other ministries, it by no means gave Phao's followers decisive supremacy. The other ministers and leaders of rival factions in the ruling circle were alert for opportunities to curb the rising power of General Phao and his clique. We should recall that it was not much more than two years later, in 1957, that Sarit's group drove Phao from the country. His position was, indeed, far from secure!

A third factor to be taken into consideration is the apparent change of posture which Phibun himself adopted early in 1955 following his return from a world tour. For whatever complex of reasons, Phibun at this time declared himself a firm believer in democracy and launched several measures designed to strengthen democratic tendencies in Thailand.

Viewed from this perspective, we can immediately see a number of ways in which the changes proposed by Phao would consolidate the growing power which his ministry had begun to gain under the newly fashionable slogans of democracy and decentralization. First, it will be seen that Phao did not actually propose any changes which would really enhance the power position of the *changwad* councils, despite the fact that he recommended the governors be recognized as the executive officers of the councils, which would shape provincial policies. We must recall the history of the *changwad* councils, how they had been started as groups of appointed advisers, and then became elected advisers, but had always remained under the easy domination of the governors. It would be surprising if Phao had imagined that the *changwad* councils would now suddenly assert their independence and bring the governors under their control. More probably, he assumed that the governors would easily continue to manipulate the councils, inducing them to adopt policies as readily as the national government obtained legitimation of its actions by the National Assembly.

If the governors already had this power, then why go through the motions of having them manipulate elected councils? The answer is that the real rivals of the governor were not elected representatives but functional specialists of other ministries in the provincial field offices. Although the 1952 act had strengthened the priority of the governor in his struggle with these officials, it by no means assured him effective supremacy. If the governor could also say, in dealing with these officials, that he was acting on behalf of the people's representatives as well as in the role of chief territorial agent of the central government, then his position would be further reinforced.

The use of elected councils by the governors, however, was only part of Phao's grand design. He also wanted to build local political parties linked with the national party. The *Seri Manangkhasila,* as an official party, would be expanded into a mass party having local branches in every province. Candidates for the Assembly would not, then, be independents—as they had previously been, despite their party labels—but would be effectively controlled and nominated as candidates of a national party machine. Since he controlled that machine, he must have considered that the expansion of the *Seri Manangkhasila* into a mass party would improve his own position in relation to his bureaucratic rivals.

If his scheme succeeded, he would be able to dominate the election of members for the *changwad* councils. Thus, his control over the governors, which he already exercised through the Ministry of Interior, would have been reinforced by supplementary controls imposed through the machinery of his official party.

Phao's memorandum, it will be recalled, proposed also that municipal governments be reorganized, by gradual stages, to approximate his image of the American system. This was designed not only to appeal to Phibun's current pro-American mood, but, in addition, to strengthen the Ministry of Interior in another way. The governors, as we have already seen, had secured by the municipal legislation of 1953 effective control over the appointment of mayors and their executive committees. No doubt Phao imagined that, as his official party succeeded, step by step, in creating effective local branches, the municipal councils could be controlled and their policies co-ordinated with those of the mayors, who were already under control by the governors. At the same time, by getting cities to assume a larger share of their own financial burdens, pressure on the central government for subventions would be alleviated.

Far from being a scheme to strengthen "democracy" and "decentralization" in Thai politics, Phao's proposal was a cleverly designed stratagem for strengthening the power of the Ministry of Interior and the *Seri Manangkhasila* Party, both of which Phao himself dominated.

Implementation.   Phao's major allies were to be the *changwad* governors. In 1953, at their national conference, the governors had asked for an increase in the decision-making authority of provincial governments, although they did not then mention the desirability of strengthening elected councils as vehicles for exercising popular control over these governments.

The following year, however, the governors laid a foundation for Phao's plan. Perhaps he had already given them some clues to his own thinking. At any rate, they urged that the "provincial assembly should be made an organ for controlling the administration of public affairs of the *Changwad* within the scope of its powers and duties, and not merely an advisory body to the executive officials."[18]

The *Changwad* Administration Act of 1955 provided for the strengthening of the role of the councils, but it also gave the governors a sharp weapon for keeping them under control. Half of their members were to be appointed, half elected. The pattern adopted in 1932 for the National Assembly, and for municipal councils in 1953, was now extended to the provincial councils.

By 1956, the governors must have gained confidence in their ability to get along with the elected councilmen, for, at their national conference, they adopted a resolution proposing that all councilors be elected. Shortly thereafter, the law was amended to provide that provincial councils should consist of at least twenty-four members, elected for five-year terms. Municipal councils were also to become all elective.[19]

The governors had learned that they could, indeed, control the councils. They were armed, for example, with authority sufficient to nullify any acts they disapproved of. Decisions of the assemblies were classified into "bylaws" and "other actions." The governor could cancel any of the "other actions" which he considered contrary to national laws, rules, or regulations as "beyond the scope" of the assembly's proper function or as "involving national politics." Moreover, the council could not review any such gubernatorial veto.

In regard to bylaws, the governor could also reject any act of his assembly, but he had to submit it to the Ministry of Interior for review. In effect, the Ministry and its agent, the governor, asserted full authority to veto, without appeal, all acts of the provincial assemblies. Under these rules, why take the precaution of appointing half the members?[20]

Against this background of gubernatorial control, it seemed advantageous to proclaim publicly the formal authority of the councils. In July, 1955, the Ministry of Interior made public an instruction to its governors that they were no longer to regard the councils as purely advisory bodies. Instead, "the governor must abide by the decisions of the assembly, which represent the will of the people in the provinces."[21]

There was clearly in the legislation some intent to give the provincial assemblies effective powers. For example, representatives of the assembly were entitled to sit in on important provincial administrative committees, and assemblymen could at any time raise questions about the provincial administration which might prove embarrassing to the governor. However, the governor and members of his administration were also authorized to attend all of the assembly's official annual one-month sessions. Arsa reaches the conclusion that the governor, "by the high prestige of his office and his personal distinction based on his traditional role as 'king of the province,' can without doubt acquire complete ascendency over the council (assembly), a locally elective body." He adds that "the people in general feel themselves inferior to government bureaucrats and generally are afraid to oppose or tangle with them."[22]

Nevertheless, the authority of individual assemblymen to raise questions to which official written answers must be given was a right which could be used to embarrass and even influence gubernatorial behavior. Hence, one of the tasks which faced every governor was how best to handle the provincial assemblymen, "especially the most obstinate and independent among them." Arsa suggests that the governor's powers over the provincial budget offered him an important weapon. He goes on to say that another method used by governors was to allow councilors "to engage in small business ventures in connection with the service of the Changwad government so that they can derive some private profits." This method was said to be particularly effective because of the very small compensation given the assemblymen for their official work—the equivalent of $1.50 per day for the few days they attended meetings. "Such cooperative and helpful action" by the governors, Arsa notes, "naturally pleases these councillors to a considerable extent, and is accountable for a certain degree of cooperation with the administration."

Arsa goes on to suggest that other officials in the provincial office and the district officers could help the governor to a considerable extent by establishing close personal relations with the elected assemblymen, which no doubt helped to "produce a degree of genial cooperation of the provincial council with the executive authority." "The informal and personal approach," Arsa continues, "constitutes the most important means for eliciting cooperation from members of the council." [23]

After reviewing all the evidence, Arsa reaches the following conclusion:

> The formal authority to sanction public servants in the province is kept entirely within the central government and its bureaucracy. The provincial council does not have the right to participate in the exercise of such authority in any manner whatsoever.
>
> The provincial council remains an institution substantially conditioned and overshadowed by the age-old traditions of centralized government and bureaucracy. One aspect of the traditional bureaucratic attitude—that public officials should be subject to the authority of the central government, not the local authority—is still prevalent. [24]

Horrigan, after studying the attempt to create a system of effective provincial assemblies, concludes:

> Changwad self-government is frankly experimental in nature at the present time. The history of the provincial assemblies does not encourage sanguine predictions of future success. The same defects are present now as were noted by observers in the past; inadequate funds, little real power, and bad parliamentary practices. It would be an overstatement to say that the assemblies are generally unpopular and ineffective since in several provinces their record has been good. Nevertheless, the civil servants for the most part consider the assembly to be "a nest of lawyers" who are totally unprepared to make policy. One informant who worked closely with the assembly of a northeastern province compared the members to "frogs under a coconut shell; they have never been anywhere or seen anything." [25]

Municipal Self-Government. As a result of the "decentralization" program of 1955, there was also a revival of interest in municipal self-government and an increase in the number of local governments. By 1958, it was reported that there were, in addition to 71 provincial assemblies, a total of 120 municipal councils in operation, 401 "sanitation districts" with more limited self-governing rights, and 4,475 commune councils. The commune councils had only the most rudimentary powers, but 59 of them had been granted official recognition as local "self-governing bodies."[26]

The precursor of the commune council, it will be recalled, was the sanitation district, which had been started on an experimental basis as early as 1905. In 1952, before the "democratization" movement of 1955, a law was adopted providing for the extension of the scheme, which was supposed to provide a training ground for municipal self-government, just as the municipalities were expected to lay a basis for democratic rule nationally. Each district was to have an elected commission with the district officer serving ex officio, as chairman. Other district officials would also be ex officio members of the commission. The elected members would include the village and commune headmen and four other persons elected directly by the people for this purpose.[27]

Under the "democratization" program, we may assume that the sanitation districts were given more support, but it is clear from their structure that they could scarcely have provided a vehicle for popular control over the district level bureaucracy. At best, they may have opened up some new channels of communication through which to influence these local agents of the central government.

The commune (*tambon*) councils were a direct manifestation of the "democratization" movement, being authorized by law in 1956. The early pattern of municipal government was duplicated on a smaller scale. Each commune was to have an elective council and an appointed executive committee. The council would consist of the village headmen and an extra elected member from each village. The executive committee, under the ex officio chairmanship of the commune headman, included five other men appointed by the district officer, plus the commune doctor and the village headmen ex officio.[28]

Evaluation. Despite this formal extension of the machinery of local autonomy, Choop reaches the conclusion that Thai local self-government has "become part of the hierarchy of the Ministry of the Interior." "All municipal institutions," he writes, as they are imposed by the central government, have no real safeguards for the rights and freedom of local self-government. They are established and attached to the hierarchy of the Ministry of the Interior for the purpose of administrative control.[29]

The control of the governor and the district officer remained sufficiently effective to guarantee that none of the elective bodies, dependent as they were on the national bureaucracy for finance and program execution, would be able to exercise significant controls over the career officials. Horrigan, reviewing the whole history of the "democratization" program, writes:

> Bureaucratic domination of local self-government is inherent in the central government controls over policy, personnel, and finances of the local units and in the strength and influence of the territorial administrators. This by no means implies that the territorial administrators and the central government agree on how the controls should be exercised, nor does it imply a lack of good will by the bureaucracy in many instances. But it is clear that the central government possesses a dominance over local political action that is checked only within the bureaucracy itself by paternalism and inertia. Overt hostility to local government on the part of some provincial governors has been inevitable in view of the role of the bureaucrat as master of the people in traditional society.[30]

This statement reflects a discerning understanding of the present pattern of government in Thailand. The final phrase, however, is troublesome because it suggests a misleading identification between the contemporary Thai polity and that of the "traditional" Siamese system. If the argument presented in this chapter is valid, the traditional system, which no longer exists, differs from the contemporary in that the present-day bureaucracy has drastically extended its control capabilities through functional differentiation of roles, whereas the former regime, however arbitrary and capricious it may have been, was unable to manipulate the behavior of the people in the villages, except for such purposes as tribute payment, *corvée* labor, and military service.

What we see, then, is not the operation of a "traditional" system, but rather the results of a "transitional" situation in which the apparatus of a modern bureaucracy has been created by virtue of a great transformation worked by the "absolute monarchy." However, the countervailing matrix of public action, whereby the interests of the people might have been imposed upon the government in a framework of law and accountability, has not come into being. The efforts of the "constitutional" reformers since 1932 to create such a system have proved abortive.

If public control over bureaucracy has been the unrealized goal of political reform since the revolution of 1932, what has been the character of the political struggle in Thai politics since that time? We have already seen that the failure of the National Assembly and political party system to impose responsibility on the cabinet at the national level resulted in a pattern of bureaucratic politics in the State Council. We can now see that the counterpart to bureaucratic politics in Bangkok is bureaucratic politics in every province and district of Thailand. The failure of formal political institutions to achieve control over the bureaucracy has not meant the elimination of "politics" and the achievement of an "administrative state." Rather, it has meant that the arena of politics, the focus of rivalry, and the struggle for power, wealth, and other public values have moved within the bureaucracy itself.

INTRABUREAUCRATIC POLITICS AND POLITICAL ACCOUNTABILITY

If the effort to impose constraints upon the bureaucracy from outside, through elected councils, has proven a failure, then it might be thought that, nevertheless, the functional equivalent could be exercised from within. Some sections of the state bureaucracy might be set up as watchdogs to supervise the actions of other sections. An auditing agency would check on financial accountability, and a personnel agency on personal responsibility. The Ministry of Interior, through its territorial administrators, would hold the field offices of specialized ministries accountable. Regional offices would check on provincial governors, and the governors in turn would check on the performance of district officers.

Let us then examine the results of intrabureaucratic rivalry within Thai local administration to determine whether or not, by this means, it could perform the functional equivalent of extrabureaucratic institutions in their role of guardians of the public interest. In launching this analysis, we will first identify three types of intrabureaucratic rivalry which no doubt arise in every state bureaucracy organized on the basis of functional specialization.

The first of these problems is a classical issue in the literature of public administration: the difficulty of reconciling the rival claims of *area and function*. The territorial administrator has a natural interest in strengthening his ability to co-ordinate the functional specialists within his area. But the professionals and technicians, for their part, prefer to deal directly with headquarters officials at the next higher level of government, bypassing the territorial generalist administrator. These conflicts at local levels have their counterparts in the center: specialized departments normally support their field agents in seeking to curtail the powers of territorial administrators; and the Ministry of Interior identifies with its governors in their attempt to limit the powers of the special program ministries.

A second type of natural conflict of interest interlaces the first. Viewed from the center, this is the familiar problem of *span of control*. From the localities, however, it is the problem of *access*. In so far as decisions in a bureaucracy are made under hierarchic authority, subordinates must win the approval of superiors to their proposals. Ultimately, this means the hierarchy in the capital, so that intervening supervisory echelons are regarded as a nuisance, for they increase the cost and time required to secure approval of desired actions. The elimination of intervening echelons, however, increases the number of units reporting directly to the center, and so the headquarters administrator may demand regional offices to co-ordinate and control the work of local areas. In Thailand, the creation and abolition of the *monthons*, followed by the creation and abolition of the *paak*, successive regional organizations, reflected a continuing struggle over span of control and access.

A third question which can also become the focus of bureaucratic conflict involves the matter of *line and staff* relationships. Staff or "overhead" organizations arise when some aspect of bureaucratic work is detached from a set of operating units in order to provide unity and coherence through centralized direction. Personnel, finance, public relations, planning—these are familiar fields of staff specialization. In the West, the activities of such staff units are treated as nonauthoritative, as based on the voluntary co-operation of "line" units, or on the role of staff agencies as "advisers" to hierarchic superiors, who then decide whether or not to use this "advice" in their authoritative decisions.

Relationships of the sort indicated above—area and function, span of control, line and staff—arise in Western countries in a context where extrabureaucratic political institutions set the goals, policies, and norms for administrative action. These goals provide sanctions for the resolution of intrabureaucratic conflicts of interest which can, therefore, be reconciled in a reasonable manner. The "science of management" is an attempt to develop guidelines for making decisions in these matters which serve the "public interest" more than the self-interests of bureaucratic protagonists. This is, at best, difficult to achieve, and intrabureau-cratic conflict is ubiquitous. Nevertheless, the tenseness of this struggle can be ameliorated to the extent that extrabureaucratic political insti-tutions and the "public interest" provide standards against which to control bureaucratic behavior, to subject the self-interests of officials to the general welfare, and to override the aspirations of bureaucrats, treating them as "value neutral," as purely instrumental, rather than as intrinsic goals of action.

In Thailand, however, as we have seen, the political instrumentali-ties for asserting public control over the expanded bureaucratic ma-chine have proved abortive. It follows, therefore, that the officials are subject to few sanctions which might compel them to harmonize their "principled interests" as civil servants with their "expediency interests" as protagonists in the usual intrabureaucratic conflicts. Accordingly, the questions of area and function and of span of control can scarcely be transformed into matters of instrumental means. They become ends in themselves.

The question of staff versus line, however, does tend to disappear. "Staff" agencies are at an inherent disadvantage against the "line" in a purely intrabureaucratic struggle. Here a "staff" unit can maintain itself only to the extent that it obtains full authority over its own operations. This means that it must transform itself into a "line" agency, with its own autonomy, without depending on someone else for implementation. Thus, the staff-line problem is resolved by the self-liquidation of staff functions. Any staff agency that limited itself to an "advisory" role would soon find itself rendered impotent by the unwillingness of anyone to heed its advice. Under conditions of intrabureaucratic politics, there-fore, the usual staff-line conflict resolves itself in favor of line agencies, at the expense of anything which might elsewhere be considered a true "staff" function.

But the area-function and span of control conflicts cannot be re-solved in such a simple manner. Both involve rival "line" activities, each with its own base of authority and control.

AREA AND FUNCTION: THE ROLE OF GOVERNOR

Let us examine the area-function question more closely in the Thai setting. We have seen how, in the period of the great transformation, the Ministry of Interior played a decisive role. At the same time, vari-ous aspects of territorial administration—finance, justice, mines, forests, canals—were detached and assigned to parallel departmental structures. In this process, the other ministries and their departments and field officers came to play a more and more powerful role.

The rise of these functional specialists in the bureaucracy had reached its peak by the time of the revolution of 1932. This event, therefore, provided an occasion for significant realignments in the intrabureaucratic distribution of power. We might expect the participants to seize upon the popular slogans of the day to reinforce their aspirations. Thus, we are not surprised to find that in the nineteen-thirties the functional specialists couched their demands in the name of democracy, whereas in the mid-fifties the countercampaign of the territorial generalists to reassert their lost supremacy was also pushed in the name of "democratization."

In 1933, shortly after the abolition of the absolute monarchy, a "committee" system in provincial government was introduced by the Administration of the Kingdom Act of 1933.[31] The presumed "democratic" significance of this change is indicated by Arsa when he writes that it resulted from "the direct influence of democracy, and stemmed from the principle that many heads are better than one." To implement "parliamentary democracy," it was decided to administer the provinces through a board or committee, rather than under one man. Why a committee of appointed officials should be more "democratic" than a single executive officer is not made clear.

The membership of the committee included, besides the governor, the public prosecutor, the police inspector, and officers for finance, revenues, excise, public health, education, land, and co-operatives. Each member was to be individually responsible to his hierarchic superiors in Bangkok for operations within his functional specialty, and collectively the provincial board was to be responsible to the central government as a whole for its administration of the province.

The governor, under this system, was merely the "first among equals." He was to abide by the "democratic decision-making" of his board. The stage was set for a severe struggle for power as the governor tried to salvage what he could of his traditional supremacy, and the newly triumphant functional specialists sought to safeguard and exercise the expanded authority granted them by the revolutionists in Bangkok.[32]

The consequences of this change are described by Arsa in these terms:

. . . because the governor was denied the powers of disciplining and re-warding technical officials, these officials, instead of attempting to cooperate closely for a consensus of agreement in eliciting the decisions of the provincial board, and subordinating their individual views to a common policy, tended to create friction and conflicts among their interests and attitudes. They felt responsible for the performance of their duties to their superiors in the central government, not to the provincial governor.

As a consequence, the provincial governor could not effectively exercise his leadership. This happened not only because the governor lacked the potential power of a chief executive, but also because he had to abide by the decision of the provincial board. Indeed, this was a severe blow to the provincial governor, who by tradition was used to exercising only his authority as the supreme chief executive of his government.[33]

This situation was scarcely conducive to effective administration or to intrabureaucratic peace. A continuing internal struggle characterized the succeeding years. The specialist officials in the governor's office, however unrepresentative in terms of democratic theory, became effective power-holders. The governors could not assure their co-operation as easily as they could bring the members of the elected provincial assembly under their domination. Here, in other words, was a crucial arena of political conflict in the provinces, however detached it might be from extrabureaucratic party and legislative rivalries, the formal "politics" of our conventional models.

The long-run instability of this alignment in which functional specialists had won the upper hand became apparent in 1952, when the governor regained his original role as the effective chief of the province. The Administration of the Kingdom Act of 1952—already referred to above—restored the governor to full authority in provincial affairs, with the right to control "all executive officials" and with full responsibility "for the administration of the government work of all ministries and departments in the province." His earlier title of *Poo Warajakarn Changwad* was restored; "under the new system," the official announcement continued, "the provincial board serves as an advisory body to the governor, and individual unit chief officials assist him in the administration pertaining to the work of their respective departments."[34]

The original slogan for this reversal of policy—designed to restore the Ministry of Interior and the provincial governors to a pivotal role in the intrabureaucratic political arena—was "administrative efficiency," not "democracy." But it was not much later, as we have seen, that the governors, at their meeting in 1954, chose to link their expediency interests to the more popular notion of "democracy." They associated "democratization" with "decentralization," arguing that strengthened provincial government, under the leadership of the governors, would contribute to the growth of Thai democracy. This development was facilitated by a legal innovation. The 1952 act had recognized the *changwad* as a juristic person. It thus acquired the right to own property and set up its own budget apart from the property and budget of the state. By 1955, it was recognized that the dual status of the *changwad* as a unit of field administration and also a juristic person created a concomitant dual role for the governor. A subordinate field official in one role, he became the head of a sub-state in a second role. Phao himself stressed this point in his 1955 memorandum, as noted above. By calling for provincial assemblies and more representative local government, the governors might gain by strengthening the second role. On the assumption that it would be easy to keep the provincial assemblies under control, the governors had little to lose and would improve their position vis-à-vis Bangkok.

The result of these developments since 1952 and 1955 has been to place the governor once more in the driver's seat. But it should not be imagined that the specialist officers accepted this reversal without protest. The maintenance of gubernatorial control against persistent efforts by the functionally specialized departments to reverse the balance remains a focus of intrabureaucratic politics in provincial government.

Arsa remarks that, although the governor is now in "firm control of the provincial board," it cannot be said that he "can autocratically exercise his authority without any 'feed back' from certain technical officials." These officials, he notes, "are directly responsible and answerable for the performance of their work to their superiors in the central government," and they are unlikely to accept the governor's will merely on the grounds of his formal authority.

They are more likely to respect the tangible controls he exercises through his power to discipline and reward his official subordinates. But the maintenance of the governor's supremacy, according to Arsa, "requires other factors, including his capacities, character and personality, as well as the psychological and administrative skills of a leader. . . . In many instances, potential problems have to be solved through means of personal and informal relationships, as called by one writer, 'whiskey-soda coordination,' which is a prominent characteristic of Thai administrative life."[35]

Horrigan also notes the "often dubious and frequently disputed relationship between the generalist and the specialist in provincial government. The trend toward increasing specialization of services and better education all around for technical personnel places the governor in fact, if not in law, more and more in the position of a general manager concerned with general supervision and control, and strengthens the independence of the technical personnel, particularly in such strong agencies as education and public health."[36]

That the potential conflicts within the provincial office between a governor and his functionally specialized staff are duplicated on a smaller scale in the district office is suggested by Prayat Smanmit's study of Thai district administration. Several years of experience as a district officer gave him a viewpoint which is relevant here. After describing the formal authority vested in the district officer to supervise and co-ordinate the work of the functional specialists assigned to work with him, Prayat writes:

> A surface appraisal of the district officer's position seems to show that he has sufficient authority to gain [assure] the success of [the] coordination process, but it is not exactly the case in practice. This is so for several reasons. The district office possesses little control over functional officers. These men are appointed by their departments. They are partly responsible to their provincial heads as well as their respective departments for the execution of their duties. As the price of coordination, the district officer has to comply with the wishes of the functional heads.
>
> The district officer who does not pay enough attention to the work of his functional subordinates invites an administrative conflict because the functional officers will choose to by-pass him in order to avoid a delay of the execution of duty. The practice poses difficulties of discipline, but they may be protected by their provincial heads. In case the provincial heads are in the good graces of the governor, the district officer finds out later on that his question of disciplinary action is not supported.[37]

SPAN OF CONTROL: REGION VS. PROVINCE

We lack as much direct evidence about the conflict between subordinate officials and superiors in the matter of "span of control" as we do for the area-function problem just presented. Nevertheless, the changes of policy on regional organization may be taken as evidence of such a conflict. We know that the creation of the *monthons* under the leadership of Prince Damrong and the Ministry of Interior constituted a frontal attack upon the old system of *Chow-muang* in the Lands. As a result of this strategy, the lord-lieutenants of the *monthons* were able to reduce the territorial lords to submission, converting them to governors and their Lands to provinces.

That battle having been won and a new corps of provincial governors created who had no option but to be loyal to the central government, a new phase of intrabureaucratic struggle commenced. The monarchy had, to a large extent, relied on princes to staff the *monthons,* just as King Chulalongkorn had turned to one of his half brothers to create the Ministry of Interior. The new governors, however, were for the most part commoners who had accepted the career system, substituting upward mobility as a career goal for the consolidation of family control over a Land. However, their prospects of promotion to the top ranks were blocked by the grip of princes from the royal family on the choice *monthon* posts. Moreover, in terms of access, the regional offices stood between them and ministry headquarters in Bangkok.

What could be more natural, under these circumstances, than for the governors to make common cause with the promoters of the revolution in Bangkok to eliminate their common rivals and bureaucratic enemies? The promoters, for their part, were not sure of their ability to gain control over the provinces. The counter-revolution of October, 1933, under Prince Boworadet was almost exclusively a result of provincial revolts. It was natural, therefore, for the revolutionists to form an alliance with the governors to eliminate the royalist lord-lieutenants of the *monthon.* Since the institution was a new one and one which the governors resented, it seemed easier to eliminate the office than to staff it with new men. Actually, Rama VII (Prachatipok) had already started to dismantle the *monthons* for economy reasons prior to the revolution.

Arsa writes that "it was apparent from the outset that the policy of the Thai government under the Constitutional regime has aimed at establishing the province as a primary unit of territorial administration and making the governor the most important man in the sphere of local government and administration." As a first step, the *monthon* was eliminated in 1933 and the office of lord-lieutenant suppressed.[38]

Arsa offers several factors as possible explanations for this step. He suggests that the spread of modern means of communication no longer made it necessary to have an intervening level between the provinces and the center in order to secure co-ordination of policy. He also points to the economies which would be made possible in a time of financial stringency (these events took place at the height of a world-wide depression which had grave repercussions in Thailand) by eliminating the high-prestige and costly *monthon* offices. Third, it was thought that the *monthon* had become an administrative and communications "bottleneck" whose removal would step up the efficiency of administrative operations. Finally, the elimination of the *monthon* was heralded as a democratic measure which would strengthen local autonomy.[39]

As we have already seen, a concurrent measure strengthened the provincial board, thereby curtailing the effective power of the governor within the provincial arena. Having won the support of the governors by eliminating the *monthon,* the promoters also made a bid for the support of the functionally specialized departments by granting them more direct access to their field personnel.

As a result of these changes, the "span of control" problem, which had earlier led to the creation of the *monthon,* now began to affect the specialized departments. Each one must have been swamped by the flow of communications from its provincial officers. Consequently, each department or ministry began to create its own regional organizations. At first they simply appointed inspectors in the headquarters office, each of whom had responsibility for the department's work in a particular group of provinces. Later, it seemed desirable to station these inspectors more permanently in the field, and accordingly, in 1941, a new regional organization, the *paak,* was created. The country was divided into five *paak,* and the ministries and departments then appointed regional inspection-commissioners for each *paak.* These *paak* inspectors were then formed into regional committees under the chairmanship of an inspector from the Ministry of Interior.

This setup, however, still provoked dissatisfaction, as governors and provincial officers continued to insist on communicating directly with Bangkok, and the headquarters offices appeared reluctant to delegate sufficient responsibility to the *paak* offices to enable them to impose co-ordinative control over the provinces in each region. The result was continuing confusion and dissatisfaction, with growing tensions between officials at the provincial, *paak,* and central levels of government. In the late nineteen-forties this regional scheme was abolished.

In 1952, the new Administration of the Kingdom Act, which, as we have already seen, restored the governor to a position of primacy in provincial administration, also created nine new administrative regions, each under the supervision of a *Poo Warajakarn Paak,* with greatly augmented powers. While the law was clearly a victory for the governors at the provincial level, it involved a defeat for them in the imposition of a stronger control authority between them and Bangkok headquarters. From the point of view of the Ministry of Interior, however, the increase in the power of the governors also meant a multiplication of the work-load at headquarters. A stronger regional authority might help to mitigate this pressure. Nevertheless, the *paak* was not given as much territorial administrative authority as was possessed by the former *monthons.* Instead, although they were supposed to regulate and supervise the provinces under their jurisdiction, it was announced that "the-day-to-day operation of public business can be transmitted through the direct channel of communication between the provinces and the central government as has been the previous practice."[40]

What an open invitation to conflict! What governor would passively submit to control by the *paak* headquarters if he retained direct access to Bangkok? At any rate, the system proved quite unworkable, provoking considerable conflict until it was eliminated in 1956. The Governors' Conference in May that year, while supporting the government's "democratization" and "decentralization" program, recommended that the regional offices be abolished. We need, therefore, be in no doubt about the views of the governors on this question. They seem, in 1956, to have been riding the crest of a wave which brought them to victory both in their struggle with technical specialists in their own office and in their contest with headquarters regarding the imposition of regional control centers over their heads.

CONCLUSION

The extent to which the Thai bureaucracy was able to create intra-bureaucratic controls that might substitute effectively for the types of extrabureaucratic political organs which in some other countries impose public accountability upon the governmental services may be left to the reader to judge for himself. We have discovered, however, that the staff services—personnel, finance, auditing, planning—which sometimes provide effective internal control systems, are weakened in a polity which lacks external power centers capable of using these "management tools" to impose sanctions for administrative responsibility. Moreover, we have seen that the characteristic "area and function" and "span of control" controversies which can be used in some administrative systems to enhance accountability were transformed, in the Thai bureaucracy, into frameworks of intrabureaucratic politics.

A more adequate judgment of the effects of intrabureaucratic politics on the Thai polity may be made if we look more closely at some of the concrete operations of the system. In the next part of this book we shall, therefore, examine the behavior of the modernized bureaucratic polity in Thailand at several levels. Starting with the central government, we shall look first at the way in which cliques and factions arose and competed with each other in the Supreme Council. We shall then examine some of the fruits of power obtained by the Siamese bureaucratic politicians. Finally, we shall review more closely the performance characteristics of the contemporary Thai polity as a working model.

PART THREE: THE MODERNIZED POLITY

CHAPTER VIII

Cliques and Factions
in the Thai Cabinet

The pattern of political rivalry in Thailand illustrates well some of the consequences of bureaucratic politics. David A. Wilson, whose book *Politics in Thailand* is not only the most recent but also probably the most comprehensive and authoritative analysis of the Thai political scene, writes:

. . . politics has become a matter of competition between bureaucratic cliques for the benefits of government. In this competition the army—the best organized, most concentrated, and most powerful of the branches of the bureaucracy—has come out on top.[1]

The revolution of 1932 substituted the idea of representative government and popular sovereignty for "the ancient and admittedly limited and outworn monarchism. But parliamentary democracy," Wilson continues, "as a process wherein diverse aroused social interests are expressed through organizations outside the government and are synthesized by representative institutions into a statement of the public power has not emerged in Thailand. Interest groups, such as they are, remain weak. . . ."[2]

Without external centers of power capable of controlling the bureaucracy, the main arena of political rivalry in Thailand has come to be the cabinet as a ruling committee of the effective heads of the ministries with their respective departments, including the armed forces, which form the apex of bureaucratic authority. To quote Wilson again, the cabinet "is the institutional focus of power in the Thai political system, both in law and in fact."[3]

The members of the Thai cabinet, therefore, exercise political power to an exceptional degree. They constitute the core of the elite. It is, consequently, a matter of some interest to examine as closely as possible just how this nuclear political elite operates. In other polities, one normally concentrates attention on such institutions as the political parties, legislatures, and pressure groups which project the force of popular political interests upon the administration, as represented in the cabinet, and one justifiably also devotes considerable attention to the ideological issues and policy conflicts reflected in the political process. Where the instrumentalities for popular control are, if not absent, at least weak or embryonic, as they are in Thailand, national politics becomes more simply a struggle for power as an end in itself among competing cliques and factions. In this context, such ideas as "right" and "left," "conservative" and "liberal," "clerical" and "anti-clerical" have no meaning. The question is merely "Who rules?" not "What does he stand for?"

If the image of Thai politics presented above is correct, cliques are to be found primarily within the membership of the cabinet itself, or at least among high officials who aspire to cabinet status. To some extent, no doubt, such rival groups do represent bureaucratic constituencies and hence espouse the interests of the officials in their respective branches or departments of government. Such interests, however, are as likely to take the form of demands for more funds and positions as they are for effective execution of programmatic values.

To some degree, more generalized policies or postures may be espoused by rival political groups in the cabinet. Thus, the alternating supremacy of Pridi (13) and Phibun (12)[4] in successive Thai cabinets has been taken as an indication of something like a two-party struggle between civilian (liberal) and military (conservative) political groups. Yet, closer inquiry indicates that the issues were much more personal and less universalistic than such an interpretation would suggest. We shall test this hypothesis, at any rate, by analyzing Thai cabinet history in terms of clique rivalry rather than competition over issues.

CABINET AS POLITICAL ARENA

In the image of a "normal" political system, the cabinet at any given moment expresses the aims of a dominant group of political contenders, whether in the form of one party or a coalition of parties. A parliament or the general electorate serves as an umpire which can, from time to time, change the composition of the cabinet, substituting one party or coalition for another. The cabinet, in other words, is not so much the central political arena itself as a prize sought by those who contend with each other in a wider arena outside the cabinet. To win the prize they must, of course, take a stand on the issues which most interest the electorate. But in the Thai system, arenas outside the cabinet are so weak that political competition is concentrated inside the cabinet itself. Rival cliques and factions seek to strengthen their own position at the expense of others who are also members of the cabinet. What determines the outcome is control over arms of the bureaucracy, especially military units—not appeals to the voters or Parliament. Success enables a victorious group to augment its position by bringing into the cabinet (co-opting) more of its own supporters, thereby placing friends and partisans in command of more departments and ministries. Defeat need not mean the elimination of a group from membership in the cabinet, but rather a reduction in the number of positions it holds, or a substitution of less important for more decisive ministries. A frequently used strategy is to weaken a rival clique by splitting it, forming a temporary alliance with one of its component factions.

Cliques and factions consist of individuals who are often bound together by ties of friendship and long-standing acquaintance, typically reaching back to school days and sometime also including kinship, frequently by marriage. Members typically hold official positions in the bureaucracy, whether military or civil. They may be in the same formal organization, as colleagues, perhaps related as superior and subordinate. More often, however, they are friends whose "informal" relationships cut across formal departmental lines. Increasingly, they have been military officials, but civilian bureaucrats have also played decisive roles in these cabinet groups. They can augment their capacity to exercise bureaucratic power by co-opting members drawn from different agencies.

A single clique is usually not strong enough to seize power by itself. Consequently, it must form an alliance with other cliques, often producing a "coup group." The members of such a "coup group" have drawn together and exchanged vows of mutual co-operation and solidarity. The very fact that they felt it necessary to take such solemn oaths suggests the artificial character of the group. We scarcely find members of each component clique in a coup group entering into such compacts.

Wilson uses the Thai term *khana*, or semiformal group, to refer to these coalitions. He writes: "In Thai politics since 1932 they have been the supreme in-group and virtually the sovereign power. For that reason they are, or more precisely their leaders are, the ruling group."[5]

Yet it is apparent that there are not enough positions in the cabinet, nor enough ruling posts in the bureaucracy, to satisfy all the members of each clique in such a coalition or *khana* which I shall call a "ruling circle" after its seizure of power. The ruling circle includes only those members of a triumphant *khana* who subsequently succeed in obtaining cabinet posts. It is not surprising that, once having eliminated their rivals and gained control over the Thai cabinet, the various cliques and factions within a ruling circle should start contending with each other to gain more favorable allocations of the key posts. Their oaths of mutual loyalty and co-operation are severely tested as they start dividing the fruits of victory.

The struggle is complicated by the presence in Thai cabinets of some men who do not belong to the ruling circle. The reason is easily seen. A coup group or *khana* which has seized power is likely to feel insecure at first. Moreover, it may lack members with enough experience to administer effectively all of the cabinet positions, especially those requiring the most technical knowledge. In addition, it wishes to prevent foreign intervention; hence, it must restore peace and order as quickly as possible. To meet all of these problems, it is likely at first to ask nonmembers—experienced bureaucrats and public men with prestige—to join the cabinet, perhaps even to take the front role of prime minister. Such "fellow-travelers" or allies of expediency are regarded as expendable as soon as the new ruling circle has gained enough experience and has consolidated its power to the extent necessary to dispense with nonmembers, thereby freeing more positions for its own members. The temporary allies, recognizing the short-term and precarious character of their appointments, may band together and form a countercircle dedicated to the overthrow of the new ruling circle. However, since a frontal attack would be unlikely to succeed, they can be expected to try to split the ruling circle by forming an alliance with one or another of its cliques in an attempt to expel a rival faction. This strategy was followed, and nearly succeeded, on only one occasion, following the formation of the first cabinets in 1932/33. More typically, and after this experience, the ruling circle moves quickly to consolidate its own power by ousting its temporary allies. However, it must first seek to legitimize its own control by obtaining international recognition. To do this, it frequently holds new elections and installs a new parliament. This enables the ruling circle to carry out a cabinet change. The prime minister submits his resignation to Parliament, and a new cabinet is formed. If the premier was merely an ally, he is replaced by a key member of the ruling circle, who is then able to claim that his power is legitimately based on democratic parliamentary procedures. Non-members of the ruling circle may be dropped from the cabinet or rotated in office with other specialists whose technical skills are required. By frequent rotation, the formation of a countercircle is prevented.

The characteristic form of political struggle in the Thai cabinet, therefore, does not involve conflict between members and nonmembers of the ruling circle. Rather, it arises out of rivalry between the component cliques of which the ruling circle is composed. Such rivalry does not create a "party" system, however, because of the difficulty experienced in recruiting new members. Wherever the base of power is popular elections, a political party strives to enhance its electoral strength by adding new members—by co-opting rising politicians. But where there is no such incentive for the expansion of membership, each clique tends to become exclusive. Since there are not enough cabinet posts to satisfy the ambitions of all members of a *khana,* the temptation is to eliminate rivals and reduce the size of the ruling circle, rather than to enlarge it. As the size of a ruling group dwindles, and the number of ambitious men excluded from access to the cabinet rises, disaffected elements begin to consider the formation of a new *khana* capable of seizing power by force or threat of force.

The new *khana* is likely to include not only factions who have actually been thrown out of office by the ruling circle, but also any clique within the existing ruling circle which feels itself sufficiently threatened to fear that it may lose in a future crisis. Indeed, the leadership of the new *khana* is customarily drawn from a threatened faction within the ruling circle. Actual possession of authority in the bureaucracy, especially in the armed forces, gives the leader of such a faction decisive bargaining power when forming a coalition with groups outside the government.

The exclusiveness of a ruling circle is perhaps based also on other considerations. Thus, the fact that members of a *khana* shared the dangerous and exciting experience of making a bid for power gives them, as veterans, a sense of comradeship that they can scarcely share with newcomers. Moreover, a new recruit might augment the strength of one of the cliques or factions within a ruling circle and hence threaten to unbalance whatever equilibrium between these groups had been previously established.

OVERTURNS, REALIGNMENTS, READJUSTMENTS, AND CONSOLIDATIONS

The displacement of one ruling circle by a new one usually, but not always, takes the form of a coup d'état. Such a displacement will be called an "overturn." Overturns have, perhaps unavoidably, commanded much attention from foreign observers as well as from the Siamese themselves. But this preoccupation diverts attention from the political struggles that take place between the overturns. These struggles typically involve realignments and readjustments, by which I mean shifts in the balance of power among the cliques and factions that constitute a ruling circle. The chief groups of which a ruling circle is composed will be called "cliques." Thus, the primary struggle for power within a ruling circle takes place between its component cliques. Whenever a clique succeeds in displacing one of its rival cliques or in drastically reducing the number of cabinet posts held by its members, we may speak of a "realignment."

Just as a ruling circle is composed of cliques, so a clique is typically composed of "factions." Factions within a clique normally co-operate with each other in order to resist a rival clique. However, should one clique triumph in a realignment, it then becomes a ruling circle, and its component factions become rival cliques. Moreover, the solidarity between factions in a clique is not necessarily so strong that leaders of a rival clique may attempt to play one faction against another in the hope of forming an alliance and disposing of a faction. It may seem more practical to eliminate a factional element within a rival clique than to dispose of the clique as a whole.

Whenever shifts in power come about as a result of factional changes, or when the relative power position of cliques changes without the actual elimination of a clique from the ruling circle, we may speak of a "readjustment." If the shift involves the dropping of nonmembers of a ruling circle from the cabinet, the event can be called a "consolidation."

The political history of Thailand since 1932, then, can be analyzed in terms of overturns, realignments, readjustments, and consolidations in the cabinet. These events may be regarded as differing from each other not only in terms of how power shifts among groups, but also in terms of degrees of intensity. Thus an overturn, in which one ruling circle displaces another, involves the most intense political struggle, whereas a consolidation of power involves the least. Realignments and readjustments reflect intermediate degrees of intensity.

Formally speaking, each of these power shifts is signalized by a cabinet change. No doubt power shifts take place during the lifetime of any particular cabinet, but it is convenient, for purposes of analysis, to focus attention on the thirty cabinet changes which have taken place between 1932 and 1963. If a cabinet change is marked by a significant shift in power, we may speak of it as a "cabinet crisis." Obviously, a Thai cabinet crisis in this sense need not involve a formal vote of confidence, resignation, and action by the Assembly, as in the parliamentary model, although these procedures may, of course, be followed. I shall refer to any overturn, realignment, or readjustment occurring during a cabinet change as a cabinet crisis, but mere consolidations or other events signalized by a cabinet change will not be called crises.[6]

CRITICAL EVENTS AND LEGITIMATIONS

Cabinet crises in Thailand are typically accompanied or preceded by events in which the power of the ruling clique (or of particular cliques and factions in it) is challenged. Among such events may be overt armed attacks upon the government, resignations of influential leaders, purported threats, international incidents, or the death of an important person. I shall refer to such occurrences as "critical events."

When the critical event takes the form of an attempted coup or uprising against the government, we may speak of a "rebellion." On occasion, the administration has moved to suppress a rebellion before it actually broke out. In such instances, it is not always clear whether an actual rebellion was contemplated. The government, because of fear that a rebellion might be planned, may have taken precautionary measures to abort it. It is convenient to refer to such events as "so-called rebellions."

We should perhaps place in a somewhat different category the promulgation of new constitutions, the holding of elections, and the convening and dissolution of Parliament. In parliamentary democracies the holding of elections and the convening of legislatures provide arenas in which political forces meet. The decisions thus made are translated into action, administratively, by the formation of new cabinets. We have already seen, however, that power in Thailand is concentrated in the cabinet and bureaucracy. Elections, therefore, serve to legitimize the rule of those in power rather than to produce a political change. A ruling group typically stages an election after it has seized power, in order to consolidate its authority, secure foreign recognition, and reduce the possibility of domestic opposition. After the elections, a cabinet is likely to resign in order to allow Parliament to ratify the appointment of a new cabinet. Since the ruling circle controls the Assembly, however, the new cabinet differs but slightly from the old. It may be a consolidation of power as the ruling circle drops some of its allies from the cabinet. However, such occasions have also been used to weaken a rival clique, causing a minor cabinet crisis or realignment.[7]

A revision of the constitution or the promulgation of a new constitution may have consequences similar to those of an election. Indeed, an election is usually called after the promulgation of a new constitution. These actions—elections, constitutional revisions, and the convening of Parliament—may be regarded as "legitimations." Whereas critical events usually threaten the power of the ruling group, causing some response that may lead to a cabinet crisis, legitimations are used by a ruling group to augment its power, to enhance the authority of its rule.

It is important to distinguish the conceptual framework presented above (focusing on the consequences of political action) from schemes based on the form of crises in which violence is used or threatened. The distinction may be clarified by looking at the typology of four kinds of overt action mentioned by Wilson. He recognizes the following: (1) a shift of power, revolution, or coup d'état; (2) an attempted coup or *kabot;* (3) a suppressed rebellion, also called a *kabot* by the Siamese; and (4) a seizure of power or *yüt amnat.*[8] Clearly, the second and third categories are equivalent to "rebellions" and "so-called rebellions," as defined above. They challenge a ruling group but do not immediately precipitate a cabinet crisis. The first and fourth categories, however, always involve cabinet crises. The four events in Wilson's first type, which took place in 1932, 1944, 1947, and 1957, brought about political overturns. Three of them (1932, 1947, and 1957) were coups d'état, but the 1944 overturn was brought about without threat of violence. The reason for classifying these four events together becomes apparent when one thinks in functional terms, rather than of "overt acts" of violence. Wilson's fourth category includes some but not all of the cases of political realignment, since some realignments were carried out without violence being invoked.

It may be observed that Wilson's classification is based on diminishing degrees of violence, except for the events of 1944, which seems out of place in his first category. By contrast, the scheme offered here classifies cabinet changes in terms of the extent to which the composition of the ruling circle was modified. Wilson's first and fourth types occur during some, but not all, political overturns and realignments. His second and third types do not accompany cabinet crises, although they may have paved the way for them. More significantly, by looking primarily for crises in which violence was used or threatened, one may not notice the political crises in which violence was not involved.

THE FIRST RULING CIRCLE

Observers of Thai politics have often noted the controversy between the "military" leadership which, until 1957, was identified with the name of Phibun (12) and the civilian leadership under Pridi (13), whose effective influence came to an end in 1947. Siamese politics has often been compared to a game of "musical chairs" in which first one and then the other of these protagonists captures the seat of power, the number of chairs being gradually reduced so that at each "play" some of the competitors are forced out. Although there is no doubt an element of truth in this interpretation, it is a great oversimplification and conceals the more interesting and theoretically significant view of events which becomes apparent when we use the model presented above as a frame of reference.

The 1932 coup group was formed by an alliance of two friendship groups which differed from each other in age, the first being composed of men about forty years old and the second of younger men of about thirty. Members of both groups had studied in Europe, the older men mainly in Germany, the younger ones chiefly in France. Their friendship grew out of mutual association there, backed by earlier school-day acquaintance in Siam. These friendship groups constituted the nuclei of what became the "senior" and "junior" cliques, respectively. Others who had not shared fully the same experience were also drawn to these groups, but they typically had some strong personal or familial link with a member of each clique.

The key leader of the senior clique was Song (10), in association with Prasard (5). The chief leader of the junior clique was Pridi (13), associated closely with Phibun (12), Prayoon (8), and Luang Tasnai Niyomseuk. Tasnai refused to join the first cabinet and died shortly thereafter, so he never became a member of the ruling circle. Khuang (47) was a good friend of the junior clique leaders during their student days in Paris, but he was not fully trusted by them and so was not asked to join in planning the revolution of 1932, but subsequently came to be regarded as a member of the junior clique, civilian faction.

Another important political leader was an army officer named Phahon (3), who was noted for his modesty, personal integrity, and pleasing personality. Although a member of the senior clique, he was not its leader. As the senior and junior clique members were quietly discussing among themselves the need for overthrowing the absolute monarchy, they became aware of each other and sought to join forces. To do this it would be necessary to accept one man as leader of the projected revolution. The active head of one clique could scarcely be accepted as leader by the other clique. It was, accordingly, necessary to choose a member of one group who could serve as a bridge with the other and therefore as "leader" of the whole *khana*. Pridi agreed to accept Phahon in this role, and Prayoon approached him to ask for his co-operation. Phahon agreed and thus became the leader of the coup group, but not the head of any clique within it.

This pattern was repeated later on several occasions when rival cliques in a ruling circle agreed to accept someone outside their own ranks as titular leader. Such a man might play a mediating role between the rival cliques, but he might also try to strengthen his own position by attracting personal followers who could serve as a third clique, helping him to manipulate and dominate the other cliques. Phibun, as leader of the third ruling circle, came nearest to succeeding in this strategy, but even he ultimately failed.

The junior clique contained three factions which became cliques after the defeat of the senior clique. These were the civilians under Pridi, the army faction under Phibun, and a naval faction, headed by Sinthu (6), Supha (21), and Thamrong (35).[9]

When the People's Committee was set up on June 28 under the Provisional Constitution, thereby constituting the first "cabinet" after the revolution, a "nonpromoter"[10] was selected as front man, serving as chairman. He was Mano (1), a high official during the absolute monarchy, an English-educated lawyer, who was at that time chief judge of the Supreme Court of Appeals. He had taught in the Law School at Chulalongkorn University, where some of the leading promoters had been his former students. He was born in 1884 and hence was nearly fifty, a decade older than the members of the senior clique. Mano was able to name three other "older officials" to the Committee, but for the rest he "appointed" promoters, including four members of the senior clique and seven members of the junior clique (one army, one navy, and four civilian faction members).

The second cabinet was named on December 10, 1932, coinciding with the promulgation of the Permanent Constitution. Mano retained the chairmanship and added four new "older officials." Thus, eight senior bureaucrats from the absolute monarchy held all the portfolios in the cabinet, while the eleven promoters received the title of ministers without portfolio. Apparently the promoters, who had seized effective power, counted on their numerical majority to retain control in the cabinet. They did not foresee that cabinet decisions could not be made by "majority rule."

A COUNTERCIRCLE FORMS

The older officials, who had been given direct administrative control over the ministries and who had had long experience in the conduct of government, did not relish the thought of being dominated by a collection of young and inexperienced bureaucratic politicians. They quickly formed a countercircle and began to curtail the power of the promoters. Recognizing that they could not make a frontal attack on the whole group, they decided to drive a wedge between its members, capitalizing on its internal tensions. They moved first to discredit Pridi and thus to separate him and his followers from the exercise of power. In this they naturally reached out for an alliance with the king, with whom they still retained long-standing bonds, and sought also to discredit the appointed Assembly and the People's Party, both of which were dominated by Pridi and his followers. Although Pridi, as a civilian, had not played a decisive role in the critical events of the military coup, he and his followers in the junior clique proved more adept in manipulating the new political symbols than their colleagues in the senior clique. Hence, Pridi moved rapidly to the forefront as the acknowledged leader of the People's Party and the Assembly and, thus, as the key figure of the revolution.

This was deeply resented by some members of the senior clique, especially its leader, Song, who soon began to feel that, after the crucial role which he had played in organizing the military revolt, he was not receiving due recognition. It seemed natural, therefore, for Mano's countercircle of older officials to seek an alliance with Song's senior clique in the hope of splitting the embryonic ruling circle from within. Clearly, the countercircle lacked sufficient political support outside the ranks of the promoters to carry out a successful countercoup. Consequently, its only chances of success lay in a strategy of alliance with a disaffected clique within the ruling circle. Because an alliance of the older officials and the monarchy with the senior clique might not have been strong enough to dislodge Pridi's's growing political influence, Mano moved also to separate some of the key men within the junior clique from their able and aggressive leader. He attempted, for example, to align the army and navy officers in the junior clique with their fellow officers in the senior clique against their age-mates. Moreover, Sinthu, the leader of the junior clique's naval faction, was a brother of the new minister of defense, through whom his neutrality, if not active support, might be gained.

Phibun, as the only junior clique army faction member in the cabinet, was granted by fate the decisive vote. Were he to line up with his fellow officers in the senior clique, he could have given them victory. By maintaining solidarity with his friends in the junior clique, he could help Pridi consolidate his power. Alternatively, by a somewhat ambiguous posture, he might augment his own weak position, bargaining with both sides, playing ultimately for larger stakes. This is the course he apparently chose at this decisive moment in Thai political history. The stage was gradually set for a showdown, which came in March, 1933, after the second cabinet had held office for less than three months. One of Pridi's first projects had been the formulation of an ambitious economic program involving an elaborate set of governmental controls. Its implementation not only required the acceptance of a radically new socio-economic philosophy, but it would also have necessitated the creation of far-reaching administrative controls for which the new government was ill prepared, a fact readily recognized by the older officials. Moreover, Pridi's scheme was seized upon as a radical, not to say a "communist," scheme. Although both the People's Party and the Assembly were divided in the subsequent controversy, it became clear that the majority favored Pridi's plan. Mano, with the tacit consent of the senior clique, secured a royal proclamation on April 1 proroguing the Assembly, which was thereby denied an opportunity to vote on the issue. Pridi was forced to resign, and he left the country on April 12. The other members of his faction, Naeb (15), Tua (14), and Det S (72), resigned with him. Thus, at the end of the first crisis, the countercircle had won a major victory, in alliance with the senior clique, against the junior clique, especially its civilian faction.[11] A major readjustment had taken place as the third cabinet was formed.

Mano's circle now began to prepare for a move against the senior clique, since it was apparent that Song and his friends, while willing to collaborate in eliminating their younger rivals within the ruling circle, were certainly not ready to turn power over to the older officials and the king. At this point, therefore, Mano sought to turn the ambivalence of the army and navy factions in the junior clique into a solid alliance. Sinthu was induced to remain in the third cabinet, where he was joined by Supha, his companion in the junior clique's naval faction. Phibun, who had resigned in protest as a gesture of solidarity with his friend Pridi, was enticed back by a substantial promotion in rank within the Army, as were many of his friends. The countercircle itself was reinforced by the addition of four older officials to the cabinet of April 3, 1933.

SENIOR CLIQUE FIGHTS BACK

These events clearly posed a challenge to Song and his senior clique. His rival for power was no longer Pridi but the "front man." Although the junior clique had apparently been removed from the arena, the Mano countercircle seemed headed for a seizure of power, perhaps in alliance with the junior clique's army and navy factions. Alternatively, Phibun himself, having by now learned more about the technique of a military coup, might launch a frontal attack upon the government which was still so precariously in power. Song faced several dangerous possibilities. Mano, in alliance with Phibun and Sinthu, might move to oust Song and thus to consolidate their power against that of the able but outflanked senior clique. Faced with such an alliance, Song would surely have gone down to defeat. But Song may well have calculated that Phibun would not lend himself to such a one-sided alliance, since left alone to face the growing power of Mano's countercircle, the junior clique's army faction, with the uncertain help of the navy faction, would probably soon have lost power to the older officials.

Phibun, confronted by this prospect, might have decided to make a frontal attack upon Mano's countercircle, hopefully with the help of Song's senior clique. But Song must have known perfectly well that the military officers of the senior and junior cliques could not govern the country without the aid of the older officials, who alone possessed the administrative experience required to handle the complex problems of the new regime. Moreover, Song could not be sure of his ability to retain the upper hand in a political alliance of the senior clique and junior clique's army faction. Hence, he was apparently unwilling to join with Phibun in such a coup. Furthermore, earlier in the game he had tried unsuccessfully to banish Phibun to a rural post as a means of curtailing his influence, and personal relations between the two men were decidedly cool. However, if Phibun should attempt to oust Mano by himself, Song would have been called upon to come to the aid of the older officials. He might have had to identify himself publicly as an ally of the old regime against his former comrades in the *khana*. This he seems to have been unwilling to do. Besides, in a government composed only of the older officials and the senior clique, Song might soon have been outmaneuvered by the skillful and ambitious Mano.

Faced with these unpleasant alternatives, Song decided to adopt a typically Siamese tactic, namely, to resign.[12] The same technique was later used, with more success, by Sarit (181) in 1957, when he decided to oust his rivals in the third ruling circle. On June 10, 1933, the four members of the senior clique in the cabinet handed in their resignations, but their army commissions were not to be surrendered until June 24. Obviously, this gave them time to maneuver and, if necessary, to use their command positions in a new coup. Phahon was commander-in-chief of the Army; Song was deputy commander. Hopefully, the Mano government, finding itself in an untenable position, would beg Song to return, and he could then have named his own terms as a price for resuming office. Song may well have counted on an alternative possibility, namely, that Phibun, who had become increasingly disaffected with the Mano regime in which he was a restive partner, would strike out desperately in a military coup against the growingly aggressive countercircle. By being out of the government, Song would have no obligation to come to Mano's defense. As long as he and his friend Phahon held the commanding positions in the Army, they could wait until Mano and Phibun were entangled in a desperate and indecisive struggle. The senior clique could then make a dramatic appearance on the stage to "save the nation." Naturally, Song's clique would then be able to impose its will upon the weakened protagonists, presumably bringing both into a new cabinet of national unity under the guidance of Song himself.

Song, of course, offered other public "explanations" for the resignation of his group. But if, as we assume, he planned to make a political comeback in the leading position, he miscalculated. The weak link in his reasoning turned out to be the behavior of his companion, Phahon, who, it should be remembered, was his senior officer as commander-

in-chief of the Army and had been accepted as leader of the ruling circle. Although a follower of Song in the senior clique, Phahon also felt
a strong sense of identification with the whole *khana* and was chagrined
to see it crumble so soon after coming to power. Song realized, of
course, that if Phahon were to join Phibun in a coup against Mano,
he could bring the Army to the side of the rebels, and Song's prospects
for a return to power would be ruined. Hence, he appears to have
exacted from Phahon a solemn promise that he would not join in any
such move against the government without the support and co-operation of Song himself. But in accepting Phahon's promise at face value,
Song failed to understand Phahon's character. Perhaps, in addition to
his desire to restore the unity of the coup group, Phahon had some personal ambitions. In any event, Phibun sought his co-operation through
intensive secret negotiations. On June 20, ten days after the resignation from the cabinet of Song's group and only four days before their
resignation from their military commands was to take effect, the second
coup took place under the joint leadership of Phahon and Phibun. This
time the full strength of the Army was officially behind the rebel group,
and Mano's government collapsed without a struggle.

JUNIOR CLIQUE WINS OUT

The fourth cabinet was formed the next day with Phahon as prime
minister and without the participation of the senior clique. Having lost
their illusions about the efficacy of "majority rule" in the cabinet, they
now included only five of the promoters: Phahon, Phibun, Sinthu, Supha,
and Narubet (30). Although Phahon belonged to the senior clique, the
omission of Song meant that this group had been dropped from the
ruling circle. Phahon, as we have seen, was not the real leader of the
senior clique. As head of the ruling circle, he exercised formal authority
as titular leader of the government, but real power now fell to the leaders of the junior clique. These included Phibun's army faction, the navy
faction of Sinthu and Supha, and the civilian faction, temporarily represented by Narubet. Pridi himself was summoned back to Thailand,
and on October 1, immediately after his joyous return, he was admitted
to the cabinet. In the interim, the power position of Phibun's army faction had risen, but the junior clique was now clearly in command; the
senior clique and the countercircle had been ousted. A major realignment of power had taken place.

That this interpretation, based on the competition of cliques and factions within the ruling circle, is different from the view which has been hitherto accepted may be seen by comparing the foregoing account with that given in the following words by Wilson:

During the year in which Phraya Mano was Prime Minister (1932–33), the ruling clique [circle], at the time the Promoters of the Coup d'Etat of 1932, left the major cabinet positions in the hands of older civil servants still deeply imbued with the traditions of the absolute monarchy. The difficulties in handling Pridi's Economic Plan, the resulting closing of the national assembly along with the period of decree rule, and evidently some suspicion of a countercoup led the Promoters of the Coup d'Etat to seize power a second time and take over the cabinet.[13]

It should now be clear that the coup of June 20, 1933, was not only a victory of the promoters over the countercircle of the older officials, but, even more significantly, it was a triumph of the junior clique over the senior clique within the ruling circle. Thus, it combined the elements of a realignment of power with a consolidation. Never again was a countercircle to come so near success, but frequently thereafter did clique rivalries lead to more realignments.

With its conquest of power, the junior clique became a ruling circle. Its former factions now became cliques. After June, 1933, therefore, we may refer to the army, navy, and civilian groups as cliques within a ruling circle still presided over by Phahon who, although originally a member of the senior clique, lacked personal followers. He retained the position of prime minister for over five years until December, 1938, but his tenure of office depended upon his ability to preserve the balance of power among the restless cliques within his circle. Eventually, as the power of the army clique rose and the civilian clique declined, Phibun displaced Phahon as prime minister.

That the promoters still required the help of senior bureaucrats is made clear by the composition of the fifth cabinet, into which Phahon brought twelve experienced officials to run the ministries. With only three exceptions, they were not members of Mano's old countercircle. They served, in effect, as agents of the reconstituted ruling circle and were unable to form a new countercircle of their own. A year after the revolution, participation in the central arena of power had been narrowed down. The senior clique had been pushed out of the circle, and the junior civilian faction, after a stunning defeat, had made a comeback with the help of fellow members of the junior clique.

The members of the prorogued Parliament were reconvened on June 22, 1933, in order to legitimize the new regime under Phahon's premiership. In November, elections for a new assembly were held, followed by the formation of Phahon's second cabinet on December 16. But this was a mere cabinet change, involving no significant shift of power in the political arena. Parliament and the national elections served to legitimize but not to disturb the control exercised by the new Thai elite. Half of the members of Parliament were appointed by the government. The clique in control of the cabinet could guarantee parliamentary approval of its acts.

REBELLION ATTEMPTED

This is not to say that the tenure of power by the junior clique was fully secure. Disaffected members of the senior clique, the royal family, and the countercircle of the old officials began to conspire together to make a comeback. In October, 1933, a rebellion organized in the provinces took place, and military units began to converge on Bangkok.[14] The leader of the rebellion was Prince Boworadet, a general who had been minister of defense before 1932 but had resigned as a result of differences with some of the other leading princes. He had even discussed collaboration with some of the commoner army officers, including Phahon, in a move to change the government, but had rejected the idea of an attempt to overthrow the monarchy by violence. After the coup in June, 1932, he expected to be made head of the People's Committee, for which post he appears to have had Phahon's support; but Pridi strongly opposed reliance on any prince and supported the nomination of Mano. When the new constitution permanently barred royal princes from political roles, the ambitious Boworadet became infuriated and turned to counter-revolutionary activity.

Another leader of the rebellion was Phya Sena Songkhram, a high officer linked with the royal family, who had commanded the First Army Corps before the revolution. He was one of the key men arrested during the coup and was the only high official to be wounded on that day. Subsequently in January, 1933, he attempted to organize an opposition political party, the *Khana Chart,* but Mano, with the king's support, took advantage of this opportunity to ban all political parties, thereby suppressing the People's Party itself, as well as the incipient opposition group. In any event, Sena was a high army officer well connected with the royal family whose attempts to lead a peaceful opposition to the revolutionary regime had failed. He now joined with Boworadet in plotting a rebellion.

A third leader of the counter-revolution was Phya Srisithi Song-khram. He also was a leading army officer and a close friend of Phahon, with whom he had joined in some early discussions of the proposed revolution. However, he failed to take an active part in the actual coup, and at the crucial moment he could not be located by Phahon when he might have been given an important role in the new regime. Disappointed in his old friend, Srisithi allied himself with Mano and the old official's countercircle. When Song and the other senior clique members resigned from the cabinet, Mano named Srisithi to take Song's post as director of military operations. When Phibun's subsequent coup on June 20 overthrew the Mano government, Srisithi's ambitions were frustrated for the second time. He had also known Boworadet in earlier days and had been privy to conversations with him about a change of regime before the coup in 1932. Thus, Srisithi joined also in the planning of the rebellion. It is apparent that the rebellion was not led by men close to the king but by men who, had circumstances been different, might well have become members of the ruling circle.

It is unnecessary to relate the events of the counter-revolution. Real fighting took place, and victory for the government forces was by no means assured. Phibun took the lead in directing the defense of Bangkok and became the hero of the day, thereby greatly strengthening his personal position within the ruling circle, as leader of the army clique. The rebellion was the most violent event in modern Thai history, yet it did not produce a cabinet crisis or even a cabinet change. Clearly, political change in Thailand has not been directly correlated with the violence of its military encounters. The ultimate defeat of Boworadet's rebellion meant the consolidation of power by the junior clique. The leaders of Song's senior clique were sufficiently identified with the revolution to make it impossible for them to give open support to the rebellion. On the other hand, they would have welcomed the collapse of the junior clique regime. Hence, a few days before the rebellion began, they left the country in order to make a "study tour." Had Phibun's defensive measures failed or had a stalemate arisen, Song's group could have returned to "save the nation." Phibun's victory, however, not only confirmed the power of the junior clique, but also ruined the chances of Song and his followers for a comeback. They had deepened the hostility and resentment of the junior clique leaders, and they now appeared to the public as men willing to desert the revolutionary government in its hour of need.

The rebellion indirectly also contributed to the growing power of the cabinet. The position of the monarchy had been compromised by the counter-revolution. Although there is no clear evidence that the king himself supported the plotters, he did not come forward to support the government either. He clearly distrusted the young men in the junior clique and resented the formalistic character of the powers granted the throne. He pressed for interpretations or revisions of the constitution that would give substance to the royal prerogatives. Taking the side of "democracy," he argued that since the elections and the Assembly exercised no real power, control having passed to a new oligarchy of young promoters, the interests of the people ought to be represented by the active participation of the Crown in the political arena. The king pushed his demands, threatening to abdicate unless they were met. He thereby confronted the regime with a dilemma, since they required the monarchic accolade as well as the vote of Parliament to give legitimacy to their rule.

The character of this constitutional crisis came into the open after January 12, 1934, when the king left the country to seek eye surgery abroad. Protracted negotiations, in which the ruling circle definitely, if politely, rejected all the king's proposals and demands, came to an end on March 2, 1935, when the king finally carried out his threat and abdicated. He had not returned home since leaving early in 1934. His abdication message was sent from England. The young Prince Ananda Mahidol, a boy of ten, who was studying in Switzerland, was then proclaimed king under a princely council of regency.

It should be clear from these events that the junior clique succeeded in eliminating seriatim from effective power in the political arena the Assembly and political parties, the royalists and old officials of the former countercircle, the senior clique, and the king himself. By 1935, the political arena was dominated by a small oligarchy of promoters, the members of the junior clique of the 1932 coup group, operating through the cabinet.

JUNIOR CLIQUE AS RULING CIRCLE

During the next three years, rivalry between the army, navy, and civilian cliques in the realigned ruling circle gradually intensified. The army and civilian cliques became the chief protagonists, with Phibun and Pridi as their respective leaders. The navy clique played a more ambiguous role, seeking the position of power balancer, harmonizer, or neutralist in the struggle.

Phahon, as prime minister, was not content to play the role of a mere figurehead, although, without a personal following, he was unable to control effectively his nominal followers in the ruling circle. He came to rely heavily upon nonpromoter older officials whom he retained in his cabinets, and he also gave increasing weight to the necessity for parliamentary support, as manifested by his willingness to resign in the face of an actual or potential negative vote. When Parliament disapproved an international convention for the control of rubber exports that had been signed by the cabinet, Phahon resigned, only to form a new cabinet, the sixth, on September 22, 1934. Again, in July, 1937, Parliament started a general debate on the selling of government land. Phahon announced his cabinet's resignation to permit "a full and free investigation," after which he formed a new cabinet, the seventh, on August 9. Elections were held on November 7, 1937, and the new parliament convened on December 10, at which time Phahon resigned again, but set up a new cabinet, the eighth, on December 21.

It would be too much to say that these events marked the formation of a new countercircle similar to the one created in 1933 by Mano. Rather, a tendency was growing to inhibit the rising power of the ruling circle, relying on the bureaucratic influence of older officials and the growing prestige of Parliament. The situation reached an impasse September 11, 1938, when Parliament insisted on certain budgetary procedures which the ruling circle found unacceptable. Phahon again submitted his resignation, but this time the ruling circle moved quickly to secure a royal order (by the regency) dissolving Parliament. The cabinet therefore continued without change, and elections were called for November 12. When the new parliament met on December 10, the ruling circle moved to consolidate its power by naming Phibun prime minister. For the first time, the members of the junior clique assumed formal authority. Twenty of them obtained cabinet posts—eight army, eight civilian, and four naval clique members—as compared with from five to nine who had held cabinet rank during the five Phahon cabinets. Since this cabinet change marked the complete elimination of any members of the former senior clique from the cabinet, it may be regarded as a realignment. The full liquidation of the former senior clique as a possible claimant for power became clear on January 29, 1939, when the Phibun administration suppressed a "so-called rebellion" led by Song. Song himself was allowed to flee the country, and the last remnants of the senior clique were destroyed.

Since Phibun's first cabinet also involved the victory of a ruling circle over nonmembers in the cabinet, it could also be considered a consolidation of power. It clearly demonstrated the inability of Parliament to gain control over the cabinet.

Although the designation of Phibun as prime minister, and concurrently as minister of defense and interior, established his personal supremacy in the ruling circle, the balancing of the number of army and civilian clique members in the cabinet symbolized their continuing partnership and equality of status in the ruling circle. Yet Pridi and Khuang were the only members of the civilian clique to obtain portfolios, while close followers of Phibun were given key supporting roles as deputy ministers of interior and defense. Four members of the naval clique were also assigned cabinet posts. Eight other cabinet positions were held by nonpromoter officials, of whom three were closely associated with Phibun: Muni (56), Wichid (57), and Boriphan (55). In a sense, these men constituted the nucleus of a personal faction which Phibun began to build, perhaps as a counterweight to help him retain personal control over the ruling circle and to escape exclusive dependence on his followers in the army clique.

ARMY CLIQUE RISES

During the course of the first Phibun cabinet, it became apparent that the power of the army clique was rising and that of the civilian clique declining, but it was not until the advent of the Japanese war that a critical realignment took place. When Phibun acceded to the demands of the Japanese, permitting them to send their armies across Siamese territory, he was also compelled to drop Pridi from the cabinet, in view of his patent sympathy for the cause of the Allies. In a delicately face-saving manner, Pridi was appointed a member of the regency council to fill a vacancy caused by death, and the next day, December 17, 1941, he resigned from the cabinet.

Other members of the civilian clique continued to serve in Phibun's wartime cabinet, which was reconstituted with minor changes on March 7, 1942. Without Pridi's leadership, however, the civilian clique played an increasingly minor role, while Phibun's army clique dominated the scene. The leading member of the civilian clique in the cabinet was

Khuang, who gradually assumed the role of mediator between Phibun and Pridi. As Phibun became ever more closely identified with the Japanese, Pridi began to organize a secret "Free Thai" resistance movement, with support from the Allies. Khuang's task was to work from within the government to protect and mask the activities of the Free Thai underground.

From the perspectives of the Free Thai leaders, most of whom were members of the civilian clique, the goal of driving the Japanese out of Thailand became inextricably mixed with the aim of gaining power in the cabinet. The wartime atmosphere of preparation for a military uprising had its obvious analogues with the conspiratorial mood of a coup group preparing to seize power. The situation was ripe for the formation of a new *khana*.

As before, a single clique could scarcely hope for success. It needed allies. Naturally enough, Khuang's group within the cabinet provided the necessary help. Under the pressure of growing army domination, Khuang identified with his fellow-members of the civilian clique in the underground. The naval clique, which had been pushed into a subordinate position, also joined Pridi's movement.

By the middle of 1944, it had become apparent to the Siamese that the Japanese would lose the war. Pridi's Free Thai organization was beginning to gather strength, but it could scarcely make an open bid for power as long as the Japanese remained in military occupation of the country. Khuang finally stepped forward, in close consultation with Pridi, to suggest to Phibun that he should resign in order that a government more acceptable to the Allies and less tainted with collaborationism might be formed. Phibun, perhaps thinking that by stepping into the background he could make a postwar comeback, whereas he would surely lose power if the war were to end with him in the premiership under Japanese tutelage, decided to accept the suggestion and resigned.

Khuang, in alliance with Pridi and with the consent of Phibun, the Japanese, and the Parliament, proceeded to form a new cabinet, Thailand's eleventh, on August 1, 1944. The members of the army clique were all conspicuously left out. Four members of the civilian clique who were secretly active in the Free Thai movement, as well as four members of the navy clique, were included in the cabinet. Phahon also was recalled from retirement to bring his prestige, if not the strength of the disintegrated senior clique, to the support of Khuang's cabinet. A new ruling circle had come to power. The second political overturn in modern Thai politics had taken place, this time without violence.

THE SECOND RULING CIRCLE

Born as it was in the limbo of the World War II Southeast Asian theater, the second Thai ruling circle was to have a confused and short-lived history. Whereas the first ruling circle had held power for twelve years, the second lasted for only three years. The first circle experienced ten cabinet changes compared with nine for the second, or an average tenure of office of more than one year for the first circle contrasted with an average duration of four months for the second circle.[15]

The second ruling circle has been called the Free Thai *khana,* but it might better be thought of as the Pridi-Khuang-Thamrong group.[16] Although Pridi was no doubt the dominant figure in the circle, and his Free Thai clique its strongest component, it lacked cohesion, and Pridi was unable to control either the naval clique or Khuang's group. Both the Free Thai clique and the naval clique possessed the inner solidarity typical of those who share the dangerous and exciting experience of plotting to seize power. But Khuang's group was of a different sort. He had never been a fully accepted member of the junior clique of the 1932 *khana.* Moreover, he had held office in earlier cabinets and made the transition to power in 1944 from the top rather than the bottom. Thus, he lacked a well-formed clique and had capitalized on his personal role in mediating between Pridi and Phibun to obtain the premiership in 1944. He was predisposed, therefore, to look for new sources of support. The result was that he turned to parliamentary politics, seeking allies among elected politicians, and eventually formed a political party.

The history of the second ruling circle is so complex that despite its short duration it cannot be described here except in briefest outline. Moreover, the reliance of Khuang upon parliamentary supporters, Pridi's own ideological commitment to parliamentary democracy, and the apparent expectation of this ruling circle that a real attempt to employ democratic procedures would help Thailand regain recognition and support from the Western Allies resulted in a short-lived florescence of parliamentary vigor. The arena of political action, as a result, expanded beyond the limits of the cabinet. Moreover, Pridi himself had been named sole regent on July 31, 1944, at the same time that the Khuang cabinet was formed. From this vantage point Pridi was able to act on behalf of the monarchy, so that his personal power reinforced the continuing prestige of the Crown. A model of Thai politics during this period, therefore, would have to take into account triangular relationships between the regency, Parliament, and the cabinet.

When the end of World War II was proclaimed on August 16, 1945, the Khuang cabinet resigned so that a new government could be formed by a man more likely to be acceptable to the Allies. Thawi (73), a member of Pridi's civilian clique who had played a leading role in the Free Thai underground, was designated prime minister of the twelfth cabinet. Khuang was not included in the new cabinet, which was dominated by the Free Thai clique. A readjustment had taken place. It was assumed, however, that someone better known to the Allies would be more acceptable to the Western powers. Accordingly, as soon as Seni (105) was able to return to Thailand from the United States, he was made head of the thirteenth cabinet as Pridi's personal choice. This was, therefore, a cabinet change with no readjustment. Seni had been ambassador to the United States before the war and had remained in America as unofficial liaison man for the Free Thai underground. He was now named foreign minister as well as premier and took over primary responsibility for the difficult negotiations with the victorious powers. Meanwhile Pridi, operating behind the scenes, directed the administration of domestic affairs through his Free Thai associates who were named to the cabinet. Seni was willing, at first, to go along with this arrangement, but differences over policy increasingly strained relationships between the two men. When the treaty with the Allies was finally signed and new elections were held on January 6, 1946, Seni resigned, and the choice of the next prime minister was left to the new parliament. In an atmosphere of free choice, the Assembly voted for Khuang, apparently not realizing that Pridi strongly favored a rival candidate, Direk (64), who had been one of his strongest associates in the Free Thai underground. For once, a significant readjustment of power had taken place by parliamentary action. Khuang utilized the opportunity to jettison members of the Free Thai clique from his cabinet, bringing in a new group of elected politicians recruited from Parliament. Parties had been authorized during the fall of 1945, and Parliament had become an authentic political arena.

There ensued a vigorous contest between Pridi as regent and Khuang as prime minister, with Parliament cast as decision-maker, not just legitimizer. The period did not last long. Pridi's followers gained a slim majority in Parliament, and on March 18, 1946, Khuang turned in his resignation.

PRIDI'S FREE THAI CLIQUE ON TOP

Pridi apparently did not want to surrender his position as regent, but after rejecting various alternatives, he decided to take the premiership himself and formed his first cabinet (Thailand's fifteenth) on March 24. An important realignment now took place, for whereas previously Khuang and Pridi's cliques had ostensibly co-operated as members of the ruling circle, now Pridi's clique assumed full power and ousted Khuang's group. Moreover, Pridi had gained a substantial majority in Parliament. He proceeded to promulgate a new constitution on May 10, 1946, providing for a two-house parliament, the Senate to be elected by the House of Representatives. Pridi had no difficulty securing the election of his own followers for the new senate.

Khuang now went into open opposition, forming the Democrat (*Prachatipat*) Party. Although Pridi had control of Parliament, he found himself confronted by a vocal opposition headed by the defeated members of his own 1944 ruling circle. The newly activated democratic process had given the losing clique in a ruling circle a forum from which to harass the victors.

When the newly constituted parliament met on June 1, it accepted Pridi's resignation, only to reappoint him prime minister on June 8. Before he had time to form his new cabinet, however, the king was killed, and so Pridi handed in his resignation the next day, June 9. The death of the king seriously undermined public confidence in Pridi's regime and reinforced the vigorous criticisms directed against the Free Thai clique by Khuang's opposition. On June 11, Pridi organized his third cabinet (Thailand's seventeenth) but retained the premiership only until August 23, when, on the plea of overwork and illness, he resigned in favor of Thamrong (35), a member of the naval clique which had become closely linked with Pridi's Free Thai clique.

Thamrong's new administration may, therefore, be considered a minor readjustment, virtually a continuation of rule by the Pridi clique. Khuang's opposition, however, stepped up its criticisms. In May, 1947, Parliament opened a general debate on government policy in response to Khuang's demands, and Thamrong, after winning a vote of confidence, resigned only to form a new cabinet on May 30, the nineteenth for Thailand and the last for the second ruling circle.

Meanwhile, army groups outside the cabinet and Parliament had become increasingly restive. Both the government and Parliament, including the opposition, were composed of civilians and the naval clique. A new *khana* now came into existence, known as the Coup d'État Group (*Khana Ratapraharn*). The group included members of the army clique which had lost power in 1944, plus younger officers who had never tasted political power. As before, the military leaders sought allies and established working relations with Khuang's opposition group. On November 8, 1947, they staged a coup against Thamrong's government, and two days later proclaimed a new cabinet, Thailand's twentieth, under Khuang as prime minister.

THE THIRD RULING CIRCLE

Khuang's third cabinet lasted from November 10 to February 21, 1948. But he now found himself allied with quite a different kind of ruling circle from the one he had formed earlier with Pridi. Leader of the circle was the old master, Phibun, who had been released from jail in March, 1946. War crimes charges against him had been dropped. Moving secretly at first, but increasingly openly, he began to lay plans for a political comeback.

But the primary instigators of the military coup were the leaders of several new cliques. A key role in the organization of the coup is attributed to Kad (60). Like Song in 1933, however, he lost out to rival factions shortly after the victory of the *khana* and was forced into exile. He was a member of the army faction in the revolution of 1932 and had held office in Phibun's two earlier cabinets. His political demands were exorbitant, however, and his followers few, so that he was unable to make a place for himself in the new ruling circle.

A second clique was organized by Phin (177), a senior army officer, with the help of his aggressive son-in-law, Phao (185). This clique, which later played a dominant role, included three other sons-in-law of Phin: Pramarn (184), Siri (187), and Lamai (182).

A third clique, composed of younger officers on the average, most of whom had studied in the Thai Military Cadet School, were followers of Sarit (181). Among the more important members of this clique were Thanom (193) and Praphas (195).[17]

Phibun, as leader of the *khana,* lacked a strong clique of his own. However, he was able to bring to his personal support in later cabinets a number of men who took part in the coup, such as Norm (111) and

Sawat (163); but perhaps more important as personal followers were Phrom Yothi (66), Boriphan (55), Muni (56), and Wichid (57), who had not joined in the coup. We may refer to this group as Phibun's personal faction, to distinguish it from the powerful cliques in the new ruling circle.

Khuang's cabinets, however, provided few opportunities for members of these army groups. Only Norm was included. Positions were filled, for the most part, by career officials who had hitherto played minor political roles. Khuang also continued to look to Parliament for political support. The Coup d'État Group, on seizing power, had proclaimed a provisional constitution. Both houses of Parliament were dissolved. A new all-appointed upper house was created, and elections were held for a new lower house on January 29, 1948. When the new parliament—in which Khuang commanded a strong majority—met on February 19, Khuang submitted his resignation, only to form a new cabinet two days later, with little change in composition. Once again, the legislature was being used to legitimize a cabinet, not to choose the power-holders.

The impotence of Parliament was conclusively demonstrated on April 6, when the Coup d'État Group informed Khuang that he must resign within twenty-four hours. After a quick check of the leading officers in the Army, Navy, and Air Force showed Khuang that he could not count on their support, he turned in his resignation. He did not even bother to ask Parliament, in which his partisans held the majority of seats, to come to his support.

KHUANG'S CLIQUE OUSTED

A major realignment now took place as Thailand's twenty-second cabinet (and Phibun's third) was formed. Khuang's clique was ousted from the ruling circle. But Phibun sought to establish his own personal supremacy by barring members of the army cliques from cabinet positions, relying on members of his personal faction and a considerable number of experienced officials. He apparently thought that his own military record would enable him to keep the army cliques under control. Unlike Phahon, he intended to be the effective master of his ruling circle, not just its figurehead.

The first major test of Phibun's administration came on February 26, 1949, when Pridi and his Free Thai followers, with the help of some supporters in the Navy, Air Force, and even the Army, staged the

"Seize the Palace" rebellion. The attempted coup was quickly suppressed, but only after some brisk fighting in Bangkok. This episode may be compared with the Boworadet rebellion in 1933, in which disappointed political figures, men who had held power at an earlier time, attempted to overthrow a newly established ruling circle. In both cases, the rebels either were killed or forced into exile.

A month later Phibun, as had his predecessors, sought to strengthen the legitimacy of his regime by promulgating a new constitution on March 23. It had been drafted by a "constituent assembly" authorized on January 23, 1948, during Khuang's administration, but not appointed until July 7, 1948, under Phibun. The new constitution was completed by December 25 and was approved by Parliament and the regent on March 23, 1949. It provided for a continuation of the bicameral legislature, with an appointive upper and an all-elective lower house, but the existing members of the House of Representatives were authorized to complete their four-year terms, 1948–52. The first regular session under the 1949 constitution met on June 15, 1949. This enabled Phibun to turn in his formal resignation and reconstitute a new cabinet, his fourth and Thailand's twenty-third, on June 24. In addition to legitimizing his regime, Phibun used the opportunity to strengthen his personal control by increasing the number of members of his own faction without adding members of the Coup d'État Group's army cliques.

The dissatisfaction of the military cliques in the ruling circle now began to grow rapidly, leading to the "Manhattan rebellion" in June, 1951. The naval clique, as we have seen, never worked in close association with the army cliques. Whatever the reason, it seems to have jumped the gun if there had been any previous agreement on tactics. Perhaps the army cliques merely wished to isolate and discredit the naval clique in advance. At any rate, the rebellion began June 26 as an attack on Phibun by the naval clique, in the form of a kidnapping attempt while he was on the American dredge *Manhattan,* during ceremonies for its transfer to Thailand. Phibun managed to escape, but not with any help from the army cliques, under Phao and Sarit, who moved to suppress the naval uprising and "restore order," no doubt hoping to gain power for themselves.

Phibun, however, took advantage of the nonco-operation between the naval and army cliques to regain power, relying heavily on his personal faction. But the consequences were disastrous for him. The naval clique was discredited. Sinthu and many ranking naval officers were arrested. The leaders of the army cliques had shown their dissatisfaction and revealed their independence of government control.

The real significance of the rebellion was not revealed until November. The Phin-Phao and the Sarit cliques were mobilizing their strength and waiting for an opportune moment to seize the power that they had almost gained during the "Manhattan rebellion." Phao had become director-general of police after the June rebellion and used this position to augment the effective power of his clique. On November 29, 1951, he moved to the fore in what has been called the "silent coup," announcing over the radio that the 1949 constitution was being suspended and the 1932 constitution reinstated. The bicameral legislature was abolished and a half-appointive unicameral parliament restored. A provisional executive group of military leaders had seized power and began planning for the new regime, while Phibun was permitted to carry on with a dummy cabinet during a transitional week. Officially this was listed as Thailand's twenty-fourth, and Phibun's fifth, dating from November 29 to December 6. It involved no significant change in membership from the twenty-third. But on December 6, the full significance of the major realignment of power which had taken place became apparent when Phibun's sixth cabinet was announced. The most dramatic change was the inclusion of the leading members of the Phin-Phao clique: Phin himself and his four sons-in-law, Phao, Siri, Lamai, and Pramarn. Of the Sarit clique, only Sarit himself was included. Phibun remained the public head of the ruling circle, but effective power was now clearly in the hands of the clique leaders.

All that remained to be done was to legitimize the new regime by holding elections under the revised 1932 constitution, which was proclaimed on March 8, 1952. Full-time officials were, for the first time, appointed to Parliament, as "second-category" members, including more than one hundred military officers belonging to the triumphant cliques. Controlled elections for the "first-category" members were held on February 26, and Parliament convened on March 18. The cabinet then resigned, to be reappointed without substantial change on March 24. This cabinet, Thailand's twenty-sixth and Phibun's seventh, was to last until March, 1957, the longest in modern Thai history.

Whereas the Phin-Phao and Sarit cliques had co-operated closely to gain power in 1951, swearing eternal solidarity, rivalry between them deepened in the ensuing years. Phibun also found that he could retain his precarious seat as prime minister only by playing them off against each other. On February 26, 1957, elections for Parliament were again held in which the Phao clique sought to use the polls as a means to buttress its power, which had come under increasingly severe pressure from the rising Sarit clique.[18] In the new cabinet, Phibun's eighth and last, which was organized on March 21, a week after Parliament met, Phao became minister of interior and Sarit minister of defense. The stage was set for a final confrontation six months later.

Sarit, having decided to make a play for full power, began to organize a new coup group which became known as the Military Group (*Khana Taharn*), which finally seized power on September 16, 1957, ousting the Phin-Phao clique. Phibun himself also fled into exile.

THE FOURTH RULING CIRCLE

As in previous overturns, Sarit's ruling circle did not move immediately into positions of authority in the cabinet. Rather, civilian allies, largely experienced bureaucrats, were assigned to man the ministries under the chairmanship of Pote (145), a highly respected civil servant who had recently been made secretary-general of the Southeast Asia Treaty Organization. This cabinet was set up only for an interim period during which new elections were organized and held on December 15. Meanwhile, two key members of Sarit's clique, Thanom (193) and Praphas (195), were named ministers of defense and interior, respectively.[19]

Parliament convened on December 26, including a new group of appointed second-category members, plus the elected first-category candidates, many of whom were "independents." Pote turned in his resignation, while Sarit mobilized a substantial majority of members in the legislature, paving the way for organization of the new cabinet on January 1, 1958, under the chairmanship of Thanom. Having legitimized their rule, the new ruling group could consolidate power and drop its temporary allies.

Sarit himself, because of serious illness, did not take the first position, but went abroad for surgery. Returning in the fall of 1958, he organized another coup on October 20 on behalf of his realigned clique, now known as the Revolutionary Group (*Khana Pathiwat*). The revised (1932) constitution of 1952 was abolished, and a provisional constitution announced on January 28, 1959, under which a "constituent assembly" was set up on February 5, authorized to act as a legislature

for an interim period of indefinite length. Political parties were abolished. The Thanom cabinet was terminated by the coup on October 20,
and the Revolutionary Group ruled in its own name until February 10,
after the promulgation of the Provisional Constitution and the creation
of the constituent assembly, when Sarit himself established a new cabinet, Thailand's thirtieth, over which he presided until his death in
December, 1963.[20]

Whether or not the Sarit regime established a new pattern of cabinet politics in Thailand remains to be seen. It seems premature to predict that factions within the Thanom regime will emerge as cliques
ready to re-enact in the future a play which, with variations, has been
seen so often before. Nevertheless, as long as major centers of nonbureaucratic power do not arise, capable of imposing discipline and
responsibility on those who rule the country, it is difficult to see how a
basically different pattern of cabinet politics in Thailand will emerge.

CHAPTER IX

Politics, Administration, and High Finance

The way in which leading Thai politician-bureaucrats have struggled to gain cabinet positions has been described in the preceding chapter. Let us next examine some reasons that cabinet posts were considered so desirable.

It may be thought that explanation is not needed. After all, there are politicians in every polity, and the quest for power seems to be so universal that one need scarcely wonder at its manifestations. Perhaps the purpose of our inquiry might be clarified by asking how, rather than why, political ambition arises and becomes satisfied.

In the model of politics which we take for granted in the Western world, there are political institutions outside the state bureaucracy through which, for the most part, aspiring politicians rise to positions of influence and authority. This is true of single-party regimes no less than of multi-party democracies. These political institutions are dominated by professional politicians. Their careers involve the quest for power to such an extent that, from an early age, ambitious men who relish political competition are attracted to this way of life. The few who reach the top are but a small portion of the large company of candidates drawn to this vocation.

By contrast, in the Thai situation, the great majority of those who reach the political pinnacle of cabinet rank emerge from careers within the bureaucracy, military and civil. If one thinks of public officials as primarily administrators, as technical specialists who typically seek career security and public service roles, then it might appear surprising that such men would be attracted to the precarious and stressful role of politician.

Another contrast between the usual image of political systems and the Thai case may be drawn in the ideological sphere. The professional politician in Western countries is expected to become a spokesman for the interests of his constituents. He is supposed to adhere to a political doctrine, whether it be the Marxist ideologies of communist and socialist politicians, or the more conservative platforms adopted by democratic and liberal parties. Moreover, a politician who must seek election at the polls becomes sensitized to the concrete demands of individual voters or blocs and exerts himself to satisfy their requests as a necessary condition for continuing in office. It is this necessity to expand the base of support, to "aggregate" the interests of clientele groups, that produces the continuous growth of leadership cadres in those political parties which actually exercise effective influence in governance.

We have already seen, however, how the ruling circle of Thai politicians tends to diminish, not grow. Furthermore, it has become apparent that the doctrines espoused by rival cliques and factions are not primarily reflections of public interests or popular doctrines designed to attract votes. Rather, they are declarations calculated to win foreign approval, as measured by diplomatic recognition and nonintervention. Whereas the professional politician in the more "modern" or "developed" polities is pushed forward by the pressure of constituents who urge their representative to serve their aspirations, the Thai politician is carried forward primarily by the dynamism of his personal quest for power. Certainly the general public is not widely involved in the rivalries between top politicians and tends to feel that changes in the ruling group are as likely to be harmful as beneficial.

Such attitudes are clearly shown in the preliminary report of the Cornell University research team working in Bang Chan, a village near Bangkok. At the time of Pridi's abortive "palace rebellion" of February 26, 1949, rumors and unbelievable official reports began to sift into the village. A few days later, two men from Bang Chan went to the city and spent a day visiting relatives and coffee shops. They returned "with a detailed, perceptive, and remarkably accurate account of the situation, obtained in spite of government censorship." They blamed the leader of the uprising for causing trouble unnecessarily. One informant, in discussing the rebellion, asked:

Why do they fight each other? They must be really fighting for their own pockets. It's not X versus Y; it's one gangster fighting against another gangster.
Another said: "The whole thing is just the result of rivalries among politicians. They fight like dogs."
A third commented more vehemently: "Curse those evil men of politics who use their position to collect wealth, and those who speak of democracy by mouth but who do not act in democratic ways."

And a priest said: "It is pitiful to see bloodshed among the Thai people. We condemn the Chinese because they fight each other, but this time history will record that we Thai did not live in peace." [1]

The Siamese attitude toward those in power is well illustrated by a fable which is sometimes told. The story goes that a beautiful girl had become the object of affection of three suitors for her hand in marriage. Her father decided to permit the marriage but to submit the young men to an ordeal in order to select his future son-in-law. He told them they would have to spend a night sleeping in the adjacent swamp, and the man who showed the greatest stamina would win his daughter's hand.

The daughter, for her part, was enamored of one of the suitors and decided to do her best to help him win the ordeal. Accordingly, during the night of the trial, she went out frequently to the swamp to drive off the mosquitoes who had settled on the bare back of her lover. Unfortunately, the swarms of mosquitoes which succeeded each other on the back of this suitor sucked away so much of his blood that he was dead by morning. By contrast, the other suitors survived in good health because the first flock of mosquitoes, having gorged themselves, remained asleep on their victim's back and prevented any other parasites from landing.

The politicians, of course, are compared with the mosquitoes and the moral is drawn that it is better to leave one gang in power than to keep changing rulers if one wishes to survive.

If the cabinet politicians of Thailand are neither the spokesmen for political ideologies and popular interests nor the victors among men who make their careers contending for electoral offices, then what alternative motivations or ways of life can account for this pattern of political struggle?

We can assume, of course, that even those who have not made their careers as professional politicians, but who have risen to high office through the ranks of the civil and military state bureaucracies, would also respond to prestige and power as effective inducements to seek cabinet posts. Yet somehow one feels that the lure of prestige and power alone cannot adequately explain the apparent eagerness of high Siamese officials to become cabinet politicians.

A telling clue may be taken from the revelations which followed the death of Marshal Sarit, prime minister of Thailand, in December, 1963.[2] It was learned that this leading military politician, who had started life with limited financial resources, had left a fortune worth some $150 million to his heirs. Certainly the meager salaries which a small and relatively poor country could afford to pay its public officials could not account for the accumulation of wealth on such a grandiose scale.

WEALTH AS A POLITICO-BUREAUCRATIC INDUCEMENT

Let us take the wealth of Sarit seriously as an indication that high office in Thailand can pay off not only in power and prestige, but also, and indeed quite handsomely, in financial terms. If we assume that public officials in Thailand, as in other countries, are motivated not only by the desire to serve the public and to develop their country, but also by expedient interests—by the hope for security and creature comforts made possible by cash income—then we might conclude that these benefits would be provided in the highest degree to those who reach the pinnacle of bureaucratic success as measured by elevation to cabinet status.

It is, of course, normal in any bureaucracy for income levels to rise with rank and status. In this respect the Siamese practice is typical, although the range of variation between the highest and lowest levels might be more than average. A salary schedule for 1900 governing the northwestern provinces, promulgated shortly after a salary system had been instituted to replace the traditional Siamese system of *biawat* (royal largess to officials), established a scale which ranged from a minimum payment of 10 baht per month for servants, through 100 baht for third-grade inspectors, to 700 for a provincial governor of the first grade, and 1,200 for a *monthon* governor of first grade. The maximum for a first-grade *monthon* governor was set at 1,600 baht.[3] Presumably, high officials in Bangkok received even more. At that time the baht was worth about thirty cents in U.S. currency.

It can be seen that, in terms of 1900 purchasing power, the new scale provided very substantial income for higher level officials. Moreover, the range of differentiation from lower to higher ranks was quite wide. Officials rising in the hierarchy became accustomed to the idea that their personal income should rise substantially. The new system had translated into payroll equivalence the rising real income that went with rank in the old *sakdi na* system, based on the *kin-muang* (eat-the-country) principle. Under that system, the lowest grade official received 400 dignity marks, as compared with a range of 25 to 400 for petty functionaries. Higher officials received *sakdi na* (up to 10,000 for ministers and a maximum of 100,000 for the prince appointed to the office of *Wang Na*). The *sakdi na* of the king was considered to be beyond computation.[4]

In theory, the *sakdi na* measured the area of land over which some-one ruled, from which he was free to extract income. In practice, the correspondence of dignity marks to territorial jurisdiction could not be maintained, but the accelerating rise in real income nevertheless prevailed.

The schedule of salaries in relation to rank has been maintained, with suitable revisions, down to the present time. According to the general salary and classification plan adopted in 1954, as subsequently modified, a scale of monthly pay grades prevails, ranging from a start-ing scale of 450 baht for fourth-class officials to 8,000 as the maximum for special-class officials.[5]

The image of career mobility and rising income in the Thai bureauc-racy can be illustrated with some figures taken from the personnel rec-ords of higher officials in the Ministry of Agriculture. These figures are not presented as in any sense a representative sample for the civil serv-ice as a whole. Rather, these were higher officials in two ministries— Agriculture and Co-operatives—as of 1958. The data illustrate the prop-osition that all began their public service at relatively low salary levels, typically as second- or third-grade officials, corresponding to their status as degree holders, and experienced a steady rise in income, although with differing rates of promotion. The key data are presented in Table 4.

The salary history of the director-generals is charted in Fig. 6 to give some indication of characteristic career patterns as far as regular salary is concerned. Nothing particularly surprising is revealed. Every-one receives a regular step increase on a seniority basis, but some are clearly raised more rapidly than others. It is notable that the highest salaries were being earned by men in their early fifties and late forties, whereas no officer born before 1902 was receiving more than 800 baht monthly. This suggests that some officials, whether because of superior education, greater diligence, more influence, or some other factor, were able to advance much more rapidly than others up the income ladder.

Salaries for cabinet members are not available to me. Moreover, information is lacking on the value of "fringe benefits" granted to Sia-mese officials. If one considers that in 1958 the baht was worth about five cents in U.S. currency, then a monthly salary of 1,000 baht was equivalent to $50 on the open exchange, or an annual salary of $600.

TABLE 4

SALARY AND PROMOTION DATA
FOR SOME HIGH OFFICIALS

Official	First Salary		Last Salary		Birth Date	Last Position
A	1916	120	1956	650	1876	superintending engineer
B	1921	30	1958	900	1902	DG
C	1923	200	1956	1200	1906	DG
D	1925	200	1958	1300	1911	DG
E	1926	240	1956	1200	1903	DG
F	1927	60	1955	700	1903	chief engineer
G	1928	20	1956	1100	1907	DG
H	1930	30	1957	1100	1911	DG
I	1930	145	1957	1100	1909	DG
J	1913	60	1958	800	1894	DG
K	1916	30	1952	750	1898	dir. of office
L	1925	150	1956	650	1905	professor
M	1926	250	1956	1200	1905	dep. DG
N	1926	30	1956	800	1905	chief engineer
O	1927	85	1956	650	1905	superintending engineer
P	1928	195	1957	700	1905	senior officer
Q	1928	215	1956	650	1906	professor
R	1929	205	1943	650	1902	DG
S	1929	45	1957	750	1916	DG
T	1930	240	1957	1400	1905	DG
U	1931	150	1957	650	1906	dep. DG
V	1931	20	1957	750	1909	special officer
W	1930	200	1957	800	1900	dep. DG
X	1931	145	1956	650	1909	dep. DG
Y	1931	140	1956	700	1902	dep. undersecretary
Z	1935	45	1957	650	1915	dep. DG
AA	1935	140	1957	1200	1912	special officer
BB	1935	140	1956	650	1911	professor

Data taken from personnel records, Ministry of Agriculture, 1958. DG means
   Director-General, the head of a department in the Ministry.

Even allowing for a somewhat higher purchasing power of the baht in
Thailand as compared with the U.S. dollar equivalent, it is doubtful
if the highest salaries were worth more than $2,000 a year in the United

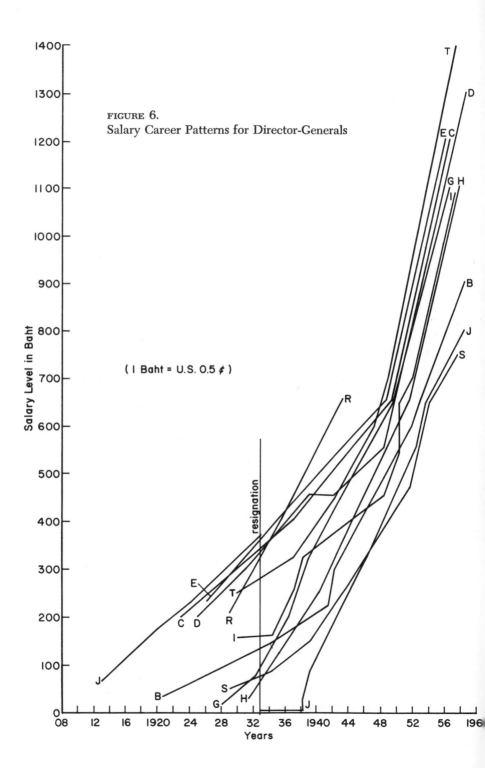

FIGURE 6.
Salary Career Patterns for Director-Generals

(1 Baht = U.S. 0.5 ¢)

States. Yet it was apparent even to casual observers that the actual scale of expenditures of high Thai officials was at a level which necessitated real incomes far above this amount.

No doubt, Thai officials were able to supplement their salaries by numerous official fringe benefits. They also frequently held several concurrent positions, thereby augmenting their income. Cost of living allowances provided a substantial supplement to salaries. The 1956 budget, for example, included an item equal to 35 per cent of the total for such allowances to officials (two billion baht out of a total of almost six billion).[6]

The complexities of Thai budgeting practice defy simple exposition. For present purposes it seems unnecessary to unravel this confused and confusing situation. What is apparent is that although a very large portion of the Thai national budget goes to pay salaries, the amount of such salaries is hopelessly inadequate and is supplemented in many ways. Even so, the formal income of most officials is insufficient to pay for socially expected costs of living. The quest for ways to augment their real income has therefore become a fundamental preoccupation of Siamese bureaucrats. When one considers that rising status and official rank are associated not only with a steeply rising scale of normal salaries but also with a rapidly rising level of conspicuous consumption, then it becomes apparent that the incentives to augment effectively the cash intake of officials is a major preoccupation.

OFFICIAL INCOME AND "PARIAH ENTREPRENEURSHIP"

Let us now consider some of the ways in which the real income of Thai officials—especially at the higher levels, notably in the cabinet itself—can be augmented. In order to make this analysis, we must examine a feature of Thai social and political structure which departs considerably from the model familiar to students of Western societies, yet one which is widely found in developing countries, namely, the phenomenon of "pariah entrepreneurship."[7]

In the implicit model which underlies thinking about relations between governmental and economic activity in the West, it is assumed that business and industrial roles, founded on the institution of private property, offer attractive careers for able and energetic individuals. Opportunities for high real income accompanied by social prestige and security make these roles appealing to members of the leading families and social strata, as well as to ambitious men of humbler origins.

An unstated premise in this model holds that the political influence of private, middle-class groups is sufficient to induce the government to adopt policies favoring the operation of market institutions, the enforcement of contracts, and the protection of property. Careers in government are also regarded as less lucrative than those in business and, in large measure, as less prestigeful also. Implicit in this model is the assumption that state bureaucrats can be held accountable for the relatively honest and efficient administration of laws and regulations which support the interests of industry and trade.

This model also implies that men are attracted to political careers because of the desire for power or public service and to bureaucratic posts in quest of security, professional goals, and a sense of duty, but not in either case to make money. It is assumed, rather, that wealth can properly be earned primarily through entrepreneurial roles, which can be filled single-mindedly: that is, entrepreneurs are subject primarily to the constraints of market mechanisms which induce them to behave in an economically rational manner—to maximize profits, to utilize scarce resources efficiently in terms of outputs—and they are not compelled to pay cash for the protection or favor of individual officials.

Any application of this model to the Thai situation leads, I believe, to grave misunderstanding. Instead, I shall apply a different model which starts from the premise that government service provides the greatest opportunities for combining high income with security, prestige, and power. It follows that anyone who can gain entry to careers in the state bureaucracies will do so in preference to alternative roles in the private sector.

It is to be expected, however, that not everyone in a given society will be permitted access to the most attractive positions in government. If, at the same time, there are reasons for encouraging the rise of a business class—such as pressure from foreign powers bent on trade—then we would expect that ambitious persons belonging to out-groups, to social or ethnic minorities, who might be denied admission to the government services, would gravitate toward entrepreneurial roles. However, precisely because of their lack of political access, a business community having such a background would be unable to gain power to the extent needed to impose constitutional restraints upon the elite, and to compel those in authority to protect the economic institutions without which private enterprise and a free market system can scarcely flourish.

This is not to say, of course, that entrepreneurial groups would not emerge. Rather, we might expect the appearance of "pariah entrepreneurship." Individual businessmen would be permitted by influential officials to carry on their activities, provided they contributed financially to the private income of their protectors and patrons in the government. The institution of pariah entrepreneurship, in other words, can become a necessary condition for making careers in government service lucrative, despite the apparent meagerness of official salaries.

The high costs of carrying on business and the extreme risks taken by anyone making long-term investments under such conditions serve to hamper the growth of the economy. Pariah entrepreneurship, then, may be considered as evidence of a socio-political syndrome with its own inner logic. It helps to perpetuate the attractiveness of governmental careers as prestigious, powerful, and lucrative roles. At the same time, it obstructs the emergence of institutions which are necessary for the growth of the economy.

CHINESE "PARIAH ENTREPRENEURSHIP" AND SIAMESE OFFICIALS

No doubt every country situation which one might wish to study differs in important ways from every other particular case. We should not expect to find a clear-cut example of the model, and certainly the Siamese case has its own distinctive characteristics. Nevertheless, the pariah entrepreneur model provides a better clue to the realities of Thai politics and administration than the conventional model outlined above. In order to test this proposition, let us begin by looking at the Chinese business community as leading candidate for the "pariah entrepreneurship" title. There are, admittedly, members of other minority groups who engage in business in Thailand—including Americans and Europeans, as well as Indians—but the Chinese community is overwhelmingly conspicuous and sets a pattern which may be regarded as decisive.

Fortunately, Skinner's detailed studies of the Chinese community in Thailand provide a wealth of data which make any independent investigation of this subject unnecessary.[8]

The picture which Skinner draws for us with painstaking detail is of a continually harassed Chinese business community, surviving only by continually buying protection from the Thai elite. As an ethnic minority, the Chinese are subject to social discrimination and to exclusion from political and administrative roles in government on the grounds that they are "aliens." They have, accordingly, been unable to secure the adoption of laws favoring their business interests or to impose effective restraints against the arbitrary exercise of power by officials.

The survival of particular concerns, therefore, has been made possible only by patrons, by influential men in government who can restrain their colleagues from touching this or that individual merchant, family, or business house. Skinner writes of the Chinese community that it is, naturally, advantageous for them to have "leaders who are business intimates of the Ministers of Education, Economic Affairs, and Interior, and of police officials." But he goes on to say that while "they may serve as intermediaries in securing this and that advantage from General Phao or General Phromyothi, they have no real hope of securing from such men any basic policy changes. They can help win skirmishes, but they are not even fighting the real battle as defined by the 100 per cent Chinese in the community." Skinner concludes that "in coming to terms individually with the Thai, many of the Chinese leaders have side-stepped rather than faced head-on the problems posed by Thai government policies."[9]

Unfortunately for the Chinese merchants, the problem is much more difficult than seems to be visualized in Skinner's comment, for it is not merely a question of inducing the Thai government to adopt specific policies. Skinner, of course, is looking at the subject primarily from the perspective of the Chinese community. By contrast, our interest here is to analyze the behavior of the Thai elite. Since the entrepreneurial community is, for the most part, Chinese, this means that in so far as a major goal of the elite is to acquire wealth, it must exact tribute from the Chinese. Since the ruling elite is not politically responsible to the business community, there is no reason to think that it would want to adopt or enforce any general rules protecting the property interests of the businessman. It prefers an unrestricted hunting license to squeeze the entrepreneur, subject to the condition that he must not be destroyed, lest this rich source of wealth be lost.

Skinner describes very well the processes by which new patterns of Sino-Thai co-optation have become established. From an earlier stage of informal and relatively unstructured symbiosis between Chinese merchants and Siamese officials there has emerged, since the nineteen-fifties, a complex superstructure of new corporations in which Thai officials and Chinese businessmen collaborate. The process began when the Chinese invited politicians to serve on their boards of directors, a development which reflected acute dissatisfaction with existing conditions and the rise of new opportunities generated by the spread of corporate forms of business organization. Thus, Skinner writes:

> Chinese leaders who have tried to "get off too cheap" or have failed to secure the backing of prominent Thai officials have themselves been arrested. The celebrated case of the nine merchants arrested in April 1952 on smuggling charges and later deported is generally interpreted in these terms. . . . These and similar incidents in 1952 pointed up to all Chinese leaders what had become increasingly apparent since 1948—the necessity for more effective measures to obtain business security. The piecemeal purchase of protection and special treatment had become unduly cumbersome, risky, and unreliable.
>
> The most popular solution to this problem found by leading Chinese businessmen was to enlist the permanent support of influential Thai officials by effecting formal business alliances with them. This was accomplished in several ways. First of all, Chinese leaders reorganized many of their major commercial and financial corporations to include on the boards of directors top government officials and other members of the Thai elite. Second, new corporations were formed on a co-operative pattern, whereby Chinese supplied the capital and entrepreneurial skill and Thai officials supplied "protection" for the Chinese, official privileges, and, in some cases, government contracts. And third, Chinese businessmen with Thai citizenship joined semi-official Thai enterprises in a managerial capacity.[10]

The advantages to the Chinese merchant of this close business relationship with members of the Thai elite could be seen in many ways. For example, it became easier to obtain quotas, permits, and licenses if officials were board members, because this created an interest in the welfare of their firms. Moreover, through honoraria, bonuses, and even salaries, the political patron acquired a predictable, easy, and respectably "legal" way of augmenting his income.

Secondly, as Skinner points out, "business ties with the Thai elite offer greater security from police interrogation, extortion, or arrest." Where communism is a crime, for example, who is to say whether or not a Chinese businessman harbors dangerous thoughts, especially with the growth of power in neighboring Communist China.

Thirdly, under the impetus of developmental initiatives by the Thai government—often in response to American economic aid and political pressure—the symbiotic Sino-Thai firm was favored to receive "government contracts and purchase orders." "And it goes without saying," Skinner adds, "that customs men and revenue officials are more likely to overlook irregularities and grant requests for special privileges to companies in which they—or their superiors—have stock or serve as directors." [11]

Although Skinner writes primarily from the Chinese point of view, he occasionally gives a clue to the motivation of the Thai officials. He tells us, for example, that "the Thai elite desire wealth and an economic base in business, and it is the influential Chinese leaders who have both in highest degree. If only on a pragmatic basis, therefore, Thai leaders seek business co-operation with the more influential Chinese leaders—ethnic prejudices and political pronouncements on the Chinese menace to the contrary notwithstanding." He writes, further:

> . . . the Thai military and political figures who came to power with Phibun in 1948—and especially those whose power was strengthened in the 1951 coup—needed an economic base to bolster their political and military power and enable them to attain higher and more enduring prestige. The active participation of Thai government officials in business had by mid-1953 reached extremes seldom attained in other countries. Insofar as the role of officials in business is thought at all peculiar by the Thai, it is condoned on grounds of economic Thai-ification: the government officials are themselves leading the way toward Thai recovery of the national economy. [12]

It is now appropriate to ask whether, and to what extent, cabinet members participate in this system. Many of the Thai elite who do take part are members of the bureaucracy below the cabinet level: career officials in the Police Department, army officers, and civil servants in the various regulatory departments. One might think that cabinet ministers would have more important matters to think about than a project to monopolize pork butchering in the city of Bangkok or a scheme involving the warehousing and ice business.

CABINET POLITICIANS ON BUSINESS BOARDS

Far from avoiding the system, however, cabinet members have been among its most active participants. To test this conclusion, I have collected data on the board memberships of cabinet members. This information can be obtained from registration data which is often announced in the press and is made a matter of official record. [13]

The registration data available here covered several years, terminating in 1957. Hence, it is not contemporary. Moreover, dates are not given for the period of membership of boards. My records may show an official as being simultaneously a member of more boards than he actually sat on at any one time. Moreover, in specifying joint participation of cabinet members on a business board, it may be that some individuals appear to have belonged at the same time, whereas, in fact, some joined after others had resigned their membership. For the most part, however, I believe that the memberships shown were concurrent.

Although the available data is rather crude, it is perhaps sufficient to establish a general pattern. A more detailed and extensive study should be done to discover the full character of the relationships which can be only roughly sketched here.

According to the available information, 61 of the 237 men who had been cabinet members between 1932 and 1962 held positions on boards of directors of business and industrial corporations during the period from 1952 to 1957. Their names and the boards with which they were identified are given in Table 5, arranged first in order of the number of board memberships which they held, and then alphabetically. After each name, which is listed in shortened form, a number is given which refers to the code number assigned it in Appendix A, where the full name is given.

The fourth column indicates whether the cabinet member was a promoter of a coup d'état. If he was a promoter, the date is provided; if not, this is shown by the letters "np," standing for "nonpromoter."

The fifth column provides the code numbers for the "leading boards" of directors on which the politician held memberships. These boards are listed alphabetically in Table 6. Any board on which, according to the available information, three or more cabinet rank politicians held memberships is counted as a "leading board." The final column gives the number of "other boards" to which the cabinet member belonged. These boards, containing only one or two cabinet politicians, are not identified separately in the table.

Reviewing the information in Table 6, we find that there were 42 companies having three or more cabinet politicians out of a total of 107 firms. The remaining 65 companies included 25 with two politician members and 40 with only one such member.[14]

COMPARISON OF PROMOTERS AND NONPROMOTERS

A direct correlation existed between the number of directorships held by cabinet politicians and their status as promoters of a coup. This is demonstrated in Table 7, which shows that only 35 per cent of the cabinet members with one or two memberships were promoters, whereas

TABLE 5

BOARD MEMBERSHIPS OF CABINET RANK POLITICIANS

Number of Memberships	Name	Code No.	Pro- moter	Major Boards*	Other Boards
26	Phao	185	47	3,7,15,16,21,23,24,25, 26,28,30,32,33,35,40,42	10
22	Sarit	181	47,57	1,3,5,6,7,13,15,16,17, 19,20,21,27,31,36,37	6
19	Praphas	195	47,57	2,6,11,13,18,19,20, 22,36,37,41	8
19	Lamai	182	47	3,8,28,38	15
17	Thanom	193	47,57	5,13,20,35,36,37,38,39	9
14	Sawai	192	47	4,5,10,11,12,13,16, 22,36,41	4
13	Siri	187	47	9,15,16,17,19,26,27, 28,34,37	3
11	Pramarn	184	47	2,9,15,16,17,24,26,28	3
9	Phin	177	47	7,8,15,16,26,27,33	2
8	Sawad	189	47	4,10,11,12,22,24,26,41	0
7	Chuang	58	32	15,18,31,32,40,41	1
7	Serm	221	np	15,25,26,27	3
7	Sunawin	167	np	7,11,25,38	3
6	Chamnan A	183	57	1,15,19,33,38,41	0
6	Chamnan Y	48	32	4,10,12,22,24	1
5	Banyat	168	47	3,15,28,29	1
5	Chitti	220	57	1,13,14,19,20	0
5	Prayoon	8	32	21,31,32,40,42	0
4	Chalerm	199	47,57	29,38,39	1
4	Xuchat	194	np	3,7,27	1
3	Chai	80	np	21,29,42	0
3	Fuen	179	np	7,23,29	0
3	Muni	56	np	3,28	1
3	Yuthasard	178	np	15	2
2	Boriphan	55	np	15,26	0
2	Bunchu	215	47,57	1,5	0
2	Chote	233	np	13,31	0

(Continued)

*Listed by code number. See Table 6.

TABLE 5 (*Continued*)
BOARD MEMBERSHIPS OF CABINET RANK POLITICIANS

Number of Memberships	Name	Code No.	Pro-moter	Major Boards*	Other Boards
2	Rak	191	np	15,42	0
2	Seri	62	32	8	1
2	Suraphong	197	np	34	1
2	Thona	144	np	21	1
2	Worakarm	160	np	2,34	0
1	Amphorn	210	57	36	0
1	Chart	134	np	33	0
1	Cherd	180	np	29	0
1	Chindarak	153	np	—	1
1	Det D	186	np	—	1
1	Det S	72	np	35	0
1	Direk	64	32,44	8	0
1	Duan	76	32,44	1	0
1	Kampanart	209	np	—	1
1	Kris	217	57	39	0
1	Kukrit	135	np	8	0
1	Leng	82	32	30	0
1	Luan	138	np	28	0
1	Mahaisawan	45	np	—	1
1	Mana	23	np	30	0
1	Norm	111	32,47	9	0
1	Phibun	12	32,47	7	0
1	Saphrang	81	32	29	0
1	Sinthu	6	32	34	0
1	Sree	31	np	39	0
1	Sriwisarn	9	np	8	0
1	Suwit	118	np	—	1
1	Thawi	219	np	—	1
1	Thewarit	79	47	—	1
1	Tiron	100	np	8	0
1	Wibun	204	np	—	1
1	Wisut	207	np	29	0
1	Yai	113	np	—	1

*Listed by code number. See Table 6.

TABLE 6

BOARDS CONTAINING THREE OR MORE MINISTERS

No.	Name of Firm	Board Members		Coup Group	Cabinets	Clique
1	Bank of Asia	Bunchu	215	47,57	25,26,27,30	Sarit
		Chamnan A	183	57	25,26	Sarit
		Chitti	220	57	28,29	Sarit
		Duan	76	32,44	10,11,12,15, 17,18,19	'32 Prom.
		Sarit	181	47,57	25,26,27,30	Sarit
2	Bank of Bangkok	Pramarn	184	47	25,26,27	PP
		Praphas	195	47,57	27,28,29,30	Sarit
		Worakarm	160	np	22,23,24,25, 26,27	Phibun
3	Cement for Irrigation	Banyat	168	47PP	23,24,25,26,27	PP
		Lamai	182	47PP	25,26,27	PP
		Muni	56	np	6,7,8,9,10,14, 20,21,24,25, 26,27	Phibun
		Phao	185	47PP	25,26,27	PP
		Sarit	181	47,57	25,26,27,30	Sarit
		Xuchat	194	np	26	tech.
4	Consumer Goods from Animals Exports	Chamnan Y	48	32S	6,7,8	'32 Prom.
		Sawad	189	47PP	26,27	PP
		Sawai	192	47	26	Phibun
5	Eastern International Development	Bunchu	215	47,57	28,29	Sarit
		Sarit	181	47,57	25,26,27,30	Sarit
		Sawai	192	47	26	Phibun
		Thanom	193	47,57	26,27,28,29,30	Sarit
6	Eastern Mine	Chitti	220	57	28,29	Sarit
		Praphas	195	47,57	27,28,29,30	Sarit
		Sarit	181	47,57	25,26,27,30	Sarit
7	Erawan Films	Fuen	179	np	25,26,27	PP
		Phao	185	47PP	25,26,27	PP
		Phin	177	47PP	25,26,27	PP
		Phibun	12	32Ja,47	1,2,3,4,5,6,7, 8,9,10,22,23, 24,25,26,27	Phibun

(*Continued*)

TABLE 6 (*Continued*)
BOARDS CONTAINING THREE OR MORE MINISTERS

No.	Name of Firm	Board Members		Coup Group	Cabinets	Clique
		Sarit	181	47,57	25,26,27,30	Sarit
		Sunawin	167	np	23,24,25,26	Phibun
		Xuchat	194	np	26	tech.
8	Farmers Bank	Direk	64	32Jc,44FP	9,10,12,13,15, 17,18	'32 Prom.
		Lamai	182	47PP	25,26,27	PP
		Phin	177	47PP	25,26,27	PP
		Siri	187	47PP	25,26,27	PP
		Kukrit	135	np	20,21,22	tech.
		Sriwisarn	9	np	1,2,3,14,20,21	tech.
		Tiron	100	np	12,13,14	tech.
		Seri	62	32Jc	9,10	'32 Prom.
9	Forest of Prachin	Norm	111	32Ja,47	14,20,21,22,23	Phibun
		Pramarn	184	47PP	25,26,27	PP
		Siri	187	47PP	25,26,27	PP
10	Import Samakhi	Chamnan Y	48	32S	6,7,8	'32 Prom.
		Sawad	189	47PP	26,27	PP
		Sawai	192	47	26	Phibun
11	Kan Kha Samakhi	Praphas	195	47,57	27,28,29,30	Sarit
		Sawad	189	47PP	26,27	PP
		Sawai	192	47	26	Phibun
		Sunawin	167	np	23,24,25,26	Phibun
12	Khosat Export	Chamnan Y	48	32S	6,7,8	'32 Prom.
		Sawad	189	47PP	26,27	PP
		Sawai	192	47	26	Phibun
13	Military Bank	Chitti	181	47,57	25,26,27,30	Sarit
		Praphas	195	47,57	27,28,29,30	Sarit
		Sarit	181	47,57	25,26,27,30	Sarit
		Sawai	192	47	26	Phibun
		Thanom	193	47,57	26,27,28,29,30	Sarit
14	Muang Rae Burapha Sethakit (trading)	Chitti	220	57	28,29	Sarit
		Lamai	182	47PP	25,26,27	PP
		Praphas	195	47,57	27,28,29,30	Sarit
		Sarit	181	47,57	25,26,27,30	Sarit
		Thanom	193	47,57	26,27,28,29,30	Sarit

(Continued)

TABLE 6 (*Continued*)

BOARDS CONTAINING THREE OR MORE MINISTERS

No.	Name of Firm	Board Members		Coup Group	Cabinets	Clique
15	NEDCOL	Phao	185	47PP	25,26,27	PP
		Phin	177	47PP	25,26,27	PP
		Pramarn	184	47PP	25,26,27	PP
		Siri	187	47PP	25,26,27	PP
		Banyat	168	47PP	23,24,25,26,27	PP
		Sarit	181	47,57	25,26,27,30	Sarit
		Chamnan A	183	57	25,26	Sarit
		Chuang	58	32Ja	8,9,10,15,17, 18,19	'32 Prom.
		Yuthasard	178	np	25,26,27	Phibun
		Serm	221	np	28,29	Sarit
		Rak	191	np	26,27	Phibun
		Boriphan				Phibun
16	NE Gunny Bags	Phao	185	47PP	25,26,27	PP
		Phin	177	47PP	25,26,27	PP
		Pramarn	184	47PP	25,26,27	PP
		Siri	187	47PP	25,26,27	PP
		Sarit	181	47,57	25,26,27,30	Sarit
		Sawai	192	47	26	Phibun
17	Phadung Sin (trading)	Pramarn	184	47PP	25,26,27	PP
		Siri	187	47PP	25,26,27	PP
		Sarit	181	47,57	25,26,27,30	Sarit
18	Provincial Bank	Lamai	182	47PP	25,26,27	PP
		Chuang	58	32Ja	8,9,10,15,17, 18,19	'32 Prom.
		Praphas	195	47,57	27,28,29,30	Sarit
19	Rajata Shipping	Sarit	181	47,57	25,26,27,30	Sarit
		Chamnan A	183	57	25,26	Sarit
		Chitti	220	57	28,29	Sarit
		Praphas	195	47,57	27,28,29,30	Sarit
		Siri	187	47PP	25,26,27	PP
20	Rajata Stone	Sarit	181	47,57	25,26,27,30	Sarit
		Chitti	220	57	25,26	Sarit
		Praphas	195	47,57	25,28,29,30	Sarit
		Thanom	193	47,57	26,27,28,29,30	Sarit

(*Continued*)

TABLE 6 (*Continued*)

BOARDS CONTAINING THREE OR MORE MINISTERS

No. Name of Firm	Board Members		Coup Group	Cabinets	Clique
21 Saeng Surat	Phao	185	47PP	25,26,27	PP
Hotel	Sarit	181	47,57	25,26,27,30	Sarit
	Prayoon	8	32Jc	1,2,3,9,10, 24,25,26	'32 Prom.
	Chai	80	np	10	tech.
	Thona	144	np	22	tech.
22 Saha Samakhi	Chamnan Y	48	32S	6,7,8	'32 Prom.
Khosat	Praphas	195	47,57	27,28,29,30	Sarit
(slaughtering)	Sawad	189	47PP	26,27	PP
	Sawai	192	47	26	Phibun
23 Sathaporn	Fuen	179	np	25,26,27	PP
Films	Phao	185	47PP	25,26,27	PP
	Siri	187	47PP	25,26,27	PP
24 Sri Ayuthia	Phao	185	47PP	25,26,27	PP
Bank	Pramarn	184	47PP	25,26,27	PP
	Chamnan Y	48	32S	6,7,8	'32 Prom.
	Sawad	189	47PP	26,27	PP
25 Sri Ayuthia	Phao	185	47PP	25,26,27	PP
Trading	Sunawin	167	np	23,24,25,26	Phibun
	Serm	221	np	28,29	Sarit
26 Sugar Industry	Phao	185	47PP	25,26,27	PP
of Chonburi	Phin	177	47PP	25,26,27	PP
	Siri	187	47PP	25,26,27	PP
	Pramarn	184	47PP	25,26,27	PP
	Sawad	189	47PP	26,27	PP
	Serm	221	np	28,29	Sarit
	Boriphan	55	np	6,7,8,9,10,22, 23,24,25,26,27	Phibun
27 Sugar Industry	Phin	177	47PP	25,26,27	PP
of Suphanburee	Siri	187	47PP	25,26,27	PP
	Sarit	181	47,57	25,26,27,30	Sarit
	Serm	221	np	28,29	Sarit
	Xuchat	194	np	26	tech.

(*Continued*)

TABLE 6 (*Continued*)
BOARDS CONTAINING THREE OR MORE MINISTERS

No.	Name of Firm	Board Members		Coup Group	Cabinets	Clique
28	Sugar Industry	Phao	185	47PP	25,26,27	PP
	of Thailand	Pramarn	184	47PP	25,26,27	PP
		Lamai	182	47PP	25,26,27	PP
		Siri	187	47PP	25,26,27	PP
		Muni	56	np	6,7,8,9,10,14 20,21,24,25, 26,27	Phibun
		Luan	138	np	20,21,24,25,26	Phibun
		Banyat	168	47PP	23,24,25,26,27	PP
29	Thai Airways	Banyat	168	47PP	23,24,25,26,27	PP
		Chalerm	199	47,57	29	Sarit
		Saphrang	81	32Jc	11,12,13,15, 17,28	'32 Prom.
		Fuen	179	np	25,26,27	PP
		Wisut	207	np	28,29	Sarit
		Cherd	180	np	25,26	tech.
		Chai	80	np	10	tech.
30	Thai Commercial	Phao	185	47PP	25,26,27	PP
	Bank	Leng	82	32Jc	11	'32 Prom.
		Mana	23	np	2,5,6	tech.
31	Thai Commercial	Sarit	181	47,57	25,26,27,30	Sarit
	Trust	Chuang	58	32Ja	8,9,10,15,17, 18,19	'32 Prom.
		Prayoon	8	32Jc	1,2,3,9,10,24, 25,26	'32 Prom.
32	Thai Financial	Phao	185	57PP	25,26,27	PP
	Syndicate	Chuang	58	32Ja	8,9,10,15,17, 18,19	'32 Prom.
		Prayoon	8	32Jc	1,2,3,9,10,24, 25,26	'32 Prom.
33	Thai Gunny	Phao	185	47PP	25,26,27	PP
	Bags	Phin	177	47PP	25,26,27	PP
		Chamnan A	183	57	25,26	Sarit
		Chart	134	np	20,21,22	tech.

(*Continued*)

TABLE 6 (*Continued*)
BOARDS CONTAINING THREE OR MORE MINISTERS

No. Name of Firm	Board Members		Coup Group	Cabinets	Clique
34 Thai Navigation	Siri	187	47PP	25,26,27	PP
	Sinthu	6	32Jn	1,2,3,4,5,6,7, 8,9,10,11	'32 Prom.
	Worakarm	160	np	22,23,24,25, 26,27	Phibun
	Suraphong	197	np	27	tech.
35 Thai Rice Co.	Phao	185	47PP	25,26,27	PP
	Thanom	193	47,57	26,27,28,29,30	Sarit
	Det S	72	np	9,10,11,20,21	tech.
36 Thai Soldiers Bank	Sarit	181	47,57	25,26,27,30	Sarit
	Praphas	195	47,57	27,28,29,30	Sarit
	Thanom	193	47,57	26,27,28,29,30	Sarit
	Sawai	192	47	26	Phibun
	Amphorn	210	57	28,29	Sarit
37 Thai Tham Distillery	Sarit	181	47,57	25,26,27,30	Sarit
	Praphas	195	47,57	27,28,29,30	Sarit
	Thanom	193	47,57	26,27,28,29,30	Sarit
	Siri	187	47PP	25,26,27	PP
38 Thailand Steel	Thanom	193	47,57	26,27,28,29,30	Sarit
	Chalerm	199	47,57	29	Sarit
	Chamnan A	183	57	25,26	Sarit
	Lamai	182	47PP	25,26,27	PP
	Sunawin	167	np	23,24,25,26	Phibun
39 United Bank of Bangkok	Thanom	193	47,57	26,27,28,29,30	Sarit
	Chalerm	199	47,57	29	Sarit
	Kris	217	57	28,29	Sarit
	Sree	31	np	4,5,8,9,11,14	tech.
40 United Civil Engineering	Phao	185	47PP	25,26,27	PP
	Chuang	58	32Ja	8,9,10,15,17, 18,19	'32 Prom.
	Prayoon	8	32Jc	1,2,3,9,10,24, 25,26	'32 Prom.
41 United Shiplines	Praphas	195	47,57	27,28,29,30	Sarit
	Chamnan A	183	57	25,26	Sarit

(*Continued*)

TABLE 6 (*Continued*)
BOARDS CONTAINING THREE OR MORE MINISTERS

No.	Name of Firm	Board Members		Coup Group	Cabinets	Clique
		Sawad	189	47PP	26,27	PP
		Sawai	192	47	26	Phibun
		Chuang	58	32Ja	8,9,10,15,17, 18,19	'32 Prom.
42	United Thai Hotels	Phao	185	47PP	25,26,27	PP
		Prayoon	8	32Jc	1,2,3,9,10,24, 25,26	'32 Prom.
		Rak	191	np	26,27	Phibun
		Chai	80	np	10	tech.

88 per cent of those with five to seven memberships and 100 per cent of those with eight or more memberships were promoters. The chief discrepancy lies in the category of men with three to four memberships, of which only 17 per cent were promoters.

If we divide the scale of board memberships into two categories— those with five or more memberships and those with four or less—we find that 89 per cent of those in the former category were promoters, and 67 per cent of the latter were nonpromoters.

The significance of the thirty promoters holding board memberships becomes more apparent if we consider the data presented in Tables 8 and 9. Only 29 per cent of all cabinet members were promoters, but

TABLE 7
NUMBER OF BOARD MEMBERSHIPS
COMPARED WITH PROMOTER STATUS

Number of Memberships	Promoters		Nonpromoters		Total
	No.	Per cent	No.	Per cent	
8+	9	100	0	0	9
5–7	7	88	2	22	9
3–4	1	17	5	83	6
1–2	13	35	24	65	37
Total	30	49	31	51	61
5+	16	89	2	11	18
1–4	14	33	29	67	43

TABLE 8

CABINET POLITICIANS, PROMOTER STATUS,
AND BOARD MEMBERSHIPS

	Number of Board Memberships, 1957						
Status	*0*	*1–2*	*3–4*	*5–7*	*8+*	*Total Board Members*	*Total Cabinet Members*
Nonpromoters	137	24	5	2	0	31	168
Promoters	39	13	1	6	10	30	69
1932 Pr.	22	5	0	3	0	8	30
1944 Pr.	6	2	0	0	0	2	8
1947 Pr.	3	3	0	2	6	11	14
1957 Pr.	8	3	1	1	4	9	17
Total	176	37	6	8	10	61	237

49 per cent of all cabinet politicians on business boards were promoters. If we define "major board members" as cabinet politicians holding three or more seats on business boards, then we find that 71 per cent of all major board members were promoters.

It is interesting to compare the degree to which promoters belonging to different coup groups had become active as board members by 1957. Table 8 shows how many promoters in each coup group held board memberships. From this table it might appear that the original

TABLE 9

RELATION BETWEEN PROMOTER STATUS
AND BOARD MEMBERSHIPS, 1957

Status	*Cabinet Members*		*All Board Members*		*Major Board Members*	
	No.	*Per cent*	*No.*	*Per cent*	*No.*	*Per cent*
Promoters						
32 & 44	38	16	10	16	3	13
1947	14	6	11	18	8	33
1957	17	7	9	15	6	25
Total	69	29	30	49	17	71
Nonpromoters	168	71	31	51	7	29
Total	237	100	61	100	24	100

TABLE 10
CABINET MEMBERS HOLDING MEMBERSHIPS
ON LEADING BOARDS

Member	Code No.	Prom.	Clique	Cabinets	Leading Boards	All Boards
PROMOTERS						
1957 Coup						
Amphorn	210	57	S	28,29	1	1
Bunchu	215	47,57	S	28,29	2	2
Chalerm	199	47,57	S	27	3	4
Chamnan A	183	57	S	25,26	6	6
Chitti	220	57	S	28,29	6	7
Kris	217	57	S	28,29	1	1
Praphas	195	47,57	S	27,28,29,30	12	19
Sarit	181	47,57	S	25,26,27,30	17	22
Thanom	193	47,57	S	26,27,28,29,30	9	17
1947 Coup—Phin-Phao clique						
Banyat	168	47	PP	23,24,25,26,27	4	5
Lamai	182	47	PP	25,26,27	6	19
Phin	177	47	PP	25,26,27	7	9
Phao	185	47	PP	25,26,27	16	26
Pramarn	184	47	PP	25,26,27	8	11
Sawad	189	47	PP	26,27	8	8
Siri	187	47	PP	25,26,27	12	13
1947 Coup—Phibun group						
Norm	111	32,47	Ph	14,20,21,22,23	1	1
Phibun	12	32,47	Ph	1,2,3,4,5,6,7,8, 9,10,22,23,24, 25,26,27	1	1
Sawai	192	47	Ph	26	10	14
1932 & 1944 Coups						
Chamnan Y	48	32	32	6,7,8	5	6
Chuang	58	32	32	8,9,10,15,17, 18,19	6	7
Direk	64	32,44	32	9,10,12,13,15, 17,18	1	1
Duan	76	32,44	32	10,11,12,15,17, 18,19	1	1

(*Continued*)

TABLE 10 (*Continued*)
CABINET MEMBERS HOLDING MEMBERSHIPS
ON LEADING BOARDS

Member	Code No.	Prom.	Clique	Cabinets	Leading Boards	All Boards
Leng	82	32	32	11	1	1
Prayoon	8	32	32	1,2,3,9,10,24, 25,26	5	5
Pridi	13	32	32	1,2,4,5,6,7,8,9, 15,16,17	1	2
Saphrang	81	32	32	11,12,13,15,17, 28	1	1
Seri	62	32	32	9,10		
Sinthu	6	32	32	1,2,3,4,5,6,7,8, 9,10,11	1	1
NONPROMOTERS						
Boriphan	55	np	Ph	6,7,8,9,10,22, 23,24,25,26,27	2	2
Chai	80	np	tech.	10	3	3
Cherd	180	np	tech.	25,26	1	1
Det S	72	np	tech.	9,10,11,20,21	1	1
Fuen	179	np	PP	25,26,27	3	3
Kukrit	135	np	tech.	20,21,22	1	1
Luan	138	np	Ph	20,21,24,25,26	1	1
Mana	23	np	tech.	3,5,6	1	1
Muni	56	np	Ph	6,7,8,9,10,14,20, 21,24,25,26,27	2	3
Rak	191	np	Ph	26,27	2	2
Serm	221	np	S	28,29	5	5
Sree	31	np	tech.	4,5,8,9,11,14	1	1
Sriwisarn	9	np	tech.	1,2,3,14,20,21	1	1
Sunawin	167	np	Ph	23,24,25,26	5	7
Suraphong	197	np	tech.	27	1	2
Thona	31	np	tech.	22	1	2
Tiron	100	np	tech.	12,13,14	1	1
Yuthasard	178	np	Ph	25,26,27	1	3
Wisut	207	np	S	28,29	1	1
Worakarm	160	np	Ph	22,23,24,25,26, 27	2	2
Xuchat	194	np	tech.	26	3	4

promoters of the revolution in 1932 had entrenched themselves in business boards and still retained their eminence in this respect by 1957. Combining the promoters of the 1932 and 1944 coups, we find that they constituted 16 per cent of all cabinet members, and that 16 per cent of all board members belonged to this group.

However, comparison with the status of the promoters of later coups reveals that they had fallen behind, relatively speaking. The fourteen promoters of the 1947 coup (excluding promoters of the 1957 coup) constituted 6 per cent of all cabinet politicians, but eleven of their number held board memberships, constituting 18 per cent of all board members. By the time of the Military Group coup in 1957, the members of this group, constituting 7 per cent of all cabinet politicians, had acquired board memberships for nine of their number, constituting 15 per cent of all political board members.

If we consider only the major board members, we find that only 13 per cent of this category were promoters of the 1932 and 1944 coups, whereas 33 per cent had taken part in the 1947 coup and 25 per cent in the 1957 coup. (If four men who took part in both the 1947 and 1957 coups were added to the list of 1957 coup members, the calculation for this group of major board members would be raised to 50 per cent.)

So important is this group of members of leading boards for an understanding of the pattern of participation by Thai cabinet politicians in business boards that it seems useful to give further details about them, as presented in Table 10. This table contains the names of all cabinet politicians who held memberships on leading boards. (The term "leading board" has been defined above as any board on which three or more cabinet politicians held memberships.) The list of members is broken into two major categories: promoters and nonpromoters. The category of promoters has been subdivided by the latest year of a coup in which the politicians concerned took part. Nonpromoters are listed alphabetically.

Cliques, as we have seen, formed within the ranks of a ruling circle. Clique affiliation is indicated in the fourth column. All participants in the 1957 coup are identified with the Sarit clique, indicated by the letter "S." Those who took part in the 1947 coup but not the 1957 coup are, for the most part, linked with the Phin-Phao (or "PP") clique. The exceptions are the two men Phibun and Norm, who also took part in the 1932 revolution, and Sawai, who appears to have been more closely associated with Phibun than with the Phin-Phao group. Some of the nonpromoters, by frequent collaboration, appear to have identified themselves with one or another of the cliques. This was particularly true of some men who belonged to one or more of the cabinets (23–27) between 1951 and 1957. Several identified with Phibun, whose group is indicated by the symbol "Ph." The dividing line between this category and the rest of the nonpromoters, who appear not to have had a strong clique identification, is rather vague. Nevertheless, the nonaffiliated nonpromoters are identified as technicians, abbreviated as "tech."

In Table 10, the cabinets on which the politicians served are indicated by number, as given in Appendix B. The last columns give the number of leading boards and the total number of boards on which the members served, according to the available data.

TABLE 11
BOARD MEMBERSHIPS BY CLIQUES AND GROUPS

Number of Memberships	Sarit Clique	PP Clique	32, 44, 47 and Phibun Groups	Technicians
26	—	Phao	—	—
23–25	—	—	—	—
22	Sarit	—	—	—
20–21	—	—	—	—
19	Praphas	Lamai	—	—
18	—	—	—	—
17	Thanom	—	—	—
15–16	—	—	—	—
14	—	—	Sawai	—
13	—	Siri	—	—
12	—	—	—	—
11	—	Pramarn	—	—
10	—	—	—	—
9	—	Phin	—	—
8	—	Sawad	—	—
7	Chitti	—	Chuang, Sunawin	—
6	Chamnan A	—	Chamnan Y	—
5	Serm	Banyat	Prayoon	—
4	Chalerm	—	—	Xuchat
3	—	Fuen	Muni, Yuthasard	Chai
2	Bunchu	—	5 men	2 men
1	3 men	—	11 men	13 men
Average Number of Memberships	7.3	11.8	3.0	1.4

BOARD MEMBERSHIPS BY CLIQUES

An analysis of the extent of board memberships by cliques is given in Table 11. For the purposes of this table, and throughout the remainder of this chapter, the structure of board memberships will be examined in terms of cliques and groups, rather than a strict promoter-nonpromoter breakdown. Thus, the Sarit clique is considered to consist of all promoters of the 1957 coup, plus Serm and Wisut; the PP clique consists of all the promoters of the 1947 clique, plus Fuen, but minus Norm, Phibun, and Sawai. The Phibun group is considered to include these three men, plus Boriphan, Luan, Muni, Rak, Sunawin, Yuthasard, and Worakarm. All the promoters of the 1932 and 1944 coups, except for Norm and Phibun, are classified as belonging to the "32" group. The remaining nonpromoters are considered to belong to the group of technicians. In Table 11, the Phibun, 1932, and 1944 groups are combined to show the range of variation in number of memberships of all cabinet politicians on business boards.

This table highlights the leading figures in each of the cliques and groups, as far as participation on business boards is concerned. It also makes possible a general comparison between the groups in regard to board memberships, showing that the average number of board memberships of the PP clique came to 11.8; of the Sarit clique, 7.3; of the Phibun group and the 1932 and 1947 promoters, 3.0; and of the technicians, 1.4.

PATTERNS OF PARTICIPATION ON BUSINESS BOARDS

Let us next scrutinize the pattern of participation by cabinet politicians in business boards. Was there, for example, any discernible significance in the choice of companies by these men? In a few instances, some fairly clear relationships appear. For example, Police General Lamai and Field Marshal Phin ran the Ministry of Agriculture as deputy minister and minister, respectively, for several years up to September, 1957. This ministry contains departments concerned with agriculture, rice, fisheries, forestry, animal husbandry, and irrigation. We find that Phin was a member of ten boards and Lamai a member of twenty. One of these firms manufactured gunny bags, which were sold to rice millers on a compulsory basis by legally requiring that a minimum percentage of the bags used for rice exports be of domestic manufacture, despite the higher cost and lower quality of domestic as compared with imported bags. Another concern manufactured plywood, taking advantage of strict limitations by the Forestry Department governing all commercial exploitation of Thai lumber resources. A third firm manufactured matches. Several warehousing companies took advantage of governmental programs to stabilize rice prices. Sugar companies were designed to exploit the government's policies for the expansion of sugar production. Another firm specialized in the sale of salted fish, presumably taking advantage of special services from the Fisheries Department. The Farmers Bank was on the list, a beneficiary of public funds for agricultural development. Shipping and insurance firms were able to take advantage of governmental programs intended to spur trade in agricultural products.[15]

Without more complete information about the business firms than can be gleaned from their titles, however, it is difficult to do more than speculate about possible relationships between the official position held by cabinet politicians and their business interests. More relevant, for present purposes, because of the light that it throws on the character of the clique structures in the Thai cabinet, is the pattern of overlapping memberships on the business boards revealed by the data given above, especially in Table 6. The information contained in this table can be used to discover how many board memberships were held in common by every possible pair of cabinet politicians. However, rather than set up an elaborate table showing all these pairs, it seemed advisable to begin with a more limited set of tables showing the number of board contacts enjoyed by the various cliques and groups.

TABLE 12

PHIN-PHAO CLIQUE: JOINT MEMBERSHIPS
ON LEADING BUSINESS BOARDS

	Banyat	Lamai	Phao	Phin	Pramarn	Fuen	Sawad	Siri	Total*
Banyat		2	3	1	2	1	0	2	11
Lamai	2		2	1	1	0	0	2	8
Phao	3	2		5	5	2	2	5	24
Phin	1	1	5		3	1	1	5	17
Pramarn	2	1	5	3		0	2	5	18
Fuen	1	0	2	1	0		0	1	5
Sawad	0	0	2	1	2	0		1	6
Siri	2	2	5	5	5	1	1		21

*Total number of board contacts.

The Phin-Phao Clique.   Because the Phin-Phao clique was clearly the most tightly knit and deeply involved in business activities, it has been selected for analysis first (see Table 12).

Table 12 shows the number of boards on which any two men are concurrently members. Thus, Phin and Phao sat together on five different boards, Pramarn and Siri on five. Whenever two men are simultaneously members of the same board, we may speak of a "board contact." The largest number of board contacts within the Phin-Phao group was made by Phao (24). This means that Phao shared a board membership twenty-four times with other members of his clique. Several of these board contacts could have been on the same board. Hence, Phao belonged to only 9 boards on which he shared a seat with another member of his clique, although he belonged to a total of 26 boards, including 16 leading boards. This means that on 7 leading boards he was the only member from the Phin-Phao clique. He may, of course, have had additional board contacts with his clique associates on his 10 "other boards." The essential characteristics of the pattern of overlapping memberships can be shown by utilizing only the "leading boards." The data becomes unnecessarily complex if all the "other board" memberships of each cabinet member are shown.

The information contained in Table 7 is shown in the form of a sociogram in Fig. 7. In this figure, the connecting lines represent the number of board contacts between each member of the clique. A dotted line represents one such contact; a single line, two contacts; a dark dotted line, three or four contacts; and a heavy line, five or more contacts. The number of board contacts made by each member of the clique is indicated by the figure under his name. It should equal the number represented by the connecting lines converging on the name.

It is apparent from this figure that Phao had the largest number of board contacts, being linked by multiple joint memberships with Siri, Pramarn, Phin, and Banyat, and by at least two board contacts with the rest: Fuen, Lamai, and Sawad. The smaller number of board contacts enjoyed by the other members is shown visually. The structure of these relationships helps to demonstrate the tightly knit character of the interlocking directorates exercised by members of the Phin-Phao clique.

The Sarit Clique.   Table 13 gives a similar presentation of the board contacts made within the Sarit clique.

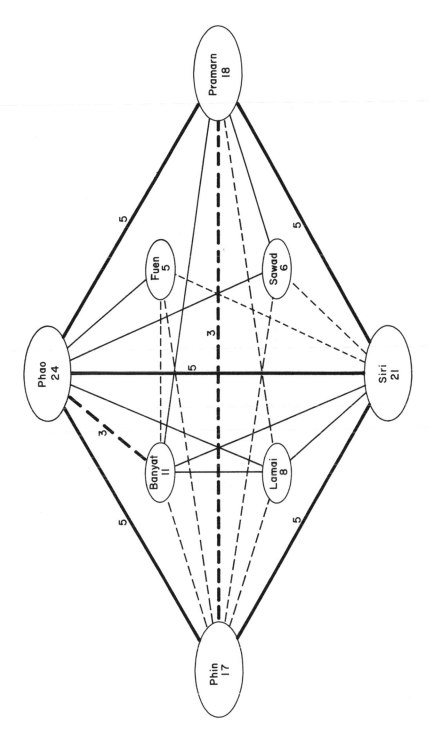

FIGURE 7. The Phin-Phao Clique

TABLE 13

SARIT CLIQUE: JOINT MEMBERSHIPS
ON LEADING BUSINESS BOARDS

	Amphorn	Bunchu	Chalerm	Chamnan A	Chitti	Kris	Praphas	Sarit	Serm	Thanom	Wisut	No. of Board Contacts
Amphorn		0	0	0	0	0	1	1	0	1	0	3
Bunchu	0		0	1	1	0	0	2	0	1	0	5
Chalerm	0	0		1	0	1	0	0	0	2	0	4
Chamnan A	0	1	1		2	0	2	3	1	1	0	11
Chitti	0	1	0	2		0	5	6	0	3	0	17
Kris	0	0	1	0	0		0	0	0	1	0	2
Praphas	1	0	0	2	5	0		7	0	5	0	20
Sarit	1	2	0	3	6	0	7		2	6	0	27
Serm	0	0	0	1	0	0	0	2		0	0	3
Thanom	1	1	2	1	3	1	5	6	0		0	20
Wisut	0	0	0	0	0	0	0	0	0	0		0

It is apparent that the dominant position was held by Sarit, with 27 board contacts; his top lieutenants, Thanom, Praphas, and Chitti, had 20, 20, and 17 board contacts, respectively. Figure 8 gives a visual presentation of the internal structure of the Sarit clique as reflected in their participation in busines boards.

Clearly, the Sarit clique had not developed as closely knit a structure as the Phin-Phao clique had created. Wisut, a nonpromoter, had no board contact with other members. Serm, also a nonpromoter, had two board contacts with Sarit and one with Chamnan A. Kris was in an isolated position, having only a single board contact each with two other members, Thanom and Chalerm. Nevertheless, the basic framework provided by Sarit, Thanom, and Praphas becomes apparent, with Chitti and Chamnan A clearly identified as major supporters.

The Phibun and "32" Groups.   Let us next examine the board contacts made by the men associated with Phibun, including Phibun himself and the men closely associated with him, plus Sawai, as shown in Table 14.

A glance is sufficient to show that the members of this group had very few board contacts with each other, a fact which is brought out even more strikingly in Fig. 9.

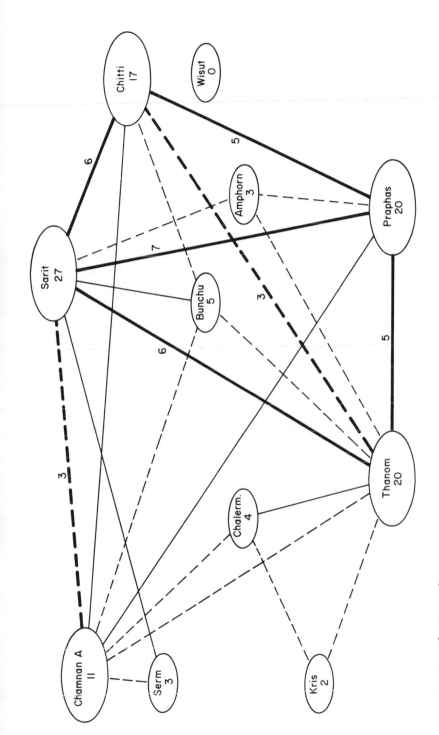

FIGURE 8. The Sarit Clique

TABLE 14
PHIBUN GROUP: JOINT MEMBERSHIPS
ON LEADING BUSINESS BOARDS

	Boriphan	Luan	Muni	Norm	Phibun	Rak	Sawai	Sunawin	Worakarm	Yuthasard	No. of Board Contacts
Boriphan		0	0	0	0	1	0	0	0	1	2
Luan	0		1	0	0	0	0	0	0	0	1
Muni	0	1		0	0	0	0	0	0	0	1
Norm	0	0	0		0	0	0	0	0	0	0
Phibun	0	0	0	0		0	0	1	0	0	1
Rak	1	0	0	0	0		0	0	0	1	2
Sawai	0	0	0	0	0	0		1	0	0	1
Sunawin	0	0	0	0	1	0	1		0	0	2
Worakarm	0	0	0	0	0	0	0	0		0	0
Yuthasard	1	0	0	0	0	1	0	0	0		2

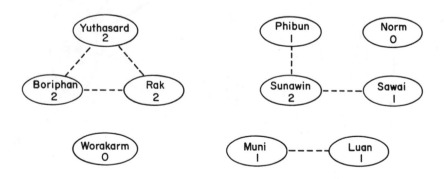

FIGURE 9.   Phibun's Group

When we examine the internal structure of board contacts of the promoters of the 1932 revolution who were members of leading boards, we find that the number of overlaps were even more limited, as shown in Table 15.

TABLE 15
1932 PROMOTERS: JOINT MEMBERSHIPS
ON LEADING BUSINESS BOARDS

	Chamnan Y	Chuang	Direk	Duan	Leng	Phibun	Prayoon	Saphrang	Seri	Sinthu	No. of Board Contacts
Chamnan Y		0	0	0	0	0	0	0	0	0	0
Chuang	0		0	0	0	0	3	0	0	0	3
Direk	0	0		0	0	0	0	0	1	0	1
Duan	0	0	0		0	0	0	0	0	0	0
Leng	0	0	0	0		0	0	0	0	0	0
Phibun	0	0	0	0	0		0	0	0	0	0
Prayoon	0	3	0	0	0	0		0	0	0	3
Saphrang	0	0	0	0	0	0	0		0	0	0
Seri	0	0	1	0	0	0	0	0		0	1
Sinthu	0	0	0	0	0	0	0	0	0		0

Except for three board contacts between Chuang and Prayoon, it appears that two or more promoters of the 1932 revolution rarely sat together on the same business board. The average number of board seats held by these men was three, admittedly well below the average of the Phin-Phao and Sarit clique members. Yet if, in any sense, they had constituted a clique, one would have expected the members of this

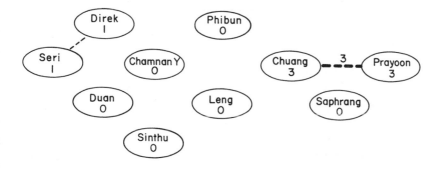

FIGURE 10. 1932 Promoters

group to have had board contacts with each other. Figure 10 demonstrates the extent to which they were mutually isolated in their business roles.

LINKAGE ROLES AMONG CLIQUES

If we think of the 1932 promoters as forming links between other groups, or as allies and partners of men in the dominant cliques, then we find that they play a more interesting role in the structure of board memberships. Let us examine this possibility (Table 16).

TABLE 16
1932 PROMOTERS: BOARD CONTACTS
WITH OTHER GROUPS

	PP Clique	Sarit Clique	No. of Board Contacts
Chamnan Y	7	1	8
Chuang	8	5	13
Direk	3	0	3
Duan	0	4	4
Leng	1	0	1
Norm	2	0	2
Phibun	3	1	4
Prayoon	4	6	10
Sawai	10	16	26
Saphrang	2	2	4
Seri	3	0	3
Sinthu	1	0	1
Total	44	35	79

These relationships are shown in Fig. 11, using boxes to represent cliques and groups, circles for individuals. Examination now clearly reveals that certain leading individuals in the group of 1932 promoters— notably Chuang (13), Prayoon (10), and Chamnan Y (8), plus Sawai (26) of the Phibun group—seem to have played significant roles as links between the Sarit and PP cliques, and, to a lesser degree, connecting also with the Phibun group and the technicians. By contrast, other men appear to have had limited board contacts with only one of the cliques. Duan, for example, had four links with members of the Sarit clique but

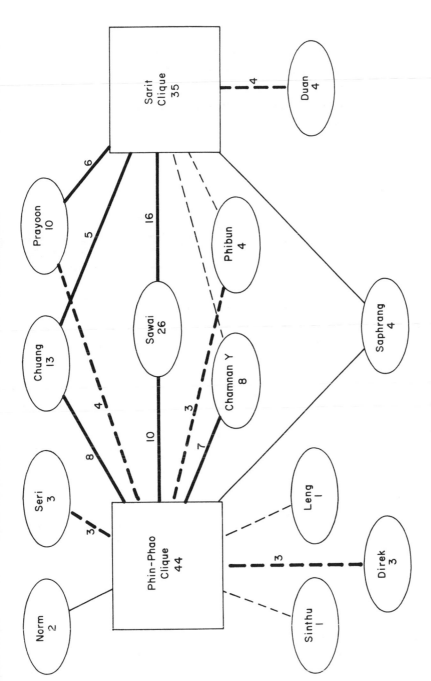

FIGURE 11. 1932, 1945, and 1947 (Non-Clique) Promoters

none with the PP clique. Norm, Direk, Seri, Sinthu, and Leng had board contacts with the PP clique but not with the Sarit clique.

Let us examine the linkage roles more closely. Instead of lumping together all members of the Sarit and Phin-Phao cliques, we will identify the specific board contacts of the leading cabinet politicians with

TABLE 17
1932 PROMOTERS: BOARD CONTACTS
WITH PHIN-PHAO AND SARIT CLIQUES

	Chai	Chamnan Y	Chuang	Phibun	Prayoon	Saphrang	Sawai	Sunawin	Xuchat	No. of Board Contacts
PP clique										
Banyat	1	0	0	0	0	1	0	0	1	3
Lamai	0	0	1	0	0	0	0	1	1	3
Phao	2	1	3	1	4	0	1	2	2	16
Phin	0	0	1	1	0	0	1	1	2	6
Pramarn	0	1	1	0	0	0	1	0	0	3
Fuen	1	0	0	1	0	1	0	1	1	5
Sawad	0	5	1	0	0	0	6	1	0	13
Siri	0	0	1	0	0	0	1	0	0	2
PP Total	4	7	8	3	4	2	10	6	7	51
Sarit clique										
Amphorn	0	0	0	0	0	0	1	0	0	1
Bunchu	0	0	0	0	0	0	1	0	0	1
Chalerm	1	0	0	0	0	1	0	1	0	3
Chamnan A	0	0	2	0	0	0	1	1	0	4
Chitti	0	0	0	0	0	0	1	0	0	1
Kris	0	0	0	0	0	0	0	0	0	0
Praphas	0	1	1	0	0	0	5	2	0	9
Sarit	1	0	2	1	2	0	4	1	3	14
Serm	0	0	1	0	0	0	0	1	1	3
Thanom	0	0	0	0	0	0	3	1	0	4
Wisut	1	0	0	0	0	1	0	1	0	3
Sarit Total	3	1	6	1	2	2	16	8	4	43
Grand Total	7	8	14	4	6	4	26	14	11	94

each member of these two cliques, as shown in Table 17. For this purpose, let us include the six promoters shown in Fig. 10 who had board contacts with both cliques and add the non-promoters holding three or more memberships on leading boards but not identified with a major clique, i.e., Sunawin, Chai, and Xuchat.

The information in Table 17 has been charted in Fig. 12. Under the name of each man in the intermediate linkage roles two figures are given e.g., 10 + 15 for Sawai. This means that Sawai had 10 board contacts with members of the Phin-Phao clique and 15 with members of the Sarit clique, a total of 25. An examination of these figures shows that nine cabinet politicians had established multiple board contacts with individuals in both of the major cliques.

Considerable difference in intensity of contacts manifests itself. Thus, Sawai, with 25 board contacts, was much more deeply involved in these relationships than Phibun himself, who had only 4. Next to Sawai, the most involved members of this intermediate group were Chuang (14) and Sunawin (14). It is notable that these men had also established board contacts with the more influential members of the two cliques: Sawai with Sarit, Praphas, and Thanom on the Sarit side, but primarily with Sawad on the PP side, although he also had at least one board contact each with Phao, Phin, Siri, and Pramarn. Similarly, Chuang had established multiple links with Phao and Sarit, augmented by fewer links with other key members of each clique. Sunawin also had his major contacts with Praphas and Phao, plus minor links with Sarit, Thanom, Phin, and Lamai. Saphrang, who had balanced his connections, had only four board contacts, and these were all with less important figures in the two cliques.

Further examination of this figure suggests the existence of several different nodes, one revolving around Sawai and Chamnan Y, a second around Chuang and Prayoon, a third around Sunawin, and a fourth around Xuchat. Let us examine all the board contacts of these men to see what kind of pattern emerges (Table 18).

CONNECTING NODES: SC, CP, SUNAWIN, AND XUCHAT

It is remarkable how few board contacts there were between these four nodes. For the SC node, Sawai had one board contact with the CP node and one with the Sunawin node, but Chamnan Y had none. Conversely, Chuang had one board contact with the SC node, but Prayoon had none. Sunawin, similarly, had one contact with the SC node but

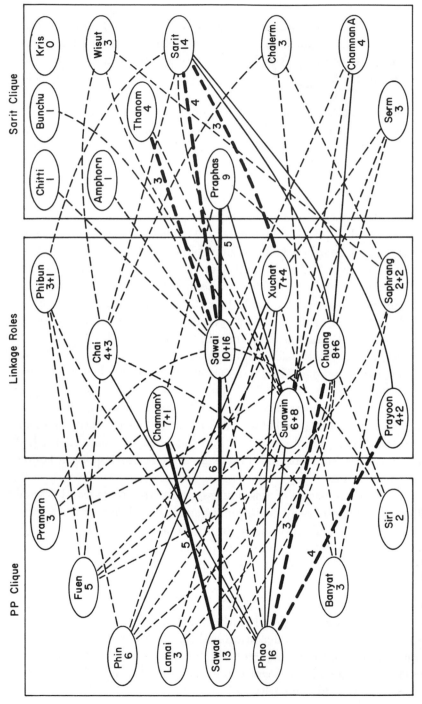

FIGURE 12. Linkage Roles

TABLE 18
BOARD CONTACTS OF THE SC, CP, SUNAWIN,
AND XUCHAT NODES

	Sawai	Chamnan Y	Chuang	Prayoon	Sunawin	Xuchat
PP clique						
Banyat	0	0	0	0	0	1
Fuen	0	0	0	0	1	1
Lamai	0	0	1	0	1	1
Phao	1	1	3	4	2	2
Phin	1	0	1	0	1	2
Pramarn	1	1	1	0	0	0
Sawad	6	5	1	0	1	0
Siri	1	0	1	0	0	1
Sarit clique						
Amphorn	1	0	0	0	0	0
Bunchu	1	0	0	0	0	0
Chalerm	0	0	0	0	1	0
Chamnan A	1	0	2	0	1	0
Chitti	1	0	0	0	0	0
Praphas	5	1	2	0	1	0
Sarit	4	0	2	2	1	3
Serm	0	0	1	0	1	1
Thanom	3	0	0	0	1	0
Others						
Boriphan	0	0	1	0	0	0
Chai	0	0	0	2	0	0
Chamnan Y	4		0	0	0	0
Chuang	1	0		3	0	0
Muni	0	0	0	0	0	1
Phibun	0	0	0	0	1	1
Prayoon	0	0	3		0	0
Rak	0	0	1	1	0	0
Sawai		4	1	0	1	0
Sunawin	1	0	0	0		1
Thona	0	0	0	1	0	0
Worakarm	0	0	0	0	0	0
Xuchat	0	0	0	0	1	
Yuthasard	0	0	1	0	0	0
Total	32	12	22	13	15	15

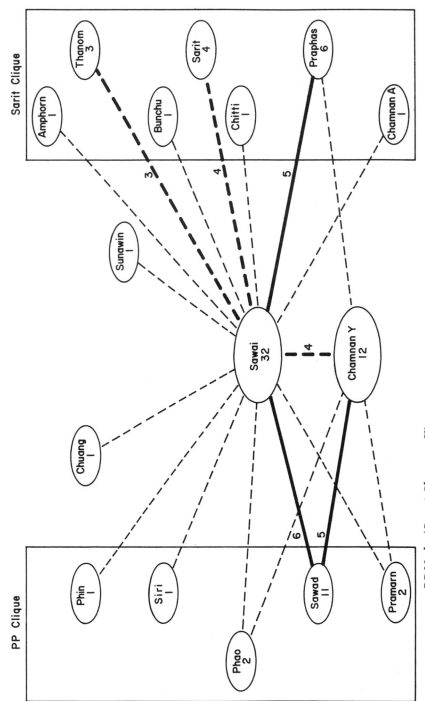

FIGURE 13. SC Node (Sawai-Chamnan Y)

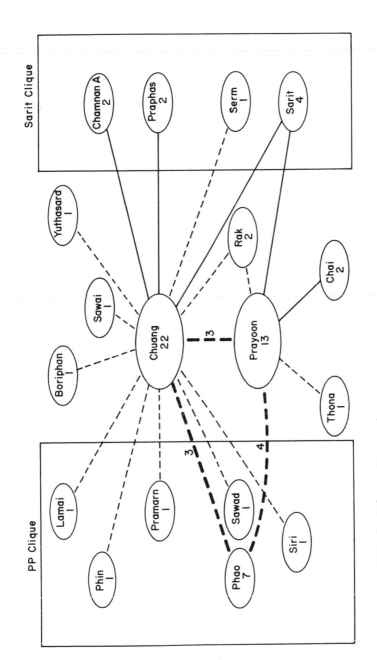

FIGURE 14. CP Node (Chuang-Prayoon)

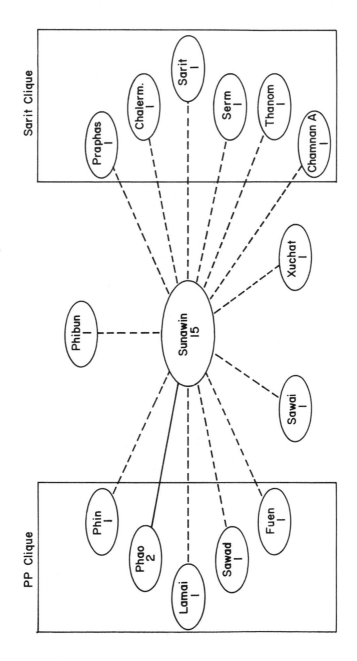

FIGURE 15. Sunawin Node

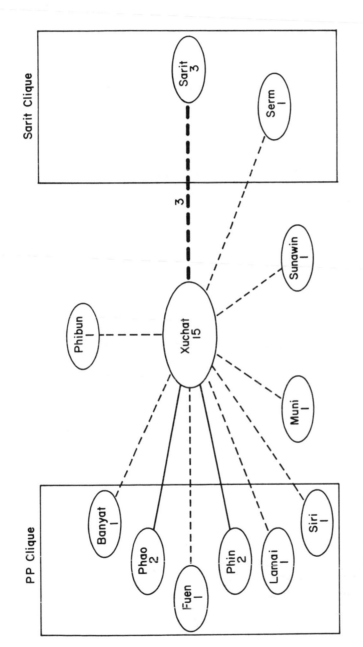

FIGURE 16. Xuchat Node

none with the CP group. Yet each of these nodes had multiple board contacts with the two major cliques and with other cabinet politicians, as illustrated in Figs. 13–16.

As Fig. 13 indicates clearly, both Sawai and Chamnan Y, although not members of either the PP or Sarit clique, had multiple board contacts in both cliques. However, Chamnan Y had most of his contacts in the PP clique, with only one link to Praphas, in the other group. Sawai, although well connected in the PP group, had his main strength in his Sarit clique connections. Both Sawai and Chamnan Y had few board contacts with nonmembers of the two leading cliques, except for their four links with each other. Sawad and Praphas appear to have been the members of the PP and Sarit cliques, respectively, with whom Sawai and Chamnan Y worked most closely.

Similar principles of organization may be discovered in the pattern of interlocking memberships for the CP, Sunawin, and Xuchat nodes, as shown in Figs. 14–16.

From these sociograms, a pattern of clique participation in business boards begins to be seen. It seems clear that nonmembers of the two dominant cliques did not form an alternative clique, working together as a bloc. Rather, individuals outside both cliques, whether because of long-standing participation in the higher levels of Thai politics or because of technical eminence as bureaucrats, were able to form links with key members of both the dominant cliques. They appear to have had little interest in forming such connections with other non-clique members, however. In playing this game, promoters like Sawai-Chamnan Y and Chuang-Prayoon appear to have done better than men who were primarily technicians, like Sunawin and Xuchat.

One is tempted, at first, to think that these marginal nodes might have performed the function of balancing between the major cliques, perhaps playing a mediating role. Yet the chief political balancer was Phibun. As prime minister it was his preoccupation, as a condition of staying in office, to preserve a balance of power between the increasingly aggressive cliques within his ruling circle. It is remarkable that Phibun himself belonged to only one business board, according to our records. He had no board contact with either the SC or CP node and only a single contact each with the Sunawin and Xuchat technician nodes.

DIRECT CONTACTS BETWEEN PP AND SARIT CLIQUES

If the members of the PP and Sarit cliques had little or no business contact with each other, then we might assume that the marginal nodes performed an important mediatory function, but analysis shows that this was not the case. Table 19 gives the direct business contacts recorded between members of the PP and Sarit cliques. Members without such contacts are not included in the table.

TABLE 19

BOARD CONTACTS BETWEEN MEMBERS OF PHIN-PHAO AND SARIT CLIQUES

	Banyat	*Lamai*	*Phao*	*Phin*	*Pramarn*	*Fuen*	*Sawad*	*Siri*	*No. of Board Contacts*
Chalerm	1	1	0	0	0	1	0	0	3
Chamnan A	0	1	2	2	1	0	1	2	9
Chitti	0	1	0	0	0	0	0	1	2
Praphas	0	2	0	0	1	0	3	2	8
Sarit	1	3	5	4	3	1	0	6	23
Serm	0	0	3	3	2	0	1	3	12
Thanom	0	2	1	0	0	0	0	1	4
No. of Board Contacts	2	10	11	9	7	2	5	15	61

The information contained in Table 19 is represented graphically in Fig. 17. It becomes immediately apparent that the individual members of both cliques had multiple board contacts with each other. It is necessary to recall here that both cliques belonged to the same ruling circle. They had frequent political, administrative, and social contacts with each other and worked for many purposes as a co-operating political elite. It was only as competition grew and the leader of the circle became increasingly unable to control the rivalry that tension between the cliques finally broke out, and one clique succeeded in ousting the other from the ruling circle.

The character of the relationships between the two dominant cliques becomes more apparent if we examine the network of board contacts made by key leaders in each of the two cliques. Let us, for this purpose, take Phao and Sarit as the two dominant figures, plus Siri and Lamai from the PP clique and Serm and Chamnan A from the Sarit clique. The choice is made on the basis that these men had board contacts with

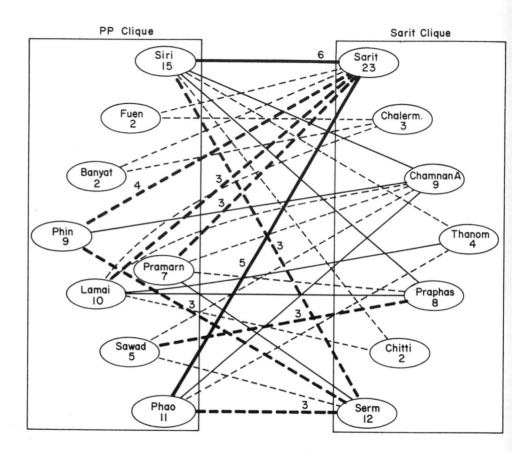

FIGURE 17.   Phin-Phao and Sarit Clique Contacts

the largest number of individuals in the other clique. The extent of their board contacts is given in Table 20.

The information contained in Table 20 has been diagrammed in Figs. 18–21, where it becomes apparent that each of the key members of the PP and Sarit cliques not only had a multiplicity of board contacts with members of his own clique, but also had established many board contacts with members of the rival clique, as well as with independent promoters, technicians, and members of Phibun's group.

TABLE 20
BOARD CONTACTS OF PHAO, SIRI, LAMAI, SARIT, CHAMNAN A, AND SERM

	Phao	Siri	Lamai	Sarit	Chamnan A	Serm	No. of Board Contacts
PP clique							
Banyat	2	1	1	1	0	0	5
Lamai	2	2		3	1	0	8
Phao		5	2	5	2	3	17
Phin	5	5	1	4	2	3	20
Pramarn	5	6	1	3	1	2	18
Fuen	2	1	1	1	0	0	5
Sawad	2	1	0	0	1	1	5
Siri	5		2	6	2	3	18
Total	23	21	8	23	9	12	96
Sarit clique							
Amphorn	0	0	0	1	0	0	1
Bunchu	0	0	0	2	1	0	3
Chalerm	0	0	1	0	1	1	3
Chamnan A	2	2	1	3		1	9
Chitti	0	1	1	6	2	0	10
Kris	0	0	0	0	0	0	0
Praphas	0	2	2	7	2	0	13
Sarit	5	6	3		4	2	20
Serm	3	3	0	2	1		9
Thanom	1	1	2	6	1	0	11
Wisut	0	0	0	0	0	0	0
Total	11	15	10	27	12	4	79
Phibun group							
Boriphan	2	2	0	1	1	2	8
Det S	1	0	0	0	0	0	1
Luan	1	1	1	0	0	0	3
Muni	2	1	2	1	0	0	6
Phibun	1	0	0	1	0	0	2

(*Continued*)

TABLE 20 (*Continued*)

BOARD CONTACTS OF PHAO, SIRI, LAMAI, SARIT,
CHAMNAN A, AND SERM

	Phao	Siri	Lamai	Sarit	Chamnan A	Serm	No. of Board Contacts
Rak	2	1	0	1	1	1	6
Sawai	1	1	0	4	1	0	8
Sunawin	2	1	1	1	1	1	6
Worakarm	0	1	0	0	0	0	1
Yuthasard	1	1	0	1	1	1	5
Total	13	9	4	10	5	5	46
1932 promoters							
Chamnan Y	1	0	0	0	0	0	1
Chuang	3	1	1	2	2	1	10
Direk	0	1	1	0	0	0	2
Duan	0	0	0	1	1	0	2
Leng	1	0	0	0	0	0	1
Norm	0	1	0	0	0	0	1
Prayoon	4	0	0	2	0	0	6
Saphrang	0	0	0	0	0	0	0
Sinthu	0	1	0	0	0	0	1
Total	9	4	2	5	3	1	24
Technicians							
Chai	2	0	0	1	0	0	3
Cherd	0	0	0	0	0	0	0
Kukrit	0	0	1	0	0	0	1
Mana	1	0	0	0	0	0	1
Sree	0	0	0	0	0	0	0
Sriwisarn	0	0	1	0	0	0	1
Suraphong	0	1	0	0	0	0	1
Thona	1	0	0	1	0	0	2
Tiron	0	0	1	0	0	0	1
Xuchat	2	1	1	3	0	1	8
Total	6	2	4	5	0	1	18
Grand Total	62	51	28	70	29	23	263

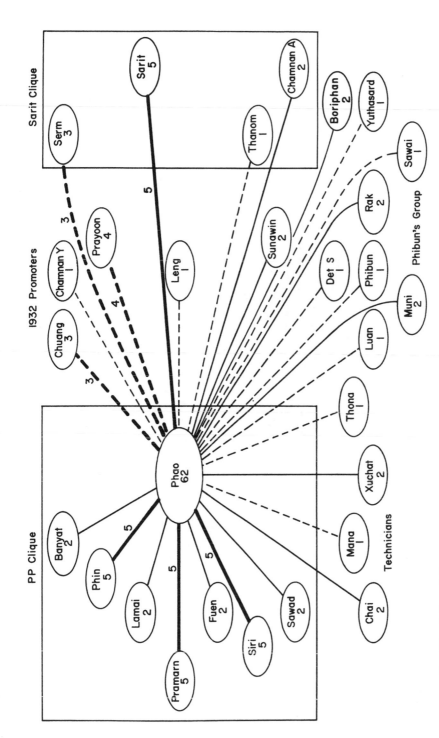

FIGURE 18. Phao's Board Contacts

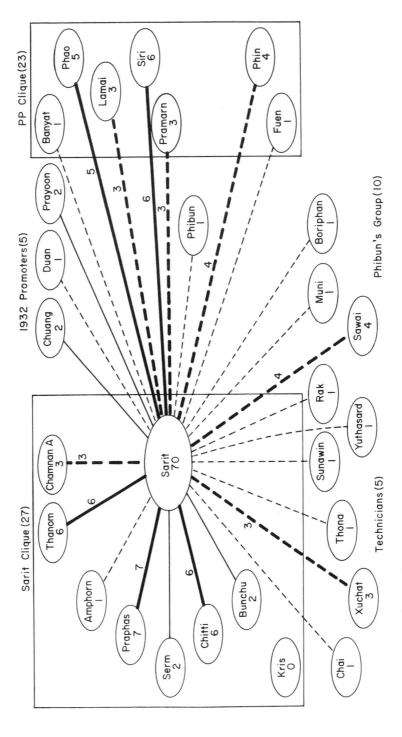

FIGURE 19. Sarit's Board Contacts

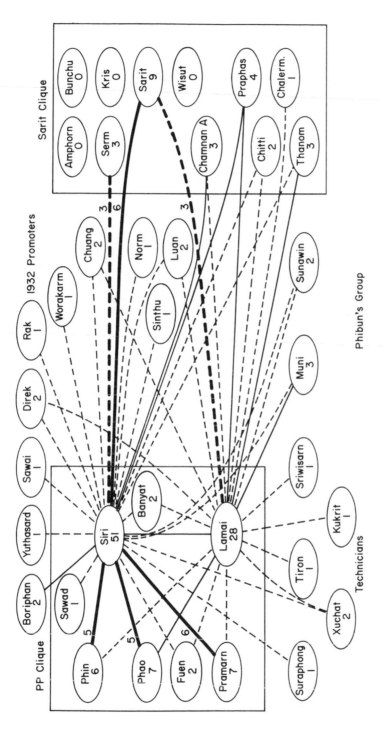

FIGURE 20. Board Contacts of Siri and Lamai

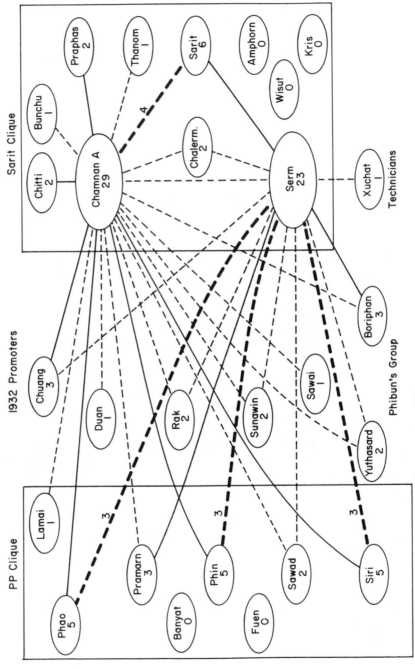

FIGURE 21. Board Contacts of Chamnan A and Serm

Comparing the positions of Sarit and Phao, we first observe that Sarit had a larger total number of board contacts (70) than did Phao (62). It is notable also that Phao had more than twice as many board contacts (23) in his own clique as he had in the Sarit clique (11), whereas Sarit had almost as many board contacts in the PP clique (23) as he had in his own (27).

SIGNIFICANCE OF MEMBERSHIP ON BUSINESS BOARDS

The major purpose of our exercise has been to demonstrate that board memberships were utilized by members of the Thai elite to enhance their income, not to augment their power. They gained power in a different way, primarily with reference to bureaucratic resources at their command, including military forces. They were invited to join business boards in order to extend the mantle of their protection to the economic activities concerned. The entrepreneurial organizers of these business concerns could scarcely afford, in the long run, to have their firms identified exclusively with one clique, for to do so was to run the risk that the other clique would emerge victorious. The defeat of their political patrons would spell ruin for their interests. Hence, we may expect that, in fact, members of both rival cliques would have been asked to take part in the board of any private firm.

Undoubtedly it was difficult to maintain a perfect balance, and it is not surprising to find that, in most boards, members of one or the other clique predominate. There were also a few boards which included only members of one clique. These firms were probably organized directly by the cabinet members concerned, rather than by independent entrepreneurs who subsequently solicited political patronage of their firms. However, adequate data are not available to test this hypothesis.

Some support for the position taken here may be inferred from comments made by Skinner in his study of the Chinese business community. He argues that several, if not all, of the Chinese power blocs were able to mobilize political support from different quarters within the Siamese elite in order to enhance their own security and prestige. In other words, each of the major Chinese groupings probably sought to win support from more than one clique within the Thai ruling circle. Whereas the Chinese leaders had to rely for influence upon their ability to pay, so that their membership on boards of directors could be taken as a direct measure of their relative power, the Thai leaders depended on direct forms of bureaucratic and political control, so that their board memberships were a consequence, not a cause, of their power position.

Skinner writes that "the largest and most powerful of these Sino-Thai business blocs turns out to be merely an expansion of the Ayutthaya Bloc. . . ." Among its political patrons Skinner lists Phao, his wife and brother, Phin and his son, Siri, and other members of the PP clique, but he also lists Sarit and officials in his clique. Skinner suggests that this bloc was composed of three constituent groups, headed respectively by Phao, Phin, and Sarit.[16]

Skinner indicates that other Chinese elite groups, allied with members of the Thai elite, could be identified, naming the "Thai-hua Bloc" and the "Bangkok Bank Bloc." I have not been able to trace any simple linkages between these blocs and cliques within the Thai elite. Perhaps this confirms the thought that each Chinese bloc sought multiple alliances with the rival groups of Siamese power-holders.

STRUCTURE OF BUSINESS BOARDS

An alternative mode of analysis of the participation of cabinet politicians on business boards may be made in terms not of the board contacts between officials but rather by examining the balance between members of the rival cliques on individual boards. If the propositions advanced in the previous paragraphs are valid, we should expect to find, in considerable measure, a balancing of participation by members of the PP and Sarit cliques on many, if not all, of the boards.

Data required for such an analysis are presented in Table 21. This table lists, for each of the leading boards, the number of cabinet politicians who were members, the percentage belonging to each of the

TABLE 21

COMPOSITION OF BUSINESS BOARDS

No.	Name	Members	*Percentage of Membership*		
			Sarit	*Non-Clique*	*PP*
1.	Bank of Asia	5	80	20	00
2.	Bank of Bangkok	3	33	33	33
3.	Cement for Irrigation	6	17	33	50
4.	Consumer Goods from Animals	3	00	67	33
5.	Eastern International Development	4	75	25	00
6.	Eastern Mine	3	100	00	00

(Continued)

TABLE 21 (*Continued*)
COMPOSITION OF BUSINESS BOARDS

No.	Name	Members	Percentage of Membership		
			Sarit	Non-Clique	PP
7.	Erawan Films	7	43	43	14
8.	Farmers Bank	7	00	57	43
9.	Forest of Prachin	3	00	33	67
10.	Import Samakhi	3	00	67	33
11.	Kan Kha Samakhi	4	25	50	25
12.	Khosat Export	3	00	67	33
13.	Military Bank	5	80	20	00
14.	Muang Rae Burapha Sethakit	5	80	00	20
15.	NEDCOL	12	25	33	41
16.	NE Gunny Bags	6	67	17	17
17.	Phadung Sin	3	33	00	67
18.	Provincial Bank	3	33	33	33
19.	Rajata Shipping	5	80	00	20
20.	Rajata Stone	4	100	00	00
21.	Saeng Surat Hotel	5	20	60	20
22.	Saha Samakhi Khosat	4	25	50	25
23.	Sathaporn Films	3	00	00	100
24.	Sri Ayuthia Bank	4	00	25	75
25.	Sri Ayuthia Trading	3	33	33	33
26.	Sugar Industry of Chonburi	7	72	14	14
27.	Sugar Industry of Suphanburee	5	40	20	40
28.	Sugar Industry of Thailand	6	67	33	00
29.	Thai Airways	7	29	43	29
30.	Thai Commercial Bank	3	00	67	33
31.	Thai Commercial Trust	3	33	67	00
32.	Thai Financial Syndicate	3	00	67	33
33.	Thai Gunny Bags	3	33	00	67
34.	Thai Navigation	4	00	75	25
35.	Thai Rice Co.	3	33	33	33
36.	Thai Soldiers Bank	5	80	20	00
37.	Thai Tham Distillery	4	75	00	25
38.	Thailand Steel	5	60	20	20
39.	United Bank of Bangkok	4	75	25	00
40.	United Civil Engineering	3	00	67	33
41.	United Shiplines	5	20	40	40
42.	United Thai Hotels	4	00	75	25

two major cliques, and the percentage who were not members of either clique.

Analyzing these data, we can distinguish at least three significant dimensions of variation: the ratio of non-clique members to clique members on each board, the ratio of members of the Sarit clique to members of the PP clique, and the total number of cabinet level politicians on each board. Utilizing each of these dimensions, we obtain the information contained in Table 22.

TABLE 22
DIMENSIONS OF VARIATION IN BOARD COMPOSITION

A. *Number of Non-Clique Members as Percentage of All Cabinet Politicians on Boards*

1.	0–9%	Most clique-dominated	8
2.	10–29%	Quite clique-dominated	10
3.	30–39%	Moderately clique-dominated	8
4.	40–59%	Little clique-dominated	6
5.	60–100%	Least clique-dominated	10
		Total	42

B. *Ratio of Sarit Clique members to PP Clique members*

1.	1/0	All Sarit, no PP clique	9
2.	1/1–1/0	More Sarit than PP clique	7
3.	1/1	Equal number from both cliques	9
4.	1/1–0/1	Fewer Sarit than PP clique	5
5.	0/1	No Sarit, all PP clique	12
		Total	42

C. *Number of Cabinet Politicians on Boards (all having 3 or more)*

1.	3 members	16
2.	4 members	9
3.	5 members	9
4.	6–7 members	7
5.	8+ members	1
	Total	42

The relationships between these three dimensions of variation may be shown in a set of two-dimensional matrices, as given in Tables 23–26.

TABLE 23

DEGREE OF CLIQUE DOMINATION COMPARED
WITH CLIQUE COMPOSITION

B. *Ratio of Sarit to PP Clique*	A. *Number of Non-Clique Members*					
	1 (0–9%)	*2 (10–29%)*	*3 (30–39%)*	*4 (40–59%)*	*5 (60–100%)*	*Total*
1 (1/0)	2	5	1	0	1	9
2 (1/1–1/0)	3	3	0	1	0	7
3 (1/1)	0	1	4	3	1	9
4 (1/1–0/1)	2	0	2	1	0	5
5 (0/1)	1	1	1	1	8	12
Total	8	10	8	6	10	42

Several observations may be based on the data in Table 23. It is striking that less than one-fifth of the boards (8) had no non-clique members. These strongly clique-dominated boards included but two (#6 and #20 in Table 21) containing only members of the Sarit clique, and just one (#23) fully controlled by the PP clique. The five others included some members of both cliques, but none in which each clique had an equal number of members. Thus, three of the five (#4, 19, 37) had more Sarit than PP clique members, and two (#17, 33) had more PP than Sarit clique members.

If we consider the first two columns together as a group of 18 relatively clique-dominated boards, we find the Sarit clique clearly in the ascendency with 7 fully dominated boards, compared with only 2 fully controlled by members of the PP clique. If we include the mixed boards (lines B2 and B4) but exclude the balanced boards (B3), and add together the first two columns (A1 and A2), we discover that the Sarit clique had more members than the PP clique on 13 clique-dominated boards, whereas the PP clique had more of its members on only four clique-dominated boards.

In marked contrast with these observations, consider the boards which were least clique dominated (column A5), in which we find that there were eight boards (#4, 10, 12, 30, 32, 34, 40, 42) containing PP clique members but no Sarit clique members, whereas there was only one board (#31) in this category containing only Sarit clique members and no PP members.

One interpretation might be that members of the PP clique preferred to co-opt technicians, 1932 promoters, and members of Phibun's group in the boards they dominated, rather than to work without associates outside their clique. But perhaps they did not like to have Sarit clique members on these boards. An alternative interpretation might be that boards in which non-clique members were influential chose to invite members of the PP clique to work with them, rather than members of the Sarit clique. The evidence seems to show, at any rate, that the Sarit clique members were more likely to be found in exclusive combinations, without either PP clique or nonmembers on the same board.

If we consider line B3, in which the number of PP and Sarit clique members were equal to each other, it is apparent that this combination was to be found chiefly in boards which were only moderately clique dominated. The seven companies in line B3 and columns A3 and A4 are #2, 11, 18, 22, 25, 29, 35. Inspection of Table 21 shows that these included the Bank of Bangkok, the Provincial Bank, Thai Airways, and the Thai Rice Company. One interpretation might be that these were official or quasi-official organizations, in which clique members were deliberately balanced with non-clique members and representation from the two rival cliques was also equalized.

TABLE 24
DEGREE OF CLIQUE DOMINATION COMPARED WITH NUMBER OF MEMBERS

C. Number of Board Members	A. Number of Non-Clique Members as Percentage					
	1 (0–9%)	2 (10–29%)	3 (30–39%)	4 (40–59%)	5 (60–100%)	*Total*
1. (3)	4	0	5	0	7	16
2. (4)	2	3	0	2	2	9
3. (5)	2	5	0	1	1	9
4. (6–7)	0	2	2	3	0	7
5. (8+)	0	0	1	0	0	1
Total	8	10	8	6	10	42

Further data may be obtained from Tables 24 and 25, which compare the number of non-clique members on business boards, and the clique ratio, with the total number of cabinet politicians.

Examining these tables first in terms of the number of members, we learn that the PP clique tended to predominate more than the Sarit

TABLE 25

CLIQUE COMPOSITION COMPARED WITH
NUMBER OF MEMBERS

C. Number of Board Members	B. Ratio of Sarit to PP Clique Members					
	1 (1/0)	2 (1/1–1/0)	3 (1/1)	4 (1/1–0/1)	5 (0/1)	Total
1. (3)	2	0	4	2	8	16
2. (4)	3	1	2	0	3	9
3. (5)	3	3	2	1	0	9
4. (6–7)	1	3	1	1	1	7
5. (8+)	0	0	0	1	0	1
Total	9	7	9	5	12	42

clique on small boards, the comparison being 10 to 2, comparing the sums of columns B_4 and B_5 with B_1 and B_2 on line C_1 in Table 25. However, the degree of clique domination of boards does not seem to vary significantly within the small board category, line C_1 in Table 24. On the other hand, if we look at the larger boards, having six or more cabinet members, we find no significant variation in the ratio of rival cliques to each other (lines C_4 and C_5 in Table 25), but a distinct tendency for these larger boards to have an intermediate degree of moderate clique domination (lines C_4 and C_5 in Table 24). The five-member boards, however, seem to show a tendency toward a Sarit clique majority (line C_3 in Table 25) and toward relative clique-domination (line C_3 in Table 24).

Looking at the tables in another way, we might consider the comparative number of cabinet politicians of business boards in terms of clique domination and the ratio of cliques. It might appear from Table 24 that the most clique-dominated boards and the least clique-dominated boards both tended to have smaller numbers of members, whereas boards with intermediate degrees of clique domination tended to exhibit greater variation in size. Looking more closely at these boards with intermediate degrees of clique domination (column A_3 in Table 24), we find that the five boards with only three politician members (#2, 9, 18, 25, 35) tended to have a quasi-governmental character. So did the three boards with six or more politician members (#3, 15, 28), but it seems possible that the latter group involved higher levels of capitalization. Most of the former (except for #9) consisted of one member each of the Sarit and PP cliques and a third non-clique member. The latter group was composed, in each case, of one-third non-clique members, but the clique members tended to belong predominantly to one or the other clique.

Examining the figures in Table 25, we can see a tendency for the Sarit-dominated boards to contain somewhat more cabinet politicians than the PP clique-dominated boards, as summarized in Table 26. As this

TABLE 26

CONDENSATION OF DATA IN TABLE 25

C. Number of Board Members	B. *Ratio of Sarit Clique to PP Clique*		
	1 & 2 (Sarit)	*4 & 5 (PP)*	*Total*
1 & 2 (3–4 members)	6	13	19
3, 4, & 5 (5+ members)	10	4	14
Total	16	17	33

table shows, of the 19 boards having 3 or 4 cabinet members, and tending to be dominated by one or the other clique, the Sarit clique prevailed in 6, compared with 13 in which there were more PP clique members. By contrast, in the 14 such boards having 5 or more cabinet members, the Sarit group prevailed in 10, compared with only 4 in which the PP clique had a majority.

No doubt, as these figures stand, they lack great significance, and their interpretation is open to some question. If comparable figures could be obtained for earlier and later periods, however, it would become possible to study the relationship between the rising or falling power position of particular cliques and the character of their participation on business boards. A number of hypotheses relating the power position of a clique in the cabinet to its ability to obtain lucrative board memberships for its members might become testable.

GOVERNMENT ENTERPRISES AND REVOLVING FUNDS

Although attention has been directed particularly to the participation of Siamese cabinet politicians on the boards of directors of private firms, it should not be thought that this device provided the only or even the primary means for enrichment. More customary means could be found throughout the operations of the governmental administration, as will be shown in the next chapter. It is worth noting, however, that the interest of Thai officials in commercial and industrial activities was not limited to private companies outside the formal structure of government. Indeed, there is evidence that, throughout the period under consideration, the number of enterprises which were capitalized from public revenues and operated as public corporations continued to grow.

Details concerning the administration of these enterprises are difficult to obtain. For the most part, they seem not to have been particularly successful and frequently had to call upon the treasury for additional subventions. Nevertheless, it can be surmised that the key officials, including cabinet members who were chiefly responsible for the organization and management of these enterprises, did not find them unproductive. At least, the evidence suggests that the chief incentives for the organization of these entities came from within the government itself, rather than from any outside groups which might have benefited from their operations.

Data concerning the number and character of these enterprises, as already indicated, are not easily obtained. An enumeration of the number of enterprises subject to audit by the Audit Council of Thailand has been consulted, yielding the following information:

TABLE 27
GOVERNMENT ENTERPRISES AUDITED IN 1957

Ministry	Number
Industry	47
Interior	30
Agriculture	18
Finance	10
Defense	6
Education	6
Public Health	6
Communications	5
Economic Affairs	4
Other ministries and agencies	9
Total	141

A listing of enterprises (compiled from sources which cannot be identified here) is given in Table 28. It should be noted that the number

TABLE 28

SOME PUBLIC CORPORATIONS AND ORGANIZATIONS,
THAILAND, 1957

Ministry	*Number of Enterprises Given in Table 27*
1. *Industry*	47
Thai Sugar Organization	
Thai Paper Mill	
Liquor and Alcohol Factory	
Gunny Bag Factory	
Provincial Liquor Factories (14 enterprises)	
Alum Factory	
Shoe Polish Factory	
Glue Factory	
Ceramic Factory	
Industrial Promotion Department Factory	
Cottage Industry Fund	
Thai Rubber Co.	
Sugar Industry Co.	
Aokam Tin Co.	
Mining Organization	
2. *Interior*	30
Marketing Organization	
Poultry Raising Organization	
Electrical Supplies Distribution Fund	
State Pawn Shop	
Police Press	
Provincial Electric Organization	
Rural Reconstruction Organization	
Bangkok Electric Works	
3. *Agriculture*	18
Fish Marketing Organization	
Naborn Rubber Plantation Organization	
Refrigeration Plant and Ice Factory Organization	
Thai Fishery Co.	
Cement for Irrigation	
Thai Plywood Co.	
Forest Industry Organization	

(Continued)

TABLE 28 (*Continued*)

SOME PUBLIC CORPORATIONS AND ORGANIZATIONS, THAILAND, 1957

Ministry	Number of Enterprises Given in Table 27
4. *Finance*	10
Industrial Bank	
Playing Card Factory	
Manufacturing Fund	
Thai Gunny Bag Co.	
Thai Product Marketing Co.	
Siam Cement Co.	
Siam Commercial Bank, Ltd.	
Provincial Bank, Ltd.	
Government Purchasing Bureau	
Government Savings Bank	
Housing Development Bank	
Tobacco Monopoly Factory	
Bureau of Lottery	
5. *Defense*	6
Tanning Organization	
Weaving Organization	
Canned-food Organization	
Fuel Organization	
Glass Organization	
Battery Organization	
War Veteran Organization	
Bangkok Dock Co.	
6. *Education*	6
7. *Public Health*	6
Pharmaceutical Factory	
8. *Communications*	5
Thai Airways Co.	
Transport Co.	
Tugboat Co.	
Express Transportation Bureau	
Telephone Organization of Thailand	
	(*Continued*)

TABLE 28 (*Continued*)

SOME PUBLIC CORPORATIONS AND ORGANIZATIONS,
THAILAND, 1957

Ministry	*Number of Enterprises Given in Table 27*
State Railways of Thailand	
Port Authority of Thailand	
9. *Economic Affairs*	4
Thai Maritime Navigation Co.	
Thai Navigation Co.	
Vorasiri Co.	
Provincial Trading Co. (22 enterprises)	
Thai Jute Co.	
Bangkok Bank, Ltd.	
Warehouse Organization	
Rice Bureau	
Agriculture Products Co.	
10. *Co-operatives*	
Thai Salt Co.	
Bank for Co-operatives	
Industrial Co-operative Organization	
Fund for Promoting Co-operative Societies	
11. *Culture*	
Musical and Choreographical Organization	
Music Fund	
12. *Office of the Council of Ministers*	
Dusit Zoo Organization	
Thai T.V. Co.	
Wire Diffusion Co.	
Southern Electric Energy Organization	
Lignite Energy Organization	
Construction Material Purchasing Fund	
Dindaeng Co.	

of enterprises identified for each ministry does not correspond with the totals given above. No explanation can be offered here for the discrepancies. However, since our main purpose is not to give a detailed picture of these operations but rather to suggest their general character, it

is sufficient to indicate the general magnitudes concerned and to identify the salient characteristics of the public enterprises.

An authoritative discussion of these public enterprises is contained
in the report of the International Bank mission to Thailand.[17] According to this report, the government plays a major role in commercial and
industrial activities.

> In manufacturing it monopolizes tobacco, potable and industrial spirits
> and playing cards; it dominates timber, sugar, paper, gunny bags and minerals
> other than tin; it has large interests in cement, glass, pharmaceuticals, bat-
> teries, tin, tanneries and textiles, sometimes in direct competition with estab-
> lished producers; and finally it operates a number of small plants making
> such diverse products as shoe polish, alum, rubber footwear, metal cabinets,
> paper clips, ceramics, and many others.[18]

Concerning the management of these enterprises, the Bank's mission
reported that "control is nominally in the hands of Boards of Directors
consisting of high-ranking military or naval officers and influential
politicians, but the effective direction is exercised by permanent officials
of the Ministries, with the factory managers having little authority." [19]

According to the Bank's report, "All of the state industries, except
the monopolies, have proved unprofitable by commercial standards."
Among the reasons cited were the following:

> The enterprises were too often initiated by persons with political influ-
> ence, who had no special knowledge of the industry or particular concern
> about ultimate success.
> . . . Because of their political origin, the projects were not properly
> studied at the beginning.
> . . . Both assets and liabilities are swollen by loans to and borrowings
> from other government agencies—a pernicious system which not only makes
> the balance sheets unintelligible but is obviously open to abuse. . . .
> Both the factory managers and the senior officials directing them at min-
> isterial headquarters lack commercial and industrial experience.[20]

Why the number of government enterprises conducted at a loss
should continue to increase is not made explicit by the Bank's report.
No doubt it was considered that the reasons would become apparent to
any reader skilled at reading between the lines, and any more direct
statement was regarded as too indelicate to make.

In the present context, however, it seems unnecessary to conceal the
fact, which has become clear from the preceding discussion, that the

higher officials in the government were caught in a squeeze between the relatively limited scale of official remuneration offered to them and the opportunities to enhance their income which increased progressively as they advanced in rank and status. The Bank's report attributed the losses of government enterprises to poor management, inadequate maintenance, inefficient use of plant, overstaffing, inappropriate utilization of skilled and professionally qualified personnel, and other administrative defects. Yet certainly, however valid such criticisms might be, the underlying reality was that those who directed and managed these enterprises found, for the most part, many ways to utilize these activities to add to their personal income even though the organizational balance sheet might show continuing losses.[21]

It has certainly not been the intention of the foregoing analysis to assert that the only motivation felt by higher Siamese bureaucrats and politicians was to increase their personal incomes. Quite the contrary, for the normal attractions of high office—prestige, power, opportunity to render public service, security—were certainly as relevant to the situation of the Siamese bureaucracy as they were in other countries. The point has been that opportunities to increase the real income of many, if not all, of the higher officials were also substantial, and that they cannot be ignored if one is seeking to understand the dynamics of bureaucratic behavior in Thailand. Certainly they help to explain the pattern of rivalry between cliques and factions described above in Chapter VIII. In the chapter which follows, an attempt will be made to provide a closer look at some of the behavioral characteristics of Thai officials in the daily work of public administration.

CHAPTER X

The Bureaucratic Polity
as a Working System

When the promoters of the coup d'état in 1932 overthrew the absolute monarchy, they issued a manifesto which revealed with rare candor the underlying objectives of the revolutionists. They wrote:

> The government dismissed a large number of officials. Students graduate from schools and find no employment; and retired soldiers cannot find jobs and must starve. This is the work of the administration of the absolute monarchy. It oppresses junior government officials including clerks and uncommissioned officers in the armed forces who were dismissed without pension. Money collected by taxation should be used to provide jobs for the people as a matter of gratitude to their sacrifice to the wealthy royalty. But the royalty does not attempt to do anything except to continue sucking blood. The savings of the royalty are deposited in foreign banks; they prepare to flee the country when the nation is in decay and starvation. This is certainly evil.
>
> Hence, the people and the officials in the civil and military services who understand such evil work of the government have organized the People's Party which has already seized the power of government.[1]

When the king capitulated and agreed to co-operate with the rebels in establishing a limited monarchy, the manifesto (with its demand for the establishment of a republican form of government) was withdrawn. Nevertheless, the popular, and especially the foreign, image of the revolution as a political upheaval similar to the earlier French and American counterparts became widespread. With this image went the assumption that the goals of the revolution were democratic and popular, including at least the establishment of a constitutional monarchy under the domination of an elected assembly, which would enhance the welfare of the people. In such a polity, the bureaucracy would serve primarily as the administrative arm of the government to implement responsibly formulated public policies.

Evaluations of the Thai government have normally rested on the premise that this was indeed the basic character of the revolution.

Siamese leaders, including Pridi himself, were at pains to maintain this international image. In this frame of reference, the successive revolts whereby cliques of politicians and military officers seized power were seen as aberrations—hopefully transitional—in a steady progress toward more stable and effective constitutional and democratic government.

There is another frame of reference, however, which is clearly implied in the very terms of the manifesto of June 25. Let us suppose that the goal of the revolution was not to establish a popular constitutional government but rather to place commoner officials in the cockpit of power and to organize a polity that would rule on behalf of the bureaucracy. No doubt such a formulation sounds paradoxical and will be rejected by many Siamese, for whom the international public image of a popular revolution has been internalized as the only proper goal of political development. Nevertheless, this paradoxical image happens to coincide with reality more closely than the official image depicted in successive Thai constitutions. It makes more intelligible the everyday behavior not only of the cabinet itself but also of the state bureaucracy, as it conducts the routine work of public administration. In this chapter I shall examine some characteristics of Thai politics and administration in the light of this model, which, for convenience, will be called a "bureaucratic polity."

THE BUREAUCRACY AS CLIENTELE SYSTEM

The actual political system that was set up in 1932 corresponds to the implicit premises of the June manifesto. Cabinet members, for the most part, have been officials who have risen to political eminence; and in the conduct of their roles as members of a ruling circle, cabinet politicians have shown themselves more responsive to the interests and demands of their bureaucratic subordinates than to the concerns of interest groups, political parties, or legislative bodies outside the state apparatus.

Commenting on this phenomenon, David Wilson concludes: "As much as the leadership of the Thai revolution might have wished things to be otherwise, it was not able to muster much popular interest outside the bureaucracy upon which to base itself. As a result, politics has become a matter of competition between bureaucratic cliques for the benefits of government."[2]

In the light of the manifesto, however, one may well ask whether the real aims of the revolutionists were to establish a system very different from the one which, in fact, they did set up. Popular revolutions have been spearheaded, in large measure, by individuals and groups outside the governmental apparatus who demanded greater access to the elite and a wider distribution of power. Is it plausible to think that those who seized power in June, 1932, were really dedicated to the establishment of effective organs of parliamentary and popular government? The question is no doubt purely academic, since, even if they had been so inspired, there was not yet available a body of organized Siamese groups capable of representing popular interests or of capturing and holding any substantial power base from which to impose their will upon the government. The system which emerged is realistically described by Wilson as follows:

> The ruling clique seizes the seats of power by a sudden coup and then uses these positions to establish and maintain its authority. But the constituencies of the members of the clique are of the bureaucracy itself. These are primarily the military . . . but also, to a greater or lesser extent, all agencies. A minister, when he steps into his ministry, possesses the traditional authority of the office, and he can expect to get the deference, respect, and obedience from his subordinates which tradition demands. He is obligated by tradition to look out for these subordinates, however. In order not to disturb his authority and perhaps that of the whole clique, he must look to this obligation. His ministry then becomes his constituency, and he represents it in the cabinet. He fights for its budget, and he protects its employees. The success with which he does this depends upon his relative position within the ruling clique, although the best he can expect is a compromise with his fellow ministers.[3]

One way of testing the validity of such statements is to look at the personal background of the men in the Thai cabinet. To what extent were they in fact bureaucrats, and to what extent did they gain this office through extrabureaucratic careers?

Of the 237 men who served in Thai cabinets between 1932 and 1958, a total of 184 may be classified as career officials, compared with 38 who were nonofficials. An additional 15 men cannot be classified at present in either category because adequate information is not available.[4] Of the career officials, 100 were civil servants and 84 were military officers.

Let us analyze these figures more closely. One might imagine that the elected politicians had played the influential roles and that officials had been designated by them to hold portfolios as technicians and functional specialists. Nothing, however, could be further from the truth.

Let us try to separate the more influential from the less influential cabinet members.

Promoters and Repeaters.   We can use two indices. As already noted, the promoters of coups d'état tended to be more influential than nonpromoters. However, all promoters were by no means equally influential, and some nonpromoters were quite influential, as has been shown in previous chapters. Let us therefore add a second criterion, namely, the number of times a man held cabinet rank. I shall refer to anyone who held such rank in three or more cabinets as a "repeater," and anyone who was a cabinet member only one or two times as a "nonrepeater."

Classifying cabinet members in terms of promoter status, we find that of the 237 men, 56 were promoters and 181 nonpromoters. Among the promoters, 53 had official careers, compared with 2 who were not officials and one not identified. These figures show that whereas 77 per cent of all cabinet members were officials, 95 per cent of the promoters who held cabinet posts were officials.

In other words, almost all of the promoters, the men who exercised greatest influence in the Thai cabinets, were military officers or civil servants. The nonofficials were, for the most part, nonpromoters (36 nonpromoters but only two promoters were not officials). The conclusion seems apparent that power was held in large measure by officials who gained cabinet rank and used their influence to secure the appointment, for the most part, of other officials, but also of some nonofficials.

If we consider the distribution of repeaters in terms of career backgrounds, we find a comparable, though less striking, picture. There were 107 repeaters among the cabinet politicians studied—i.e., men who had served on three or more cabinets. Of this number, 94, or 88 per cent, were career men, as compared with 11 who were not and 2 not identified. The extent to which bureaucrats prevailed over nonbureaucrats among the repeaters is not as great as among the promoters, yet the percentage of repeaters who were officials was higher than the percentage of all cabinet members—88 compared with 77 per cent. By this measure of cabinet participation, then, we again find that officials tended to hold office more frequently than nonofficials. However, the figures indicate that a significant number (11) of nonofficials, who were also nonpromoters, did manage to hold office on several occasions. We may assume that these men were effective "technicians" whose services were in demand to such an extent that a ruling circle required them fairly often.

If we look at those who were both promoters and repeaters, we find that there were 41 men in this category, 40 of whom were officials and none of whom can be identified as nonofficials. One only is not identified in my records. Fifteen of the promoters were nonrepeaters, showing that all of the promoters did not necessarily hold office frequently. Of this number, two were not officials.

TABLE 29

BUREAUCRATIC PARTICIPATION IN THAI CABINETS

A. *Summary Figures*

	Total	Promoters	Nonprom.	Repeaters	Nonrepeaters
Civil Servants	100	14	86	51	49
Military Officers	84	39	45	43	41
All Officials	184 (77%)	53 (95%)	131 (72%)	94 (88%)	90 (69%)
Nonofficials	38	2	36	11	27
Unidentified	15	1	14	2	13
Total	237	56	181	107	130

B. *Analysis*

	Total	REPEATERS		NONREPEATERS	
		Promoters	Nonprom.	Promoters	Nonprom.
Civil Servants	100	12	39	2	47
Military Officers	84	28	15	11	30
All Officials	184	40	54	13	77
Nonofficials	38	0	11	2	25
Unidentified	15	1	1	0	13
Total	237	41	66	15	115

TABLE 30
COMPOSITION OF THAI CABINETS

			All Cabinet Members				Promoters		
No.	Prime Minister*	Total	Non-Off.	Officials	Mil. Off.	Civ. Off.	Promoters	Mil. Off.	Civ. Off.	Total Officials

No.	Prime Minister*	Total	Non-Off.	Officials	Mil. Off.	Civ. Off.	Promoters	Mil. Off.	Civ. Off.	Total Officials
	FIRST RULING CIRCLE									
1.	Mano I	15	0	15	7	8	11	6	5	11
2.	Mano II	20	0	20	8	12	11	6	5	11
3.	Mano III	20	0	20	11	9	8	7	1	8
4.	Phahon I	20	0	19	9	10	7	5	2	7
5.	Phahon II	20	0	20	7	13	7	5	2	7
6.	Phahon III	31	1	30	13	17	11	7	4	11
7.	Phahon IV	20	1	19	10	9	7	6	1	7
8.	Phahon V	21	1	20	12	8	12	8	4	12
9.	Phibun I	32	1	29	15	14	16	11	5	16
10.	Phibun II	30	1	26	17	9	17	11	5	16
	SECOND RULING CIRCLE									
11.	Khuang I	24	2	22	11	11	4	0	3	3
12.	Thawi	23	8	15	4	11	13	0	7	7
13.	Seni	25	9	16	2	14	13	0	7	7
14.	Khuang II	21	5	15	5	10	2	0	2	2
15.	Pridi I	16	0	14	3	11	6	0	6	6
16.	Pridi II									
17.	Pridi III	15	1	13	4	9	7	0	6	6
18.	Thamrong I	19	6	12	4	8	3	0	3	3
19.	Thamrong II	19	4	13	4	9	6	0	3	3
	THIRD RULING CIRCLE									
20.	Khuang III	24	4	17	7	10	1	1	0	1
21.	Khuang IV	25	4	20	8	12	1	1	0	1
22.	Phibun III	31	5	25	11	14	3	3	0	3
23.	Phibun IV	26	5	19	9	10	4	4	0	4
24.	Phibun V	15	1	14	7	7	3	3	0	3
25.	Phibun VI	25	1	24	17	7	8	8	0	8
26.	Phibun VII	31	1	30	20	10	11	11	0	11
27.	Phibun VIII	29	8	20	16	4	13	13	0	13
	FOURTH RULING CIRCLE									
28.	Pote	26	2	24	14	10	6	6	0	6
29.	Thanom I	37	8	27	13	14	6	6	0	6
30.	Sarit I	15	1	7	5	2	4	4	0	4
31.	Thanom II									

If we compare the total number of civil servants with military officers in our collection of cabinet politicians, we find that more were civil servants—100 compared with 84. However, using our two categories of influence, we find that 39 promoters were military men, compared with 14 who were civil servants. By contrast, more repeaters were civil servants than were military men, 51 compared with 43. Thus, military officers constituted 74 per cent of the promoter officials holding cabinet positions but only 46 per cent of the repeater officials. The conclusion is suggested that, although military officers tended to gain greater power through participation in coups d'état, a relatively larger number of civil servants managed to hold office repeatedly in the Thai cabinets.

The figures given above are summarized and additional data given in Table 29.

The Changing Composition of Succeeding Cabinets. A more detailed picture of the composition of the Thai cabinets in terms of officials and nonofficials can be obtained by analyzing each cabinet in turn. Such an analysis is presented in Table 30, inspection of which reveals some interesting trends. During the period of the first ruling circle, from 1932 to 1944, almost all cabinet positions were held by officials. Subsequently, officials continued to hold most of the cabinet seats, but the number of nonofficials tended to increase, notably during the period of the second ruling circle, between 1944 and 1947. Thereafter, although fluctuating, the number of nonofficials in the succeeding cabinets of the third and fourth ruling circles tended to be greater than during the first period, but fewer than during the second.

The significance of the number of nonofficials holding cabinet positions during the 1944–47 period becomes more apparent when we discover that only during this period were any of these nonofficials also

---

*Succeeding columns refer to: total number of cabinet members; number of nonofficials in cabinet; number of bureaucrats in cabinet; number of military officers; number of civil servants; total number of promoters in cabinet; number of military officers among promoters in cabinet; number of civil servants among these promoters; and total number of public officials among the promoters in the cabinet. Men whose careers are unidentified are included in the first column but not in any subsequent columns. For dates of cabinets, see Appendix C.

promoters. During the Thawi and Seni cabinets (Nos. 12 and 13, August, 1945, through January, 1946) the number of nonofficial promoters rose to six. There was one in the first Khuang cabinet, No. 11; one in the third Pridi cabinet, No. 17; and three in the second Khuang cabinet, No. 19. (The exact dates of these cabinets are given in Appendix C.)

It has already been shown, in Chapter VIII, that Parliament and the political parties began to play a more influential role during this period. It was a time when the grip of Phibun's clique over the government was shattered, and a new civilian ruling circle anxiously sought the approval of the Western democracies in order to avoid having to pay a heavy penalty for Thailand's collaboration with Japan during the war. Under these circumstances, the rise of parliamentary and nonbureaucratic power was signalized by the recruitment of nonofficials into the cabinet.

However, even during this period, there were always more officials in the cabinet than there were nonofficials; the number of official promoters was at least equal to the number of nonofficial promoters; and usually there were more official than nonofficial promoters. Pridi appointed no nonofficials to his first cabinet and only one to his third. (We omit analysis of his abortive second cabinet.) During the third and fourth ruling circles, moreover, the nonofficials in the cabinet never included any promoters.

A basic shift in the intrabureaucratic composition of the ruling circle took place in succeeding periods. Although the ratio of civil servants to military officers in the cabinet fluctuated, there were always some members of both categories. But this balance in the general composition of each cabinet was not reflected in the selection of promoters for inclusion in the cabinet. Thus, during the period of Pridi's third ruling circle, the promoters in each cabinet were always civilians, whether officials or nonofficials, and no military officers in these cabinets were promoters.

By contrast, the cabinets of the third and fourth ruling circles always included military officer promoters but no civilian promoters. This obviously reflected the fact that the third and fourth ruling circles consisted exclusively of military officers who had staged the coups which caused the overturns of 1947 and 1957. Similarly, the overturn of 1944 which ended the first Phibun era was largely brought about by civilians, without a military coup.

It may be possible by further scrutiny of the data in Table 30 to discover certain characteristic patterns of variation during, for example, the life cycle of a ruling circle. However, further elaboration seems unnecessary for the purposes of this analysis. The crucial point has been the extent to which members of the state apparatus, whether civil servants or military officials, have dominated the Thai cabinet. The foregoing analysis provides additional evidence to support Wilson's general proposition that the political elite were drawn from and reflected the interests of the bureaucracy, rather than political groups or the general public outside the formal government.

IMPLICATIONS OF A BUREAUCRATIC POLITY

"What," the reader may well ask, "is the significance of the number of officials in the Thai cabinet? Is it not possible in any political system for the members of a cabinet to be recruited in large part from career officials without this having any notable consequences for the character of the political system?" The answer, I believe, is that this measure gives us a clue to the essential characteristics of Thai politics, characteristics which are suggested by the term "bureaucratic polity."

Elsewhere I have attempted to characterize the modernity of a political system by referring to the extent to which the functionally specialized state bureaucracy has been brought under effective control by political institutions outside the governmental bureaucracy.[5] This conception holds for totalitarian polities as well as democratic. To meet the definition, however, it is necessary to be able to consider the dominant political party in a totalitarian regime as falling outside the governmental bureaucracy. The fact that such parties may have a bureaucracy of their own by no means disqualifies them from meeting this definition; so do the parties and other organizations outside the state administration which, in democratic polities, impose their will upon the government.

The significance of such extrabureaucratic institutions lies not only in the fact that they are able to formulate demands and rules which become government policies—important as this is—but also, and perhaps equally important, that by serving as the spokesmen and leaders of such extrabureaucratic institutions, the key authorities of a political system gain the requisite power to activate the bureaucracy. An implicit premise of this proposition is that the administrative duties which officials are called on to perform are always onerous and the resultant rewards never enough to satisfy all their wishes. Consequently, unless the government possesses effective sanctions by means of which it can secure a substantial level of conformity to official policies, it will not be able to rely upon its bureaucracy as an instrument of administration capable of reliably translating policies and rules into reality. Lacking any major center of power and policy-making outside the bureaucracy, a governmental elite must become the spokesman and instrument of the bureaucracy. The predominance of officials in a cabinet reflects this reversal of roles.

To the extent that such a reversal of roles has become normal in the Thai government, we may expect it to explain many phenomena which strike the Western observer—accustomed as he is to a different image of political systems—as bizarre and outlandish. So difficult is it for us to perceive the significance of this paradoxical type of political system that we tend to look elsewhere for explanations. Some, for example, holding to an ethnic or racial theory of civilization, may try to find reasons for the idiosyncratic features of the Thai polity in some alleged traits of the Siamese "race." It goes without saying that such an explanation can scarcely find support in the light of contemporary science, save from the racist extremists.

The Cultural "Explanation." A more widely accepted idea, however, strikes me as almost equally invalid, because it seeks in the acquired beliefs and practices of a society, its cultural system, an explanation for its behavior. This type of theory has gained extensive support on the basis of arguments that impute to any cultural group a set of learned patterns of behavior, which members of the group cling to in the face of any pressures or suggestions that they could or should be changed. Why, one might ask, should they learn these, rather than some other items of belief and practice?

Such a point of view is analogous to the idea of inertia in physics. No doubt a billiard ball will rest without motion on a level pool table if no one touches it. But if it is struck by a cue, it begins to move and continues until it collides with another ball, strikes the side of the table, or is in some other way deflected from its course or moved.

Similarly, I submit that members of any culture are sensitive to pressures and considerations that can induce them to revise patterns of thought and action which they have previously learned, although they may also resist such changes. Certainly the history of Siam during the last one hundred years has witnessed many fundamental changes in the system of government and the cultural practices of the people. We may postulate that the established cultural system imposes resistance to any innovation, and yet the question must always be raised why, despite this resistance, some innovations became institutionalized while others did not.

The absolute monarchy was overthrown, and the center of power moved from the throne into the hands of a ruling circle of commoners. The promoters of the revolution were even ready, as indicated by their manifesto, to destroy the monarchy and replace it by a republic. It was not so much a cultural abhorrence of republicanism as the shrewd complaisance of a realistic king which preserved the monarchy.

The establishment of an elected assembly also violated cultural norms of the Siamese, who had previously viewed authority as coming from above, not as being based upon popular sovereignty. Nevertheless, despite this incongruence between the traditional culture and the new ideas of constitutional government, the assembly was established, elections were held, political parties formed, and parliamentary practices institutionalized. So firmly did this formal apparatus of government become rooted in contemporary Thai thinking that some kind of parliamentary or constituent body was created in every one of the subsequent constitutional charters by which different ruling groups sought to legitimize their authority to govern. Indeed, the idea was perceived as so essential to the process of modernization that succeeding governments sought to extend the idea to local government, establishing a variety of provincial and municipal assemblies with the apparent intent of diffusing the principle of popular and responsible government at local as well as central levels.

The fact that these representative bodies were never able to gain enough power to impose effective control over the cabinet and the bureaucracy cannot, it seems to me, be explained in terms of cultural predispositions or the influence of attitudes and ideas held by the contending leaders, except in so far as these attitudes reflected underlying interests and the prevailing distribution of power. Consider the following statement by two leading authorities on Thailand which, in my view, correctly states the facts but does not fully indicate their significance.

In 1932 . . . an ostensibly representative national assembly was established in Thailand by popular election and with the authority to control legislation and administration. From the very beginning, however, the attitude of the new Thai leaders toward the national assembly was somewhat ambivalent. Their bureaucratic background inclined many of them toward a strong executive government and nourished their suspicions of an unprecedented and unpredictable body of men, each of whom had his personal sources of power. These new leaders would have preferred an assembly consisting of wise and gentle counselors who, by expressing the consensus of the nation, would provide the administration with the guidance and information it needed in governing the country. Their view ran counter to the *doctrinaire belief* that an assembly's proper function was to serve as a watchdog for the public interest and as the embodiment of a general will that commanded government. This *radical viewpoint, which had little basis in Thai tradition* but had come home in the luggage of students returning from Europe, turned out to be the prevalent one among the men who were elected to the national assembly. The *tensions* between the executive and the legislative side of the government that arose from this conflict of basic attitudes have *resulted* in rendering the national assembly ineffectual. [*Italics added.*] [6]

The authors, Phillips and Wilson, go on to describe how the assembly has repeatedly been dissolved or reorganized whenever its views clashed with those of the government. The lack of party organization and popular support outside the assembly are mentioned as contributory factors. Consequently the cabinet, "bearing the immense prestige of His Majesty's government and supported by the bureaucracy in general and the military in particular . . . is usually able to prevail over the assembly. It has managed, with rare exceptions, to impose by various means an iron discipline on its majority and to ignore whatever opposition there may have been. The assembly, therefore, has had little effect on the making and implementation of policy." [7]

The "doctrinaire belief" which returning students imported from Europe was, of course, a key idea requisite to effective modernization of the polity. Although this idea lacked a basis in Thai tradition, so did many other imported ideas. The reasons which made it impossible to institutionalize this idea as the effective basis of the Siamese government are precisely the reasons which have prevented Thailand from creating a modern political system, and which have transformed it from a traditional into a bureaucratic polity. The outcome of the struggle between the cabinet and the assembly cannot be explained by the "tensions" which arose between them. That there were tensions goes without saying, for tensions accompany any competition for power. The outcome can be explained, rather, by the forces which gave political supremacy to the cabinet rather than to the assembly. The cabinet, indeed, as a ruling institution, was as foreign to Siamese tradition as an assembly. The king had been the center both of authority and of effective power. Both were wrested from him in the name of the "people." The assembly was designed to be the spokesman of the people, and the cabinet its executive arm.

But it proved impossible for the assembly to control the cabinet. The cabinet, instead, gained control over the assembly. It was able to do so because the cabinet had an effective constituency, the bureaucracy (military and civil), whereas the assembly lacked any effective constituency (electorate and political parties). The resultant system of government, which I have termed a "bureaucratic polity," is in a sense a nameless system. It is nameless because no one dares ascribe to it a basis of political legitimacy which corresponds to the facts of effective control.

The Problem of Authority. The traditional Siamese polity was legitimized by the royal or supernatural authority of its kings. A modern polity, which the students returning from Europe hoped to create, rests for its authority upon the idea of popular sovereignty. It is notable that in both conceptions the bureaucracy is supposed to serve an instrumental function: as the slaves of the king in the former, as the servants of the people in the latter. No one has presumed to formulate a doctrine of government in which the bureaucracy is conceived of not only as a ruling group, but also as the seat of sovereignty.

Who is brash enough to declare openly that a government derives its just powers to rule from the interests of the rulers? Who can formulate an argument that would induce both the king and the masses to concede that the right of the government to govern rests on its mastery of the means to power? Was this not the opinion of Thrasymachus in his famous argument with Socrates when he declared: ". . . in all states there is the same principle of justice, which is the interest of the established government; and as the government must be supposed to have power, the only reasonable conclusion is that everywhere there is one principle of justice, which is the interest of the stronger"? [8]

The Socratic argument against the position of Thrasymachus appears to have been so devastating that it has rarely, if ever, been seriously propounded as the basis of a political formula. Yet many ruling groups, in both traditional and modern polities, must have secretly endorsed the validity of Thrasymachus' view. In Thailand, however, no official would publicly endorse such a heresy. Those who remain traditionally oriented—primarily the peasant masses—continue to believe that the government rules justly only by virtue of the royal mandate, whereas those in the cities who have imbibed most fully of the heady doctrines of Western liberalism proclaim that the government's right to rule derives from a popular mandate formulated by elected assemblies. Both recognize, of course, that in fact those in power may not always be under the effective control of either the king or the assembly, but then they may conclude that, to this extent, the rulers have unjustly seized power and ought to be overthrown.

There seems, however, to be some basis in Thai culture for legitimizing the authority of those who rule simply because they actually hold power.[9] On the village level, for example, we are told by Phillips and Wilson that the Siamese peasants "look to their government as a source of gentle benevolent concern," as a body possessed, ideally, of "the attributes of a strong, wise, but indulgent father." Indeed, they are quoted as saying to the authors, " 'The government is like our father, we are like its children.' " The ritual importance of field visits by district officers to the villages is emphasized. The peasants apparently believe that when an official visits them,

. . . he does so not only to express his benevolent concern but also because he needs them to reaffirm and legitimate his own position. Whether he be a district officer or a deputy minister, as official he thus provides them with the opportunity to play out their part of the political dialogue, for villagers actually enjoy making known to those in power their willingness to be ruled. Indeed, this is to them one of the major pleasures of being a citizen.[10]

Such attitudes are no doubt characteristic manifestations of certain generalized values and beliefs which prevail throughout the Siamese culture. Although the dominant Buddhist faith has become a vehicle of these norms, they are probably more deeply ingrained in the traditional heritage of the Siamese. It seems unnecessary to describe these beliefs here. They are well summarized as they relate to political behavior in Wilson's book on Thai politics.[11]

Wilson summarizes his discussion of the Thai system of cultural values by noting:

These generalized virtues manifest themselves in the social behavior of the Thai by their adherence to the belief that the proper manner of ordering specific social relations is by expression of respect. Symbols and gestures of respect from lower to higher status are the very stuff of the actual relationships between persons. Even in the language, as has been mentioned, differences of status and the respectful aspect of these differences are an integral part of the vocabulary.[12]

More specifically, this attitude is rooted in a fundamental metaphysical view of the nature of reality, a view based on the shared Hindu and Buddhist idea of karma, the inherent justice of underlying reality, manifested through chains of reincarnation and the cause-effect sequences which occur throughout life. Thus, as Wilson asserts, ". . . one's place is a result of one's own will" and "one is therefore ultimately responsible for one's own position in society. . . ."

The position of a being, human or otherwise, in this universe may be measured by the degree to which he is subject to the will and power of others. This conception is the one which must be referred to throughout this discussion of Thai politics, i.e. the necessary and just unity of virtue and power. *Those who have power are good and deserve their good fortune. Power justifies itself.* This idea is not to be understood in a cynical sense which would lead to the view that might is right. It is rather a magico-religious view that right is might. [*Italics added.*] [13]

Wilson attributes certain characteristics of Thai politics to these underlying views. "One of these characteristics," he writes, "is a strong tendency toward ceremonial correctness in political relationships and political activities."

In the political world these characteristics have a profound effect on the fundamental attitude toward law and institutions. Although scrupulous attention is given to the formalities of procedure, there appears to be little faith in the necessary regularity of the working of law and institutions. Intervention by persons of power in the application of law appears to be accepted without disturbance. In such an attitude toward law lies some explanation of the easy recourse to periodic *coups d'etat* for the modification of political structures and for adjustment of constitutions.[14]

As I have argued above, we must not impute to such culturally defined attitudes a deterministic relation to patterns of political and administrative behavior. Such patterns and institutions are subject to change. Nevertheless, prevailing cultural norms do provide an easy rationalization for acceptance of a *status quo* which violates other norms of political and constitutional behavior to which lip service may also be paid. Thus, when the political doctrines of monarchic or parliamentary authority give way to the actual practices of bureaucratic rule, it becomes possible for the "average" Siamese to console himself with the idea that, after all, those who rule must in some way have earned their success; their power is its own justification. It is both right and expeditious to defer to those in power.

To challenge the justice of a regime conducted by and on behalf of officials would be to raise difficult metaphysical problems and, perhaps more important, to ask for trouble. Another Thai cultural value involves admiration for a posture of noninvolvement. One should respond to embarrassing or difficult situations by aloofness, by appearing to be detached.[15] If, therefore, one finds the actions of officials oppressive, unjust, or lacking in legitimacy, would it not be better to sit back and ignore the problem than to become personally involved in a situation which could not help but be frustrating, humiliating, or costly?

This argument from cultural values is not intended, clearly, as an explanation of the emergence of a bureaucratic polity in Thailand. It is offered, however, to explain why, after such a polity has emerged, for whatever reasons, it could have been accepted by the population with relative equanimity. But even this much explanatory value needs qualification. Had the bureaucratic rulers of Thailand chosen to exercise their power so as to cause acute difficulties for the population, I do not doubt that serious movements of protest and revolt would have arisen.

As a matter of fact, the various Siamese administrations have chosen to exercise their power in a moderate fashion, showing enough consideration for the interests and susceptibilities of the public to avoid outraging them. Such moderation is, of course, no proof of democratic responsiveness, but even openly absolutist regimes have exhibited concern for public opinion. The reasons for such moderateness may become more apparent as we examine the operational code which we might expect a bureaucratic polity to pursue.

Operational Code.   Let us make an assumption, which we can assume, for the moment, need not be true of the Thai situation. We can reserve judgment as to whether or not, despite all the evidence offered above, the Thai polity was in fact a bureaucratic polity. But to carry the argument forward, let us ask what would be the operational code of a bureaucratic polity? Let us then examine some actual operations of the Thai bureaucracy to see whether or not they can be explained as reasonable in terms of such a code. If they can, the possibility that some other reasons might actually give rise to the same behavior would not be ruled out, but at least the case for thinking that the Thai government was a bureaucratic polity would be strengthened. Given the additional grounds advanced in previous chapters of this book, plus the evidence presented above in this chapter, the case might at least seem highly probable.

Reasoning from the presumed character of the self-interest of officials, let us offer some guiding norms which might be adopted by any bureaucratic ruling group. These norms can be expressed in four propositions, as follows:

1. As much as possible, reduce the work load for officials. This refers especially to the content of bureaucratic work—i.e., avoid the necessity of making hard decisions, of having to choose between alternatives which would necessarily alienate and antagonize other officials, especially those higher in the hierarchy.

2. As much as possible, reduce tensions between the bureaucracy and the public, since any measures which incur the wrath or resistance of the people would only make life more difficult for the officials. For example, it is better to provide "services" to the public than to impose "regulations" on them, since the latter create difficult and embarrassing situations. Reliance on such a norm might also help to explain the compliant attitude of the public toward the Thai officials.

3. The foregoing norms have to be qualified by the necessity of extracting from the public the means of subsistence for the officials. Consequently, the public must be compelled to pay taxes, and pressure may be imposed on other officials to secure as much income as possible. The need for income is so great that one may justifiably impose tributes upon others for direct payments, but one should do so in moderation to avoid violating the first two norms. It is apparent from this rule that one should squeeze the hardest where the victims are least able to make trouble and avoid putting pressure on those who can create difficulties.

4. Finally, in order to succeed in applying the first three norms, it is important to be well situated within the bureaucracy, since all positions are not equally desirable from the point of view of the incumbents. Hence, it is an operating rule to seek promotions, transfers, and changes or revisions of one's job assignments if thereby the prospects of satisfying the other norms can be enhanced.

Rules of seniority and security of tenure may be regarded as a corollary to this norm, since a dominant bureaucracy must have a relatively simple and easily applied set of rules for deciding whom to promote and for protecting attained privileges. Perhaps equally important, status must be rewarded. If the essential rewards of the system are to be accorded to those who rise within its hierarchy, then the rule of deference to superiors follows as an inflexible norm. Such deference reflects the admiration and respect anyone who is "upward-mobile" feels for those who have succeeded. Perhaps more important, those below know that the pace of their own climb upward depends upon the support and patronage of superiors whom they cannot, therefore, afford to antagonize. Finally, if cultural values prevail which induce ordinary citizens to defer to officials on the principle that "right makes might," then how much more surely will subordinate officials pay homage to higher officials on the same grounds.

In postulating such norms I do not wish to imply that they have ever been engraved in a rule-book or made the object of public declarations, like an Athenian oath. Indeed, public declarations are more likely to contradict these norms. Rather, I am postulating that while such rules may be the secret guides to behavior of officials in any bureaucracy, they are likely to become the apparent operational code only in a bureaucracy not under effective control by extrabureaucratic institutions. In other words, such rules become manifest in the administrative behavior of officials in a bureaucratic polity, but not in either traditional or modern polities, where other countervailing norms stand a better chance of sublimating these rules.

Let us now examine some evidences of the actual politico-administrative practices of the Thai bureaucracy, including the cabinet, in order to ascertain whether or not these norms apply. In so doing I shall not attempt to examine comprehensively the structure and operations of the Siamese governmental bureaucracy. These have been well described in other works, which may be consulted for further clarification.[16]

Here I propose only to test the norms presented above, to ask whether or not they apply to characteristic patterns of Thai administrative behavior. But before doing so, a few words may be in order to characterize the general magnitude of the bureaucracy as related to the total population. In very rough figures, there were some 350,000 civil and military officials of the Thai government in 1958, or about 1.4 per cent of a population estimated at around 25 million.

Of this total, some 150,000 were in the armed forces under the Ministry of Defense. Details are not available, but it is assumed that this figure includes only officers, not enlisted men. Of the remaining 200,000 civil servants, about 174,000 were fourth-class officers and probationers, including some 85,000 teachers and 40,000 police officers. These men and women had little or no chance to rise in the bureaucratic hierarchy. We may therefore exclude them from further consideration.

Our primary concern is with approximately 26,000 higher officials of the third class and above and an equivalent number of military officers. As we have seen, a college or university degree was necessary for admission to the third class, except for the small number who may have succeeded in winning promotion from the fourth to the third class. Military officers would have had equivalent academic attainments based on graduation from a military academy.

Within the category of 26,000 higher civil servants, the most important group consisted of less than 700 special-class officers and around

1,750 first-class officers. In a sense, the first-class officers, who typically held positions as chiefs of the several hundred divisions within departments and as district officers in some 500 *amphurs,* were men who had reached the top of the pyramid of predominantly administrative jobs.

The posts of director-general of approximately 85 departments and offices, of secretary-general to the dozen or more ministries, of governorships in the 71 *changwads,* and a variety of related high status positions were filled by the special-grade officers. The men moving into these positions were the ones who began to feel acute political constraints and for whom the possibility of moving up into the cabinet became a tantalizing lure. To become a special-grade officer one needed endorsement by the cabinet itself, and hence some entree to that innermost circle.

The bureaucracy as a ruling group, therefore, constituted but a tiny fraction of the total population. At its core were the dozen or two who, at any given time, were cabinet members. The next larger circle consisted of perhaps a thousand special-grade and high military officers, followed by another two or three thousand men holding key administrative posts, being drawn gradually closer to the inner circle. Outside this circle one found more than 25,000 career men with good prospects, the rank-and-file administrators, all of whom expected to move up gradually in terms of salary and status, and some of whom expected, in due time, to join the more influential and rewarding inner circles.

The routine work of government was performed, in large part, by the even larger circle of 200,000 or more lesser civil servants and military "noncommissioned" officers, whose prospects for crossing the line into the inner circle were almost nil.[17]

It is in the context of this bureaucratic system that we must interpret the data which follow. I have chosen to use some conventional administrative categories—finance, personnel, organization, management— as root concepts for organizing the treatment of a subject which could have been broken down in many other ways. Let us begin, therefore, by looking at some aspects of financial administration, with special reference to budgeting and planning.

FINANCE: BUDGETING AND PLANNING

The allocation of scarce funds to competing purposes is a difficult and crucial function in any government. We cannot view finance, therefore, as simply a technical or administrative matter; we must consider it in the context of the economy as a whole. In an age when economic planning and the availability of foreign financial assistance keyed to development projects have become commonplace, it is perhaps logical to begin this analysis by looking at the structure of planning. For this purpose we can turn to the perceptive reports of a foreign economic adviser who worked for some years in the Thai government under a personal contract. In a memorandum to the Ministry of Finance he once wrote as follows:

> Economic development needs are not widely felt throughout the country; development schemes do not well up out of long-felt and long-suppressed hopes of regional groups; projects do not originate in the grass roots of the provinces; the provinces are not importuning the central Government to find funds to carry out programs locally conceived.
>
> Instead, everything is done by a benevolent bureaucracy in Bangkok. Ministries think up development schemes. Departments of Government decide what is good for the people and then try to get it done.[18]

On the basis of his analysis, the adviser concluded: "Since development schemes are formulated by Ministries, arguments about which scheme is more important become inter-Ministerial arguments, and there is no automatic mechanism for adjudicating them." "In short," he continued,

> . . . when development projects originate, as they do in Thailand, in Ministries, the conflicting claims of different projects against limited financial resources give rise to inter-Ministerial arguments; and no machinery exists for resolving these disputes rationally. Even the Council of Ministers does not suffice, because after all the Council is only the Ministers assembled together. The best they can do to resolve their differences is to compromise. But the compromise is not likely to be rational or best to serve the interests of the nation.[19]

If we start with the premise that power rests fundamentally, in the Thai polity, in the bureaucracy, then it is not surprising that development projects should arise within the ministries, nor is it surprising that they should not reflect any ground swell of popular demand from the provinces. Moreover, if we assume that development schemes cost money and that the protagonists of development schemes can use them to justify their demands for larger budgetary allocations, then we can see how the third bureaucratic norm given above would provide reason enough for each ministry to formulate and present its development schemes.

When we consider, however, that the cabinet was the political arena in which intrabureaucratic struggles took place, then it is scarcely surprising that budget decisions regarding the allocation of available funds should have taken place within the cabinet on the basis of "compromise," i.e., as "pork-barrel" appropriations. On the basis of our first norm, moreover, we should not expect the cabinet (including the prime minister, who needed to maintain the support of members of his ruling circle) to make the hard decisions required to establish rationally oriented priorities for deciding how to use limited funds.

Nor can we expect that any other administrative structures to which these key budgetary decisions might have been referred would have succeeded in making the tough decisions which the prime minister and cabinet would not make, since they could have enforced their decisions against the disappointed ministers only if they had possessed the backing of some superior center of power. In a modern political system, we expect to find such a power center in the dominant political party or in the legislature. But we should not expect the Thai assembly to succeed in exercising this function as long as it remained politically subject to the cabinet.

Accordingly, we are not surprised to read in the economic adviser's report about the helplessness of the assembly as it sought to review the government's budget. On the first reading of the budget bill, a vote of agreement "in principle" to the measure was apparently always obtained. The bill was then submitted to the Budget Committee, which deliberated on the measure for some time but was not permitted to make any substantial alteration in the magnitude of the major items in the budget, although it did make minor adjustments. The adviser concluded:

> This system reduces the usefulness of the Assembly's Budget Committee. It probably enhances the opportunities for energetic and articulate Ministries to prevail upon the Assembly to increase their appropriations at the expense of other Ministries. In any case it deprives the Assembly's Budget Committee of the opportunity to exercise what should be the primary function of a parliamentary budget committee, namely, to consider and decide, upon broad grounds of national interest, whether the levels of contemplated expenditure and/or revenue-collection should be materially higher or lower than what is proposed by the Government.[20]

It would appear that the assembly was used, under these circumstances, to help remove some of the weight of decision-making from the shoulders of the prime minister and the cabinet by permitting the legislators to mediate between competing bureaucratic interests and to exercise some slight influence in enhancing the position of some at the expense of others. The reason for the inability of the assembly to do more than this, however, would appear not to have been the rules or customs which limited the legislature to this secondary role, but rather the lack of effective parliamentary support by organized political parties or other groupings outside the legislature who could have upheld its decisions whenever they were rejected by an angered council of ministers. As long as the balance of power remained thus one-sidedly in the hands of the bureaucracy, no amount of tinkering with the procedures of the assembly could have been counted on to change effectively the process of allocating funds.

The adviser went on to describe the budgetary procedures within the administration, where the budget measure was considered first by a screening committee of the National Economic Council and then by a budget committee of the Ministry of Finance. He then indicated that the proposals of the National Economic Council appeared to have no more than an "advisory" effect. Moreover,

> The Finance Ministry for its part does not have, in practice, the authority to rule out some projects altogether in order to permit other more important projects to be done adequately and at an adequate developmental pace. Hence the Finance Ministry's Budget Committee is necessarily reduced to "nibbling" at the requests for funds emanating from other Ministries. No executive officer has antecedently made the more drastic decisions to accept or reject certain projects *in toto*. The Finance Ministry has no authority to do so.[21]

In 1959, a new Budget Procedures Act was adopted which transferred this function from the Ministry of Finance to the office of the prime minister. In principle, this strengthened the power of financial allocation enjoyed by the head of the government, who could presumably carry out this function more effectively than could a minister who was forced to adjudicate among his peers. If, however, the prime minister himself depended for the maintenance of his own power position on the support of his ministers and their bureaucratic constituencies, then there would have been real limits to his own power to reshape the budget presented to him by his cabinet members.

As in the past, legislation designed to "modernize" the structure of government failed to grapple with the basic issue, the allocation of power between the bureaucracy and extrabureaucratic institutions. In practice, even the decisions of the prime minister on such crucial matters (politically) required ratification by the cabinet.

The Cabinet as a Typical Committee.   If, in the final analysis, it was the cabinet as the center of the power structure which had to allocate resources, then it would appear to have been crucial to the system that the cabinet operated effectively. Yet the economic adviser reported that the cabinet was unable to deal adequately with the many issues that came before it. "I find," he reported,

. . . that in the period from 2 July 1955 through 26 November 1955–a period of less than five months–no fewer than 185 issues were submitted to and considered by and more or less unequivocally decided by the Council of Ministers. When allowance is made for the number of four-to-seven-day intervals during which the Council did not meet at all, this number of issues is impossibly large. It is not merely the number of issues but the quality of the issues. Many of the matters brought up for discussion are of the type that can and should be assigned to some responsible Ministry. There are, for example, items recorded as having been discussed in the Council of Ministers which involve promotions in the civil service, assignment of foreign advisers to particular Ministries, and comparable items which would not appear to be necessarily matters for consideration by the Council of Ministers.

But more important perhaps than either the number or the quality of the issues coming before the Council of Ministers is the fact that decisions taken in that body, as recorded, appear to lack binding force in many instances; and this lack of binding force is attributable primarily to a lack of clarity in the formulation of the decision taken.[22]

It appears from the adviser's report that the pattern of committee action which he attributes to the cabinet is typical for a large number of committees which had been established throughout the government. He characterizes the work of these committees in the following terms: "Issues arise orally; the facts develop only in a casual and slipshod way as the discussion goes on; the committee frequently has no clear idea of what are the alternative decisions available to it; issues are discussed and then abandoned without any clear decision being taken; or if a clear decision is taken there is no written record of it and therefore no subsequent assurance that it will be carried into execution."[23]

To overcome these deficiencies, the adviser recommended the use of a set of rules for good committee procedure, including reliance on effective documentation, the use of a secretariat, the need for an agenda distributed in advance of meetings, and so forth. Yet there was no evidence that mere knowledge of such rules would have brought about a transformation in committee operations. We can assume that committee members were familiar with the rules of good procedure but unable to employ them. If not, why not?

The use of committees in the Thai government was, indeed, endemic and ubiquitous. If procedural reforms would have made them work better, then surely there must have been foreign advisers to suggest such improvements long since.[24]

A more plausible hypothesis would be that the apparently indecisive mode of committee operations practiced in Thailand served some useful function from the point of view of the bureaucrats involved. Evidence on this point is provided by Siffin:

> If there were no committees, the Thais would have been forced to invent them, for the committee device is exquisitely suited to the Thai administrative system and its setting. The use of committees obscures the exercise of responsibility at subordinate levels, thereby meeting the need for deference to the power and prerogatives of the center, and protects individuals against action and its possible consequences. . . .
>
> The use of committees in many situations at higher administrative levels also enables a negotiated approach to decision-making, in a system where power and values are often much more important than facts. . . .
>
> . . . most significant committee actions are necessarily contingent, and must be referred to higher authority for ratification. Thus the minister signs the paper and takes the official responsibility for the tentative acts and decisions of groups operating obscurely in the remote bowels of the organization.[25]

An underlying reason both for the pervasive use of committees and for the apparently inconclusive manner of their operation may well be the first norm of a bureaucratic polity, as proposed above: namely, avoid making tough decisions. (Note that this norm is rooted in structure, not in any alleged racial or cultural trait.) If a question involves the competing or incompatible interests of several officials, then a definite decision by any individual in the hierarchy would subject him to possible criticism and resentment. To avoid being placed in this unpleasant position, an official may call on a committee representing the interested parties to make a recommendation. Thus, the very fact that an issue came before a committee might be taken to reflect the unwillingness of an official to make a tough decision. He might hope that, in committee, the interested parties would work out a compromise which subsequently could be authorized officially, without risk. But if such a compromise could not be reached, then the committee need not make a decision, nor would it risk the loss of prestige incurred by open revelation of its failure. The rules of good committee procedure necessitate the making of decisions and the revelation of decisions that have been made. The apparently slipshod norms of committee procedure, however, appear to have been more functional for Thailand by enabling officials to maintain their prestige and to avoid hard decisions, while continuing to seek compromise solutions to difficult problems.

It would appear, therefore, that the procedures of the cabinet, as the supreme committee of the bureaucratic polity, reflected in its operating norms patterns of conduct which prevailed throughout the system. Continuing his discussion of cabinet procedures, the economic adviser stated:

. . . the majority of the matters discussed in the Council—and therefore the majority of the decisions taken—have the character of either ad hoc modifications of the budget or of decisions about the disbursement of unbudgeted funds. In either case the consequence is to stultify the budget process. If the Council of Ministers has at its disposal substantial revenues which are excluded from the general and normal budget (and this seems to be the case), the budget process has little significance as a mapping and planning exercise for the utilization of all revenues that can be obtained. If, on the other hand (and this seems to be also to some extent the case), the Council of Ministers makes expenditure decisions during the budget year for which no funds are in sight, this also is a stultification of something—either of the budget which must be altered ad hoc, or else of the Council of Ministers' decision which cannot be executed because there are no financial resources with which to execute them.[26]

Committees as Agents or Arenas.   It is assumed in the image of a modern government that committees, including the cabinet itself, are agents of rational administration. They bring together the technical information required so that decisions can be made which maximize the achievement of values prescribed by a political authority, typically embodied in a representative legislature, a dominant political party, an elected chief executive, or some such extrabureaucratic "principal." If one assumes that the political authority has the power to reward effective administration and to punish ineffective administration, then one can assume that the occupants of bureaucratic posts and committee memberships would have a strong inducement to adopt rules of procedure which would enable them to increase the flow of rewards from the power-holders and to reduce the pressure of constraints.

But if one assumes that the bureaucrats and committee members are themselves the power-holders, then the improved rules of procedure become irrelevant. What is going on is a ubiquitous political struggle in which committee sessions become political arenas. The outcome is determined by a process of compromise and adjustment reflecting the continuously changing power or alignment of the major protagonists. Shifting budgetary allocations and the exclusion of funds from budgetary manipulation may be seen as natural consequences of the politicization of intrabureaucratic decision-making.

The picture of Thai financial procedures and committee processes given by the economic adviser is corroborated by the report of the International Bank's economic survey mission to Thailand. The following passage comments on the procedure for preparing the annual budget.

Government departments request appropriations with only vague justification and in amounts that are consciously set beyond any expectation of achievement. These requests are then transmitted by the Ministry within which they originate without sufficient screening and coordination. And the Ministry of Finance lacks personnel with the necessary competence and detailed knowledge of departmental requirements to evaluate adequately the reasonableness and priority of request. In these circumstances it is almost axiomatic that requests for appropriations will be cut; but the nature and extent of cutting involves substantial elements of *arbitrary judgment and political pressure*. Hence some appropriations may be unrealistically low and in important cases almost certain to be exceeded, while others may be well in excess of any reasonable justification. The result has invariably been the enactment of total appropriations substantially beyond the available non-inflationary sources of financing.

Fortunately, inflationary spending has, in fact, been avoided in recent years. This has been achieved by holding disbursements below appropriations. But this introduces *expediency and political* pressure into the disbursement as well as the budgeting process. The consequence is not only serious year-to-year discontinuity and uncertainty as to appropriations for particular functions and services, but additional uncertainty whether funds appropriated will be actually forthcoming. [*Italics added.*] [27]

The basic facts suggested by this statement coincide with those described by the economic adviser. The implicit assumptions behind the statement, however, repay scrutiny. What, for example, is meant by such terms as "arbitrary judgment" and "political pressure"? It is customary in our political thought to distinguish between "political" and "administrative" processes. If a scene of action is defined as a political arena, then the rivalry between competing interests is not usually spoken of as "political pressure," nor is the outcome of a political contest likely to be referred to as an "arbitrary judgment."

It is only in respect to an administrative process, a situation in which the politically defined goals have been specified in advance, that one uses these terms. A judgment is regarded as "arbitrary" if it fails to make optimum use of scarce resources to achieve a prescribed goal. One speaks of "political pressure" in such circumstances, when the rational process of resource allocation is disrupted because of special interests, typically not those of the bureaucratic participants in the administrative process but rather those of interest groups or partisan elements outside the bureaucracy.

To use these terms in the Thai context, therefore, is to imply that in the budgetary process we are dealing with an administrative situation, and that the prescribed pattern for handling such matters has gone awry. If, by contrast, one were to recognize the budgetary process as a central arena for political competition, then these terms would scarcely seem appropriate. The outcome simply reflects the relative power position of the rival bureaucratic protagonists, and as such it is no more arbitrary than any other outcome of a political contest. Moreover, if the process is inherently a political one, it would appear gratuitous to speak of it as involving political pressure, any more than one might refer to the outcome of an election in the United States as involving "substantial elements of political pressure."

Yet if the Thai system was in fact a bureaucratic polity, as argued here, then the budget-making exercise was indeed an arena for political rivalry. And if this could be considered an accurate description of the situation, then clearly the idea that the underlying reason for the behavior described was a lack of personnel in the Ministry of Finance with "the necessary competence and detailed knowledge" would scarcely hold up. Rather, one would see the limitations of the Ministry's personnel as a consequence, not a cause, of these phenomena. One might reasonably conclude that, until centers of power capable of imposing direction on the bureaucracy came into existence, manipulation of the organization and staffing of the Ministry of Finance would be unlikely to have more than marginal impact on the system.

Not, of course, that the Ministry of Finance would be inclined to reject advice to enlarge its staff and create new administrative units. Quite to the contrary, it would welcome such recommendations—especially in so far as they might be accompanied by external assistance—since they would tend to enhance the power position of the Ministry in its continuing struggle with other ministries. Indeed, such was the situation reported by the Bank's mission, for they found that the government had already launched plans to build up a budget department in the Ministry—on recommendation of its fiscal advisers. This was to be accompanied by a strengthening of the Comptroller General's department and enhancement of the Audit Council. Whether this proliferation of new financial control units would affect the distribution of power between the bureaucracy and its external rivals remains subject to question.

PERSONNEL: COMPETENCE, SENIORITY, OR INFLUENCE

References to the personnel needs of the Ministry of Finance suggest a parallel between the budgetary and the personnel processes of the Thai government. The International Bank's mission tells us that "it is simple in principle to ensure that scarce skills are put to their most important uses. All that is required is a rational placement policy." Again we see that the implicit model of the Thai polity held by the advisory group was of an administrative process. In the allocation of personnel to bureaucratic posts one could and should use rational criteria. The procedure to be followed is described in these terms:

Each civil service position that demands special qualifications should be carefully analyzed, then described in terms of the skills needed. Only candidates who meet these specifications should be appointed. . . .

Clearly, these are tasks that should be performed by the Civil Service Commission. But at present this agency has no technical staff. Hence there is no one who can write a satisfactory job description or who can appraise applicants for positions. There are no well-formulated techniques of placement, and the Commission, like so many government agencies in Thailand, exercises little independence of judgment. Not only difficult decisions, but also even minor ones, are passed on to the Council of Ministers for determination.[28]

It is only when one views personnel assignment as an administrative process that one can talk of assigning "skills" to their "most important uses" or can view personnel decisions as "minor." If one uses a political process model, then "skills" can be translated into "protagonists," contenders in a political arena. One cannot decide which uses are "most important" if there is no external political process by which the goals of administrative action are set. What is important is, rather, the interests of the protagonists, and the outcome is determined by their relative power and their views about the relative value, to them, of gaining this or that available post.

Whether a particular decision is minor or major cannot, in this view, be determined by an outside observer's opinions about the intrinsic significance of a given job. Rather, it is determined by the degree to which contenders for an assignment can gain access to the top influentials. Imagine the risks a personnel officer in the Civil Service Commission would run should he seek to block an appointment on the grounds of incompetence, when that candidate had the ear of a powerful cabinet member, perhaps the hierarchic superior of the personnel officer himself! To pass such a "minor decision" up to the Council of Ministers would indeed be an act of political discretion, not of administrative bungling.

Nevertheless, since the Bank mission defined the problem as inherently administrative, the treatment it prescribed was also administrative. The Civil Service Commission, it suggested, should be reformed. "This reform should concentrate upon turning the Commission into a professional body, by providing it with a staff adequate in size and, in particular, adequate in professional competence to perform the tasks outlined above. No reorganization will ensure independence of judgment, but this might come as a by-product of increased technical competence." [29] What the report overlooked was that in a political arena the most technically competent person is pushed aside if he lacks power. The question, of course, is what kind of skills are required. In a political arena, one needs the skills that command votes, other skills being irrelevant. In a bureaucratic polity, the most relevant skill is capacity to exercise influence. A man with technical skills but without influence in a position whose maintenance requires the ability to secure resources from one's rivals would soon find himself deprived of any opportunity to exercise his skills.

I recall a personal encounter with such a man who was employed by one of the major industrial development enterprises of Thailand, a combine which had been established with strong governmental support. This person was reputed to be a highly competent industrial engineer. I found him in his office, apparently unoccupied. As our interview proceeded, I discovered that he had been brushed aside as a nuisance by those in effective control of the organization. He had criticized many of their methods, and so they had simply removed him from effective contact with actual operations. Yet they found it useful to keep him on the payroll as a decoration or prestige symbol that could be exhibited to critical foreign advisers and the agents of international banks. Moreover, why look for trouble by trying to discharge him? Following the first norm of a bureaucratic polity, he was simply allowed to continue drawing his salary checks. Since the bosses of the firm counted on a government subvention to cover their losses, they were apparently unconcerned about the waste. The man himself felt trapped, since he could neither afford to resign and lose the income nor could he make public his criticisms of the organization's management as long as he remained on the payroll.

In such a setting it seems ironic to read the following statement by the Bank mission: "Far too frequently, unskilled individuals are assigned tasks whose performance requires highly developed skills. This practice has been conspicuous in the government-run industries, where men with little or no experience in management have been put in charge of factories. That the results have been almost uniformly bad is hardly surprising."[30] That the results were bad from the point of view of economic growth and rationality or technical efficiency was no doubt true. But were these the relevant criteria in the system that existed? If we postulate the existence of a bureaucratic polity, then assignment to posts as managers of factories must have been among the most avidly sought-after political plums. Men of influence were clearly needed for these assignments: first, because they could not otherwise have obtained the posts in competition with their rivals; and second, because they needed influence to obtain repeated subventions from the public treasury to make up for their regular losses. Mere technical and managerial efficiency would not enable such a manager to secure such subventions.

Nor, indeed, would they enable him to run the enterprise profitably. I recall a Siamese government enterprise which I once studied. The manager of this enterprise was widely reputed to be one of the most effective and knowledgeable men in his field. Indeed, it was known that, on the side, he ran a private enterprise in this field and make substantial profits in it. However, in the public enterprise he found himself subjected to so much pressure to appoint protégés of others to key positions in the establishment that he could not, in fact, gain effective control over operations. The result was that the concern operated at a loss, which could be made up only by government grants. To obtain these grants, the manager had to conciliate influentials. Clearly, one of the ways in which he did this was by providing posts for their protégés. In effect, then, this man was able to survive as manager of a public enterprise because he could exercise influence. He was also technically qualified—as he proved by his private operations—but these qualifications were not the key ones for his survival in the government service.

The Relevance of Academic Degrees. Let us examine the questions of personnel administration a bit more closely. The International Bank's mission reports:

Job descriptions, which outline the responsibilities and qualifications of various positions, are virtually non-existent. Government agencies needing technically trained people accordingly now put in a request stated in terms of university degrees, not in terms of the functions to be performed and the training and experience needed.[31]

"In Thailand today," the report continues, "there is far too much stress on academic degrees as such. . . ." As a corrective the report suggests that more attention should be paid to the quality of the institutions awarding degrees and the specific relevance of academic training to the positions assigned.

What the authors of this report perhaps overlooked is that even the academic institutions of highest standards were unlikely to offer the kinds of training that would actually qualify their graduates for effective service in the Thai bureaucracy. If, as I have argued above, the bureaucracy was indeed a political arena, then success in this arena required political skills: the ability to wield influence, to win the support of the powerful, and to counteract the opposition of one's rivals. If technical competence was in fact irrelevant to successful performance, then what good would the highest standard education have been?

Yet the emphasis on academic degrees was functional for the operation of a bureaucratic polity in another way. If admission to the bureaucracy was in effect admission to the ruling class, then one can understand that the pressures for admission might have been great. If everyone were eligible for admission, then the decisions facing those in power as to whom to admit and whom to reject would have been difficult indeed. By making academic degrees a prerequisite for admission, and by relating the degree level to a graded hierarchy of administrative classes, it became possible to simplify the problem of screening applicants for admission to the bureaucracy. Indeed, those without appropriate degrees could not even apply and thereby removed themselves from the competition. According to law, candidates for appointment as fourth-grade officials must be graduates of a secondary school, and candidates for admission to the bureaucracy as third-grade officials must normally hold a bachelor's degree. It is technically possible, though very difficult, for a fourth-grade official to rise into the third grade. For the most part, all officials in the second, first, and special grades must have started as third-grade officials.[32]

The degree system, in other words, can be viewed as primarily a device for screening the initial entrants into the civil service. Since a college degree is unlikely to be acquired by anyone without a fairly substantial family background, and since the university education confers on all graduates some common denominators of acquired tastes and social graces, it may be thought to assure a degree of homogeneity and compatibility among members of the bureaucracy. Academic education, moreover, provides recruits who can be expected to understand and abide by the rules of a political game which they have to learn after entry. For the system, this may be far more important to learn than whatever technical competence is also brought from studies in a university.

In this connection, a personal episode may be worth recounting. One day a Thai division chief who held a Ph.D. in biology from a leading American university invited me to accompany him on a trip into the countryside to see a village fair. I accepted gladly, for it was my first chance to observe such an activity, and I hoped it would also provide an opportunity to get to know my host much better. To reach the village, we had to drive for a long distance across parched rice fields, it being the dry season. Every time the jeep crossed a dike between fields, it landed with such impact that I feared the frame would be cracked. Nevertheless, after what seemed an interminable trip and after having had to hail nearby farmers many times to ask directions, we finally arrived at the village, where a substantial fair was in gay and noisy progress.

Although our conversation ranged over many topics, I had been unable to learn from my host the real purpose of his trip, but soon after we arrived it became clear enough. I discovered that the guest of honor at the fair was the vice-minister of the ministry in which my host worked. Shortly after our arrival, he introduced me, and thereafter attached himself to the vice-minister for several hours. The fair, in other words, afforded him an opportunity to gain the ear of an influential cabinet member whom he could not see under such favorable circumstances in Bangkok.

As I recall this episode, one observation made by my host during our long cross-country trek stands out in my mind. I had directed our conversation to a review of his educational and career experiences. At one point he told me of the initial disillusionment he had felt shortly after his return home. He had received a good assignment in an agricultural research laboratory and had started with great energy and enthusiasm to carry on some experiments. In due course, his work began to show positive and surprising results. At this point, he told me, he noticed that his colleagues were shunning him and showing manifest signs of dislike. It did not take him long to discover that the success of his own work in contrast to the routine failures of others was perceived by them as a threat. In short, he was made to understand that matters would not go well for him if he persisted in being a "rate buster." He soon felt obliged to make some mistakes which brought his own work to a level not much better than that of his associates, and thereby he reinstated himself in their good graces.

That this was no isolated case became clear to me in conversations I had with a highly regarded American adviser working among the agricultural experiment stations. One day when we were on an extended field trip, he began to tell me how discouraged he felt with the work done in most of the experiment stations. He pointed out that the men concerned often had the most advanced technical training, and that the equipment at their disposal, provided by American aid, was of the best quality. Indeed, he felt envious, because in the stations where he had worked in the United States the available equipment was not nearly as good. Nevertheless, he lamented, the results were disappointing. There was little cumulation of findings over any period of time, so that it appeared the stations were always starting anew on experiments which had been done earlier many times, but never with conclusive results. He was careful to point out some exceptions, but the picture as a whole was disappointing and frustrating.

It could be shown that, as individuals, the Siamese experimental scientists were as capable as their counterparts in the United States, where, under different environmental constraints, they have done and can do excellent work. Moreover, there are circumstances in Thailand which induce the Siamese to display great energy and persistence. I could not help thinking of my official host who had showed such determination in seeking out a remote village. Clearly, it had become apparent to him that such expenditures of energy, when the goal was to gain access to an influential person, were quite worth while, whereas equivalent energy spent in the research laboratory was useless, perhaps even dangerous.

If we recall the norms of a bureaucratic polity, we can see how this pattern fits the norms. One should avoid acting in such a way as to shame or anger one's colleagues in the bureaucracy. One should cultivate influence in order to improve one's position in the hierarchy.

Seniority or Merit.   At one point in its report, the International Bank's mission comments that "the outmoded civil service system of promotion should be altered to permit the advancement of promising young teachers on the basis of ability rather than seniority."[33] Yet in principle the Thai civil service system did stress ability in promotion. According to the civil service laws, as described by Udyanin and Smith, promotions from the third grade to the second grade were made by a ministerial civil service subcommission on the nomination of the undersecretary of the ministry or the director-general of a department. Candidates must have had at least three years of government service (a modest recognition of seniority), but they must also have shown "exceptional ability and efficiency." Similar criteria were prescribed for promotions from second to first grade, and from first- to special-grade officers, but the cabinet itself had to approve this highest level of promotion. Within grades, a less elaborate procedure was followed, but again the basis of promotion was supposed to be diligence, efficiency, discipline, alertness, quality of work and tenure of office. . . ."[34]

The real question here is whether, in a bureaucratic polity, it is possible simply "to alter" the civil service promotion system. Who is to decide the criteria of "efficiency"? What tests can be used to determine "exceptional ability"? If one frankly recognizes the bureaucracy as a political arena, then the essential criterion of efficiency and ability is the capacity to make friends and influence the influential. Energy and efficiency displayed in the laboratory or working over statistics may be highly irrelevant. It is only under conditions where goals and policies can be clearly formulated outside the bureaucracy and the officials held strictly to account for their ability to fulfill these goals and follow these policies that promotion based on "merit" becomes possible. In this context, the kind of technical virtuosity which impresses a foreign observer as evidence of competence may have little relevance to the job requirements perceived by an official as his own requisites for promotion or even survival. Indeed, the man who devotes himself too conscientiously to technical proficiency in his work may soon find that this leaves him too little time for those tasks which experience, not the classroom, teaches him to regard as crucial for success.

Seniority, it is true, does provide a fundamental criterion for promotions. But this must be true, I submit, in any bureaucratic polity, for it is the norm which can most easily be applied. If hard choices must be made among contending candidates for promotion, and the criteria for advancement are so elusive as to be evanescent, then what simpler solution can be found than to choose the man who has served longest? But seniority provides only the floor of the promotion system. Everyone's salary automatically rises a step a year. To justify an increase of more than one step, special reasons must be found. At this level, will the reasons be technical competence and efficiency, or influence and "pull"? One suspects that in a bureaucratic polity, influence will count for more than virtuosity.

There is, indeed, plenty of evidence that, despite the various safeguards promulgated by the Civil Service Commission, influence played a substantial role in promotions in Thailand. Shor described the situation in these terms:

> The most debilitating set-backs to an effective civil service system in Thailand are doubtless the numerous incursions of political and personal favoritism. Legal subterfuge and extra-legal arrangements frequently circumvent elaborately prescribed procedures for protecting the merit system in placement, promotion and other personnel actions. Ubiquitous partisanship is a dominant fact of life in the Thai public service. Although considerable professionalization of the service has been achieved, the career opportunities of the civil servant are subject to capricious political and personal influences. Recurrent subversion of the merit principle through evasion and contravention of the civil service law and rules have stunted the growth of protective traditions. . . .
>
> Within the service, career advancement generally requires the personal support of superiors or the political leverage of influential relatives or friends. Such support is also essential to obtaining preferred assignments. Favored officials may obtain normally difficult transfers to other ministries for the purpose of advancement. . . .[35]

As has been suggested above, the higher the grade of the official, the more politicized his office becomes. Not only is he called upon more often to use his influence on behalf of particular cliques or "political" groups within the bureaucracy, but his own career prospects depend increasingly on the character of his own system of alliances and alignments. Shor takes note also of this phenomenon:

> Favoritism is particularly conspicuous at the top levels of the departments and ministries where it has induced the close identification of political and

administrative officials. Many civil service posts at these levels are allocated as a reward for partisan loyalty and service. Tenure in these positions, however, is consequently somewhat precarious. A change of regime is likely to result in the removal of incumbents who are out of favor with the new leadership, or whose position is needed for another with a stronger claim to reward.[36]

One can think of systems—and some of the governments in Latin America today come to mind—where there has been virtually no career service, and everyone in the government's employ is liable to displacement with a change in the political leadership or military junta in power. Perhaps, to avoid such evils of rampant spoils or patronage, a civil service system which stresses the rule of seniority may have a stabilizing effect and even enhance moderately the over-all effectiveness of the bureaucracy as an administrative machine.

ORGANIZATION: FUNCTIONALISM FOR WHOM?

In every system of government there are perplexing problems of organization. In a framework of administrative rationality, one may find modes of organization which most economically and effectively facilitate the achievement of politically prescribed goals. Similarly, under the canons of economic rationality, a firm operating within the constraints of a market is under continual pressure to find patterns of organization which enhance productivity and performance, since failure in this respect can mean bankruptcy and disappearance of the organization. But in a bureaucratic polity, what are the constraints which promote rationality? Indeed, by what criteria can one recognize the rational or distinguish the effective from the ineffective, the efficient from the inefficient? Costs, after all, can be measured only comparatively, and relative to some specified standard. If one cannot determine the output, how can one measure the input?

The International Bank's mission boldly confronted this organizational question, enunciating the principle that "effective organization should concentrate, not disperse, the responsibility for getting particular jobs done." By this test, the mission gave poor marks to the organizational patterns which it discovered in Thailand, as indicated in the following paragraphs:

This principle of organization is not sufficiently observed in Thailand. Too many Ministries are trying to do the same thing. Both the Ministry of Cooperatives and the Department of Public Welfare (Interior) have elaborate land settlement schemes, government industries are scattered among several

Ministries, and in some Ministries there are two or three small statistical units with no apparent connection. On the other hand, in the Northeast of Thailand, two parts of a single function—the provision of irrigation water—were allocated to separate Ministries. Tanks were built by the Royal Department of Irrigation, but the construction of canals was left to the Ministry of Cooperatives. Since the latter lacked the engineering competence to do the job, it was not done. This situation is now being corrected by transferring canal construction to the Department of Irrigation.

In general, dispersal of functions leads to a duplication of staff, thus to extra expense, and usually to less than optimum results. It also tends to breed a senseless rivalry, dedicated to "empire building" rather than getting on with the job.

Good organization requires that, as a general rule, where a particular function needs to be performed, a specific governmental unit be made responsible for it. Otherwise (unless the task in question is quite minor) either the work will not get done, or it will be intermingled with other tasks and be done half-heartedly. Thus we have already stressed the planning function, and recommended an organization to perform it. A corollary to the need for a specific agency to perform a complex function is the need to abolish organizations that have little or nothing to do.[37]

Needless to say, the specific factual statements and implications of these paragraphs appear to have been precisely correct. The question raised here, however, is whether the implicit value assumptions and the explicit prescriptions were realistic and rested on an accurate analysis of the Thai bureaucratic polity.

From one point of view, the structure of the government of Thailand seemed to be a model of organizational symmetry and structural simplicity. If one were to compare this structure with that of the United States government, for example, one might render a verdict in favor of the rationality of the Thai system and against the hopeless irrationality of the American. If the American system works better, it is probably despite, rather than because of, its organizational design.

The essential question is not the formal or intrinsic rationality of the organizational design, but rather the motivational forces which give it life. Any organization, presumably, grows or persists only because someone wants it that way. Unless we can relate a structure to the purposes it serves, we cannot evaluate it. Purposes, however, are not ethereal bodies floating in space like Greek gods but the concrete aspirations and objectives of real men. Our first question, therefore, is who wanted the prevailing pattern of organization in Thailand? What objectives of theirs did it serve?

The automatic answer which one gives when looking at governmental organization is that public administration is designed to meet the needs of the people. In a democratic polity it is the public interest, as determined by due political and legislative processes, which provides the touchstone for evaluating administrative organization. Even in a totalitarian system, the dominant political party may be viewed as the client system for which the state apparatus is designed and to which it is responsive.

But in a bureaucratic polity must we not assume that the organization of government is shaped by the interests of the bureaucrats themselves? In so far as Thailand had a bureaucratic polity, we would therefore expect its public organizations to reflect the needs and purposes of its official beneficiaries. The mission report states that "where a particular function needs to be performed," a specific governmental unit should be made responsible for it. But who determines what the function is which needs to be performed? A function, after all, is a relationship between an action structure and a system of which the structure is a part. There can be no agricultural function, for example, unless there are farmers with fields and consumers who use the crops. There is no statistical function without users who require the data collected. Merely to collect figures and process them in a machine is not a statistical function unless the results produced serve someone's need. To carry on experiments in a laboratory is a functionless activity unless the results are perceived as significant to some consumers of the end product. In this sense, a babbling brook is a nonfunctional system of action until some poet perceives it with aesthetic delight or a miller harnesses its power to grind flour.

When the IBRD report speaks of the "need to abolish organizations that have little or nothing to do," one is entitled to ask who can decide whether an organization has anything to do. On my arrival in Thailand, I surveyed all the public agencies that had anything to do with rice. In a country where rice was the primary product, I was not surprised to find many such agencies. My next task was to investigate the functions performed by each. In this quest I came across the "Rice Office," which, after the war, had been set up to monopolize and control the export of rice. Subsequently this activity was returned, in large measure, to the private enterprise and market system. Nevertheless, the Rice Office remained as an organizational structure, fully housed and staffed. After the military coup in 1957, however, it was closed down.

Investigation soon showed that the director of the office was a key military officer, a former cabinet member, hence one of the influentials. The office was staffed with men who supported him and whom he, in turn, felt obligated to help. As a member of the ruling circle, he also had a claim on the cabinet members for support. In terms of the bureaucratic polity as a model, it became apparent that this office did have a function—namely, to provide jobs for an influential group of men. No doubt any foreign adviser, thinking in terms of a modern polity, would regard such an office as a costly luxury, since it no longer carried out the public service for which it was originally chartered. The office was, indeed, subsequently abolished, but not because its manifest function had vanished. It was abolished when an overturn in the power structure destroyed the influence of the men whom the office employed. At this point the office lost its latent—and more vital—function, which was to provide posts for men of influence. The new cabinet no longer cared about the men affected and happily abolished their positions.

For Whom Is the Function Performed?   The mission's report speaks also of dispersed functions leading to "a duplication of staff" and to "senseless rivalry, dedicated to 'empire building' rather than getting on with the job." But it is only if one sees "the job" as public service that one can castigate this form of organization as "senseless." In a bureaucratic polity the real "job" may be to provide more employment opportunities for public officials. If dispersal of functions leads to staff duplication, well and good, for thereby the number of positions is increased! As to "empire building," is this not "the job" in a bureaucratic polity? The public service which results can be regarded as a useful spin-off effect, but secondary in importance. Thus, a bureaucratic polity reverses the scale of priorities set by modern polities.

The public service spin-off, moreover, may be recognized as significant for reasons different from those visualized by foreign experts. If a service can be performed that will generally please the public and make it more docile, easier to get along with and manipulate, then the interests of the dominant bureaucracy are served. In this sense, the public service motive is recognized as valid in a bureaucratic polity. Just as the citizen public in a modern polity concedes that, if bureaucrats are to be effective and helpful public servants, their needs must be cared for also, so the ruling officials in a bureaucratic polity recognize that if the subject population is to perform the productive labor required to generate income which can be taxed—the food, clothing and other amenities needed by the governing class—then some public services must be provided in exchange to keep the people contented and willing to comply with official requirements.

Moreover, if foreign aid missions provide additional funds, fellowships, equipment, and prestige as a condition for carrying out development projects, then by all means the officials concerned find it worth while to praise and support such programs.

However, organizations designed to enforce regulations which provoke resistance by the public are to be avoided, except in so far as such regulations can be used directly to enhance the income and welfare of officials. For example, laws that generate tax revenues should be enforced within reasonable limits. Moreover, in view of the scarcity of budgeted funds in a low income country, officials will promote regulations and programs which assure them their own special or ear-marked revenues. Hence the proliferation of income-collecting activities in different agencies and the use of "revolving funds" and state enterprises—for these all enhance the immediate expediency interests of the officials concerned.

The Bank's report found several occasions to complain of such practices in Thailand. It stated, for example, that

. . . various sources of public revenue are not included in the budgeting operation. This has recently been corrected in the case of special taxes earmarked for health and education purposes. But other substantial public receipts and disbursements remain outside the budget, the most important of which are the financial operations of the State Lottery and numerous special funds operated by various government departments for a variety of income producing purposes.[38]

For similar reasons, government officials in a bureaucratic polity may even welcome the existence of laws which they cannot actually enforce. A forest guard may relish regulations prohibiting the extraction of timber from public forests, since this enables him to exact tribute from the loggers. He may even work out complicated deals. For example, after the loggers have cut their timber, the guard will "discover" the illegal operations, report his findings, and have the logs removed at public expense, to be subsequently sold at auction. Inquiry might reveal that the purchasers were the ones who had cut the logs and paid the forest guard to help them solve their transportation problem. Everyone directly concerned makes a profit, and the guard gains a reputation as an effective watchdog.

Laws which are difficult to enforce and bring no tangible benefits to the enforcing agents, however, are unlikely to receive much attention in a bureaucratic polity. I recall inquiring once in a Thai agricultural agency about certain regulations which had come to my attention. They called for the enforcement of certain safety and health standards in the storage and distribution of rice and other grains. The officials in the agency concerned seemed eager to please and made a diligent search of their files, but they were never able to discover copies of the laws in question. I was finally advised to buy the text at the bookstore of the university law school, where an adequate supply was presumably maintained for the use of the students. My curiosity was not sufficient to induce me to follow up this lead, but I did inquire further about the reason for this curious lapse. The explanation I was finally given was that such laws were difficult to enforce and only created trouble. The agency in question preferred to concentrate on the service aspects of its duties which brought respect and affection from the people.

Commenting on this problem in relation to social and industrial legislation in Thailand, the Bank's mission stated:

With the quite proper intention of raising social standards, laws have been passed that are too advanced for the present stage of development. Because the machinery to enforce them does not exist, they have often failed to achieve their objectives, and instead have actually put a brake on progress.[39]

When Is Rivalry "Senseless"?   When the Bank's report speaks of "senseless rivalry" it calls attention to the prevalence of interagency competition within the Thai bureaucracy. When I arrived in Thailand, I was also struck by various evidences of poor communication and apparent rivalry between ministries, departments, and divisions within the government. Yet familiarity with internecine struggles and prevalent "in-fighting" in the bureaucracies of the United States and other Western countries should teach one to expect intrabureaucratic competition as a normal characteristic of government. Readers of the reports of the Inter-University Case Program in the United States will be familiar with the ubiquitous and frequently tense character of interagency competition in American administration.[40]

Comparative analysis suggests that intrabureaucratic rivalry in Thailand is no more acute than in a modern polity. Perhaps the key

word to be stressed is "senseless" rather than "rivalry." Yet to whom is
the rivalry senseless? Perhaps only in the perspectives of foreign observers who expect rivalry to be concerned with issues of public welfare. In the King's River case, to take one American example, the U.S.
Corps of Engineers did battle with the Bureau of Reclamation for the
privilege of building a dam in California. Both agencies, no doubt, had
expediency interests to consider. But what gave the case its particular
vigor and complexity was the pattern of alignments between the Corps
of Engineers, a complex of local interests in the King's River valley,
and co-operating members of Congress, as contrasted with the more
subtle and comprehensive view of the public interest held by the Bureau
of Reclamation and the president. At stake were complex issues involving the distribution of costs and benefits in terms of irrigation facilities,
public power, and flood control.[41]

Such issues are, for the most part, weak or absent in the intrabureaucratic contests of the Thai state apparatus. A case involving agricultural
experimentation may illustrate the point. The leading agency for experimentation regarding rice production was the Rice Department in the
Ministry of Agriculture. This department maintained a network of stations which engaged in plant breeding and had a remarkably impressive record in the production of improved species of rice. The criteria
of research had to do largely with the quality of the grain. American
technical assistance had been given quite generously in the building up
of this program and had, indeed, been indirectly responsible for the
emergence of the department as a separate agency. When the assistance
program started, the rice program had been carried out by a section,
later a division, in the Department of Agriculture. The expansion of
staff which resulted from the successful, American-advised, research
program led to a minor organizational explosion and the birth of the
Rice Department.

Meanwhile, the Irrigation Department, also in the Ministry of Agriculture, had an interest in rice, but from a different point of view. This
department, which happened also to be one of the most effectively administered agencies in the government, wished to expand the area of
the central plain under rice cultivation. Such an expansion, which had
been a persistent concern of the Siamese government from the time of
King Mongkut, would increase the production of Thai rice available
for domestic use and for export. The premium tax on rice exports and
the customs duties on imports (paid for with the foreign exchange

earned by rice exports) provided a lion's share of the revenues available to the government. Hence, the expansion of rice acreage was not only in the interests of the country as a whole but also promised direct benefits to everyone who worked for the government.

The system of irrigation on which the Siamese traditionally relied did not require the impounding of water in storage reservoirs. Rather, it involved the building of a vast network of canals which distributed water during the rainy season throughout the rice-growing central plains. Rice in Thailand, as elsewhere in Asia, was grown for the most part in flooded paddy fields. (Dry rice, of course, was grown on the hillsides by shifting cultivators, but this was culturally defined as a different crop. Indeed, the Agriculture Department continued to carry on some experimental work with dry rice after the Rice Department split off, with its focus on wet rice cultivation.)

The limits of irrigation by diversion canals had been reached when the Irrigation Department, in the mid-fifties, began to explore with the World Bank the possibility of securing a large loan to finance the construction of a high dam in northern Thailand. The director-general of the Irrigation Department was Xuchat (194, Appendix A), whose name has already been mentioned as a technician influential, a one-time cabinet member, and the holder of several board memberships. He was also a man of unusual vision who perceived some of the ranging implications of the proposed giant reservoir. The idea of such a dam had, indeed, been proposed as early as 1903 by the Dutch adviser, J. H. van der Heide, but was never implemented.[42] Xuchat was able to persuade the World Bank to make a large loan, but with the assumption that programs to assure optimal utilization of the stored water would be launched at an early stage.

The most significant innovation that stored water would make possible was the provision of irrigation water during the dry season. During the rainy season, the water supply was ample to flood the paddy fields over an extensive area. However, at best the newly impounded water would not be sufficient to flood the rice fields of the central plains during the dry season. It would quite obviously be necessary to discover crops that could be grown with limited supplies of water, in rotation with rice. In order to identify such crops, to explore their market and processing requirements, and to find out whether Siamese farmers could be induced to cultivate them, a vigorous experimentation program was clearly needed.

After approaching several foreign aid agencies for help, including the USOM, Xuchat finally succeeded in persuading the Food and Agriculture Organization to supply a foreign adviser qualified to render assistance. An Indian agronomist arrived and was assigned to look into this question. Proposals were made to the Rice and Agriculture departments to undertake the needed experimental work, but both apparently refused. Eventually, the Irrigation Department undertook to set up its own experiment station under the direction of the FAO adviser.

Rice Experimentation.   Although the primary emphasis in this station was to be on crops which might be grown during the dry season with a limited supply of water, it was also considered necessary to learn more about the growing seasons of rice in order to determine what crops could most advantageously be rotated with rice. Different varieties of rice can be planted and harvested at different times. Moreover, some varieties have markedly shorter growing seasons than others. As long as it was assumed that only one crop, rice, would be grown, the time factor was not regarded as significant. No advantage was to be gained by combining experiments on rice quality with other experiments designed to study the duration and timing of the growing season.

The experimental station of the Irrigation Department embarked, then, on a program designed to produce rice varieties which could most readily be rotated with dry season crops. Meanwhile, the Rice Department had already embarked on its "seed multiplication" program designed to distribute among the farmers the improved seed that had been grown in its stations. To the Rice Department, the introduction of a new criterion for experimentation greatly complicated the technical problems which in large part it had already mastered.

The confusions which might have resulted from these two different programs are apparent. Rival extension agents from the two departments might have urged contradictory courses of action upon the farmers, recommending different varieties of rice seed. But important advantages in a rice economy can be gained by standardization. One of the chief criteria used by buyers in grading milled rice is the percentage of broken grains in a sample. But the rate of breakage in the mills is influenced significantly by the extent to which all grains of rice are of the same size. Therefore, it is in the interest of the farmers, the millers, and the country for farmers to use a single variety of rice, rather than a mixture of seeds, and for all farmers in a given milling area to use the same variety, since in buying from small-scale farmers the output from different suppliers tends to become mixed.

From an over-all point of view, then, it was in the interest of the Thai economy to agree on standardized rice varieties and to induce all or most farmers in a given area to grow the same variety for the market. Yet the proliferation of experimental programs, each stressing a different set of criteria, was not calculated to achieve this result.

Despite this apparent conflict of interest between the rival experimental programs, however, there seemed to be little tension. I worked often in both agencies during my field work in Thailand, and I was rarely able to detect any feeling of hostility or even rivalry between them, at least nothing comparable to what might have been expected under similar circumstances in the United States. Indeed, I was often struck by each agency's apparent lack of knowledge of and interest in what the other was doing, although their spheres of interest obviously overlapped extensively. Nor did I find evidence of an interagency committee or other mechanism which might have been used to co-ordinate their work. (The reader must bear in mind that this was the situation in 1957/58, and the state of affairs has probably changed in many respects since then.)

How can we explain this multiplication of overlapping experimental programs and their apparent lack of mutual liaison? If we were considering a comparable situation in the United States, we would expect the farmers concerned to have formed an influential organization whose agents would be working in close touch with the experiment station people. Moreover, there would be a unified extension service whose agents would be talking with farmers and establishing communication between them and whatever different facilities or services might have become available through the several experimental programs. The millers or processors of agricultural products would also have applied pressure for the standardization of grain varieties, if this appeared to be desirable. Rivalry between competing government agencies, under such conditions, would have been motivated by eagerness to win the support of organized clientele groups.

But in the Thai setting, there was little evidence of such clientele organization. The farmers, for the most part, were quite unorganized. It was true that the government had sponsored the formation of some rice marketing co-operatives, but these were organized by the Ministry of Co-operatives, quite outside the Ministry of Agriculture, and I found no evidence that the agencies concerned with rice cultivation ever collaborated with the agency responsible for improved rice marketing. Moreover, the millers, who were organized to a greater degree, were virtually all Chinese and hence were not regarded with favor by the government officials. Rather, they were regarded as obnoxious aliens who exploited the people and therefore were not proper subjects for governmental assistance. The government might seek to establish its own milling facilities, and indeed the rice marketing co-operatives were obliged, at least in principle, to sell their rice to the Siam Rice Company, a state enterprise in which the co-operatives were supposed to own shares.

Extension Services. A unified extension service might, presumably, have served an intermediary function by carrying the results of different experimental programs to the farmers and interpreting to the officials what the farmers' needs were. However, each of the product-oriented departments in the Ministry of Agriculture had its own extension division. Various foreign advisers, it is true, did recommend the establishment of a single extension department or service which would deal directly and exclusively with the farmers and harmonize the diverse programs of the different departments concerned respectively with livestock, fishing, forests, rice, irrigation, and "agriculture."

The International Bank mission also had something to say about the organization of extension services, which aptly provides additional information on this subject.

At present there are less than 300 extension officers in the whole of Thailand, including those who do some extension work incidental to their main assignment on experimental farms. Most of the extension staff belong to the Rice Department of the Ministry of Agriculture and are engaged mainly in the Government's program for propagating the use of improved varieties of rice seed.

We recommend, as the minimum objective of a satisfactory extension service, two general purpose extension officers in each of the 448 districts (amphurs) of the Kingdom. We emphasize "general purpose" because we see little merit in prolonging the present division of extension activities among the Agriculture, Rice, Livestock, and Irrigation Departments of the Ministry. We would certainly not wish to minimize the importance of the program of distributing improved rice seed and urge that it be given every possible support by the Government. We believe, however, that this program could be carried out as effectively, and perhaps more so, if its officers were part of a general purpose extension service rather than a specialized staff of the Rice Department. We have also been impressed with the interest of the Irrigation Department in experimental and extension work. But this work has grown up of necessity, because the other agencies of the Ministry of Agriculture have failed to provide such services. As an effective general purpose extension service is built up, it should take over these activities from the Irrigation Department.[43]

Here again we find an organization structure which seems well adapted to the needs and purposes of a bureaucratic polity, although not that of a modern political system. A separate extension service would have required a type of functional specialization necessitating intensive interdepartmental co-ordination. One department would have to disseminate information prepared in several other departments. The existing organizational structure, by contrast, enabled each department to be relatively self-contained. The Rice Department could carry out its own plant breeding experiments and propagate the improved seeds to farmers in those districts where it happened to have its own agents. The fact that it lacked agents elsewhere created the basis for a future claim on the national budget. Meanwhile, since farmers were not organized and clamoring for service, the Department experienced no acute discomfort.

The other product-oriented departments were in the same position. Even the Irrigation Department, which had invited the Rice or Agriculture departments to undertake the new experimental programs, was probably relieved to have its own autonomous program, since it involved careful regulation of the flow of irrigation water, and it was easier to locate a new station near irrigation facilities than to try to provide water for a station already situated with other criteria in view.

The existing organizational structure was functional from the point of view of bureaucratic interests, since it simplified the technical problems with which each department had to contend. By reducing the degree of functional interdependence between departments, it helped the officials in these departments to get along well with each other by eliminating many possible occasions for conflict of interest. Under these circumstances, a reorganization scheme which increased the interdependence of administrative units without at the same time changing the political basis of the regime would probably have intensified intrabureaucratic conflict and confusion without significantly improving the services provided to the general public.

A change in the political basis of these programs would require the organization of effective interest groups, political parties, and legislative assemblies so that the needs of farmers, merchants, and millers might become articulate and politically effective. If such a political transformation could have been effected, the existing organizational machinery, whatever its illogic, could probably have been made to work far more effectively in providing needed agricultural services. But without such a political transformation, even the most "rational" and beautifully designed organizational structure would probably not have been able to render public services any more effectively than the structures which already existed.

At one point, in discussing the failure of a national housing program to accommodate its program to the plans of the Bangkok Planning Commission, the Bank's mission noted sadly: "As so often in Thailand, one agency of government seems not to have known or cared about the intentions of another agency."[44] This, then, was the special character of the "senseless rivalry" in Thai bureaucratic organization. It was a form of rivalry which seemed almost benign, for it minimized clientele-oriented outputs. In the mythology of the market system, vigorous competition is regarded as a healthy phenomenon. May the same not be true within a bureaucracy? Energetic or "sensible" rivalry betokens some effort on the part of different agencies to win the favor of the politically influential outside the bureaucracy. Such efforts are likely to result in better public service. The interagency rivalries of the Thai bureaucratic polity were conducted according to a set of operating rules designed to eliminate major points of friction and to maintain the system at a low level of tension.

MANAGEMENT: CENTRALIZATION AND DEFERENCE

One of the perennial complaints about the management of public affairs in every underdeveloped country—and in this respect Thailand is no exception—is the degree to which the decision-making process is excessively centralized. Despite many comments made by foreign advisers regarding the urgency of this problem and recommendations submitted for overcoming it, the situation appears to persist. Perhaps if the dynamics of a bureaucratic polity were taken into account, it would be seen that the empirical reality is not nearly as simple as the advisers have described it, nor do the solutions proposed come to grips with the essentials of the problem.

In this connection, let us review a series of recommendations made by foreign advisers, chosen somewhat at random from a considerable list of such reports. An early discussion of this subject is contained in Reeve's book dealing with public administration in Siam before the revolution of 1932.

One very important defect in the system as it operates in Siam is that the requirement, or rather the practice, to refer so many matters to a higher authority for approval slows down the work of many of the departments. The ministries get bogged down with masses of papers on more or less unimportant issues nearly all of which have to pass through the bottleneck of an overworked Permanent Under-Secretary's office. And then an unnecessarily large number of questions are submitted for the prior approval of a Minister who is often more pre-occupied with the political crisis of the moment than with the routine administration of his ministry.

Each State Councillor in charge of a ministry could be instructed to have a regular weekly conference with all his subordinate Director-Generals and the Heads of Divisions in his ministry. At these conferences all outstanding matters could be put on the agenda and discussed and usually a final and definite decision could be made on the spot, and confirmed in the minutes of each meeting. This would abolish much unnecessary paper work and obviate much delay.[45]

The first administrative study of the Thai government made after the war was carried out by the Public Administration Service under a contract with the Mutual Security Agency. Its report, submitted early in 1952, contained the following paragraphs:

It has become increasingly apparent that individually and collectively the Council of Ministers are so seriously burdened with a heavy weight of administrative detail that the Cabinet, as the central directing force of the Government, is diverted from its deliberations of the major policies which the Cabinet alone can decide. It also appears that the work of the Cabinet and of the individual ministers is retarded and their effectiveness in carrying out urgently needed programs of government services is badly impaired by the large volume of trifling matters which are referred to the individual ministers and to the Cabinet for consideration and decision. . . .

The reference of detailed decisions to Cabinet members, both individually and collectively, is but a part of the larger problem of a very high degree of centralization of authority in the Government. This situation can be demonstrated from a number of sources. For one thing, it is commonplace to discover that the permanent under-secretaries of ministries, the director-generals, and even the division heads, are diverted from consistent and serious consideration of their major problems by the need to give personal approval to many actions of a routine matter arising out of the normal course of departmental operations. This is so whether those matters relate to the assignment, transfer, or discipline of personnel, or to such routine matters as the issuance of permits for legitimate activities which are subject to surveillance by the State. The same situation prevails in relation to the changwad governors. The changwad governors have a tremendous volume of paper work signatures and approvals, much of which might be well delegated to subordinates with authority to act. Other matters which now must be referred through the governor to a Bangkok department and ministry might well be decided in the changwad, whether it be the case of a proposed transfer of a secondary teacher from one school to another within the changwad or the institution of a new health clinic even though local funds may be available for its support.[46]

Interestingly enough, the authors of this report recognized that it was "a far-reaching" problem which would require the services of "Thai officials with real imagination and ability." However, they proposed a number of steps which might be taken to cope with it and estimated that if two advisers were assigned "to work at the Cabinet level and in one ministry, to serve as an example to others, the work might be completed in 9 to 10 months. . . ."[47]

Whatever may have been done to implement these recommendations, the problem appears to have persisted, for the International Bank's report, in 1959, contains the following exposition:

A further cause of inefficiency in the public service is the habit of passing all questions upwards for decision. This results in great delays. Even Ministers have been known to refuse to decide matters that are clearly within their jurisdiction, preferring instead to pass them on to the Cabinet for collective resolution. The result is an inordinate volume of work for that body, including a large proportion of petty matters with which it should not be bothered—such as civil service promotions, foreign leave for subordinate officers, and other issues that should in many instances be decided by heads of departments.[48]

The Bank's mission thought that reform in this area should not be too difficult, and it offered some suggestions on how to achieve better co-ordination at lower levels of government without throwing so much of the burden on the overworked cabinet. Its proposals were formulated in these terms:

Just as good organization usually requires a specific agency to perform a specific function, so good management requires that someone supervise the work of different agencies, and, in particular, that he prevent them from working at cross purposes. Such coordination is inadequate in Thailand. . . .

The principal coordinating body is of course the Cabinet. If the Cabinet were to draw up a list of matters it would refuse to consider, as being insufficiently important to warrant its attention, and would then abide by this policy, it would have much more time for the exercise of its primary function of coordination. Moreover, a start would have been made toward forcing decisions to be taken at the appropriate level.

Within each Ministry, it is the duty of the Permanent Undersecretary to coordinate the activities of the different departments. The performance in this regard is very uneven. If each Undersecretary were to refuse to act on, or to pass on to his superior, decisions that should be taken by department heads, he, too, would have more time to do his real job, and it would be easier for his Minister to hold him to account for it. His department heads might also become more effective administrators—or resign.[49]

Readers of this book will immediately recognize that the prescriptions offered by the Bank's mission flout the first norm of a bureaucratic polity—to avoid making hard decisions. If the ministers, undersecretaries, and director-generals were, indeed, willing to make hard decisions, they might act as the advisers suggest without having to be so prodded by foreigners. But the advice proffered implies that this is a matter over which they have control, as though by an act of will or self-discipline they could make themselves more decisive.

If, as postulated here, there are powerful institutional sanctions which would penalize any official who acted in such a manner and offer few if any rewards for acting differently from the way he does, then the advice offered might amount to an invitation to martyrdom. Moreover, if the institutional sanctions are as postulated, then persons who took personal responsibility for unpopular decisions might soon find themselves transferred to other positions. In other words, there may be forces which regularly recruit to the key positions men constitutionally disposed to act precisely in the manner against which the foreign advisers protest.

An Equivocal Distribution of Power. The image presented in the foregoing quotations, however, seems to be an oversimplification of reality. It was only the formal authority structure that was highly centralized in the Thai bureaucratic polity. To a considerable degree, each of the subordinate agencies of the government was relatively autonomous in actual operations. The effective control of the center over its subordinate operating units was not very great. In other words, the real pattern of power distribution was highly equivocal.[50]

The ambiguities of this mode of distributing power in the Thai polity have been well characterized by Siffin, who describes and explains the centralization of authority in these terms:

Decision-making and the *right* to exercise initiative are both highly centralized. For one thing, rank and authoritative status go hand-in-hand. Secondly, subordinate level officials cannot generally afford to exercise much responsibility; it might reflect upon superiors. . . . Third, arrangements for delegating functional responsibility down the line, and for controlling the results, are neither systematic nor otherwise very adequate. . . . Finally, there is the strong tradition of centralization. [*Italics added.*] [51]

But Siffin is also aware of the decentralization of effective control which leads him to characterize the Thai polity as displaying a "peculiar combination of centralization and autonomy, which is as real as it is difficult to describe. . . ." In explaining the effective decentralization of control, he writes:

. . . within subordinate units of organization in the Thai civil service there is much autonomy and freedom from continuing intervention and control by management. Generally, the chief of a division or even a section expects freedom from close scrutiny or "ordering around" by his superior, so long as he maintains the proper personal relationship with that superior and does not otherwise get into trouble. Seldom in the Thai administrative system does one find reporting arrangements deliberately planned to give the supervisor a continuing picture of the work status and substantive accomplishments of subordinate units. Means for positive, continuing, program-oriented management control are very limited.

Superiors are not supposed to interfere persistently in the work of their subordinates, but it is entirely proper for them to submit specific orders for execution. . . . Orders which would have significant, lasting effects on the goals and work methods of a unit would not be likely to be effective unless reinforced over a period of time by other measures than the direct order. And complex formal systems for reinforcing such orders do not exist to any great extent. [52]

The reasons for the equivocal distribution of power become more apparent if one considers the essential logic of a bureaucratic polity. The first norm of action—to avoid making difficult decisions—clearly militates against any official, even at the highest level, taking on himself personal responsibility for measures certain to antagonize any substantial number of colleagues. By the same rule, superiors avoid setting up any permanent and continuous machinery for close supervision and control over their subordinates. If the government is being run on behalf of the officials, then they must, for the most part, be permitted to do what they want, within a general framework that legitimizes their operations. Thus, the very processes which appear to produce centralization also have the paradoxical effect of producing localization. One of the reasons that high officials and even committees are reluctant to announce tough decisions is that they know they cannot enforce them. Rather than be caught in the embarrassing position of promulgating unenforceable policies, officials prefer to delay, to "pass the buck," or to formulate apparent decisions in nonoperational terms so that they can be ambiguously interpreted. In refusing to decide on an issue, moreover, a subordinate official rarely takes much risk that his superiors will decide it in an intolerable way.

The fourth operational norm of the bureaucratic polity—to seek higher rank and to respect those who have already won superior status —may also be considered in this connection. If, in a bureaucratic polity, the incentives are powerful to defer to those of higher rank, then subordinates will seek at all times to please those above them. Hence, they will avoid making decisions which might offend their superiors and will insist on referring them up the hierarchy.

But the same norm also leads subordinates to avoid passing information to superiors or giving them information which might displease them. The result is that the superiors will be poorly informed about the actual state of affairs in units under their nominal control, so that subordinates are able, in practice, to do much as they please as long as unpleasant situations do not come to the attention of those above them in the hierarchy. The fourth norm, then, would also help to explain the paradox of an equivocal distribution of power: the simultaneous propensity toward centralization of deferential authority and localization of actual control.

It seems apparent that in Thailand such an attitude of deference to superiors was pervasive. Among many writers who have commented on this point, Mosel provides a particularly apt description:

The legitimacy of the superior's authority is probably the more important basis of conformity. The "ideology" which establishes this legitimacy is derived from the hierarchial status system and "vertical orientation" of the larger society. The "decision from above" tradition implies obedience from below. Compliance with authority is not merely a matter of regulations; it is an expression of respect for the dignity of rank. Submission to higher rank is seen as natural and proper; it is a carryover of habits acquired elsewhere in the Thai culture. So important is this cultural feature that it has been given formal embodiment. Civil Service Regulations explicitly require that civil servants display both respect and obedience to superiors. Such a system automatically lays great stress on the externalization of status symbols. Thus, civil servants wear uniforms which clearly announce their grade.[53]

While Mosel stresses the influence of the cultural system on the deferential attitudes of Thai bureaucrats, it should be added that the social system also institutionalized powerful rewards for those who most consistently pleased their superiors. Siffin has commented very perceptively on this point:

Rewards in the Thai system are heavily not based upon positive program accomplishment, although a gross and glaring failure can sometimes lead to sanctions. To a great degree, rewards are based upon one's relations with his superiors, as expressed in terms of deference, support, avoidance of trouble, compliance with Thai ideals, and similar matters. Although the West usually is described as highly materialistic in contrast with Buddhist Thailand, the rewards sought by Thais in top management positions appear to be prestige, power, and material well-being, and not necessarily in that order. More often than not, these positions are essentially instrumentalities for the advancement of the personal aims of the holder. The concept of service to the public is not very potent; this is certainly understandable—it is not part of the tradition of the society.[54]

Power, Sanctions, and Policy. All of this statement provides support for the view that the Thai political system was a bureaucratic polity— except for the final clause. Whether or not the expedient reasons for deference to superiors were traditional, it was also, and more importantly, true that the public was not organized politically and hence was unable to provide, through extrabureaucratic institutions, any positive rewards or punishments which would have compelled public officials to consider that their personal advantage was linked with public service rather than with deferential postures toward their superiors.

Various other recommendations for management improvement offered by foreign advisers fall as wide of the mark as those mentioned above, precisely because they misconstrue the reasons for the difficulties which they perceive. Administrative experts, for example, frequently criticize the operation of "staff" agencies, which are supposed to render technical advice to top management. Although some agencies in the Thai government were technically set up as staff units, they have not worked effectively, according to the standards set in modern governments.

Advisers often seem to think that this is owing to unfamiliarity with the principles of public administration, and that a change in the laws or regulations, or training of personnel, could bring about an improvement in the staff function. Yet the principle of deference to superiors makes it unlikely that a subordinate Thai official could bring himself to offer "advice" which would appear to those above him as critical. Thomas remarks shrewdly upon this point when he points to "the failure of high officials to make use of staff advice, research and planning though units may exist which supposedly perform these functions." By way of explanation, he states:

> For a subordinate to offer advice to his superior is deemed presumptuous, and of course if this advice ran counter to the opinion of the superior or contradicted advice given by other officials, with higher rank than the subordinate, the latter would be at odds with the vertical orientation of society and exaggerated system of deference.[55]

But Thomas fails to notice that it is not only the stress on deference to superiors but also the characteristic pattern of bureaucratic power which undergirds the inability to use staff services as well as the equivocal distribution of power and other management problems, as seen in the Thai government. Perhaps the most fundamental consequence of this pattern is that there is no way for extrabureaucratic organs of political action to carry out the functions which Gabriel Almond has so well described—the functions of interest articulation and aggregation, of political socialization and communication, and of rule-making.[56] When these functions are carried out predominantly within a state bureaucracy, then the same persons both make and implement policy. When this happens, we can assume that they will tend to take it easy, to adapt both the formulation and execution of policy to their own expedient interests. It will be difficult, under such circumstances, to determine just what public policy is.

If there are explicit rules to be applied, and if sanctions can be imposed from outside the bureaucracy to assure their enforcement, then top management will welcome staff advisory services which help them to improve their level of performance. But in the absence of such clear guidelines and of any sanctions to reward or punish the administrators, there are few standards by which a staff man can tell what kind of advice to offer, and few rewards for the high officials to induce them to listen to unwelcome words from their underlings.

The equivocal distribution of power is similarly based on this lack of externally imposed policy guidelines. For a subordinate officer to make a clear-cut determination on a controversial issue, he needs to rest his decision on a sound basis in law or policy. He needs to know that there are influential groups—or a dominant party—who backed the law and who will uphold his efforts to enforce it. Without such sharply defined criteria for judgment, the low-level official merely has his own preferences to pit against those of his superiors. If he is confident that they will sustain them, he can go ahead and make a decision, but not if he has reason to think that his decision might be overruled. Hence, if in doubt, he passes the question up the line.

Alternatively, if he thinks he can keep the matter from being known, he can also go ahead and make a decision on his own. But then he has an incentive to prevent his superiors from finding out about his actions, thereby reinforcing the resistance to upward communication about which Siffin has written. We find, in other words, that the lack of externally sanctioned laws and policy guidelines undergirds the centralization of authority and the decentralization of control in a bureaucratic polity. The evidence from the Thai case confirms the impression that these characteristics prevailed there.

It seems unnecessary to explore further the extensive list of characteristics of the Thai bureaucracy and administrative system which have been variously noted by foreign advisers and scholars analyzing the working practices of Siamese government. In many cases, these patterns have been viewed as the result of ignorance, and technical assistance programs have been suggested in the expectation that an infusion of "know-how" and expertise might lead to a correction of administrative defects. Others, influenced by historical or anthropological perspectives, have stressed the impact of tradition and cultural conditioning, as they have sought to explain the prevalence of such patterns as extreme centralization of authority or deference to superiors.

The view advanced here is that, although there may be some validity to these interpretations, a more fundamental explanation is likely to be found if we examine the socio-political structure of Thai society and the way in which power, wealth, and prestige are distributed. In particular, it is suggested that the model of a bureaucratic polity can be used with considerable explanatory power in providing a new understanding of the characteristics of the Thai government and its distinctive patterns of modernization.

CHAPTER XI

Conclusion:
The Theory of Modernization

In writing this book, I have sought to understand and interpret the processes of change in Thai politics and public administration. I have become convinced that what we see in Thailand today is no longer the Siamese traditional society or polity. Inexorably, and in common with the rest of Asia and Africa, Thailand has responded to the impulses of modernization that have appeared everywhere as a consequence of the industrial revolution and the spread of Western military and political power.

But the characteristics of this change process have been infinitely complex. They have manifested themselves in different countries in quite diverse patterns. To speak of modernization is, then, not to speak of one dimension of change or a single type of transformation. Rather, it is to associate a variety of responses to a common challenge. That challenge has been the example, the threat, the fascination, the pervasive influence of the modern world. The reactions to that challenge have been kaleidoscopic in their constantly changing and multifarious manifestations.

So diverse have been these responses that some scholars have abandoned any attempt to discover the common elements in them. Each response, it has been claimed, is totally unique. It is as impossible to compare and classify the varied patterns of modernization as to compare an orange with an ostrich, or an abacus with a zebra. In this mood, the history and peculiarities of each country as it has responded to the Western impact can and have been described with infinite care and patience.

But the task of a social scientist is to theorize, to discover uniformities in social behavior and to state testable propositions about relationships between variables. In this context, a case study of one country may be useful for two quite different reasons. It may suggest hypotheses which can be tested by inductive methods through the analysis of comparable data about other countries. It may also be used, if one starts with previous generalizations, as a basis for testing propositions already stated. Both procedures require one to identify some key variables and imagine how they are related to each other.

This book attempts to straddle both approaches. To some extent, I have been content merely to describe, with illustrative detail, some highlights of the continuously shifting contours and undulating surfaces cast up by the recent history of a fascinating and friendly country. But this narrative will scarcely be counted worth the effort unless it can be used also to illumine some perplexing theoretical problems which, in recent years, have attracted the attention of students of political and administrative development.

Directing our attention now toward this theoretical concern, can we identify some of the dimensions of change that have interpenetrated the processes of transition in Thai history, and suggest ways in which they have been related to each other? If we can, then this exercise may have a broader interest than its merely descriptive account of conditions and events in one country. It will capture as in a cameo the figure of Thai modernization against the ground of a world transformation.

What, then, are some of the variables which may be subsumed under the general heading of "modernization," and how are they plausibly related to each other? In answering, I must use words which are often bandied about and given vague connotations that defy definition or operationalization. Yet in such an analysis, we scarcely have any option but to use such words: development, progress, change, modernization, Westernization, industrialization, differentiation, transformation, democratization, integration. If the meanings I propose to assign to them depart from common usage, I can ask only that the reader try to grasp the concept, the meaning, for which the word is used only as a convenient label. The alternative is to invent neologisms, to assign letters of the alphabet or to borrow terms from optics or biology, a course which is likewise strewn with danger. But let disputation over terminology not distract our attention from the crucial substantive issues involved.

MODERNIZATION: CULTURAL AND SOCIAL CHANGE

In speaking of "modernization" I refer broadly to all the processes of change which result from the impact of more upon less advanced societies. The objection will be raised that the word "advanced" carries a value loading, that it cannot be used for an empirically identifiable referent. Agreed. But it is precisely the subjective evaluation by one subject or society of another as "advanced" that creates the phenomenon of modernization. As long as the Chinese looked with disdain upon the crude customs of the Western barbarians who infested their shores, there was no phenomenon of modernization; but when the Chinese began to emulate the science and technology of the Europeans and found them superior to their own, then a process of modernization began.

In this sense, when Hellenic culture spread to the barbarians; when the Japanese launched the Taika reforms of the eighth century, following the model of T'ang China; when the Thai states first began to emulate the achievements of the great Khmer empire—then processes of modernization took place.

Modernization, then, may refer not to a particular kind of change, like "industrialization," Westernization, or Hellenization, but to a phenomenon of historical relativity, to the processes which result whenever a society or state launches—willingly or unwillingly—a chain of transformations designed to reduce the cultural, religious, military, or technological gap between itself and some other society or state which it admires as more powerful, advanced, or prestigious.

The processes of modernization may be classified into two large categories: cultural and social. Cultural changes occur whenever some patterns of learned belief and practice diffuse as a consequence of the modernizing process. Social changes involve transformations in the structures and dynamic characteristics of a system. In a sense this is a distinction between the cultural form and the social content of modernization, its institutional patterns and substantive functions.

Cultural changes may be classified in several ways. One important mode of classification is in terms of the place of origin of the diffused characteristics. In this sense, Sinicization meant the spread of Chinese cultural traits to surrounding areas such as Korea, Japan, and Vietnam. Today Westernization means, in the same way, the spread of cultural practices from western Europe to other parts of the world. Certainly the modernization of Thailand involved a large element of Westernization. The importation by returned Thai students and foreign advisers of innumerable specific Western practices constituted a process of Westernization. Whenever we look at the constitutional charters, legal codes, administrative regulations, or educational institutions of the country, we immediately recognize familiar patterns and techniques that came from the West.

Westernization, Neotraditionalism, and Industrialization.   However, in varying degrees, these imported Western institutions and practices operate differently from the way they did in their original home countries. We have seen, for example, how the Thai assembly, though patterned after a European model, did not become the central political instrumentality of the Thai polity. We have discovered that administrative agencies formally identified as "staff units"—such as civil service and budgeting committees—did not perform the same functions in Thailand that they fulfilled in the countries emulated.

In so far as this diffusion of Western institutional structures was accompanied by changes in their functions, the exclusive study of Westernization becomes misleading and uninteresting. The changing functions of the Thai polity arouse greater interest than the remade structures —although the diffusion of Western cultural practices is not, of course, without some intrinsic interest. As far as this book is concerned, however, our main concern has been to identify some of the changes in Siamese social and political structures. Why has not Westernization brought to the emulating country the same results that the original practices had in their countries of origin?

One reason is, perhaps, that cultural diffusion has never been complete or unchallenged. Diffusion is always selective. Only some Western cultural traits have been imported, and they have not affected all parts of the population equally. Thus, Bangkok was much more Westernized than remote villages and tribal areas. The upper strata of society became more Westernized than the lower strata.

But there was also at work a contrary type of diffusion conveniently referred to as "neotraditionalism." Neotraditionalization must be seen as part of the process of modernization. Whereas much of the population may remain traditional in its orientations, neotraditionalism involves a conscious effort to rescue from history a set of doctrines and practices, long since lost sight of, with which to launch a counterattack against the intrusive alien values and practices. In the Siamese case we have seen how King Mongkut sought to revitalize and restore earlier and more vigorous forms of Buddhist practice and belief and to remake the throne in terms of purified Buddhist ideas, rather than Hindu accretions. In doing so Mongkut was a neotraditionalist.

It is usually the case, however, that modernizers are eclectic, that they try in some way to harmonize alien values and practices with their own history. Mongkut and Chulalongkorn both worked as eclectic modernizers, seeking to unite Western with neotraditional cultural materials. Of the two, Mongkut was no doubt more neotraditional than Westernizing, whereas Chualongkorn was certainly more of a Westernizer than a neotraditionalist.

There are other ways to classify cultural diffusion. One of the most important is in terms of technological change. The spread of new scientific ideas and the use of nonhuman power harnessed to increasingly productive methods and materials have produced the industrial revolution. This process of diffusion may be called industrialization.

The key goal of modernization in many countries is precisely industrialization, because it is thought that this transformation will make possible much-cherished gains in productivity, military power, and prestige. In respect to industrialization, however, we have seen that Thailand has not gone as far as many other countries, including neighbors such as the Philippines, Malaya, Formosa, and Korea, to say nothing of Japan, India, or China.

This is not to say that there has been no industrialization in Thailand. The processing of rice for export did, indeed, require one of the earliest and most important forms of Thai industrialization, namely, the establishment of power-driven rice mills. Nevertheless, in large part, the economic modernization of Thailand was carried out by expanding the area under rice cultivation with traditional methods, thereby making possible a rise in exports and in import of manufactured and consumer goods. If we add the other new industries (largely extractive and operated by aliens) of teak, tin, and rubber, we can account for most of the economic changes which accompanied Thailand's modernization. These changes entailed a minimum of industrialization.[1]

The cultural change processes inherent in the modernization of Thailand, then, involved a substantial overlay of Westernization, an important element of neotraditionalism, and a limited amount of industrialization. All of these patterns of cultural change have left their mark on the structure of the Thai polity. The successive constitutional charters, for example, have received their deepest impression from Western models, borrowed either directly from Europe or indirectly by way of Russia and China. The changing monarchic institution showed a great impact from neotraditionalism. To a marked degree, the administration of public services has been influenced by technological changes and the effects of industrial innovations. The introduction of telecommunications and modern means of transportation, for example, have had far-reaching effects on the structure of the bureaucracy.

Dimensions of Development.   Despite these important influences, the most interesting transformations which have accompanied modernization in Thailand and have had the most fundamental impact on its politico-administrative processes have been those which reflect social, rather than cultural, changes. It is convenient to lump them together and to deal with them under the broad heading of "development."

In referring to development, however, it must be stressed that we are not talking about a single dimension of change or variation, but rather about several. I shall distinguish four such dimensions, although closer analysis would enable us to identify more.

These four dimensions of developmental variation will be referred to as "diffraction," "power distribution," "growth," and "integration." Each of these types of change is sometimes identified with "development." It seems more exact and probably just as reasonable to use the word "development" to refer to all these kinds of change.

The only disadvantage of this usage is that we must then probably abandon the comparative forms of the word: less and more developed. A society which is highly developed in terms of one of these dimensions of variation may deserve a low rating in terms of another. To illustrate in another field, we might say that "development" in the human individual involves age, size, intelligence, and health. How should we then compare, as more or less developed, a stupid small old man in good health with a middle-aged large intelligent but sick man? We might equate development with one of the variables—age or size, for example—or say that we cannot compare degrees of development, but only degrees of the four variables subsumed under this heading.

In this sense, the study of development can be considered a form of multivariant analysis. If this convention is adopted, such designations as "undeveloped," "underdeveloped," and "highly developed" become logically impossible, even though grammatically permissible. However, one might speak of different patterns of development, suggesting various combinations of the component dimensions of change lumped together under this term. Direct comparisons of different systems would have to be made in terms of the constituent variables, such as more or less diffracted, more or less integrated.

Despite this logical position, we do need a convenient way of referring to the countries of Asia, Africa, and Latin America, which have been the object of so much attention in recent years through technical assistance and foreign aid programs. Such a widely used phrase as the "underdeveloped countries" and the various euphemisms substituted for it—developing countries, lesser developed countries, low-income countries, transitional societies, emerging nations, new states, to name the most usual ones—can scarcely be ignored. Although there are logical absurdities in all these phrases, and none is acceptable to everyone, the economy of having some such term is apparent. I propose to use the phrases "developing countries" and "transitional societies" as synonyms for this group of countries, using quotation marks to show that the precise meaning of the adjectives is not intended.

So much by way of introductory comment. Let us now examine, in turn, each of the four developmental variables and ask how one might rank Thailand, what relation the variables have to each other, and what light this might throw on the future.

"DIFFRACTION" AND THE "PRISMATIC" CONDITION

Such terms as "increasing specialization," "division of labor," and "social differentiation" have been widely discussed in the literature of economics and sociology. Their relation to economic development and social change has, accordingly, become generally recognized. It is their application to the analysis of political and administrative change that remains more problematical.

Looking at the structure of the Thai polity, for example, we can discover a wide range of specialized organs of administration which parallel, although admittedly on a smaller scale, the similar range of differentiated structures of government in America and Europe. Indeed, when we start examining the more sophisticated of the classical civilizations, we discover that there was also a great deal of specialization in the governments of imperial China and Rome, or, in a different way, in the immensely complex caste system of India. It seems clear that to relate the economic and sociological concepts of increasing specialization or social differentiation to the analysis of political change is not a simple matter.

Moreover, it is tempting to mix other dimensions of change with this variable. For example, one may assume that increasing specialization is regularly associated with greater efficiency or with rising outputs, with economic growth. Let me illustrate by reference to a supple and sophisticated treatment of development offered by Binder. He starts by identifying economic development with increased efficiency and increased complexity in the processes of production. He defines increased efficiency as "increased output for the same quantity of input." Complexity is described as "the division of labor, economic interdependence, a money economy, lengthier and costlier production processes requiring long-range planning, coördination, and market predictions."[2]

Binder then asserts that political development is similar to economic development in that it also involves rising efficiency and complexity. Efficiency is treated as the ability of a political system to legitimize social power. Complexity is characterized as follows:

> In a developed system, politically functional activity requires greater planning, better organization, larger resources, and certain technical skills. This complexity is best evidenced in the operation and scope of institutional groups. The bureaucracy, especially, increases in size, in specialization and the division of tasks, and in the professionalization of its personnel. The military and other security forces also increase their ability to use violence, so that the potential for control over other structures of power relationships by these two institutional groups increases greatly.[3]

We need, I believe, to enrich our vocabulary in order to deal more simply with the range of phenomena encountered here. The word "development" has taken on such a variety of important meanings that it is scarcely feasible to narrow its denotation to one of them. If efficiency and complexity are, indeed, two dimensions of variation, then we cannot limit the use of the word "development" to one of them.

Perhaps analysis can be clarified by introducing a technical term borrowed from optics, namely, "diffraction." In earlier writings I have used this word to refer to an increase in the functional specificity of the institutional structures of a social system.[4]

Let us now use the word "diffraction" to suggest a relationship between degrees of variation in differentiation (which I shall use in place of Binder's "complexity") and levels of performance (which may be substituted for "efficiency"). In Fig. 22 a co-ordinate field is presented in which the two axes may be taken to represent these primary dimensions of variation.

Consider, first, the question of direction of change. If, starting from any point in the field (x), a system were to increase in degree of differentiation but not to experience any change in level of performance, as symbolized by the line (c), one would have a pure case of increasing

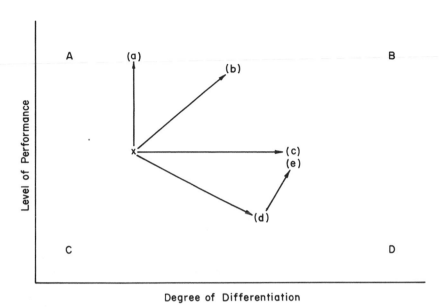

FIGURE 22.   Patterns of Developmental Change

differentiation. By contrast, vertical movement upward, as represented by line (a), would be interpreted as an improvement in performance without change in degree of differentiation. Neither of these types of change is regarded as very probable. More typically, both dimensions of variation occur simultaneously in any concrete social system, but not necessarily in direct covariance. In other words, although performance might rise with differentiation, as in line (b), it might also decline, as represented by line (d).

Let us then define "diffraction" to refer only to a type of change which combines increasing performance and differentiation, type (b). If differentiation increases but performance declines, as symbolized by (d), we would have what I call "negative development,"[5] or an increase in "prismatic" traits.

This terminological framework enables us to distinguish between a system of considerable differentiation but low performance, as at D in Fig. 22, and a system marked by a high level of differentiation and performance, as at B. I would call such a system (b) highly diffracted, but the system (d), quite prismatic.

It is also useful to distinguish between a particular location on the field represented in Fig. 22, and a direction of movement. For example, the line (e) represents a type of change in which both levels of performance and differentiation are rising, and hence the system is "diffracting," although the position near (d) is rather prismatic. In other words, we can refer to a direction of movement by a verb, in contrast to a location, as expressed by a noun or adjective. Thus, to "be diffracted" would refer to a location near B, whereas "to diffract" would be to move in that direction, as at (b) or (e). To "be prismatic," similarly, would refer to a location near D. There is no standard verb for movement in a prismatic direction. We could invent one, like "to prismaticize," but this sounds atrocious, and I prefer a more euphonious construction like to "em-prism."

What is it about a political system that enables it to attain higher levels of both differentiation and performance, i.e., to diffract? Clearly the more differentiated a system becomes, the more difficult and delicate becomes the task of co-ordinating the highly specialized roles. One of the major functions of government for a differentiated system becomes precisely the task of assuring the reciprocal adjustment of highly interdependent structures. This task can be accomplished only in part by the voluntary co-operation of the interacting units, because it seems unavoidable that, at certain points, their interests would diverge. Hence, there must be someone—some institutions or roles—standing outside the interdependent units to define the "rules of the game" and assure their observance.

At one level, of course, the state bureaucracy performs this role in relation to voluntary citizen groups and organizations—as in the policing of a market system or the enforcement of traffic regulations. But at another level, the various parts of a modern bureaucracy are themselves highly interdependent, specialized units. A society cannot make certain that these units will mesh harmoniously and efficiently unless it has some means to police the bureaucracy. It is precisely in this sense that the importance of extrabureaucratic political institutions rises in direct ratio with the increase in functional differentiaton.

In so far as a society may be successful in establishing such control organs, it becomes more diffracted. It can take advantage of the increased productivity and flexibility made possible by specialization because it has the necessary institutional framework for assuring the reciprocal co-ordination of the differentiated units.

Put another way, a diffracted polity is a constitutional regime in the sense that the holders of authority operate under effective restraints. These restraints not only provide the necessary sanctions to induce the officials of government to mesh their interdependent activities in a reasonably coherent fashion, but also prevent powerful persons from using their power arbitrarily to threaten, intimidate, or abuse those who wish to focus their energies on a specialized type of activity, provided they abide by the known rules established in advance for the regulation of this type of activity. Such constitutional restraints upon the key authority figures in a government would scarcely be possible without the rise of powerful institutions outside the formal government and the official state bureaucracy. A diffracted polity, therefore, is capable of being not only complex but also efficient, because it has institutionalized constitutional restraints on the exercise of power by the elite.

In the process of modernization, in the effort to transform a society, to industrialize, it can happen that more rapid progress will be made in creating specialized units than in building the institutional nexus necessary for their co-ordination. It becomes apparent, from this point of view, that the preponderant impact of technical assistance programs has been upon the proliferation of specialized units. When the United States invested money and time in training and building a Siamese governmental unit qualified to carry on successful experiments in the breeding of rice seeds, a new group of specialists was created, and a new department budded off from its parent department. But equivalent effort was not invested in the building of co-ordinative institutions capable of integrating the newly created centers of specialized capability and concern.

It may be argued that staff services, such as budgeting, auditing, and personnel offices, or, even more important, the office of the prime minister, serve these co-ordinative functions, and that technical assistance has been provided in helping to create or strengthen these entities. To some degree this is true, but the expenditure of funds and effort has been relatively minor in contrast to the amount spent to build the specialized units.

Moreover, if the general argument of this book is valid, the prime minister's office itself is not really capable of generating the co-ordinative impulses which are required, because it is not backed by a major center of power outside the bureaucracy. If, indeed, the prime minister heads a power structure in which the bureaucracy is the primary constituency, then how can the prime minister also generate the power position he needs to impose sanctions on bureaucrats which will be effective enough to assure their reciprocal co-ordination of effort even though they do not want to co-operate?

In short, Thailand provides almost a classical case of a situation in which the external pressures which have induced modernization—including a substantial movement of Westernization—have quite unconsciously produced an imbalanced pattern of development, one in which the rate of differentiation of structures within the bureaucracy has proceeded more rapidly than the compensatory growth of co-ordinating institutions outside the bureaucracy which could assure a high level of performance by these new, functionally specialized units.

The result, clearly, has been to produce, through modernization, a system which is no longer traditional (or fused), but which has become quite highly prismatic, not diffracted. The general conclusion reached is that, in the process of modernization, the Thai society has built a bureaucratic polity which approximates many features of the prismatic model. It has not created a modern polity resembling the diffracted model.

DEMOCRATIZATION AND THE DISTRIBUTION OF POWER

A second type of social change which has often been equated with "political development" involves a different dimension of variation, namely, the extent to which power is widely or narrowly distributed in a social system. For many scholars, the most significant pattern of change in the processes of modernization is the sequence of events which leads from traditional authoritarian regimes to a democratic form of government.

Writers on the modernization of Thailand have often been more concerned with the prospects for the emergence of democratic government in the kingdom than they have with its economic growth or the emergence of social differentiation. For example, they have noted that under the absolute monarchy the Siamese kingdom was an authoritarian regime. With the revolution of 1932 and the adoption of a constitutional charter based on the Western parliamentary model, they perceived a sudden and progressive transformation whereby the new Thai limited monarchy emerged, like a butterfly from its chrysalis, as a beautifully shimmering democracy.

How disappointed they were when, in succeeding years, coup followed coup, army officers rose to power, and parliaments were dissolved when they clashed with the ruling oligarchy. A tendency then arose to visualize Thai politics as a kind of tug-of-war between heroic and villainous forces. Pridi was cast as the captain of the "good" team, and Phibun emerged as an "evil genius," whose collaboration with Japan during the war and whose military following proved his alliance with the powers of darkness. Subsequently, when Pridi fled to Communist China and Phibun aligned himself as an ally of the anticommunist West, this estimate of his government had to be seriously revised. When Phibun finally was overthrown by Sarit's Military Group, the whole tug-of-war mythology broke down, and the Thai government was variously explained as a dictatorship to be compared with Hitler's Germany, or a democracy bravely defending the free world in Southeast Asia.

The interpretation offered in this book regards this view as largely irrelevant to the pattern of modernization in Siam. For a long time the Siamese polity has had a pattern of power distribution intermediate in character between the concentrated and dispersed extremes. The absolute monarchy, as I sought to show in Chapter II, was not so highly centralized as a traditional bureaucratic empire, nor so localized as a fully feudalistic system. The major transformation of the polity was not the revolution of 1932 but the bureaucratic reorganization of 1892, which increased the centralization of the regime by functionalizing the bureaucracy. The events of 1932 completed the process of secularization by substituting a bureaucratic ruling circle for the throne as center of the emergent bureaucratic polity. The reforms which were subsequently promulgated to create institutions of popular control over the bureaucracy proved unsuccessful as successive legislative assemblies and abortive political parties rose and fell.

A bureaucratic polity, it should be noted, cannot impose a tight system of centralized control, as can a single-party dictatorship. Such a control system requires that the state officials themselves be subjected to iron discipline so that they can be relied upon to carry out the unpleasant and arduous tasks imposed upon them by the ruling party. A bureaucratic polity, run in the interests of the state officials, is so self-indulgent that such discipline is impossible.

However, a bureaucratic polity is not as dispersed in its power structure as a modern democracy, for it does not permit the rise of a large number of autonomous centers of power—interest groups and political parties—outside the state apparatus itself. The Thai political system, then, may be classified as intermediate on a scale measuring power distributions between democratic and totalitarian extremes.

Seen from this perspective, the struggles of rival bureaucratic cliques to gain control of the cabinet appear not so much like a tug-of-war between the powers of light and darkness, or rivalry between the forces of militarism and civic virtue, or the "right" and the "left," as like the duels by which successive kings or chiefs in some traditional polities contended with and succeeded one another. It would be as futile to impute ideological significance to the dreary Wars of the Roses between the houses of Lancaster and York in fifteenth-century England, or the long-lasting struggle between Guelph and Ghibelline in pre-Renaissance Florence, as to spend time probing the inner meaning of successive Thai regimes.

Apart from the intrinsic interest which one may have in studying the pattern of modernization in Thailand as it affects the outlook for democratization, one may also be concerned about the pattern of power distribution as it affects the processes of economic growth. One school of thought holds that industrialization takes place most readily through the operation of a free enterprise system and under the constraints set by market institutions. A free market, however, seems to be possible only in association with a democratic polity. At least, the communist form of authoritarianism has reduced the market to a marginal role, stressing the planned organization of economic growth.

However, the example of the Soviet Union also shows that industrialization is possible in a society subject to highly concentrated control by a single-party dictatorship. Many leaders in the developing countries, impressed by the Russian example, have concluded that they can achieve their economic goals more rapidly and surely by emulating the communist pattern rather than the model set by the democratic Western countries.

One response to this point is to argue that political development and economic development are quite different ideas and goals. If, as has just been suggested, there is an element of incompatability between the two, then one or the other must be given priority. Defenders of human and social values may argue that it is better to be free and poor than rich and a slave. Others, taking a more materialistic point of view, answer that there can be no freedom for a man who is starving. An inconclusive debate rages.

From the point of view adopted in this book, the controversy is largely irrelevant. If, as has been argued above, the Thai polity is intermediate in power distribution between the democratic and totalitarian extremes, then is such a political system likely to be conducive to economic growth? It seems clear from the example of both the Soviet Union and the Western democracies that industrialization can, in fact, take place under both concentrated and dispersed patterns of power distribution, although we might also argue that if power is excessively concentrated (as the Soviet Union perhaps became during the late Stalin period) or excessively dispersed (as the United States perhaps became by the late nineteen-twenties, when the world depression took place), then successful industrialization might indeed be gravely hampered. However, with an intermediate level of power distribution, as in Thailand, we can consider this fact neither an impediment nor an asset for industrialization and economic growth.

It is not, in other words, the power distribution as such which constitutes the basic obstacle to further diffraction and, hence, to the emergence of an efficiently differentiated—i.e., diffracted—society. The difficulty lies in the pattern of power allocation, the lack of effective centers of institutionalized power outside the state bureaucracy, rather than in the extent to which a relatively small or large number of individuals share substantially in the exercise of power.

This, of course, is not to dismiss the question of democratization as a proper and important subject of analysis. It is merely to say that changes in the distribution of power, as one dimension of development, may have little to do with changes in the level of differentiation of function and efficiency of performance. The latter type of change has much to do with economic growth, whereas the former may have little relevance to the prospects of a country for industrialization.

GROWTH AND THE LEVEL OF OUTPUTS

There is another scale of variation on which contemporary polities have come increasingly to be measured. This, of course, is the scale of "development" most favored by the economists who appear to have almost monopolized the term for the concept of "economic growth." Such a scale has been used to place an economy within a series of stages ranging from traditional subsistence through "underdeveloped" to highly "developed." More recent schema, such as Rostow's, provide a series of stages in which the crucial point for developmental purposes is that of the "take-off," when economic growth becomes self-sustaining. On such a scale one might judge that Thailand has begun to fulfill the "preconditions" but has not yet entered the "take-off" stage.[6]

When economists look at a political system, they tend to judge it in terms of its relation to the economy. Thus, the political system of a society having a traditional subsistence economy might be judged an "undeveloped" system; the polity of a society whose economy was entering the take-off stage might be regarded as "developing"; and the government of an industrialized nation, by the same token, would be regarded as necessarily "developed."

Why this should be so becomes apparent if we consider the political and administrative requisites of economic growth. The government may be thought of as a kind of gigantic corporation. Just as a business firm produces outputs in the form of marketable goods and services, so a government also supplies a range of public services or "outputs." However, the government differs from a business firm in that its "inputs" are not primarily in the form of cash payments made by consumers for direct benefits received, but taxes collected on some other basis, such as relative ability to pay. However, the government, like the firm, is a productive organization whose inputs must be sufficient to provide the required level of outputs.

As economic growth and industrialization take place, the required level of governmental outputs—the "infrastructure"—increases. As the economy expands, the tax base also rises, but perhaps not as rapidly as the need for public services. Consequently, from an economic point of view, one might stress the need for government in an expanding economy not only to raise the level of its outputs, but also to lower the ratio of inputs to outputs—to increase efficiency—so that the increase in inputs need not be as large as the growth of outputs.

From an economic point of view, then, political and administrative development are basically similar to, or instrumental for, economic development. In both cases we are referring to rising levels of output and to increased efficiency in the utilization of inputs. A further refinement may be added. As output levels rise, a point is reached at which additional increments of output are not consumed but are invested so as to produce more outputs. This is what happens at the "take-off" stage, when economic growth becomes "self-sustaining."

The relevance of these ideas to the concept of political development is explicitly stated by the sociologist Eisenstadt, who writes as follows:

. . . political development will be used in a specific way. It will be used, if with less precision, as the economist uses "self-sustained" growth to mean a continuous process of growth which is produced by forces within the system and which is absorbed by the system.

Within the political sphere, the equivalent of such self-sustained growth is the ability to absorb varieties and changing types of political demands and organization. It also includes the skill to deal with new and changing types of problems which the system produces or which it must absorb from outside sources.[7]

It should be clear that this concept of political "development" as a rise in the output level of a political system is a different dimension of change from the two dimensions which have been previously considered: levels of diffraction and of democratization. It is certainly apparent in economic analysis that a country blessed with rich natural resources might produce a much higher per capita gross national product than another country with equally efficient productive organization but much less natural endowment per capita. Thus, the level of performance or efficiency of an economy is certainly different from the output level, and both are different from the degree of specialization or social differentiation. The famous Hawthorne studies have shown that, beyond a critical threshold, increasing specialization can cause a decline in productivity.

The same relationships hold in the analysis of political and administrative behavior. To demonstrate the point, let us consider as an example the extreme case where an entrenched elite blocks political progress, however defined. The only way to proceed is to overthrow this elite by revolutionary means. During and for some time after the revolution, the ability of the government to perform its political functions is seriously disrupted by dissentience, the inexperience of the new rulers, and general disorganization of the bureaucratic machinery. A change process which results in a more differentiated and possibly, in due course, a more diffracted polity has, in the interim, suffered an acute decline in outputs.

The point to be made is that, although in the long run, it may be assumed that increasing differentiation varies directly with a rise in governmental outputs and levels of performance, in the short run a decline in outputs may be a necessary condition for further differentiation. If this be the case, policy-makers might have to make a hard choice between policies favoring increased differentiation at the cost of a short-run decline in outputs, and a course of action designed to increase outputs, even though this might seriously delay any increase in differentiation.

The argument for this paradoxical relationship between a rise in differentiation and increasing outputs can be related to information contained in Chapter X, above. We saw there that an official who might be highly qualified technically, who was personally motivated to work hard and to be productive, could become discouraged from such work by the counter-productive pressures exercised on him in the framework of a bureaucratic polity. He comes to realize that the use of his time to cultivate influence and build a political support base within his agency is, in terms of this system, the key requisite for success, if not for mere survival.

Under such circumstances, even output-oriented policies ought to take into account the need for changing the political alignment of forces within the polity as a prerequisite for raising both economic and administrative performance levels. They should recognize also that because of the delicacy and, indeed, the traumatic character of such changes in a political system, the immediate effects of a system change may well be a drop in performance and output levels. By contrast, direct efforts to raise program outputs, where the performance, in each case, is to be that of government officials, heightens the power position of bureaucrats by increasing their numbers and specialization, and hence increases the complexity and difficulty of the task of imposing co-ordination. Thereby the obstacles to successful creation of extrabureaucratic institutions capable of bringing the gigantic "administrative" apparatus under control are intensified.

If "development" is viewed, rather simplistically, as merely a matter of raising output levels, this dilemma will not be appreciated. In essence, this appears to have been the basic frame of reference of the International Bank's mission to Thailand. The direct relation of governmental services to economic growth is an apparent premise of the observations made in that report. The nine men who composed the team were, for the most part, economists, and the governing criteria of the Bank itself were clearly economic. The title of the report might well have been "An Economic Development Program for Thailand," rather than "A Public Development Program." From this point of view, it is clear that the same kinds of criteria were applied in judging the government's administrative organization and performance as might have been applied by a consulting firm called upon to help overhaul a business corporation that was experiencing difficulties in selling its products.

The weakness in this approach, I believe, is not only that it fails to understand the political requisites for raising governmental outputs, so that many of the recommendations for administrative reform are irrelevant in terms of their stated objectives. Perhaps more important, the proposals to raise the outputs of functionally specialized governmental services would increase the prismatic tendencies in the government, because effective political institutions for co-ordination and goal attainment are not available. In other words, while heightening levels of differentiation, the levels of performance might actually decline if these proposals were adopted.

However, if the proposals to raise outputs—governmental and economic—were successful, forces might be generated that would have other problematical effects on the level of diffraction. The argument for this point rests on the significance of the level of "integration" of a political system, introducing a fourth dimension of development which must now be examined.

INTEGRATION LEVELS AND PRESSURES FOR CHANGE

It is apparent that some countries are more receptive to change than others, and the rate of change in one country can vary strikingly between different periods. Clearly, the Japanese response to the impact of the West after the mid-nineteenth century was far more receptive to the challenges and opportunities of industrialization than was the Thai response. Yet the Siamese, as we have seen, were much more effective in responding to British and French imperialism than were the Burmese. Moreover, the ability of the Japanese to make dramatic changes in the late nineteenth century contrasts strikingly with their determination to resist change prior to their confrontation with Perry's small fleet.

We are familiar with the phenomenon of a critical point in other fields. Water, for example, remains a liquid until the temperature rises above a given point, when the fluid suddenly begins to change into a gas. The analogy suggests that we might look for some characteristic of social systems whose changes might help explain varying propensities to engage in structural change.

Such a variable is important for our purposes, also, because one of the aims of development in many societies may be to increase the level of integration.

The word "integration" unfortunately has a variety of overlapping meanings. It has been used above in a somewhat different sense to refer to social assimilation and to the effective co-ordination of the differentiated parts of a system. The emphasis, if not the meaning, intended here is somewhat different. Perhaps an analogy in another field might clarify the idea. Consider the meaning in biology of the concept of "health" or "well-being." It is apparent that health represents a different dimension of variation than age or size. Adults as well as children may become sick. Big men are no more likely to be healthy than small men. Is there any social counterpart of health? Can we imagine that a highly developed social system might be "sick," and that an undeveloped system might be in good "health"? These words, of course, suggest organismic analogies which may be misleading. Consequently, I shall use the concept of "level of integration" to designate the extent to which the actual performance levels of a given social system are adequate to maintain the system at its established level of differentiation. A very low level of integration will be called "disintegration," a moderately low level, "malintegration."

It seems clear that if a system is well integrated, its performance, by definition, is adequate to maintain the system at the prevalent level of differentiation. Consequently, we can assume that a well-integrated system will resist change. It will be in a state of equilibrium. However, a malintegrated system might precipitate forces of dissatisfaction and a restless search for alternatives which could lead to system change. If this reasoning makes sense, then a necessary condition for the propensity to seek fundamental changes—such as an increase in the level of differentiation of a society—might be a degree of malintegration.

One evidence for the extent of malintegration in a society could be the degree to which its members feel dissatisfaction with the prevalent state of affairs. Such dissatisfaction might manifest itself in movements of protest, reform, or even revolution, and in outbreaks of violence. The prevalence of violence in a society, by this reasoning, would not be a measure of underdevelopment, but rather a possible indicator of the extent of malintegration. One should, of course, recognize that other variables would also affect the incidence of violence, such as the existence of external threats or a culturally conditioned predisposition to resort to or avoid displays of violence.

The existence of malintegration should probably be regarded as only a necessary, but not a sufficient, condition for increasing diffraction. Moreover, if the level of integration fell too low, a society might become so disorganized and demoralized that it could not take the necessary steps to bring about its own further development.

Looking at some concrete examples, we might consider that the French system, although highly developed in terms of social differentiation, has been subject to malintegration for the last century and a half. This has rendered the polity particularly unstable and subject to frequent realignments of its constitutional structure. By contrast, the Thai system, while much less differentiated than the French, has been more highly integrated. It has apparently become a relatively stable bureaucratic polity. The low level of tensions within the system give evidence of substantial integration. The successive coups d'état by which ruling circles are modified and replaced have become as much a constitutional formula for changing elites as the periodic electoral battles which take place in the United States, or the cabinet crises of France during the Third and Fourth Republics. The succession of constitutional charters in the Thai polity have, correspondingly, scarcely more systemic significance than a change of party in England—perhaps less. The effective constitutional structure, which is unwritten, appears to have taken shape as a relatively stable pattern.

It may be that a high level of integration of the traditional Siamese polity enabled its rulers to adapt to the pressures of aggressive European empires more successfully than the Burmese. In other words, their level of diplomatic performance was relatively high for a traditional polity with a low level of social differentiation, because of the high level of integration which prevailed. By contrast, Burmese society was suffering from so much malintegration that it could not respond effectively. The result was an outbreak of warfare which cost the Burmese their independence, leading to major structural changes—under the direct control of British rulers.

The diplomatic success of the Siamese also enabled them to maintain their traditional way of life. Put another way, the vast majority of Siamese have felt little disruption because of the pressure of European economic and military imperialism. The absolute monarchs and the small ruling oligarchy, of course, felt sufficiently threatened to take the lead in launching a process of controlled and moderate system-change which resulted in the emergence of a bureaucratic polity and the low-tension form of modernization described in this book. Paradoxically, the very achievement of integration by the Siamese which enabled them to respond quite successfully to the Western impact—if my formulation is correct—also impeded any dramatic transformation of the society and polity. In so far as the tension level in contemporary Thailand remains low and the level of integration high, we may expect the present bureaucratic polity to continue with only marginal changes in the years ahead.

There are, however, reasons for thinking that the tension level will rise and that, consequently, the Thai polity will become more dynamic in the future than it has been in the past—perhaps a generation or even a decade from now.

THE FUTURE: PRESSURES FOR MALINTEGRATION

Perhaps a useful point at which to initiate a few speculations about some likely sources of increasing tension in the Thai polity is the discrepancy between the rising output of university graduates compared with the less rapidly growing increase in acceptable job opportunities. Siffin has commented persuasively on this point in the following statement:

. . . at this time the total number of students in Thai universities, exclusive of the medical school and police and military academies, is about equal to the total number of third grade positions in the entire civil service, which was about 16,500 in 1957. The majority of these students appear to prefer civil service employment, although the current annual rate at which vacancies occur in the third grade (the customary civil service entry grade for college graduates) is estimated at about four per cent. Under these conditions it does not take any elaborate analysis or highly refined data to show that the shoe is already pinching. Furthermore, enrollment trends in the institutions are generally upward, the trend curve of matriculations is in some cases even more sharply upward, and there seems every likelihood that the higher education system is going to expand at a greater rate than the absorptive capacity of the civil service.[8]

The prospects of an increasing flow of university graduates confronts the government and the polity with some awkward problems. Roughly speaking, there are three streams into which these graduates can flow. Each stream will generate serious problems.

The government may expand considerably and take in many more graduates than it now absorbs. However, there is already evidence of very substantial overstaffing in the bureaucracy, and such an expansion would be malintegrative for the public services. The flow of revenues is unlikely to grow rapidly enough to maintain the present level of per capita income. A general decline in the real income of public officials would contribute to demoralization and increasing corruption.

A second stream flows into private occupations, notably into industry and trade and, to some extent, the professions. However, these have been traditionally low-status occupations—except for the professions, which tend to be combined with government employment—and fundamental changes in attitudes will be necessary to attract a large number of graduates to private roles. As in many other "developing countries," these occupations have been largely in the hands of low-status minorities, notably Chinese in the Thai case. Most of the Chinese firms are small family enterprises, and the opportunities for the employment of Siamese university graduates in these establishments, even if both parties were willing to co-operate, are quite limited. The chances are that opportunities for Siamese in private business and industry will largely be found in non-Chinese firms, often headed by ex-officials who, for one reason or another, found it expedient to leave the public service after having accumulated substantial fortunes.

If such a trend begins to gather force, it could result in the emergence of a growing and substantial Siamese business and industrial community. Almost certainly it would operate at a higher unit cost level than its Chinese competitors and could survive only by securing preferential advantages over the Chinese through direct governmental intervention and discriminatory policies. Tendencies in this direction have already manifested themselves, and they might well grow rapidly.

Tensions within the over-all business community would rise without necessarily giving birth to a coherent "middle class" capable of organizing itself politically so as to exercise significant controlling influences in or over the government, except in highly particularistic ways.

Just as the expansion of the stream of graduates into public employment creates threatening problems, so a substantial build-up of private commerce and industry confronts the government with a real dilemma. The case is nicely stated by the International Bank's mission in these words:

Some Thai leaders have a very real fear that an indiscriminate policy of encouraging industry might lead to dangerous predominance of the Chinese community in this field. The problem is a difficult one. It is clearly desirable to encourage greater participation in industry on the part of Thais. At the same time, any attempt to do so by excluding Chinese from the benefit of

Government help is unlikely to produce the economic results which Government industrial policy should aim to achieve. Thailand has been very successful in the past in the assimilation of Chinese into the Thai community, and the most hopeful solution of the problem would appear to lie in encouraging the acceleration of this process.[9]

One could scarcely be less than enthusiastic for a policy of assimilating the Chinese, for if a real Sino-Thai business community could emerge, it might well lay the basis for an effective transformation of the polity in the direction both of a more diffracted and a democratic system. However, this belief and cautious statement by the Bank's mission appears incredibly optimistic.[10]

A more likely prospect appears to be the encouragement of industrial development under the control of Siamese officials and entrepreneurs, using a select group of co-opted Chinese as managers and agents. This group, caught in an ambivalent role between the Siamese and Chinese communities, might well vacillate between efforts to guide and promote Chinese assimilation and efforts to contain the alien Chinese community.

In so far as such policies involve direct or indirect subsidies from public funds to uneconomic (because inefficiently managed) enterprises, the cost to the Siamese taxpayers will mount. The Bank's report notes that "all of the state industries, except the monopolies, have proved unprofitable by commercial standards."[11] Without fundamental change in the structure of the polity, it is difficult to see how administrative or legal manipulations can change this situation fundamentally. In other words, a flow of university graduates into commercial and industrial enterprise in mounting numbers is likely to heighten the intercommunal tensions in Thai society and politics.

The third stream for college graduates is, of course, into unemployment and low-paying jobs, whether in government or elsewhere, giving rise to the phenomenon of the disaffected intelligentsia. Experience in other developing countries suggests that these elements, as their numbers and the acuteness of their dissatisfaction rise, become the leaders of revolutionary and radical movements against the government in power, whether it be indigenous or alien in personnel. If the mass base of discontented urban workers and/or rural peasants should rise, such protest organizations can become exceedingly disruptive. With external financial help and guidance, communist-led movements can be readily formed in such a matrix. The exposure of Thailand to infiltration by communist agents from neighboring countries and the recent history of Vietnam, Laos, and Cambodia make this prospect a serious cause for alarm.

Wilson has explained quite persuasively why Marxism so far has had little appeal in Thailand. Among the arguments he offers is the following:

A social fact of supreme importance in the history of modern Thailand is the absence of a frustrated, unemployed educated class. The traditional occupation of the educated is government. . . . At the same time, control over the education system, the primary upward pathway and recruiting agency for new members of the elite, has permitted the maintenance of an approximate balance between qualified applicants for positions of responsibility and jobs.[12]

Yet, as Siffin has pointed out, the rise in university enrollments means that this happy situation will not persist into the foreseeable future. Wilson himself concedes that a "tiny group of 'pure intellectuals' among the educated people in Thailand" has emerged. Many are journalists and writers, a few are "leisured and aristocratic full-time intellectuals." Some are journalists who failed to obtain their university degrees. As a group they have become a "rather querulous and irresponsible critic of the government." They constitute, Wilson adds, "a potential flaw in the structure of the educated class."[13]

What is today a small and "querulous" group of intellectuals could, in the future, become a large and revolutionary intelligentsia. To prevent the formation of such a group, the government must either retrench in the provision of educational opportunities for its people—a course of action also fraught with dangerous consequences—or expand opportunities for employment along the lines which we have already reviewed, each of which again opens up dangerous consequences.

POPULATION GROWTH, URBANIZATION, AND ECONOMIC PRESSURES

In selecting problems likely to be generated by the increasing output of university graduates, I have merely pointed to one of several possibly explosive potentialities in the Thai situation. The growing university population is only one manifestation of a general increase in the population of the country which has mushroomed in a century from something like 5 million in 1850 to 25 million in 1962. Current projections anticipate a population level between 34 and 37 million by 1977.[14]

These figures, although dramatic, do not portend a pattern of population density in the near future even approximating that of neighboring countries such as China and India. Population density in rural areas is less than 95 persons per square mile, and the land under cultivation is not more than 20 per cent of the total area of the country. Yet, some implications of future population growth are suggested by Siffin when he writes that, if the present ratio of agricultural to urban population were to continue and the present organization of agricultural production in small farm holdings were to be maintained, then "between 1957 and 1977 about 5,675,000 additional persons in the economically productive age groups would enter agriculture. . . . They would require from 16 million to 20 million additional acres of farmland—in comparison with a total of about 24 million acres now being cultivated. . . ."[15]

Unfortunately, there is little arable land which can be added to the area now in irrigated rice cultivation. Two important consequences follow: the volume of rice production cannot continue to keep pace with population growth; and new crops must be grown in greater measure. But the expansion of new crops will necessitate important changes in the way of life of the farm population. Already in the central plains some of the potential consequences of crop rotation made possible by the provision of water during the dry season have become evident.

Early results of the experimental work of the Irrigation Department, to which reference was made in Chapter X, demonstrated the feasibility of growing sugar cane in rotation with rice. On the basis of this demonstration, plans were made for the launching of a sugar industry, and a modern factory has been built under the management of the National Economic Development Company (NEDCOL). A succinct statement about this firm in the International Bank's report suggests the difficulties which have arisen:

To prevent bankruptcy, the Government has had to take over the whole concern. NEDCOL's affairs have now been analyzed by foreign industrial consultants, and it is apparent that the Government has on its hands a group of expensive factories, the cost of which will have to be met from public funds without prospects for an adequate return on the total investment.[16]

Difficulties in the area arose shortly after plans for the sugar industry were made. Farmers were induced, somewhat reluctantly, to start planting sugar cane against promises of payment by a sugar mill yet to be built. When the first crops ripened, the mill was not yet ready for operation, and the farmers concerned lost their investment of time, effort, land, and funds. After the mill opened, the terms of payment and other arrangements made with the company left more farmers dissatis-fied. From the mill's side, the quantity and quality of the cane avail-able proved inadequate, and technical problems in the mill were not fully solved, so that the sugar produced did not reach the quality stand-ards expected. Many farmers then refused to plant sugar cane again, and the mill faced the necessity of acquiring land and cultivating its own cane on a plantation basis. A labor supply had to be imported into the area.

In other words, the introduction of a new technology and crop brought with it a host of problems, many of which promised to become sources of acute tension. Yet the spread of double cropping, as the irri-gation potentialities of the great Yanhee dam begin to materialize, prom-ises to raise many similar problems as various programs are launched to find means of increasing food and related industrial production.

The implications of the decline in rice production per capita also justify concern. The situation has been succinctly described by Siffin:

Average per capita consumption of milled rice, plus wastage and other unaccounted-for diversions, now amounts to about one and one-half pounds per day. In three recent years an estimated average population of 21 mil-lion persons apparently accounted for an average of 5 million tons of rice per year. On this basis, consumption in 1972 would be about 8 million tons, and by 1977 it would approach 10 million tons. In recent years, Thai rice production has averaged around 7 million tons with a rather small upward production trend (about two per cent annually), and normal exports have ranged around an average of about 1 million tons, earning about half Thai-land's foreign exchange. These figures are only approximations, but if the trends they reflect were to run their future courses, within the coming twenty years Thailand would cease to have a rice export surplus *and might soon thereafter be faced with domestic shortages.* [Italics added.] [17]

The dangerous implications of this prospect become apparent when we stop to think of the extreme degree to which the Thai economy has been dependent on rice, notably, the export of rice as a major source of government revenues and the foreign exchange earned thereby as the major resource to pay for imported manufacturing and consumer's goods.[18]

The pressure of a declining rice surplus available for export will in-tensify pressure within the country for new forms of agricultural pro-duction based on dry farming and, at the same time, for the develop-ment of new types of manufacturing and processing industries. Such changes will prove highly disturbing to the established social order and hence will set in motion forces of malintegration which could decisively affect the political structure of the country.

Although it has been estimated that more than 90 per cent of the Thai population is rural, the rate of urbanization is as striking as in other developing countries. Between 1947 and 1958, according to a recent study, the population of Bangkok grew at an annual rate of 7.1 per cent, more than twice the rate of population growth for the country as a whole. In 1955, the urban population in the Bangkok metropolitan area was over one million. Between 1955 and 1965 it was estimated that this population would double. Siffin observes that, "in such rapid growth dismaying social, economic, political, and administrative problems are likely to be inherent." [19]

The creation of a national network of primary schools and highways, reaching into the villages, serves to accelerate the migration of rural folk to the cities, and especially to Bangkok. In 1936, Thailand's highways were "negligible in quantity and poor in quality," but by 1957, a national road network of 7,450 kilometers had been opened, augmented by municipal and subsidiary provincial roads. In education, there are now enough primary schools so that 90 per cent of the children in the compulsory age group are able to attend. According to law, children from eight to fifteen must go to school until they finish the four years of primary education.[20]

Although the beneficial effects of rural schooling are stressed in the development plans of the Ministry of Education and the recommendations of foreign advisers, it is also true that school graduates often acquire aspiration levels which cannot be readily satisfied in a village setting. They bring home new ideas which clash with the traditional views of their parents and neighbors. New sources of tension are often thereby introduced into rural life, heightening whatever traditional sources of dissatisfaction were already present in the rural society. The spread of the road system and inexpensive public bus and railroad transportation make it possible for the more energetic young people to migrate to the city.

A likely consequence of this pattern of change is to make the metropolitan area an increasingly restive focus of discontent as the immigrants find that they cannot fulfill their aspirations in this new setting. Meanwhile, the rural areas are drained of some of the most enterprising members of the younger generation.

The full political implications of all these possible sources of rising discontent have yet to be realized. It is not my intention to suggest here that the consequences will necessarily be disastrous. Indeed, if the level of malintegration rises only moderately, forces of structural political transformation may well be set in motion which could launch Thailand on a future course of modernization that might reshape its bureaucratic polity into a modern-type political system whereby the state apparatus would be brought under the control of extrabureaucratic political institutions. If such a course of events were to be anticipated, it should be taken into account in the forward planning of Thai policy-makers and their foreign advisers.

A BUREAUCRATIC POLITY: FRUIT OF MODERNIZATION IN THAILAND

Meanwhile, before these tension-producing problems become acute, it seems likely that the Thai political system will continue without major change as a relatively well-integrated and hence stable bureaucratic polity, a prismatic society in equilibrium, at a low level of industrialization and economic growth and an intermediate level of power distribution between the democratic and authoritarian extremes. As such, it is no longer a traditional polity or society. The road traversed during the last one hundred years has wrought far-reaching and irreversible changes in the process of modernization. The impact of the Western world has produced substantial Westernization in the formal structures of government and administration, and the introduction of the products of industrial technology has brought far-reaching changes in public administration and daily life. An influence of neotraditionalism has also been important in creating a distinctive, Buddhistic cultural environment as a setting for these transformations.

In closing, it may be useful to recapitulate the main propositions presented in earlier chapters, on the basis on which the conclusion has been reached that a bureaucratic polity has replaced the traditional, as a result of the processes of modernization in Thailand. In Chapters IV and V we saw how the traditional, cosmologically oriented courts of the Siamese monarchy were transformed into a functionally specialized and secular bureaucracy. We saw in Chapter VI and VII how the efforts to impose accountability on the bureaucracy by the creation of new political institutions—primarily legislative in character—proved largely ineffective.

In Part Three, we examined the behavioral characteristics of the polity which emerged from this historical process of modernization.

Considering the cabinet as the focal political arena of this system, we saw how its ruling circle was self-recruited, in large measure, from among the upper bureaucracy, both civilian and military. We examined the process of intrabureaucratic struggle as it manifested itself in the formation of cliques and factions within the ruling circle, and we traced, historically, the succession of these circles from 1932 to 1958.

In the expectation that it would shed some light on the dynamism and motivation of this system, we examined, in Chapter IX, some of the rewards of office obtained by the higher officials, especially those who gained cabinet rank. In doing so, we learned something about the mechanisms by which these rewards—especially the financial gains—became available. Finally, we postulated that a government having a secularized and functionally specialized bureaucracy, staffed by career officers but not subject to control by extrabureaucratic political institutions, would have the characteristics of a "bureaucratic polity." Such a polity was defined in terms of the domination of the official class as a ruling class, even though formal constitutional charters and ceremonial doctrines of government might give lip service to modern ideas of popular sovereignty or traditional concepts of royal and divine sovereignty. A set of norms was then specified and postulated as a reasonable operational code for a bureaucratic polity; and, somewhat at random, evidence of bureaucratic organization and behavior in Thailand was presented which seemed to fit these norms.

Despite this accumulation of evidence, we should not regard the Thai political system as a perfect example of a bureaucratic polity. It may well be that there are other societies in which we might find patterns of behavior that approximated more closely the constructed type of a bureaucratic polity. Certainly there is evidence of public servants in Thailand who take their obligations to serve the public, and the king, very seriously.

It is doubtful, I think, that we shall ever find in real life an actual political system which conforms exactly to the logic of an abstracted model. Nevertheless, the model and the series of cultural and social variables postulated as concomitants of modernization have helped us, I believe, to obtain a better understanding of the Thai polity and, at the same time, to clarify some concepts and propositions which may prove useful in the study of other political systems and, perhaps, in the formulation of public policies.

APPENDIXES, NOTES, AND INDEX

APPENDIX A

THAI CABINET MEMBERS

Code No.	Name*	Cabinet No.	Coup Group Promoters†	No. of Board Memberships
1. Manoprakorn, Nitithada, Phya มโนปกรณนิติธาดา, พระยา		1,2,3		
2. Preechachola Yuth, Rear Adm., Phya ปรีชาชลยุทธ, พระยา		1,2,3,4		
3. Phahon Phonpha Yuha Sena., Gen., Phya พหลพลพยุหเสนา, พระยา		1,2,3,4,5,6,7,8,11	32S	
4. Ritthi Akaney, Col., Phya ฤทธิอัคเณย, พระยา		1,2,3,6,8	32S	
5. Prasard Phidthayuth, Lt. Col., Phra ประศาสน์พิทยายุทธ, พระ		1,2,3	32S	
6. Sinthu Songkhramchai, Adm., Luang สินธุสงครามชัย, หลวง		1,2,3,4,5,6,7,8,9, 10,11	32Jn	(1)

Key

1 = cabinet number (see App. C)	32Jn = naval faction (junior clique)
1 = prime minister	32S = senior clique
(1) = no. of board memberships	44FT = Free Thai clique
32, 47, 57 = years of coups	47K = Kad clique
32J = junior clique	47Phib = Phibun clique
32Ja = army faction (junior clique)	47PP = Phin-Phao clique
32Jc = civilian faction (junior clique)	47S = Sarit clique

Bold-face type indicates members of coup groups

* and † See note p. 419

Code No.	Name*	Cabinet No.	Coup Group Promoters†	No. of Board Memberships
7. Det Sahakorn, Luang เดชสหกรณ, หลวง		1,2,9	32Jc	
8. Prayoon Phamon Montri, Lt. Gen. ประยูร ภมรมนตรี		1,2,3,9,10,24, 25,26	32Jc	(5)
9. Sriwisarnwaja, Phya ศรีวิสารวาจา, พระยา		1,2,3,14,20,21		(1)
10. Songsuradet, Col., Phya ทรงสุรเดช, พระยา		1,2,3	32S	
11. Pramuan Wichaphul, Phya ประมวญวิชาพูล, พระยา		1,2		
12. Phibun Songkhram, Field Marshal, Luang พิบูลสงคราม, หลวง		1,2,3,4,5,6,7,8,9, 10,22,23,24,25, 26,27	32Ja, 47Phib	(1)
13. Pradit Manutham, Luang (Nai Pridi) ประดิษฐมนูธรรม, หลวง (นายปรีดี พนมยงค์)		1,2,4,5,6,7,8,9, 15,16,17	32Jc, 44FT	(1)
14. Tua Laphanukorm, Nai ตั้ว ลพานุกรม, นาย		1,2,9	32Jc	
15. Naeb Phahonyothin, Nai แนบ พหลโยธิน, นาย		1,2,	32Jc	
16. Thammasak-Montri, Chao Phya ธรรมศักดิ์มนตรี, เจ้าพระยา		2,3,4		
17. Thebwithun Pahunsarutra- baudee, Phya เทพวิทุรพหลศรุตาบดี, พระยา		2,3		

Code No.	Name*	Cabinet No.	Coup Group Promoters†	No. of Board Memberships
18.	Radwangsan, Vice-Adm., Phya ราชวังสัน, พระยา	2,3		
19.	Wongsanupraphat, Chao Phya วงษานุประพัทธ์, เจ้าพระยา	2,3		
20.	Jasaenyabaudee, Phya จาแสนยบดีศรีบริบาล, พระยา	2,3		
21.	**Suphachalasai, Capt. R.N., Luang** ศุภชลาศัย, หลวง	3,4,5,6,7,8,10, 11,12,14,20,21	32Jn	
22.	Udomphong Phensawad, Phya อุคมพงศ์เพ็ญสวัสดิ์, พระยา	3,4		
23.	Manavaraj Sevee, Phya มานวราชเสวี, พระยา	3,5,6		(1)
24.	Phichai Songkhram, Maj. Gen., Phya พิชัยสงคราม, พระยา	3		
25.	Srisithi Songkhram, Col., Phya ศรีสิทธิสงคราม, พระยา	3		
26.	Prasert Songkhram, Maj. Gen., Phya ประเสริฐสงคราม, พระยา	4,5		
27.	Komarnkun Montri, Phya โกมารกุลมนตรี, พระยา	4,5		
28.	Suriyanuwatt, Phya สุริยานุวัตร, พระยา	4,5,6		
29.	Sidthiryang Detphon, Col., Phra สิทธิเรืองเคชพล, พระ	4,5,6		

Code No.	Name*	Cabinet No.	Coup Group Promoters†	No. of Board Memberships
30. **Narubet Manit, Luang** นฤเบศร์มานิต, หลวง		4,5,6,8,9	32Jc	
31. Sreethammathibet, Chao Phya ศรีธรรมาธิเบศ, เจ้าพระยา		4,5,8,9,11,14		(1)
32. Nitisard Phaisarn, Phya นิติศาสตร์ไพศาลย์, พระยา		4,5,6		
33. Sirirajamaitri, Luang สิริราชไมตรี, หลวง		4		
34. Wichit Cholathi, Capt. R.N., Phya วิชิตชลธี, พระยา		4,20,21		
35. **Thamrong Navasawat, Rear Adm., Luang** ธำรงนาวาสวัสดิ์, หลวง		4,5,6,7,8,9,10, 17,*18,19*	32Jn	
36. Aphaiban Radchamaithree, Phya อภิบาลราชไมตรี, พระยา		4,5		
37. Sarasarth Phraphan, Phra สารสาสน์ประพันธ์, พระ		5,6,7,8		
38. Woraphong Piphad, Chao Phya วรพงศ์พิพัฒน์, เจ้าพระยา		5,6		
39. Dunlayatharn Preechawai, Phra ดุลยธารณปรีชาไวท์, พระ		5,6		
40. Samantarat Burinthorn, Phya สมันตรัฐบุรินทร์, พระยา		5,6,7		
41. Sarasart Polakharn, Phra สารสาสน์พลขันธ์, พระ		5		

Code No.	Name*	Cabinet No.	Coup Group Promoters†	No. of Board Memberships
42.	Samaharn Hitakhadi, Khun (Nai Po)	6,7,9,10,11		
	สมาหารหิตะคดี, ขุน (นายโป)			
43.	Sorayuth Seni, Rear Adm., Phya	6		
	ศรยุทธเสนี, พระยา			
44.	Sukhonthawit Sugsakarn, Khun	6,7		
	สุคนธวิทศึกษากร, ขุน			
45.	Mahaisawan Sombudsiri, Phya	6,10,22		(1)
	มไหสวรรย์สมบัติศิริ, พระยา			
46.	Srisena, Phya (Nai Srisena Sombudsiri)	6,7,11,14, 20.21		
	ศรีเสนา, พระยา (นายศรีเสนา สมบัติศิริ)			
47.	Kowit Aphaiwong, Luang (Nai Khuang)	6,8,9,10,*11*, *14,20,21*	32Jc	
	โกวิทอภัยวงศ์, หลวง (นายควง)			
48.	Chamnan Yuthasil, Col., Luang	6,7,8	32S	(6)
	ชำนาญยุทธศิลป์, หลวง			
49.	Nadniti Thada, Luang	6,7		
	นาถนิติธาดา, หลวง			
50.	Wicharn Chakrakit, Capt. R.N., Phya	6,7,8		
	วิจารณจักรกิจ, พระยา			
51.	Adundetchtarad, Pol. Gen., Luang	6,8,9,10,12,13	32Ja	
	อดุลเดชจรัส, หลวง			

Code No.	Name*	Cabinet No.	Coup Group Promoters†	No. of Board Memberships
52. Aphai Songkhram, Col., Phya	6,7,8			
อภัยสงคราม, พระยา				
53. Chaiyod Sombat, Phya	6,7,8			
ไชยยศสมบัติ, พระยา				
54. Mahithorn, Chao Phya	6,7			
มหิธร, เจ้าพระยา				
55. Boriphan Yutthikit, Gen., Phra	6,7,8,9,10,22,23, 24,25,26,27		(2)	
บริภัณฑ์ยุทธกิจ, พระ				
56. Wetchayan Rangsit, Air Marshal, Phra (Muni)	6,7,8,9,10,14,20, 21,24,25,26,27		(3)	
เวชยันต์รังสฤษฎ์, พระ (มุนี)				
57. Wichid Wadthakarn, Maj. Gen. (Hon.), Luang	7,8,9,10,24,25			
วิจิตรวาทการ, หลวง				
58. Chawengsak Songkhram, Col., Luang (Chuang)	8,9,10,15,17, 18,19	32Ja	(7)	
เชวงศักดิ์สงคราม, หลวง (นายชวง)				
59. Sajaphirom, Phya	8			
สัจจาภิรมย์, พระยา				
60. Kadsongkhram, Lt. Gen., Luang (Kad or Thein Kengradomying)	9,10	32Ja, 47K		
กาจสงคราม, หลวง (นายกาจ หรือ เธียร เก่งระดมยิง)				
61. Sarit Yuthasin, Col., Luang	9			
สฤษฎ์ยุทธศิลป์, หลวง				

Code No.	Name*	Cabinet No.	Coup Group Promoters†	No. of Board Memberships
62. Seri Roengrit, Gen., Luang เสรีเริงฤทธิ์, หลวง		9,10	32Ja	(2)
63. Chamnan Nitikased, Luang ชำนาญนิติเกษตร, หลวง		9,15		
64. Direk Chainam, Nai ดิเรก ชัยนาม, นาย		9,10,12,13,15, 17,18	32Jc, 44FT	(1)
65. Navawichit, Rear Adm., Luang (Pun) นาวาวิจิตร, หลวง (ผัน)		9,11	32Jn	
66. Phrom Yothi, Gen., Luang (Mungkorn) พรหมโยธี, หลวง (มังกร)		9,10,22,23,24, 25,26	32Ja	
67. Sangworn Yuthakit, Rear Adm., Luang (Suwanacheep) สังวรยุทธกิจ, หลวง (สังวร สุวรรณชีพ)		9,10,12	32Jn	
68. Wilas Osathanond, Nai วิลาส โอสถานนท์, นาย		9,18		
69. Kriengsak Phichit, Lt. Gen., Luang (Phichit) เกรียงศักดิ์พิชิต, หลวง (พิชิต เกรียงศักดิ์พิชิต)		9,10,14	32Ja	
70. Wanit Pananond, Nai วนิช ปานะนนท์, นาย		9,10		
71. Uthai Seangmani, Nai อุทัย แสงมณี, นาย		9,10		

Code No.	Name*	Cabinet No.	Coup Group Promoters†	No. of Board Memberships
72. Det Sanitwong, M.L. เดช สนิทวงศ์, ม.ล.		9,10,11,20,21		(1)
73. Thawi Bunyaket, Nai ทวี บุณยเกตุ, นาย		9,10,11,*12*,13, 15,17	32Jc, 44FT	
74. Boonchiem Komolmitra, Air Vice-Marshal บุญเจียม โกมลมิตร์		9,10		
75. Sawat Ronnarong, Gen., Luang สวัสดิ์ สวัสดิ์รณรงค์, หลวง		9,10	32Ja	
76. Duan Bunnag, Nai เดือน บุนนาค, นาย		10,11,12,15,17, 18,19	32Jc, 44FT	(1)
77. Udomyotha Ratanawadi, Col. อุดมโยธา รัตนาวดี		10		
78. Kri Dechatiwong, M.L. กรี เดชาติวงศ์, ม.ล.		10,15,17,18	32Jc	
79. Thewarit Phanluek, Air Marshal, Luang (Kap) เทวฤทธิ์พันลึก, หลวง (กาพย์)		10,11,12	47Phib	(1)
80. Chai Prathibprasen, Maj. Gen. ไชย ประทีปเสน		10		(3)
81. Saphrang Thebhasadin Na Ayuthaya, Nai สพรั่ง เทพหัสดิน ณ อยุธยา, นาย		11,12,13,15, 17,28	32Jc, 44FT(?)	(1)
82. Leng Srisomwong, Nai เล้ง ศรีสมวงศ์, นาย		11	32Jc	(1)

Code No.	Name*	Cabinet No.	Coup Group Promoters†	No. of Board Memberships
83.	Udom Sanitwong, M.L.	11,13,20,21		
	อุคม สนิทวงศ์, ม.ล.			
84.	Sri Thammarat, Phya (Kanchanachot)	11		
	ศรีธรรมราช, พระยา (นายศรีธรรมราช กาญจนโชติ)			
85.	Amorn Wisai Soradet, Maj. Gen., Phya (Pin)	11		
	อมรวิสัยสรเดช, พระยา			
86.	**Thaharn Khamhiran, Rear Adm.**	11	32Jn	
	ทหาร ขำหิรัญ			
87.	Chalit Kulkamthorn, Rear Adm.	11		
	ชลิต กุลกำม่ธร			
88.	Sinat Yotharak, Lt. Gen., Luang (Chit Munsilp)	11,12,13,14,20		
	สินาดโยธารักษ์, หลวง (ชิด มันศิลป์ สินาดโยธารักษ์)			
89.	**Prachuab Bunnag, Nai**	11,12,13,14,20	32Jc, 44FT	
	ประจวบ บุนนาค, นาย			
90.	Rueng Ruengveerayudth, Col.	11		
	เรือง เรืองวีระยุทธ			
91.	**Thongin Phuriphat, Nai**	11,12,13,17, 18,19	44FT	
	ทองอินทร์ ภูริพัฒน์, นาย			
92.	Chira Wichit Songkhram, Gen., Luang	11,13,15,17, 18,19		
	จิระ วิชิตสงคราม, หลวง			

Code No.	Name*	Cabinet No.	Coup Group Promoters†	No. of Board Memberships
93. Thawi Tawethikun, Nai ทวี ตะเวทิกุล, นาย		12,13	44FT(?)	
94. Attakari Niphon, Phya อรรถการีย์นิพนธ์, พระยา		12,13,20,21, 28,29,30		
95. Thawin Udol, Nai ถวิล อุคล, นาย		12,13	44FT(?)	
96. Thong Kanthatham, Nai ทอง กันทาธรรม, นาย		12,13,18,19	44FT(?)	
97. Bunnakorn Kowit, Luang บรรณกรโกวิท, หลวง		12		
98. Wuthi Suwannarak, Nai วุฒิ สุวรรณรักษ์, นาย		12		
99. Wichit Lulitanon, Nai วิจิตร ลุลิตานนท์, นาย		12,13,15,17, 18,19	44FT(?)	
100. Tironnasarn Wisawakam, Phra ตรีรณสารวิศวกรรม, พระ		12,13,14		(1)
101. Tiang Sirikhan, Nai เตียง ศิริขันธ์, นาย		12,13,18	44FT	
102. Phueng Sirichan, Nai พึ่ง ศรีจันทร์, นาย		12,13		
103. Sanguan Tularak, Nai สงวน ตุลารักษ์, นาย		12,13	32Jc, 44FT	
104. Chamlong Dao-Ryang, Nai จำลอง ดาวเรือง, นาย		12,13,18,19	44FT(?)	
105. Seni Pramot, M.R. เสนีย์ ปราโมช, ม.ร.ว.		*13*,14,20,21	44FT	

Code No.	Name*	Cabinet No.	Coup Group Promoters†	No. of Board Memberships
106.	Norarat Suwat, Phya นลราชสุวัจน์, พระยา	13		
107.	**Charoon Sueb Saeng, Nai** จรูญ สืบแสง, นาย	13,18	32Jc	
108.	Worathat Na Lampoon, Chao วรทัศน์ ณ ลำพูน, เจ้า	13		
109.	Suthi-at Narumon, Phra สุทธิอรรถนฤมนตร์, พระ	13,14		
110.	Chit Wetprasit, Nai ชิต เวชประสิทธิ์, นาย	13,19		
111.	**Norm Ketunut, Maj. Gen.** น้อม เกตุนุติ	14,20,21,22,23	32Ja, 47Phib	(1)
112.	Angkhananurak, Luang อังคณานุรักษ์, หลวง	14,20		
113.	Yai Sawitchart, Nai ใหญ่ ศวิตชาต, นาย	14,20,21		(1)
114.	Boontheng Thongsawat, Nai บุญเท่ง ทองสวัสดิ์, นาย	14,21		
115.	Atcharart Songsiri, Phya อัชราชทรงสิริ, พระยา	14		
116.	Chom Charurat, Nai ชม จารุรัตน์, นาย	14,20,21		
117.	Liang Chayakarn, Nai เลียง ไชยกาล, นาย	14,22,23,27		
118.	Suwit Phanthasset, Nai สุวิชช พันธเศรษฐ, นาย	14		(1)
119.	Forng Sithitham, Nai ฟอง สิทธิธรรม, นาย	14,21		

Code No.	Name*	Cabinet No.	Coup Group Promoters†	No. of Board Memberships
120. Sunthorn Phiphit, Phya สุนทรพิพิธ, พระยา		15,17,18,19		
121. Radab Khadi, Khun ระดับคดี, ขุน		15,17,19		
122. Thuan Wichai-Khatthaka, Col. ทวน วิชัยขัทคะ		15,17,18,19		
123. Sanguan Chutatemi, Nai สงวน จูฑะเตมีย์, นาย		15		
124. Wirote Kamonphan, Nai วิโรจน์ กมลพันธ์, นาย		15,17,18,19		
125. Surapan Seni, Col., Phya สุรพันธเสนี, พระยา (อั้น บุนนาค)		15,17	32Jn	
126. Thongpleo Cholaphum, Nai ทองเปลว ชลภูมิ์, นาย		18	32Jc, 44FT	
127. Yuean Phanitchawit, Nai เยื้อน พาณิชวิทย์, นาย		18,19		
128. Nonthiyawat Sawastiwatana, H.S.H. Prince นนทิยาวัต สวัสดิวัฒน์, ม.จ.		18,19		
129. Athakit Phanomyong, Nai อรรถกิตติ พนมยงค์, นาย		19	44FT(?)	
130. Sang Suthipongse, Nai แสง สุทธิพงศ์, นาย		19		
131. Prakit Kolasart, Phya ประกิตกลศาสตร์, พระยา		19		
132. Norat Raksa, Luang นรัตถรักษา, หลวง		19		

Code No.	Name*	Cabinet No.	Coup Group Promoters†	No. of Board Memberships
133.	Wiwatchai Chaiyan, H.S.H. Prince วิวัฒนไชย ไชยันต์, ม.จ.	20,21,22,23		
134.	Chart Nag-Rob, Gen., Luang ชาตินักรบ, หลวง	20,21,22		(1)
135.	Kukrit Pramot, M.R. คึกฤทธิ์ ปราโมช, ม.ร.ว.	20,21,22		(1)
136.	Lek Sumit, Rear Adm. เล็ก สุมิตร	20,21		
137.	Saraphaiwanit, Phya (Luan) ศราภัยวาณิช, พระยา (เลื่อน)	20		
138.	Luan Phongsophon, Nai เลื่อน พงษ์โสภน, นาย	20,21,24,25,26		(1)
139.	Sitthiporn Krisdakorn, H.S.H. Prince สิทธิพร กฤดากร, ม.จ.	20,21		
140.	So Setthabut, Nai สอ เศรษฐบุตร, นาย	20		
141.	Chawalit Aphaiwong, Nai ชวลิต อภัยวงศ์, นาย	21		
142.	That Phrommanob, Nai ถัด พรหมมานพ, นาย	21		
143.	Rangsiyakorn Apakorn, Air Marshal, H.S.H. Prince รังษียากร อาภากร, ม.จ.	21,22		
144.	Thonawanik Montri, Phya โทณวนิกมนตรี, พระยา	22		(2)

Code No.	Name°	Cabinet No.	Coup Group Promoters†	No. of Board Memberships
145.	Pote Sarasin, Nai พจน์ สารสิน, นาย	22,23,28		
146.	Sanitwong Seni, Col., Mom สนิทวงศ์เสนี, หม่อม	22		
147.	Phana-Nuchorn, Phya พจนานุจร, พระยา	22		
148.	Sri Phichai Songkhram, Col., Phya ศรีพิชัยสงคราม, พระยา	22		
149.	Polasinthawanat, Adm., Luang พลสินธวาณัติก์, หลวง	22		
150.	Pridithepphong Thewakun, Maj. Gen., H.S.H. Prince ปรีดิเทพพงษ์ เทวกุล, ม.จ.	22		
151.	Borirak Wetchakarn, Phya บริรักษ์เวชชการ, พระยา	22,23,24,25,26		
152.	Prasit Chakrkarn, Capt. R.N., Luang ประสิทธิ์จักรการ, หลวง	22		
153.	Chindarak, Phya จินดารักษ์, พระยา	22		(1)
154.	Manupharn Wimonsard, Phra มนูภาณวิมลศาสตร์, พระ	22,23		
155.	Khemchad Bunyaradtaphan, Nai เขมชาติ บุณยรัตนพันธุ์, นาย	22,23,24,25,26		
156.	Che Abdulla Langputeh, Nai เจะ อับดุลลา หลังปูเต๊ะ, นาย	22,28,29		

Code No.	Name*	Cabinet No.	Coup Group Promoters†	No. of Board Memberships
157.	Kitcha Wathanasin, Nai กิจจา วัฒนสินธุ์, นาย	22		
158.	Prathom Pokeo, Nai ปฐม โพธิแก้ว, นาย	22,23,29		
159.	Fuen Suwanasarn, Nai ฟื้น สุพรรณสาร, นาย	22,23		
160.	Worakarm Bancha, Col. (Hon.), Nai วรการบัญชา, นาย	22,23,24,25, 26,27		(2)
161.	Sukit Nimmanhemin, Nai สุกิจ นิมมานเหมินท์, นาย	22,23,24,25, 26,28,29		
162.	Sawet Piamphongsarn, Nai เสวตร เปี่ยมพงศ์สานต์, นาย	22,23,27,29		
163.	Sawat Sawattironachai Sawattikiet, Gen. สวัสดิ์ สวัสดิ์รณชัย สวัสดิ์เกียรติ	22,23,24	47Phib	
164.	Thebhasadin, Lt. Gen., Phya เทพหัสดิน, พระยา	22,23		
165.	Chuang Kaset Silpakarn, Phra ช่วงเกษตรศิลปการ, พระ	22,23		
166.	Plot Poraphak, Lt. Gen., Khun ปลดปรปักษ์, ขุน	23	32Ja	
167.	Sunawin Wiwat, Vice-Adm., Luang สุนาวินวิวัฒ, หลวง	23,24,25,26		(7)

Code No.	Name*	Cabinet No.	Coup Group Promoters†	No. of Board Memberships
168.	**Banyat Thebhasadin Na Ayuthaya, Lt. Gen.** บัญญัติ เทพหัสดิน ณ อยุธยา	23,24,25,26,27	47PP(?)	(5)
169.	Atthaporn Pisarn, Luang อรรถพรพิศาล, หลวง	23,29		
170.	Kongrithi Suksakorn, Khun คงฤทธิศึกษากร, ขุน	23,27		
171.	Prasert Sutbanthad, Capt. ประเสริฐ สุดบรรทัด	23		
172.	Theb Chotinuchit, Nai เทพ โชตินุชิต, นาย	23		
173.	Songkarn Udomsit, Pol. Maj. สงกรานต์ อุดมสิทธิ์	23		
174.	Seri Israngkun Na Ayuthaya, Nai เสรี อิศรางกูร ณ อยุธยา, นาย	23		
175.	Samer Kanthathan, Nai เสมอ กัณฑาธัญ, นาย	23		
176.	Nititharn Phiset, Phra นิติธารณ์พิเศษ, พระ	24,25,26		
177.	**Phin Chunnahawan, Field Marshal** ผิน ชุณหะวัณ	25,26,27	47PP	(9)
178.	Yuthasard Koson, Fleet Adm., Luang ยุทธศาสตร์โกศล, หลวง	25,26,27		(3)
179.	Fuen Ronnaphakard Ridthakni, Air Marshal ฟื้น รณนภากาศ ฤทธาคนี	25,26,27		(3)

Code No.	Name*	Cabinet No.	Coup Group Promoters†	No. of Board Memberships
180.	Cherd Wuthakard, Air Chief Marshal, Luang เชิดวุฒากาศ, หลวง	25,26		(1)
181.	Sarit Thanaratchata, Field Marshal สฤษดิ์ ธนะรัชต์	25,26,27,30	47S, 57	(22)
182.	Lamai Udthayananon, Pol. Maj. Gen. ลม้าย อุทยานานนท์	25,26,27	47PP	(19)
183.	Chamnan Atthayuth, Adm., Luang ชำนาญอรรถยุทธ, หลวง	25,26	57	(26)
184.	Pramarn Adireksarn, Maj. Gen. ประมาณ อดิเรกสาร	25,26,27	47PP	(11)
185.	Phao Sriyanonda, Pol. Gen. เผ่า ศรียานนท์	25,26,27	47PP	(26)
186.	Det Detpradiyuth, Gen. เดช เดชประดิยุทธ	25,26		(1)
187.	Siri Siriyothin, Maj. Gen. ศิริ สิริโยธิน	25,26,27	47PP	(13)
188.	Wan Waithayakorn, Maj. Gen. (Hon.), H.S.H. Prince วรรณไวทยากร, พระองค์เจ้า	26,27,28,29,30		
189.	Sawad Sorayutha, Gen., Luang สวัสดิ์สรยุทธ, หลวง	26,27	47PP	(7)
190.	Ladphli Thammaprakan, Phya ลัดพลีธรรมประคัลภ์, พระยา	26,27		
191.	Rak Panyarachun, Maj. รักษ์ ปันยารชุน	26,27		(2)

Code No.	Name*	Cabinet No.	Coup Group Promoters†	No. of Board Memberships
192.	Sawai Swaisaenyakorn, Gen. ไสว ไสวแสนยากร	26	47Phib	(14)
193.	Thanom Kitikhachorn, Gen. ถนอม กิตติขจร	26,27,28,29,30	47S, 57	(17)
194.	Xuchat Kuamphu, M.L. ชูชาติ กำภู, ม.ล.	26		(3)
195.	Praphas Charusathien, Gen. ประภาส จารุเสถียร	27,28,29,30	47S, 57	(19)
196.	Chalerm Phongsawad, Maj. Gen. เฉลิม พงศ์สวัสดิ์	27	47Phib	
197.	Suraphong Triratana, Nai สุรพงษ์ ตรีรัตน์, นาย	27		(2)
198.	Sawad Khamprakob, Nai สวัสดิ์ คำประกอบ, นาย	27,29		
199.	Chalermkiart Watthanang-kun, Air Marshal เฉลิมเกียรติ วัฒนางกูร	27	47S, 57	(4)
200.	Burakarm Kowit, Col. (Hon.), Luang บุรกรรมโกวิท, หลวง	27		
201.	Yots Intharakomalasud, Nai ยศ อินทรโกมาลสุต, นาย	27		
202.	Chuen Rawiwan, Nai ชื่น รวิวรรณ, นาย	27,29		
203.	Pin Malakun, M.L. ปิ่น มาลากุล, ม.ล.	28,29,30		

Code No.	Name*	Cabinet No.	Coup Group Promoters†	No. of Board Memberships
204.	Wibun Thammabut, Nai	28,29		(1)
	วิบูลย์ ธรรมบุตร, นาย			
205.	Sawatkolayuth, Gen., Luang	28		
	สวัสดิ์กลยุทธ, หลวง			
206.	Sanong Thanasak, Adm.	28,29	57	
	สนอง ธนศักดิ์			
207.	Wisut Atthayuth, Nai	28,29		(1)
	วิสูตร อรรถยุกติ, นาย			
208.	Pong Punnakan, Lt. Gen.	28,29,30	47S, 57	
	พงษ์ ปุณณกันต์			
209.	Kampanart Saenyakorn, Gen., Luang	28,29		(1)
	กัมปนาทแสนยากร, หลวง			
210.	Amphorn Chintkanom, Lt. Gen.	28,29	57	(1)
	อัมพร จินตกานนท์			
211.	Pachern Nimibut, Lt. Gen.	28,29	47S, 57	
	เผชิญ นิมิบุตร			
212.	Chalaw Charuklas, Lt. Gen.	28		
	ชลอ จารุกลัส			
213.	Sanguan Chantra Saka, Nai	28,29	57	
	สงวน จันทรสาขา, นาย			
214.	Chalerm Prommas, Nai	28,29		
	เฉลิม พรมมาศ, นาย			
215.	Bunchu Chantharubeggsa, Air Chief Marshal	28,29	47S, 57	(2)
	บุญชู จันทรุเบกษา			

Code No.	Name*	Cabinet No.	Coup Group Promoters†	No. of Board Memberships
216. Chiem Yanothai, Lt. Gen. เจียม ญาโนทัย		28,29	57	
217. Kris Punnakan, Lt. Gen. กฤช ปุณณกันต์		28,29	57	(1)
218. Charoon Chalermtiarna, Adm. จรูญ เฉลิมเตียรณ		28,29	57	
219. Thawi Raengkham, Nai ทวี แรงขำ, นาย		28,29		(1)
220. Chitti Nawisathien, Gen. จิตติ นาวีเสถียร		28,29	57	(5)
221. Serm Vinitchaikun, Nai เสริม วินิจฉัยกุล, นาย		28,29		(7)
222. Prakas Sahakorn, Phra ประกาศสหกรณ์, พระ		29,30		
223. Net Khemmayothin, Lt. Gen. เนตร เขมะโยธิน		29	57	
224. Thim Phuriphat, Nai ทิม ภูริพัฒน์, นาย		29		
225. Aree Tantiwetchakun, Nai อารีย์ ตันติเวชกุล, นาย		29		
226. Dulyapak Suwamant, Phra ดุลยพากย์สุวมันต์, พระ		29		
227. Tongthang Tongtham, M.R. ทองแท่ง ทองแถม, ม.ร.ว.		29		
228. Norm Uporamai, Nai น้อม อุปรมัย, นาย		29		

Code No.	Name*	Cabinet No.	Coup Group Promoters†	No. of Board Memberships
229.	Prasidth Karnchanawat, Nai ประสิทธิ์ กาญจนวัฒน์, นาย	29		
230.	Thanad Kormanda, Nai ถนัด คอมันตร์, นาย	30		
231.	Soonthorn Hongladarom, Nai สุนทร หงสลดารมภ์, นาย	30		
232.	Bamras Naradura, Phra บำราศนราดูร, พระ	30		
233.	Chote Kunakaserm, Nai โชติ คุณะเกษม, นาย	30		(2)
234.	Sawad Mahaphol, Nai สวัสดิ์ มหาผล, นาย	30		
235.	Boon Chareonchai, Nai บุณย์ เจริญไชย, นาย	30		
236.	Kaserm Sripayak, Nai เกษม ศรีพยัคฆ์, นาย	30		
237.	Surachit Charuserani, Gen. สุรจิตร จารุเศรณี	30	57	

*Since the official transliteration of Siamese names in English often results in forms quite far from actual pronunciation, a method of "translation" has been used which approximates the sound and sometimes follows personal usage of those concerned. Royally conferred titles such as Khun, Luang, Phra, and Phya, and royal titles such as M.L. and M.R., as well as designations of military rank, properly should precede rather than follow the name. However, for convenience in reference, these titles have been placed after the name. Long Siamese royally conferred names have been separated into parts to facilitate pronunciation. The word "Nai" simply means "Mr."

†All membership in cliques and factions is based on informal and unofficial information and is therefore subject to correction. The author would welcome information that might lead to later revisions.

APPENDIX B

CHRONOLOGY OF THAI POLITICAL HISTORY, 1932–63

Date	Cab. No.	Types	Date	Prime Minister	Overturns Realignments Readjustments	Critical Events	Legitimations
1932	1	ov	June 28	**Mano I	Revolution of June 24		Prov. Const. June 27
	2	lg	Dec. 10	Mano II			Perm. Const. Dec. 10
1933	3	rd	Apr. 3	*Mano III	Junior clique weakened	Mano ousts Pridi Apr. 1	Parl. prorog. Apr. 1
	4	rl cn	June 21	*Phahon I	Phibun's coup June 20	Resig. of Song June 10	Parl. convenes June 22
	5	lg	Dec. 16	Phahon II		Boworadet reb. Oct. 12–27	Elections Nov.–Dec.
1934						King leaves Jan. 12	
	6	lg	Sept. 22	Phahon III		Parl. debate Sept.	Phahon resigns
1935						King abd. Mar. 2	
1936							

Year	Cabinet		Date	Cabinet name			
1937	7	lg	Aug. 9	Phahon IV		Parl. debate Aug.	Phahon resigns
							Elections Nov. 7
	8	lg	Dec. 21	Phahon V			Parl. convenes Dec. 10
1938						Phahon resigns Sept. 11	Dissol. of Parl. Sept. 11
							Elections Nov. 12
	9	rd cn	Dec. 16	*Phibun I	Rise of jr. clique		Parl. convenes Dec. 10
1939						Song's "rebellion" Jan. 29	
1940							
1941		rd	Dec. 17	*(no cabinet change)	Pridi resigns Dec. 17	Japanese occupation Dec. 8	

Key
* cabinet crisis
** major cabinet crisis: overturn
ov overturn
rl realignment
rd readjustment

cn consolidation
lg legitimation
reb. rebellion
Roman numerals following a name refer to the number of that prime minister's cabinet

Date	Cab. No.	Types	Date	Prime Minister	Overturns Realignments Readjustments	Critical Events	Legitimations
1942	10	lg	Mar. 7	Phibun II			
1943							
1944	11	ov	Aug. 1	**Khuang I	Resig. of Phibun July 26	Allied victory predicted	
1945	12	rd	Aug. 31	*Thawi I	Rise of Free Thai	Allied victory Aug. 16	
	13	lg	Sept. 17	Seni I			
1946	14	rd lg	Jan. 31	*Khuang II	Return of Khuang		Elections Jan. 6
	15	rd	Mar. 24	*Pridi I	Defeat of Khuang		New Const. May 10
	16	lg	June 8	Pridi II		King's death June 9	Parl. convenes June 1
	17	lg	June 11	Pridi III			
	18	rd	Aug. 23	Thamrong I			
1947	19	lg	May 30	Thamrong II		Debate in parliament May	

Year	No.		Date	Cabinet	Coup	Rebellion	Constitution / Parliament
1948	20	ov	Nov. 10	**Khuang III	coup d'etat Nov. 8		Prov. Const. Nov. 9
							Elections Jan. 29
	21	lg	Feb. 21	Khuang IV	Khuang resigns		New Parl. Feb. 19
	22	rl cn	Apr. 8	*Phibun III		coup de main Apr. 6	
						Staff rebellion Oct. 1	
1949						Pridi's palace reb. Feb. 26	New Const. Mar. 23
	23	lg	June 24	Phibun IV			New Parl. June 15
1950							
1951						Manhattan reb. June 26	
	24	lg?	Nov. 29	Phibun V	"silent coup" Nov. 29		1932 Const. proc. Nov. 29
	25	rl	Dec. 6	*Phibun VI			Elect. Feb. 26
1952							Rev. of '32 Const. Mar. 8

Date	Cab. No.	Types	Date	Prime Minister	Overturns Realignments Readjustments	Critical Events	Legitimations
	26	lg	Mar. 24	Phibun VII		Peace reb. Oct.	New Parl. Mar. 18
1953–56							
1957							Elections Feb. 26
	27	lg	Mar. 21	Phibun VIII			New Parl. Mar. 14
	28	ov	Sept. 21	**Pote I**	**Milit. Group coup Sept. 16**		Const. susp. Sept. 16
							Elections Dec. 15
							New Parl. Dec. 26
1958	29	cn	Jan. 1	*Thanom I			
		rd	Oct. 20	(abolition of cabinet)	Revol. Group coup Oct. 20		Const. susp. Oct. 20
1959							Prov. Const. Jan. 28
	30	lg	Feb. 10	Sarit I			Const. assem. Feb. 5
1960–63							

APPENDIX C

TABLE 1

PROMOTERS IN THAI CABINETS (1932 COUP GROUP)

Cabinet	Total members	Total prom.	Senior Clique	Junior Clique Total	Army	Civil.	Navy
I. *The First Ruling Circle*							
1. Mano I 6/24/32–12/10/32	15	11	4	7	1	4	1
2. Mano II 12/10/32–4/1/33	20	11	4	7	1	5	1
3. Mano III 4/1/33–6/21/33	20	8	4	4	1	1	2
4. Phahon I 6/21/33–12/16/33	20	7	1	6	1	2	3
5. Phahon II 12/16/33–9/22/34	20	7	1	6	1	2	3
6. Phahon III 9/22/34–7/9/37	31	11	3	8	2	3	3
7. Phahon IV 7/9/37–12/21/37	20	7	2	5	1	1	3
8. Phahon V 12/21/37–12/16/38	21	12	3	9	3	3	3
9. Phibun I 12/16/38–3/6/42	32	20	0	20	8	8	4
10. Phibun II 3/7/42–8/1/44	30	17	0	17	8	5	4

TABLE 2
PROMOTERS IN THAI CABINETS (1944–1947)

Cabinet	Total members	Total prom.	Free Thai Clique	Navy Clique	Seni	Khuang
II. *The Second Ruling Circle*						
11. Khuang I	24	10	4	5	0	1
8/1/44–7/31/45						
12. Thawi	23	8	7	4	0	0
7/31/45–8/17/45						
13. Seni	25	7	6	5	1	0
8/17/45–1/31/46						
14. Khuang II	21	5	1	3	1	1
1/31/46–3/24/46						
15. Pridi I	16	6	3	4	0	0
3/24/46–6/8/46						
16. Pridi II*						
6/8/46–6/9/46						
17. Pridi III	15	7	4	4	0	0
6/11/46–8/23/46						
18. Thamrong I	19	6	5	3	0	0
8/23/46–5/30/47						
19. Thamrong II	19	2	2	0	0	0
5/30/47–9/8/47						

*Data on this very brief (two-day) interim cabinet have been omitted.

TABLE 3
PROMOTERS IN THAI CABINETS (1947 AND 1957)

Cabinet	Total members	Total prom.	Phin-Phao	Sarit	Phibun
III. *The Third Ruling Circle*					
20. Khuang III 11/10/47–2/6/48	24	1	0	0	1
21. Khuang IV 2/21/48–4/8/48	25	1	0	0	1
22. Phibun III 4/8/48–6/23/49	31	3	0	0	3
23. Phibun IV 6/24/49–11/29/51	26	4	1	0	3
24. Phibun V 11/29/51–12/6/51	15	3	1	0	2
25. Phibun VI 12/6/51–3/23/52	25	8	5	1	1
26. Phibun VII 3/24/52–2/26/57	31	11	6	2	2
27. Phibun VIII 3/21/57–9/16/57	29	13	6	4	2
IV. *The Fourth Ruling Circle*					
28. Pote I (Phoch) 9/21/57–12/26/57	26	5			
29. Thanom I 1/1/58–10/20/58	37	5			
30. Sarit I	15	4			

NOTES

INTRODUCTION

1. Howard Wriggins, "Foreign Assistance and Political Development," in *Development of the Emerging Countries: An Agenda for Research* (Washington, D.C.: Brookings Institution, 1962), p. 185.
2. The field work was made possible by a grant from the Comparative Politics Committee of the Social Science Research Council. Needless to say, however, I am personally responsible for the views offered in this study. The Committee and Council should therefore be held blameless for what follows.
3. See my "Agraria and Industria: Toward a Typology of Comparative Administration," in *Toward the Comparative Study of Public Administration,* William J. Siffin, ed. (Bloomington: Indiana University Press, 1957), pp. 23–116.
4. A series of articles giving preliminary shape to these ideas were published in Philippine and Thai journals. In *The Ecology of Public Administration* (Bombay: Asia Publishing House, 1961), based on lectures given at the Indian Institute of Public Administration on my way home from the Philippines, I put these ideas together in a somewhat more comprehensive fashion. More recently I have attempted to pull together the content of scattered essays in a systematic exposition of the prismatic model, entitled *Administration in Developing Countries: The Theory of Prismatic Society* (Boston: Houghton-Mifflin, 1964).
5. John Loftus, "Report of the Economic Adviser," August to December, 1956 (mimeo.), p. 5.
6. Lucian W. Pye, *Politics, Personality, and Nation Building: Burma's Search for Identity* (New Haven: Yale University Press, 1962); and Leonard Binder, *Iran: Political Development in a Changing Society* (Berkeley and Los Angeles: University of California Press, 1962).
7. David A. Wilson, *Politics in Thailand* (Ithaca: Cornell University Press, 1962); and William J. Siffin, *The Thai Bureaucracy: Institutional Change and Development* (Honolulu: East-West Center Press, *in press*).

CHAPTER I

1. In this connection, see Robert Heine-Geldern, "Conceptions of State and Kingship in Southeast Asia" (Cornell University, Southeast Asia Program, Data paper no. 18, 1956).

2. The complicated dynastic histories of these countries are described in W. A. R. Wood, *A History of Siam* (Bangkok, 1924?); John F. Cady, *A History of Modern Burma* (Ithaca: Cornell University Press, 1958); and D. G. E. Hall, *A History of South-East Asia* (New York: St. Martins, 1956).

3. Hall, *op. cit.*, p. 579, and David A. Wilson in *Politics in Thailand* (Ithaca: Cornell University Press, 1962), p. 4, quoted from Sir John Bowring, *The Kingdom and People of Siam* (London: Parker & Son, 1857), II, 227.

4. Cady, *op. cit.*, p. 10.

5. Walter F. Vella, *The Impact of the West on Government in Thailand* (Berkeley and Los Angeles: University of California Press, 1955), p. 325. The royal stipends, Vella writes, were "regarded not as a salary but as an indication of royal favor." Describing the traditional revenue system, Wales writes: "The tax-farmers employed their own staff of collectors who, although they were nominally under the supervision of government officers, usually managed to exact more than the just portion of tax due. In the same way the official tax-gatherers, though they were not under the same necessity of handing over a certain agreed sum to the treasury, were equally interested in making a profit for themselves. The higher officials of the various *glans* (*kroms*), in the absence of anything in the nature of a budget system, had even greater opportunities of enriching themselves. . . . In short, every conceivable species of corruption was in vogue amongst the army of officials who handled the king's revenues at one stage or another, with a result that only a comparatively small proportion of the amount collected became available for legitimate government expenditure." H. G. Quaritch Wales, *Ancient Siamese Government and Administration* (London: Bernard Quaritch, 1934), p. 224.

6. Hall, *op. cit.*, p. 581: "In the days of the great chartered companies of the seventeenth and eighteenth centuries rulers in South-East Asia had preferred that each community of foreign merchants—and this included the Chinese as well—should be under the control of a chief, with whom the ruler could deal directly in all matters concerning them."

7. The sequence of judicial reforms is summarized by Vella, *op. cit.*, pp. 347–48.

8. Hall, *op. cit.*, pp. 538–39. See also Maung Maung, *Burma in the Family of Nations* (Djambatan and Amsterdam, 1958), p. 46.

9. Cady, *op. cit.*, p. 101.

10. Mongkut was serving in a monastery when his father died, and his brother became king in 1824. He decided to remain in the Order, where

he rose to high rank, until his own enthronement in 1851. Abbot L. Moffat, *Mongkut: The King of Siam* (Ithaca: Cornell University Press, 1961), pp. 9–22; and A. B. Griswold, *King Mongkut of Siam* (New York: Asia Society, 1961), p. 12.

11. Cady, *op. cit.*, pp. 88–89.
12. *Ibid.*, p. 103.
13. Hall writes (*op. cit.*, p. 444) that "Siam at the beginning of the nine-teenth century had so far recovered from the Burmese invasions that she was reviving her ancient claims to dominion over the whole penin-sula."
14. *Ibid.*, p. 446.
15. Maung Maung, *op. cit.*, p. 34.
16. Hall, *op. cit.*, pp. 519–20.
17. *Ibid.*, p. 396.
18. Maung Maung, *op. cit.*, p. 158. Text from Georg F. Martens, *Nouveau Recueil de Traites*, VI, pt. 2 (Göttingen: Dieterich, 1828), 894–98.
19. Hall, *op. cit.*, p. 399.
20. *Ibid.*, p. 448.
21. *Ibid.*, pp. 525–26.
22. *Ibid.*, pp. 527–29; Cady, *op. cit.*, pp. 86–89.
23. Hall, *op. cit.*, p. 401.
24. Moffat, *op. cit.*, p. 43.
25. Quoted *ibid.*, p. 44.
26. *Ibid.*
27. In 1883, Phayre published a *History of Burma* (London). Henry Yule, *A Narrative of the Mission Sent by the Governor-General of India to the Court of Ava in 1855* (London, 1858) contains an account of this mis-sion. See Hall, *op. cit.*, pp. 531–32.
28. *Ibid.*, pp. 538–41.
29. Mongkut set up a Royal Mint in 1860 to issue flat silver coins in place of the bullet-shaped ticals and cowrie shells previously in use: Moffat, *op. cit.*, pp. 25–26. Mindon introduced coined money in 1861: Cady, *op. cit.*, p. 102. See also Hall, p. 583.
30. J. S. Furnivall, *Colonial Policy and Practice* (New York: New York University Press, 1956), pp. 64–65.
31. Cady, *op. cit.*, p. 102.
32. *Ibid.* See also Ma Mya Sein, *Burma* (London: Oxford University Press, 1944), pp. 10–12, 27.
33. Cady, *op. cit.*, p. 115. The ranks accorded to the highest officials in the Burmese and Siamese systems of government had symbolic and cosmo-logical significance, as will be explained in more detail in chap. II. Cor-responding to the Burmese *Atwinwuns, Wungyis,* and *Wundauks,* we may place the Siamese *Akkhramaha Senabodi, Senabodi,* and *Montri.*
34. *Ibid.*, pp. 115–16.
35. Moffat, *op. cit.*, p. 105.

36. *Ibid.,* pp. 105–12.
37. Hall, *op. cit.,* p. 452.
38. *Ibid.,* pp. 562–63.
39. Moffat, *op. cit.,* pp. 119, 122.
40. *Ibid.,* pp. 123–24.
41. *Ibid.,* p. 124.
42. Hall, *op. cit.,* p. 604.
43. *Ibid.,* p. 607.
44. *Ibid.,* p. 608.
45. *Ibid.,* p. 609.
46. Cady, *op. cit.,* pp. 88–89.
47. Curiously, this role could be compared with that of the American vice-president in the Senate.
48. *Ibid.,* pp. 102–3.
49. *Ibid.,* p. 111.
50. Quoted by Moffat, *op. cit.,* p. 173.
51. *Ibid.,* p. 176.
52. *Ibid.*
53. *Ibid.,* p. 177.
54. *The Journal of the Siam Society,* XXXVIII, pt. 2 (1951), 92. Quoted in Wilson, *op. cit.* (above, n. 3), p. 6.
55. Hall, *op. cit.,* p. 502.
56. Cady, *op. cit.,* p. 23.
57. Hall, *op. cit.,* p. 525. See also Cady, *op. cit.,* p. 80.
58. Taksin imagined that he was developing into a Buddha. He "commanded the priests to pay him divine honors. Some, through fear, assented, but many refused. These, to the number of over five hundred, were cruelly flogged, and the head priests among them were degraded and imprisoned. . . . The King began to suspect everybody of carrying on illicit trade. As he accepted the sworn statement of a single person as conclusive evidence of this, a detestable band of informers soon grew up, who waxed rich on fines extorted from their victims. The latter were not only plundered, but often flogged to death. Burning people alive became a common event. One of the King's own wives was consigned to the flames on a [false] charge of stealing money from the treasury. On every side were heard the lamentations of innocent victims, groaning under the insensate tyranny of a madman." Wood, *op. cit.* (above, n. 2), pp. 269–70.
59. *Ibid.,* p. 272.
60. *Ibid.,* p. 277. See also Hall, *op. cit.,* p. 399.
61. Dates from *ibid.,* p. 733.
62. Cady, *op. cit.,* p. 22.
63. *Ibid.,* pp. 557–59.
64. John F. Cady, *Supplement to A History of Modern Burma* (Ithaca: Cornell University Press, n.d.), p. 1.

65. John H. Badgley, "Burma: The Nexus of Socialism and Two Political Traditions," *Asian Survey*, III (February, 1963), 90.
66. For a detailed analysis of these events, see chap. VI, below.
67. (Stanford: Stanford University Press, 1955).
68. A picul is equal to 132 pounds or 60 kilograms. It was formerly defined as equal to 133 and ⅓ pounds. One metric ton equals 16.67 piculs. Data are taken from James C. Ingram, *Economic Change in Thailand Since 1850* (Stanford: Stanford University Press, 1955), p. 38.
69. *Ibid.*, pp. 37, 40.
70. *Ibid.*, p. 44.
71. The best land for rice cultivation is in the central plain of the Chao Phya river. As the limits of cultivation were reached here, new lands were brought into rice production, primarily in the north and northeast. Only good lands were used initially, for domestic consumption with a relatively high level of productivity. But as submarginal lands in the outer areas were brought under cultivation, productivity declined. Thus, in 1931–34, yield per rai was 4.24 piculs in the center but 4.90 in other areas. By 1948–50, average yield in the center was 3.90 piculs compared with 2.88 in other areas. Ingram concludes, quite cautiously: "The apparent decline in yield per rai lends some support to the hypothesis that an unchanging technique was applied to a larger amount of land, and that the increments of cultivated land were of poorer quality *for rice growing.*" *Ibid.*, pp. 48–49.
72. *Ibid.*, p. 93.
73. *Ibid.*, p. 22.
74. See *ibid.*, pp. 113–32 for a comprehensive analysis.
75. *Ibid.*, p. 216.
76. *Ibid.*, p. 75.
77. *Ibid.*, pp. 76–79.
78. *Ibid.*, p. 60.
79. *Ibid.*, pp. 61–63.
80. *Ibid.*, pp. 79–85.
81. *Ibid.*, pp. 108–9.
82. Reginald Le May, *An Asian Arcady: The Land and Peoples of Northern Siam* (Cambridge, England: W. Heffer & Sons, 1926), p. 60. Le May calls attention to the important role that the new Forest Department played in strengthening the administration of the Siamese monarchy in the northern provinces, where local hereditary chiefs had hitherto largely held sway (p. 62). See also Ingram, *op. cit.*, pp. 110–11.
83. Cady, *op. cit.*, p. 47.
84. *Ibid.*, p. 48.
85. After 1852, "the free export of rice from Rangoon to foreign markets tended to raise the price of this staple food in Upper Burma. It also established the possibility of marketing overseas the rice output from Lower Burma's expanding paddy acreage, a boon which had never before been permitted to the delta area." *Ibid.*, p. 95.

CHAPTER II

1. See, for example, George McT. Kahin, Guy J. Pauker, and Lucian W. Pye, "Comparative Politics of Non-Western Countries," *American Political Science Review*, XLIX (Dec., 1955), 1022–41; and Lucian W. Pye, "The Non-Western Political Process," *Journal of Politics*, XX (Aug., 1958), 468–86.

2. Consider, for example, the typology proposed by Gabriel A. Almond, "Comparative Political Systems," *Journal of Politics*, XVIII (Aug., 1956), 391–409. He suggests that most, if not all, political systems can usefully be categorized under four headings: the Anglo-American; the Continental European; the totalitarian; and "the pre-industrial, or partially industrial." Here we find the "non-Western" and the "underdeveloped" categories implicitly juxtaposed. Leonard Binder organizes his analysis of political systems about two dimensions: behavior and legitimacy. For him, political behavior involves a range of variation between "underdeveloped" and "developed," whereas system-legitimacy revolves about the "traditional" pole at one extreme and, at the modern level, "rational" and "conventional" orientations. *Iran: Political Development in a Changing Society* (Berkeley and Los Angeles: University of California Press, 1962), p. 37. For a discussion of Binder's approach, see my "The Theory of Developing Polities," *World Politics*, XVI (Oct., 1963), 147–71.

3. Arthur S. Banks and Robert B. Textor, *A Cross-Polity Survey* (Cambridge, Mass.: The M.I.T. Press, 1963), pp. 112–13, and FC 183.

4. Abbot L. Moffat, *Mongkut: The King of Siam* (Ithaca: Cornell University Press, 1961), pp. 172, 178, 181.

5. Published in the *Siam Rath Weekly Review*, Aug. 29, 1957, p. 12.

6. Robert Heine-Geldern, "Conceptions of State and Kingship in Southeast Asia" (Cornell University, Southeast Asia Program, Data paper no. 18, 1956), p. 1.

7. H. G. Quaritch Wales, *Siamese State Ceremonies: Their History and Function* (London: Bernard Quaritch, 1931).

8. *Ibid.*, pp. 78–79.

9. Quoted *ibid.*, p. 107.

10. *Ibid.*, pp. 162–63.

11. Heine-Geldern, *op. cit.*, p. 4; Wales, *op. cit.*, p. 48.

12. Walter F. Vella, *The Impact of the West on Government in Thailand* (Berkeley and Los Angeles: University of California Press, 1955), p. 322.

13. James N. Mosel, "Thai Administrative Behavior," in William J. Siffin, ed., *Toward the Comparative Study of Public Administration* (Bloomington: Indiana University Press, 1957), p. 287.

14. David A. Wilson, *Politics in Thailand* (Ithaca: Cornell University Press, 1962), p. 95.

15. William J. Siffin, *The Thai Bureaucracy* (draft ms., 1963; Honolulu: East-West Center Press, *in press*).

16. H. G. Quaritch Wales, *Ancient Siamese Government and Administration*
     (London: Bernard Quaritch, 1934), p. 70.
17. Heine-Geldern, *op. cit.*, p. 3.
18. *Ibid.*, pp. 4–5.
19. Vella, *op. cit.*, p. 322.
20. *Ibid.*, p. 323.
21. Wales, *Ancient Siamese Government*, pp. 35–43.
22. In modern usage, a "department" is normally divided into sub-units,
     each performing a function logically included within the scope of the
     more inclusive unit. Thus, in contemporary Thai administration, each
     "ministry" contains a number of "departments" which, in turn, are sub-
     divided into "divisions," and each division is composed of a number of
     "sections." But a "palace" need not be divided into "courts" or a court
     into "chambers." Let us visualize a palace complex as consisting of sev-
     eral major buildings surrounded by minor ones, each containing a set
     of rooms, typically laid out in a geometrical pattern. Surrounding the
     central or royal palace we might then discover a number of secondary
     palaces, front and rear, right and left (or east and west, south and north).
     Between and around these palaces might be found some humbler struc-
     tures which we could call "courts" and within and among the courts, a
     multitude of "chambers." Each structure would be assigned an occupant
     with his retinue carefully graded in hierarchic terms. All would come
     under the direct control of the king, although he might, at will, ask any
     palace or court to take charge of some combination of chambers.
23. Wales, *Ancient Siamese Government*, p. 79.
24. *Ibid.*, p. 86.
25. *Ibid.*, p. 81.
26. Thawatt Mokarapong, "The June Revolution of 1932 in Thailand: A
     Study in Political Behavior" (Indiana University, Ph.D. diss., 1962),
     p. 76.
27. Wales, *Ancient Siamese Government*, p. 79.
28. For further details, see *ibid.*, pp. 80–81, 93–102.
29. *Ibid.*, p. 81.
30. *Ibid.*, p. 83.
31. Arsa Meksawan, "The Role of the Provincial Governor in Thailand"
     (Indiana University, Ph.D. diss., 1961), p. 52.
32. For details, see James W. Fesler, "French Field Administration: The
     Beginnings," *Comparative Studies in Society and History*, V (Oct.,
     1962), 76–111.
33. *Ibid.*, pp. 80–83, 111.
34. A. M. Hocart, *Kingship* (London: Oxford University Press, 1927), esp.
     pp. 113–29. See also *idem, The Life-Giving Myth* (New York: Grove
     Press, n.d.), pp. 129–38.
35. McKim Marriott, "Little Communities in an Indigenous Civilization,"
     in Marriott, ed., *Village India* (Chicago: University of Chicago Press,
     1955).

36. Fesler, *op. cit.*, pp. 82–85.
37. Wales, *Ancient Siamese Government,* p. 184.
38. See p. 69 and n. 11, above.
39. Vella, *op. cit.* (above, n. 12), p. 327.
40. Arsa, *op. cit.,* p. 82.
41. See Gabriel A. Almond and James S. Coleman, eds., *The Politics of the Developing Areas* (Princeton: Princeton University Press, 1960), pp. 16–17, 26–58.
42. R. Lingat, "Evolution of the Conception of Law in Burma and Siam," *The Journal of the Siam Society,* XXXVIII, pt. 1 (Jan., 1950), 26.
43. Sir Henry Maine, *Lectures on the Early History of Institutions* (London: John Murray, 1893), pp. 380–81.
44. *Ibid.,* pp. 282–83.
45. Lingat, *op. cit.,* p. 27.

CHAPTER III

1. Harold D. Lasswell and Abraham Kaplan, *Power and Society: A Framework for Political Inquiry* (New Haven: Yale University Press, 1950), p. 205.
2. Henry Pratt Fairchild, *Dictionary of Sociology* (Ames, Iowa: Littlefield, Adams, 1955), p. 29.
3. Florence Elliott and Michael Summerskill, *A Dictionary of Politics* (London: Penguin Books, 1957), p. 53.
4. Lucian W. Pye, *Politics, Personality, and Nation Building: Burma's Search for Identity* (New Haven: Yale University Press, 1962), affords a graphic portrait of the social and psychological anguish through which the Burmese have passed in their quest for a viable political order. By contrast, the Siamese appear to have entered the modern world with relative aplomb and nonchalance, unperturbed by the Dostoyevskian soul-searching of their Burmese neighbors.
5. Walter F. Vella, *The Impact of the West on Government in Thailand* (Berkeley and Los Angeles: University of California Press, 1955), p. 317.
6. *Ibid.,* p. 330.
7. *Ibid.,* p. 327.
8. *Ibid.,* p. 331.
9. H. G. Quaritch Wales, *Siamese State Ceremonies: Their History and Function* (London: Bernard Quaritch, 1931), p. 166.
10. Vella, *op. cit.,* p. 334.
11. A. B. Griswold, *King Mongkut of Siam* (New York: Asia Society, 1961), p. 18.
12. *Ibid.,* pp. 24, 25.
13. *Ibid.,* p. 19.
14. *Ibid.,* p. 30.
15. *Ibid.,* p. 29.

16. A. M. Hocart, *Kingship* (London: Oxford University Press, 1927), pp. 120–21.
17. Wales, *op. cit.*, pp. 200–201.
18. Lauriston Sharp, Hazel M. Hauck, Kamol Janlekha, and Robert B. Textor, *Siamese Rice Village: A Preliminary Study of Bang Chan, 1948–1949* (Bangkok: Cornell Research Center, 1953), pp. 51, 59, 67.
19. William Klausner, "Report of Nong Khon: A Thai Village in Ubol" (Bangkok: 1956, mimeo.), p. 11.
20. Wales, *op. cit.*, p. 316.
21. *Ibid.*, p. 214.
22. Quoted in Thawatt Mokarapong, "The June Revolution of 1932 in Thailand: A Study in Political Behavior" (Indiana University, Ph.D. diss., 1962), pp. 299–304. Translated by the author from the *Siam Rath*, June 25, 1932.
23. *Ibid.*, p. 53.
24. *Ibid.*, p. 141.
25. Vella, *op. cit.*, p. 349.

CHAPTER IV

1. Walter F. Vella, *The Impact of the West on Government in Thailand* (Berkeley and Los Angeles: University of California Press, 1955), pp. 332–51; and William J. Siffin, *The Thai Bureaucracy* (draft ms., 1963; Honolulu: East-West Center Press, *in press*).
2. Siffin, *op. cit.*
3. *Ibid.*
4. Sir John Bowring, *The Kingdom and People of Siam* (London: Parker & Son, 1857), II, 227.
5. Vella, *op. cit.*, p. 334. Information taken from Malcolm Smith, *A Physician at the Court of Siam* (London: Country Life, 1947), p. 26, quoting from *Bangkok Calendar*, 1868.
6. Reginald Le May, *An Asian Arcady: The Land and Peoples of Northern Siam* (Cambridge, England: W. Heffer & Sons, 1926), p. 65.
7. H. G. Quaritch Wales, *Ancient Siamese Government and Administration* (London: Bernard Quaritch, 1934), pp. 234–35.
8. Siffin, *op. cit.*
9. Prince Damrong Rajanubhab, *Tesaphiban* (Provincial Administration in Thailand During the Period 1892–1932), trans. by Rampa, Cornell Research Center, Bangkok. See slightly different translation quoted by Siffin, drawing from Prince Damrong, "Ministries in the Old Times" (1914), in Somdej Krom Praya, compilation of Damrong's writings.
10. Siffin, *op. cit.*
11. *History of the Ministry of Agriculture* (in Thai: Bangkok), Part I: "Agriculture in Ancient Times."
12. Wales, *op. cit.*, p. 89.

13. *History*, pp. 21–22; *Government Gazette*, Vol. 8, p. 462.
14. *History*, pp. 54–55; *Gazette*, Vol. 13, p. 599.
15. *History*, p. 57; *Gazette*, Vol. 16, p. 302.
16. *History*, pp. 64, 69–70.
17. *Ibid.*, pp. 70–73.
18. *Ibid.*, pp. 74–77; *Gazette*, Vol. 25, p. 1069 (C.E. 127).
19. *History*, pp. 79–80, 88; *Gazette*, Vol. 25, p. 1431.
20. *History*, pp. 126–27.
21. *Ibid.*, pp. 169–72.
22. *Ibid.*, pp. 158–59, 162–66.
23. Siffin, *op. cit.*
24. *History*, p. 185; *Gazette*, Vol. 49, p. 180.
25. *History*, pp. 187, 190–91; *Gazette*, Vol. 50, p. 172.
26. *History*, pp. 238, 240, 316–18.
27. *Ibid.*, p. 258; *Gazette*, Vol. 59, p. 1023.
28. *History*, p. 330; *Gazette*, Vol. 70, p. 1077.

CHAPTER V

1. R. Lingat, "Evolution of the Conception of Law in Burma and Siam," *The Journal of the Siam Society*, XXXVIII, pt. 1 (Jan., 1950), 30.
2. René Guyon, *The Work of Codification in Siam* (Siam, Ministry of Justice, published by authority of the Code Commission [Paris: Imprimerie nationale, 1919]), p. 14.
3. Quoted in Abbot L. Moffat, *Mongkut, The King of Siam* (Ithaca: Cornell University Press, 1961), p. 33.
4. Prince Damrong Rajanubhab, *Tesaphiban* (Provincial Administration in Thailand During the Period 1892–1932) (ms. of translation from Cornell Research Center, Bangkok), p. 14 (Bangkok: Klang Vidhya Press, B. E. 2495 [1952]).
5. *Ibid.*, pp. 14, 16.
6. *Ibid.*, p. 17. See also Arsa Meksawan, "The Role of the Provincial Governor in Thailand" (Indiana University, Ph.D. diss., 1961), p. 92.
7. Reginald Le May, *An Asian Arcady: The Land and Peoples of Northern Siam* (Cambridge, England: W. Heffer and Sons, 1926), p. 62.
8. Damrong, *op. cit.*, p. 23.
9. *Ibid.*, p. 26. See also Arsa, *op. cit.*, p. 104.
10. *Ibid.*, p. 114.
11. William J. Siffin, *The Thai Bureaucracy* (draft ms., 1963; Honolulu: East-West Center Press, *in press*).
12. Arsa, *op. cit.*, pp. 231–32.
13. *Ibid.*, p. 68.
14. Siffin, *op. cit.*
15. Prayat Smanmit, "District Administration in Thailand" (University of the Philippines, unpublished Master's thesis, 1959), p. 148.

CHAPTER VI

1. Elsewhere I have attempted to show how a prematurely expanded bureaucracy in a developing country can block the growth of extra-bureaucratic centers of political power: "Bureaucrats and Political Development: A Paradoxical View," in Joseph LaPalombara, ed., *Bureaucracy and Political Development* (Princeton: Princeton University Press, 1963), pp. 120–67. Thailand offers a case study par excellence of this pattern of development.
2. "Interest and Clientele Groups," in Joseph L. Sutton, ed., *Problems of Politics and Administration in Thailand* (Bloomington: Indiana University, Department of Government, 1962), pp. 153–92. The data on which this essay was based are presented separately in my *Census and Notes on Clientele Groups in Thai Politics and Administration* (Bloomington: Indiana University, Department of Government, 1963, mimeo.), 42 pp.
3. "Interest and Clientele Groups," *loc. cit.*, p. 184.
4. *Census*, pp. 40–41.
5. David A. Wilson, *Politics in Thailand* (Ithaca: Cornell University Press, 1962), pp. 267–68.
6. More details about the leading Thai political figures, including Pridi, are given in chap. VIII.
7. Wilson, *op. cit.*, p. 233.
8. Thawatt Mokarapong, "The June Revolution of 1932 in Thailand: A Study in Political Behavior" (Indiana University, Ph.D. diss., 1962), p. 156.
9. Thawatt, *op. cit.*, pp. 163–66.
10. *Ibid.*, pp. 171–72.
11. Wilson, *op. cit.*, p. 236. See also John Coast, *Some Aspects of Siamese Politics* (New York: Institute of Pacific Relations, 1953), p. 31.
12. Wilson, *op. cit.*, p. 237.
13. *Ibid.*, p. 238.
14. *Ibid.*, p. 243.
15. The history of these party organizations is given in more detail, though in a different analytic framework, in *ibid.*, pp. 233–43, and Coast, *op. cit.* It is worth noting that individual M.P.'s were able to shift back and forth between official, factional, and oppositional parties, but not always with great ease. The personal history of Liang Chayakarn may be used to illustrate this point. Liang was elected to the Assembly from Ubon as early as 1933 but, being a nonpromoter, had difficulty gaining access to perquisites or power. Khuang at last included him in his cabinet, in January, 1946, as a minister without portfolio. After his resignation in March, Khuang joined forces with Kukrit to form the *Prachatipat* as an opposition party. Liang came in as an ally. In mid-1947, Pridi was in serious trouble and anxiously seeking parliamentary support. Liang then led a defection which split the *Prachatipat,* and formed a new group, the *Prachachon* (People's Party), which allied itself with Pridi.

Thawi, one of Pridi's close friends, became an adviser to the new party. The *Prachatipat* accused Pridi of having paid for the split. See Coast, *op. cit.*, p. 38.

In November, 1947, it will be recalled, the military coup took place, and Khuang was named prime minister. Khuang, presumably, had no love for Liang, who had deserted him earlier in the year. The *Prachachon,* under Liang's leadership, therefore joined with Phibun's *Tharmathipat* and some independents in forming an avowed opposition group. (Wilson mistakenly asserts [*op. cit.*, p. 242] that Liang "cooperated with the Khuang government until it was overthrown in 1948.") After the *coup de main* which brought Phibun to the premiership, Liang was able to join the official United Parties, and Phibun named him deputy minister of interior, then minister of education in January, 1951. When the "silent coup" in November, 1951, humbled Phibun and brought Phao to the fore, Liang again lost out to the coup promoters and went into opposition. In February, 1957, Liang stood for re-election on an opposition platform, but subsequently joined Phao's official *Seri Manangkhasila,* receiving a cabinet position as deputy minister of justice, in March, 1957. After the Sarit coup, Liang was again re-elected to the Assembly in December, 1957.

16. *Bangkok World,* December 21, 1957.
17. *Bangkok Post,* January 7 and 8, 1958.
18. *Ibid.,* January 10, 1958.
19. *Ibid.,* January 18, 1958. The number of appointed members seems to have been reduced from 123 to 121 at this time, but the author of this report was either uninformed or poor in arithmetic!
20. *Ibid.,* January 6, 1958; *Bangkok World,* January 10, 1958.
21. *Bangkok Post,* December 17, 1957.

CHAPTER VII

1. That the kings may have toyed with the idea of parliamentary government, as an abstract principle, is suggested by a whimsical experiment in self-government conducted by King Wachirawut in 1918 when he established a mock government in his court as part of the winter fair. A royal "constitution" was promulgated authorizing the courtiers in the palace to establish an elected municipal government with a two-party system. The king himself headed the Blue Ribbon party, and a high official was asked to lead the opposition Red Ribbon. Rival papers were published, and electioneering was carried on. A legislature containing elected and appointive members was established (perhaps creating a precedent for the similar constitution of the National Assembly some fifteen years later). It should be remembered that this king had an English education and was no doubt intrigued by the British parliamentary system, including its appointive House of Peers and elected Commons, which provided a model for his political game. He was moved to enact as a royal play what he was unwilling to launch as a

reality in the political arena. See Choop Karnjanaprakorn, "Municipal Government in Thailand as an Institution and Process of Government" (Indiana University, Ph.D. diss., 1959), pp. 20–23.

2. *Ibid.*, pp. 7–8.
3. Frederick J. Horrigan, "Local Government and Administration in Thailand: A Study of Institutions and Their Cultural Setting" (Indiana University, Ph.D. diss., 1959), p. 237.
4. Choop, *op. cit.*, p. 14.
5. *Ibid.*, p. 93.
6. *Ibid.*, p. 29.
7. Wendell Blanchard *et al., Thailand: Its People, Its Society, Its Culture* (New Haven: Human Relations Area Files, 1957), p. 191. See also Horrigan, *op. cit.*, p. 237.
8. Walter F. Vella, *The Impact of the West on Government in Thailand* (Berkeley and Los Angeles: University of California Press, 1955), pp. 379–80.
9. Virginia Thompson, "Rural and Urban Self-Government in Southeast Asia," in Rupert Emerson, *Representative Government in Southeast Asia* (Cambridge, Mass.: Harvard University Press, 1955), p. 127.
10. Blanchard, *op. cit.*, p. 192. See also Thompson, *op. cit.*, p. 148.
11. Choop, *op. cit.*, p. 99.
12. *Ibid.*, p. 100.
13. *Ibid.*, p. 27.
14. Horrigan, *op. cit.*, pp. 269–70.
15. Thompson, *op. cit.*, pp. 148–49. See also Blanchard, *op. cit.*, p. 192.
16. Full text of this memorandum is reproduced in Horrigan, *op. cit.*, pp. 318–22.
17. *Ibid.*, pp. 321–23.
18. Arsa Meksawan, "The Role of the Provincial Governor in Thailand" (Indiana University, Ph.D. diss., 1961), p. 317.
19. *Ibid.*, pp. 317–18; 284.
20. *Ibid.*, pp. 321–22.
21. *Ibid.*
22. *Ibid.*, p. 326.
23. *Ibid.*, pp. 330–31.
24. *Ibid.*, p. 333.
25. Horrigan, *op. cit.*, p. 274.
26. Arsa, *op. cit.*, pp. 279–80.
27. Choop, *op. cit.*, pp. 31–32.
28. *Ibid.*, pp. 32–35.
29. *Ibid.*, pp. 37, 54.
30. Horrigan, *op. cit.*, p. 294.
31. Sec. 18. Provisions summarized in Arsa, *op. cit.*, p. 153.
32. *Ibid.*, pp. 155–57. At the same time, the title of the governors was officially changed from the more prestigeful *Poo Warajakarn Changwad* to that of *Kha-luang Prachum Changwad* (provincial commissioner), which, by implication, carried less authority.

33. *Ibid.*, p. 160.
34. *Ibid.*, p. 163.
35. *Ibid.*, pp. 178–79.
36. Horrigan, *op. cit.*, p. 155.
37. Prayat Smanmit, "District Administration in Thailand" (University of the Philippines, unpublished Master's thesis, 1959), pp. 141–42.
38. Arsa, *op. cit.*, pp. 140–41.
39. *Ibid.*, pp. 141–42.
40. Official letter from the Ministry of Interior, April 8, 1952, quoted *ibid.*, p. 149.

CHAPTER VIII

1. David A. Wilson, *Politics in Thailand* (Ithaca: Cornell University Press, 1962), p. 277.
2. *Ibid.*
3. *Ibid.*, p. 143.
4. Only abbreviated names will be used in the text followed by a number referring to the full name as given in the list of cabinet members reproduced in Appendix A. This list includes all cabinet members from 1932 to 1962, arranged chronologically according to the date when they first held cabinet posts. Names are given in forms current in Thailand, not in a standardized transcription.
5. Wilson, *op. cit.*, p. 248. Wilson (p. 246) names four *khanas:* the Promoters of the Revolution in 1932, the Coup d'État Group in 1947, the Military (or Revolutionary) Group in 1957, and the Free Thai *khana* of 1944–47.
6. A list of the cabinet changes is given in Appendix B, together with a brief indication of the relevant political events. Cabinet crises are indicated by asterisks. After the names of cabinet members in Appendix A are given the numbers of the cabinets in which they served and a tentative identification of the cliques and factions to which members of the various ruling circles belonged. The data on cabinet dates and membership are taken from: Thailand, House of Representatives, *Smutpaab-Smachic-Rathsapa, 2475–2502* (Pictorial Book of Members of Parliament, A.D. 1932–59 [Bangkok, 1960]).
7. David A. Wilson and Herbert P. Phillips, "Elections and Parties in Thailand," *Far Eastern Survey*, XXVII (Aug., 1958), 113–19.
8. Wilson, *Politics in Thailand*, p. 255.
9. The Thai *khana* is an informal rather than a formal group. Hence, membership is unofficial, and official lists of members are scarcely published. Nevertheless, through journalistic sources, lists of members have become available. Such a list of the promoters is given in Thawatt Mokarapong, "The June Revolution of 1932 in Thailand: A Study in Political Behavior" (Indiana University, Ph.D. diss., 1962), pp. 286–98. Membership in component cliques and factions is even more difficult to verify. The following list is based on information collected by

Thawatt from a variety of Thai sources, supplemented in consultations with Amara Raksasataya and other Thai scholars and informants. The numbers refer to names in Appendix A.

Senior clique: 3, 4, 5, 10, 48.

Junior clique, civilian faction: 7, 8, 13, 14, 15, 30, 47, 64, 73, 76, 78, 81, 82, 89, 103, 107, 126.

Junior clique, army faction: 12, 51, 58, 60, 62, 66, 69, 75, 111, 166.

Junior clique, navy faction: 6, 21, 35, 65, 67, 86, 125.

10. Siamese refer to members of the 1932 *khana* as the "initiators" or "promoters."

11. Thawatt, *op. cit.*, p. 165.

12. This analysis of the events leading to and following Song's resignation is based on Thawatt, pp. 216–48. The use of resignation as a tactic in Thai politics is discussed by G. William Skinner in his analysis of the Chinese community in Thailand, where he explains how the leaders of Chinese groups also used this technique. Whenever a resigning leader can leave the organization in an untenable situation, he can strengthen his own position by bargaining for new powers as a condition of resuming office. *Leadership and Power in the Chinese Community of Thailand* (Ithaca: Cornell University Press, 1958), pp. 121–22.

13. Wilson, *Politics in Thailand*, pp. 158–59.

14. For details, see Thawatt, *op. cit.*, pp. 248–71.

15. The primary source of data for the latter years of the first ruling circle, as well as for the remainder of this essay, is a manuscript by Amara Raksasataya entitled, "Major Political Events in Thailand, 1932–1962." It is derived in large part from the official work cited above, n. 6. Thawatt's detailed study deals only with the period up to 1933. Supplementary data have been taken from John Coast, *Some Aspects of Siamese Politics* (New York: Institute of Pacific Relations, 1953), and Wilson, *op. cit.*

16. Among the leading members of the Free Thai clique were: 64, 73, 76, 89, 91, 101, 103, 126.

17. Members of the Coup d'État Group probably included:

Kad: 60.

Phin-Phao clique: 168(?), 177, 182, 184, 185, 187, 189.

Sarit clique: 181, 193, 195, 199, 208, 211, 215.

Phibun's personal faction: 12, 79, 111, 163, 192, 196 (plus non-coup members: 55, 56, 57, 66).

18. For background, see Albert Pickerell and Daniel E. Moore, "Elections in Thailand," *Far Eastern Survey*, XXVI (June, July, 1957), 92–96, 103–11.

19. Members of the Military Group included: 181, 183, 193, 195, 199, 206, 208, 210, 211, 213, 215, 216, 217, 218, 220, 223, 237.

20. A somewhat extremist but detailed interpretive account of these events is contained in Frank C. Darling, "Marshal Sarit and Absolutist Rule in Thailand," *Pacific Affairs*, XXXIII (Dec., 1960), 347–60. Darling's

essay also gives a typically oversimplified account of modern Thai political history in terms of continuing rivalry between civilian and military factions.

CHAPTER IX

1. Lauriston Sharp, Hazel M. Hauck, Kamol Janlekha, and Robert B. Textor, *Siamese Rice Village: A Preliminary Study of Bang Chan, 1948–1949* (Bangkok: Cornell Research Center, 1953), p. 50. Commenting further on this episode, the Cornell report observes (*loc. cit.*) that "Bang Chan people universally favor the incumbent regime over any other possible contenders, while at the same time many earnestly condemn (and often exaggerate) war- and inflation-bred corruption, bureaucratic inefficiency and cynicism, arbitrary police actions and unkept promises of improved conditions. While there is dissatisfaction with the government, at the same time there survives, though with some ambivalence, the old Southeast Asian respect for those of higher status, including government authorities."
2. *New York Times*, December 9, 1963, p. 12e.
3. William J. Siffin, *The Thai Bureaucracy* (draft ms., 1963; Honolulu: East-West Center Press, in press).
4. H. G. Quaritch Wales, *Ancient Siamese Government and Administration* (London: Bernard Quaritch, 1934), pp. 21–43.
5. The full scale, showing salary steps in each grade for each class, is given in Siffin, *op. cit.* Taken from Civil Service Act B.E. 2497 (1954), Schedule 1, as subsequently amended.
6. Wendell Blanchard *et al., Thailand: Its People, Its Society, Its Culture* (New Haven: Human Relations Area Files, 1957), p. 257. According to PAS report no. B-1, "Budget Administration in the Government of Thailand" (unpublished, 1956) p. 13, an item of 2 billion baht in the 1956 budget for "readjustment of salaries and special allowances" amounted to 80 to 90 per cent of all government salaries and almost half of the "ordinary expenditure" budget. The "salaries" item under each department reflected the nominal basic salaries only, i.e., only some 10 to 20 per cent of actual payments.
7. This phenomenon is discussed in my book *Administration in Developing Countries: The Theory of Prismatic Society* (Boston: Houghton-Mifflin, 1964), pp. 141–49, 184–93.
8. G. William Skinner, *Leadership and Power in the Chinese Community of Thailand* (Ithaca: Cornell University Press, 1958). See also his earlier companion volume, *Chinese Society in Thailand: An Analytical History* (Ithaca: Cornell University Press, 1957). Additional information on this topic, more directly focused on the present theme, is contained in Joseph Ping-lun Jiang, *Political Change and Pariah Entrepreneurship* (Indiana University, Ph.D. diss., 1962); cf. pp. 65–95, 213–48.
9. *Leadership and Power*, p. 246.

10. *Ibid.,* pp. 191–92.
11. *Ibid.,* pp. 303–5.
12. *Ibid.,* pp. 244; 192.
13. David Wilson, who was carrying on independent research in Thailand while I was there, had collected the names of board members for a large number of firms. Although the criteria relevant to his studies were different from mine, he kindly permitted me to use his data to add to my records on cabinet members the names of the corporations on whose boards they were directors.
14. The 42 firms with three or more cabinet level directors included 16 with three ministerial members, 9 with four, 9 with five, 3 with six, 4 with seven, and 1 with twelve. The most elaborate setup was that of the National Economic Development Co., Ltd., usually known as NEDCOL, which had twelve members who were, or had once been, cabinet members. This company, with an initial capitalization of 50 million baht, was technically a private firm but enjoyed a guarantee from the Ministry of Finance which enabled it to borrow funds from foreign banks, including the Bank of America.
15. To indicate the scope of the business interests of these politicians, here is a list of board memberships formerly held by Lamai:

> Cement for Irrigation
> The Bangkok 96 Co., Ltd. (construction)
> The Bangkok Technical Consultant Co., Ltd.
> The Farmers' Bank
> The Mai-ad Sriracha Plywood Co., Ltd.
> The Provincial Bank Co., Ltd.
> The Ruam Chai Thanya Co., Ltd. (selling rice)
> The Saha Monkon Insurance and Warehouse Co., Ltd.
> The Sugar Industry of Thailand Co., Ltd.
> The Thai Mineral Co., Ltd.
> The Thai Plywood Co., Ltd.
> The Thai Vehicle Transportation Co., Ltd.
> The Thai Welfare Trading Co.
> The Thailand Steel Co., Ltd.
> The Thanya Warehouse Co., Ltd.
> The United Burapha Matches Co., Ltd.
> The United Construction Co., Ltd.
> The Wibunsathid Warehouse Co., Ltd.
> The Wimanfa Restaurant Co., Ltd.
> The Yanyon Insurance and Trading Co., Ltd.

16. Skinner, *Leadership and Power,* p. 306.
17. International Bank for Reconstruction and Development, *A Public Development Program for Thailand* (Baltimore: The Johns Hopkins Press, 1959).
18. *Ibid.,* pp. 90–91.

19. *Ibid.*
20. *Ibid.*, pp. 92–94.
21. In addition to the public enterprises, many government agencies were authorized to establish "revolving funds," based on an initial grant, with the prospect of renewal or even profits due to the sale of some commodity or service generated by the program carried out in conjunction with the fund. Needless to say, such revolving funds could provide a degree of flexibility and autonomy for the officials controlling them, to say nothing of incidental side benefits for those concerned. No sharp line appears to have been drawn between these revolving funds and the public enterprises. At least, a list of some 42 funds established since 1933, and still in operation in 1956, includes some titles which appear to duplicate those in the list of enterprises given in Table 28. This list of funds includes the following:

Agricultural Journal	Fuel Oil
Aid to Members of Self-Help Settlements	Glue Factory
	Government Housing Bureau
Animal Husbandry	Government Pawn Shop
Bamboo Products Pilot Plant	Gunny Bag Weaving
Boot Polishing Cream Factory	Industrial Promotion Department
Cattle Breeding Promotion	Factories
Children's Textbooks	Manufacturing
Cloth for Farmers	Medical Supplies and Appliances
Construction Equipment	Musical Entertainment
Construction Materials	Narcotic Drugs Revolving Fund
Co-operatives Promotion	National Livestock Promotion
Cottage Industry	Paddy Seeds Expansion
Cotton Industry	Paper Manufacturing
Cotton Purchasing	Para Rubber Improvement
Earthenware Promotion in Northeast	Peoples Vocational Promotion
	Playing Cards
Educational Broadcasting	Revenue Department Slaughter
Electric Power Distribution	House
Electrical Appliances and Equipment	Rice for Relief
	Slaughter House
Elementary School Texts	Thai Dictionary Publishing
Farm Labour Saving	Undertaking Farm Work
Fertilizer Purchasing	

CHAPTER X

1. The manifesto, said to have been written by Pridi, was published on June 25, 1932. Translation by Thawatt Mokarapong in "The June Revolution of 1932 in Thailand" (Indiana University, Ph.D. diss., 1962), p. 3.
2. David A. Wilson, *Politics in Thailand* (Ithaca: Cornell University Press, 1962), p. 277.

3. *Op. cit.*, p. 161. Elsewhere (p. 137) Wilson contrasts the Thai polity with European parliamentary systems in these words: "In contrast to its model, however, the Prime Minister of Thailand draws power from bureaucratic constituencies by means of cliques rather than from popular constituencies by means of parties."

4. Because definite career information on all these men is not available, I have had to draw inferences in order to classify some of them. I have included in the category of civil officials all men carrying titles of official rank. These titles were given during the absolute monarchy, and one had to have achieved a given rank in the civil service in order to be eligible. Thus, the title of *Phya* was awarded only to officials at the level of departmental director-general or above, *Pra* to division chiefs or above, *Luang* to men at or above the rank of section chief, and *Khun* to assistant section chiefs, chief clerks, and similar ranks. After the revolution of 1932, such titles were no longer given, but we know that anyone having such a title was a civil servant before 1932 and presumably continued his service career afterward. Men carrying titles of military rank were easily classified in the military services. Definite information was available for some of the nonofficials. Where such information was lacking, but the man had held a parliamentary seat at least once as a first-category, elected member, he was classified as a nonofficial. Some officials also ran for election to the Assembly, but they were classified as officials if there was evidence that they held career portions.

5. "Bureaucrats and Political Development," in Joseph LaPalombara, ed., *Bureaucracy and Political Development* (Princeton: Princeton University Press, 1963), pp. 120–67.

6. Herbert P. Phillips and David A. Wilson, "Certain Effects of Culture and Social Organization on Internal Security in Thailand" (Santa Monica, Calif.: The Rand Corporation, Memorandum RM-3786-ARPA [abridged], 1964), pp. 15–16.

7. *Ibid.*, p. 17.

8. Plato, *Republic*, I, 338E–339A. (Trans. B. Jowett [Oxford: The Clarendon Press, 1953], Vol. II, p. 177.)

9. This statement, of course, does not imply any cultural determinism. It is not asserted here that any beliefs held by the Siamese make the triumph of a bureaucratic polity necessary. Rather, it is suggested that if, for completely extraneous reasons, a bureaucratic polity has come into existence, there are elements in the learned beliefs and attitudes of the Siamese which make it easier to accept this fact as right and proper than might otherwise be the case.

10. Phillips and Wilson, *op. cit.*, pp. 8–9.

11. Wilson, *Politics in Thailand*. On pp. 72–73, Wilson provides a selected bibliography of the literature in English bearing on the basic cultural values and beliefs which prevail among the Siamese people.

12. *Ibid.*, p. 79.

13. *Ibid.,* p. 74.
14. *Ibid.,* pp. 80–81.
15. *Ibid.,* p. 79.
16. See especially William J. Siffin, *The Thai Bureaucracy: Institutional Change and Development* (Honolulu: East-West Center Press, *in press*). Other relevant works include: *idem.,* "The Civil Service System of the Kingdom of Thailand," *International Review of Administrative Sciences,* XXVI, No. 3 (1960), 225–68; *idem.,* "Personnel Processes of the Thai Bureaucracy," in Ferrel Heady and Sybil L. Stokes, eds., *Papers in Comparative Public Administration* (Ann Arbor: University of Michigan, I.P.A., 1962), pp. 207–28; Edgar L. Shor, "The Thai Bureaucracy," *Administrative Science Quarterly,* V (June, 1960), 66–86; M. Ladd Thomas, "Thai Public Administration," *New Zealand Journal of Public Administration,* XXV (Sept., 1962), 3–33; Malai Huvanandana and William J. Siffin, "Public Administration in Thailand," in S. S. Hsueh, *Public Administration in South and Southeast Asia* (Brussels: International Institute of Administrative Sciences, 1962), pp. 157–88; and James N. Mosel, "Thai Administrative Behavior," in William J. Siffin, ed., *Toward the Comparative Study of Public Administration* (Bloomington: Indiana University Press, 1957), pp. 278–331. For background information, see also: Kasem Udyanin and Rufus D. Smith, *The Public Service in Thailand: Organization, Recruitment and Training* (Brussels: International Institute of Administrative Sciences, 1954); Joseph L. Sutton, ed., *Problems of Politics and Administration in Thailand* (Indiana University, Department of Government, 1962); Walter F. Vella, *The Impact of the West on Government in Thailand* (Berkeley: University of California Press, 1955); W. D. Reeve, *Public Administration in Siam* (London: Royal Institute of International Affairs, 1951); and my *The Ecology of Public Administration* (Bombay: Asia Publishing House, 1961), pp. 98–143.
17. Information on the structure of the Thai bureaucracy has been gleaned from a variety of unpublished sources, often not consistent with each other. Since our purpose here is to ascertain general orders of magnitude, it seems unnecessary to examine the figures in detail or to show changes from year to year. The most helpful source has been Siffin, *The Thai Bureaucracy.* Siffin relied extensively on Chap Tharamathaj, "The Composition of the Civil Service of Thailand" (Bangkok: Thammasat University, unpublished Master's thesis, 1959). The thesis was not available to me in the preparation of this work.
18. "Report of the Economic Advisor," August 11 to December 31, 1956 (Bangkok: mimeo., 1957), Annex I, p. 1.
19. *Ibid.,* pp. 2, 3.
20. *Ibid.,* p. 12.
21. *Ibid.*
22. *Ibid.,* p. 11.

23. *Ibid.*, p. 10.
24. For example, W. D. Reeve, the British adviser, had recommended that the number of governmental committees be reduced to a minimum. He wrote: "Matters which could more expeditiously and efficiently be decided by one man who has studied the problem in all its aspects, are often referred to a large committee. . . . More often than not, committees drag on for month after month and produce in the end an inconclusive or even useless report on which no action is taken." Reeve also noted the tendency of the bureaucracy to refer issues to the cabinet: "Far too many more or less minor questions which could and should be decided on at once at lower levels are referred above, particularly by Ministers to the Cabinet. The latter gets overloaded with the necessity of debating points of detail." The explanation which Reeve offers, however, begs the question, for he attributes these phenomena to the inclination of Siamese officials "to avoid making a decision on any unpleasant or controversial question." *Op. cit.* (above, n. 16), pp. 21, 83.
25. Siffin, "The Civil Service System of the Kingdom of Thailand," *loc. cit.* (above, n. 16), p. 263.
26. *Op. cit.* (above, n. 18), p. 11.
27. International Bank for Reconstruction and Development, *A Public Development Program for Thailand* (Baltimore: The Johns Hopkins Press, 1959), p. 202.
28. *Ibid.*, pp. 222–23.
29. *Ibid.*, p. 223.
30. *Ibid.*, p. 222.
31. *Ibid.*, pp. 221–22.
32. For a detailed explanation of these rules, see Udyanin and Smith, *op. cit.* (above, n. 16), pp. 41–44.
33. *Op. cit.* (above, n. 27), p. 159.
34. Udyanin and Smith, *op. cit.*, pp. 43–44.
35. Edgar L. Shor, "The Public Service," in Joseph L. Sutton, ed., *Problems of Politics and Administration in Thailand* (Bloomington: Indiana University, Department of Government, 1962), p. 34.
36. *Ibid.*
37. *A Public Development Program for Thailand*, pp. 223–24.
38. *Ibid.*, p. 199.
39. *Ibid.*, pp. 100–101.
40. See, for example, the cases published in Harold Stein, ed., *Public Administration and Policy Development* (New York: Harcourt, Brace & Co., 1952), and other cases published more recently by the Inter-University Case Program, Syracuse University, Syracuse, N.Y.
41. Stein, *op. cit.*, pp. 533–72.
42. This story is told by James C. Ingram, *Economic Change in Thailand Since 1850* (Stanford: Stanford University Press, 1955), pp. 79–85.
43. *A Public Development Program for Thailand*, p. 56.
44. *Ibid.*, p. 162.

45. Reeve, *op. cit.* (above, n. 16), pp. 38–39.
46. Public Administration Service, "A Program for Strengthening Public Administration in the Kingdom of Thailand" (mimeo., May, 1952), p. 21.
47. *Ibid.,* p. 23.
48. *A Public Development Program for Thailand,* p. 225.
49. *Ibid.,* pp. 225–26.
50. In *Administration in Developing Countries: The Theory of Prismatic Society* (Boston: Houghton-Mifflin, 1964), pp. 280–83, I have described an equivocal distribution of power as one in which formal authority is relatively concentrated and centralized, whereas effective control is relatively dispersed and localized. Such a power distribution cannot be simply described as "centralized," yet it is probably the most characteristic pattern in the governments of underdeveloped countries, and is a logically necessary structure of power in the "prismatic model."
51. Siffin, "The Civil Service System," *loc. cit.* (above, n. 16), pp. 262–63.
52. *Ibid.,* p. 264.
53. Mosel, "Thai Administrative Behavior," *loc. cit.* (above, n. 16), p. 322.
54. Siffin, "The Civil Service System," *loc. cit.* (above, n. 16), p. 265.
55. Thomas, "Thai Public Administration," *loc. cit.* (above, n. 16), p. 29.
56. Gabriel A. Almond and James S. Coleman, eds., *The Politics of the Developing Areas* (Princeton: Princeton University Press, 1960), pp. 26–52.

CHAPTER XI

1. For details, see James C. Ingram, *Economic Change in Thailand Since 1850* (Stanford: Stanford University Press, 1955).
2. Leonard Binder, *Iran: Political Development in a Changing Society* (Berkeley and Los Angeles: University of California Press, 1962), p. 47.
3. *Ibid.*
4. *Administration in Developing Countries: The Theory of Prismatic Society* (Boston: Houghton-Mifflin, 1964), pp. 22–28. In the analogy, diffracted light is separated by its component wave lengths, appearing in the form of a spectrum or rainbow bands. Fused or "white" light, by contrast, mixes all the frequencies together. The terms seemed convenient to distinguish between contrastive-type social systems in which all functions are performed by a single structure and in which every function has its distinctive structure. It is recognized, of course, that no concrete social system is, in this sense, completely and utterly functionally diffuse or specific. Consequently, the term "prismatic" was introduced to refer to intermediate-type systems which mix, in various proportions, the fused and diffracted characteristics. We might speak of historical social systems as being prismatic in varying degrees, some tending toward the fused model, others toward the diffracted.

A further characteristic implied by the model is significant here. Both the fused and diffracted models appear to be relatively static or fixed, whereas the prismatic model implies an unstable and dynamic quality of change or disequilibrium.

5. *Ibid.,* pp. 120–21.
6. W. W. Rositow, *The Stages of Economic Growth: A Non-Communist Manifesto* (Cambridge, England: Cambridge University Press, 1960).
7. S. N. Eisenstadt, "Bureaucracy and Political Development," in Joseph LaPalombara, ed., *Bureaucracy and Political Development* (Princeton: Princeton University Press, 1963), p. 96.
8. William J. Siffin, "The Civil Service System of the Kingdom of Thailand," *International Review of Administrative Sciences,* XXVI, No. 3 (1960), 267.
9. *A Public Development Program for Thailand* (Baltimore: The Johns Hopkins Press, 1959), pp. 95–96.
10. The ups and downs of Sino-Thai relationships are well described by G. William Skinner in *Chinese Society in Thailand: An Analytical History,* and *idem, Leadership and Power in the Chinese Community of Thailand* (Ithaca: Cornell University Press, 1957 and 1958). See especially chap. 9 in the latter work. The sources of persistent tension between the Chinese business community and the Thai elite are examined in terms more directly relevant to the present discussion by Joseph Pinglun Jiang, *Political Change and Pariah Entrepreneurship* (Indiana University, Ph.D. diss., 1962), pp. 213–48.
11. *Op. cit.* (above, n. 9), p. 92.
12. David A. Wilson, "Thailand and Marxism," in Frank N. Trager, ed., *Marxism in Southeast Asia* (Stanford: Stanford University Press, 1959), p. 66.
13. *Ibid.,* p. 68.
14. The somewhat shaky data on which these figures are based are presented by William J. Siffin in "Economic Development," Joseph L. Sutton, ed., *Problems of Politics and Administration in Thailand* (Bloomington: Indiana University, Department of Government, 1962), pp. 130–31.
15. *Ibid.,* p. 132.
16. *A Public Development Program for Thailand,* p. 92.
17. Siffin, "Economic Development," pp. 133–34.
18. The International Bank report states: ". . . it is difficult to exaggerate the importance of rice in Thailand's past economic development and present economic well-being. Probably about two-thirds of the population earns a living from rice farming: it is by far the largest single contributor to the national income; it provides nearly half of Thailand's export earning; and is a major support, directly and indirectly, of government revenues." *Op. cit.,* p. 34.
19. Siffin, "Economic Development," p. 135.
20. *A Public Development Program for Thailand,* pp. 131, 176.

INDEX

Numbers in parentheses following cabinet members' names refer to their code numbers in Appendix A.

70
71
72
74
75
76
77
79
80
83
85

88